The Philosophy of Tim Burton

THE PHILOSOPHY OF
TIM BURTON

Edited by

Jennifer L. McMahon

Scholarly publisher for the Commonwealth,
serving Bellarmine University, Berea College, Centre College of Kentucky, Eastern Kentucky University, The Filson Historical Society, Georgetown College, Kentucky Historical Society, Kentucky State University, Morehead State University, Murray State University, Northern Kentucky University, Transylvania University, University of Kentucky, University of Louisville, and Western Kentucky University.

Editorial and Sales Offices: The University Press of Kentucky
663 South Limestone Street, Lexington, Kentucky 40508-4008
www.kentuckypress.com

Library of Congress Cataloging-in-Publication Data

The philosophy of Tim Burton / edited by Jennifer L. McMahon.
pages cm
Includes bibliographical references and index.
ISBN 978-0-8131-4462-7 (hardcover : alk. paper) —
ISBN 978-0-8131-4464-1 (pdf : alk. paper) — ISBN 978-0-8131-4463-4 (epub)
1. Burton, Tim—Criticism and interpretation. I. McMahon, Jennifer L. editor of compilation.
PN1998.3.B875P55 2014
791.4302'33092—dc23 2014005231

This book is printed on acid-free paper meeting the requirements of the American National Standard for Permanence in Paper for Printed Library Materials.

Manufactured in the United States of America.

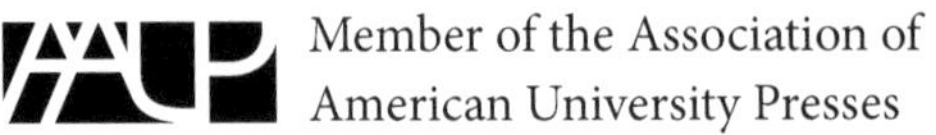

Contents

Part 3. Burton and Aesthetics

Introduction

No contemporary director-producer has as deliciously macabre a signature as Tim Burton. Known for his quirky characters and delightfully sinister settings, Burton displays an undeniable knack for the fantastic. Alluding to sources as varied as Lewis Carroll, Mary Shelley, Washington Irving, Edward Gorey, Salvador Dali, and Dr. Seuss, Burton's creations fascinate audiences by virtue of their ability to elicit both alarm and wonder. And Burton's influence extends beyond the screen. After over a decade spent establishing a reputation primarily in the cinematic arts, in 2007 Burton released *The Melancholy Death of Oyster Boy and Other Stories*, a collection of short fiction. Then, in 2009, he received critical acclaim for an exhibition of his original artwork at the Museum of Modern Art (MoMA) in New York. This multimedia collection was exhibited at the Los Angeles County Museum of Art in 2011. The next year, 2012, brought the release of several Burton productions, including *Dark Shadows, Abraham Lincoln: Vampire Hunter* (co-produced with Timur Bekmambetov), and a feature-length 3-D remake of *Frankenweenie.* As the variety and popularity of his works suggest, whether in an offbeat animated feature, a box-office hit, a collection of short fiction, or an exhibit in the visual arts, Burton pushes the envelope of the imagination with his uncanny productions and in doing so has emerged as a powerful force in contemporary culture.

This collection examines the philosophical significance of Burton's corpus, a body that includes *Beetlejuice* (1988), *Batman* (1989), *Edward Scissorhands* (1990), *Batman Returns* (1992), *The Nightmare Before Christmas* (1993), *Mars Attacks!* (1996), *Sleepy Hollow* (1999), *Planet of the Apes* (2001), *Big Fish* (2003), *Corpse Bride* (2005), *Charlie and the Chocolate Factory* (2005), *Sweeney Todd* (2007), *9* (2009), *Alice in Wonderland* (2010), and *Dark Shadows* (2012). Burton's work invites philosophical consideration for a variety of reasons. Clearly, to the extent his most prominent achievements have been within the visual and performing arts, his work invites aesthetic analysis. Aesthetics is the philosophical discipline that studies art. Philosophers who specialize in aesthetics consider questions such as What is the nature of art? What is the nature of artistic genius? Can art educate? And what role do negative emotions play in art? Certainly, when one considers Burton's unique style, often disturbing content, and popular appeal, one can see how the aforementioned questions can be directed to Burton's corpus. We can ask whether his work should be considered art, whether he should be regarded as a genius, whether his works educate, and whether his ominous style augments or compromises the aesthetic value of his work. But Burton's work inspires more than aesthetic examination. In a less disturbing fashion than *Sweeney Todd,* Burton's characters and plots provide ample "meat" for satisfying discussions regarding other long-standing philosophical topics, including identity and authority. Indeed, this collection is organized around these three core topics: identity, authority, and art.

Part 1 looks at the issue of identity. Philosophers have been debating the nature of the self for centuries. Historically, there have been two schools of thought on the subject. The essentialist viewpoint asserts that individuals have an essential identity, namely, a core self that endures and is immune to empirical influence. Conversely, the empirical viewpoint maintains that the self is an emergent phenomenon and mutable entity, one predicated on, and modified by, experience. Ken Hada's "Fishing for the [Mediating] Self: Identity and Storytelling in *Big Fish*" exemplifies the empirical viewpoint. Drawing primarily from the works of Jean-Paul Sartre (1905–1980), George Herbert Mead (1863–1931), Mitchell Aboulafia (1951–), and Walter Benjamin (1892–1940), Hada argues that Burton's film *Big Fish* illustrates the fact that personal identity emerges within a social or intersubjective context and is intimately connected to linguistic activities. In particular, Hada argues that *Big Fish* illustrates that the self has a narrative structure; namely, it is a conceptual figure that develops in and through experience. Ryan Weldon directs readers' attention to the topic of gender identity, particularly feminist theory and ideals of feminine identity, in "Catwoman and Subjectivity: Constructions of Identity and Power in Tim Burton's *Batman Returns.*" Drawing from the works of Jean-Paul Sartre and Simone de Beauvoir (1908–1986), Weldon examines the implications of Selina Kyle's transformation into Catwoman for feminist theories regarding identity and agency. In the final two essays in the section, contributors Daniel Sullivan and Mark Walling return readers to broader issues of identity. In "The Consolations and Dangers of Fantasy: Burton, Poe, and *Vincent,*" Daniel Sullivan compares the gothic aesthetic of Burton to that established by Edgar Allan Poe (1809–1849). Sullivan explores the psychological appeal of this aesthetic to insecure individuals, particularly insecure children. Drawing primarily from Søren Kierkegaard

(1813–1855) and R. D. Laing (1927–1989), Sullivan argues that a preoccupation with fantasy worlds offers both dangers and delights. Finally, in his comparative essay, "Johnny Depp Is a Big Baby! The Philosophical Significance of Tim Burton's Preoccupation with Childhood Consciousness in *Edward Scissorhands* and *Ed Wood*," Walling examines current research in cognitive science that suggests that, rather than perceiving less than their mature counterparts, children perceive more, and their cognitive apparatus is epistemologically unique for this reason. Walling argues that Burton's nostalgia for childhood is not anchored primarily in nostalgia for the innocence of youth but instead in the unique cognitive awareness that children exemplify and that warrants further examination.

Part 2 expands consideration of Burton's work from the domain of the individual to the domain of the social. Specifically, it looks at the way in which works in Burton's corpus comment on authority and supplements influential philosophy on the subject. In the opening chapter in the section, well-known theorist of popular culture Paul A. Cantor argues that *Mars Attacks!* illustrates Burton's tendency to champion the underdog and critique the establishment. Drawing primarily from Alexis de Tocqueville's (1805–1859) *Democracy in America*, Cantor's essay, "*Mars Attacks!*: Burton, Tocqueville, and the Self-Organizing Power of the American People," asserts that Burton's work typically conveys a grassroots antielitist message that empowers ordinary individuals. Steve Benton's "'Pinioned by a Chain of Reasoning'? Anti-intellectualism and Models of Rationality in Tim Burton's *Sleepy Hollow*" continues the discussion of the ways in which Burton at least appears to challenge authority. Benton examines how Burton's *Sleepy Hollow* seems to invert the anti-intellectual message implicit in Washington Irving's (1783–1859) classic. Despite appearances, Benton argues, Burton's remake of Irving's classic fails to reverse a dynamic prevalent in American culture, namely, the tendency to denigrate intellectuals, and it instead reproduces it. Kevin S. Decker's "Culture, Hermeneutics, and the Batman" expands the conversation Benton initiated regarding remakes and Weldon's discussion of *Batman* by focusing on Burton's adaptation of the DC Comics hero. Drawing primarily from the hermeneutical theories of Martin Heidegger (1889–1976) and Hans-Georg Gadamer (1900–2002), Decker argues that the salient differences between the Batman character in the original comic, the television serial, Burton's *Batman* and *Batman Returns*, and Christopher Nolan's *Batman Begins* and *The Dark Knight* are expressive of divergent cultural moments out of which these works emerged. Thus, Decker argues that we can discern information regarding our cultural self-understanding from the iconic figure of the Caped Crusader. Finally, in "Burtonology: Metaphysics, Epistemology, Essences, Christmas, and Vincent Price," Kimberly Baltzer-Jaray turns the conversation to broader epistemological issues, specifically questions regarding what we can and cannot know. Focusing primarily on Immanuel Kant's (1724–1804) distinction between noumena and phenomena and incorporating material from Thomas Nagel's (1937–) "What Is It Like to Be a Bat?," Baltzer-Jaray looks at *The Nightmare Before Christmas* and *Vincent* to see if we have any authority to claim knowledge of anything outside our own minds.

Part 3 focuses on the most obvious link between Burton and philosophy: aesthetics. In "A Symphony of Horror: The Sublime Synesthesia of *Sweeney Todd*," Jennifer L. Jenkins uses Edmund Burke's (1729–1797) theory of the sublime as a framework with which to analyze Burton's horrific tale. Jenkins argues that Burton employs synesthesia, or sense mixing, in order to create an impression of sensory excess that heightens the aesthetic effect of the film. Deborah Knight and George McKnight also offer an aesthetic analysis of Burton's work. In "Tim Burton, Johnny Depp, and the Fantastic," Knight and McKnight argue that Burton's films illustrate Tzvetan Todorov's (1939–) concept of the fantastic and that the actor Johnny Depp is central to Burton's personal expression of the concept. Jennifer L. McMahon also examines the aesthetic effects that Burton's work elicits and introduces an existential dimension to the conversation. In "It's Uncanny: Death in Tim Burton's Corpus," McMahon draws primarily from the works of Martin Heidegger to argue that Burton's unique ability to arouse the experience of the uncanny allows him to instruct audiences regarding mortality and help them achieve authenticity. In "Affect without Illusion: The Films of Edward D. Wood Jr. after *Ed Wood*," David LaRocca examines Burton's critically acclaimed *Ed Wood*, a film that LaRocca argues not only celebrates Wood's ability to use unreal settings to prompt heightened awareness of the world we inhabit but also demonstrates Burton's ability to do the same. Finally, in an expanded version of an already published essay, Debbie Olson examines the effects that Burton's dramatic color palette might have on young viewers. In "Little Burton Blue: Tim Burton and the Product(ion) of Color in the Fairy-Tale Films *The Nightmare Before Christmas* and *Corpse Bride*," Olson links back to the childhood theme established in Walling's essay in part 1 and expands the discussion to explore not only how Burton idealizes childhood but also how his works might affect children.

Overall, the essays in this collection aim to invite unique and provocative discussion of one of this century's most provocative and unique figures. Tim Burton's singular style and range of influence warrant examination of his work from a philosophical perspective. Philosophers trade in, or at least aim at, the discernment of truth. There is no doubt that Tim Burton has helped shape our popular perceptions of identity, authority, and the aesthetic. The essays herein seek simply to encourage the same degree of critical reflection on Burton that Burton encourages in his audiences.

Part 1

Burton and Identity

Fishing for the [Mediating] Self

Identity and Storytelling in *Big Fish*

Ken Hada

> The selfhood of oneself implies otherness to such an intimate degree that one cannot be thought of without the other.
>
> —Paul Ricoeur

No son wants a delusional or dishonest father, but this seems to be the situation that Will Bloom (Billy Crudup) faces in Tim Burton's film *Big Fish* (2003). Will is convinced that his father, Ed Bloom (Albert Finney), is an irresponsible liar whose self-proclaimed fantastic identity is delusional. The film's setting brings father and son together one last time as Ed is confined to his deathbed. Though Will has not spoken to his father in three years, he returns home to be with him during his last days. In addition to dealing with the emotional intensity of preparing to bury his father and comfort his grieving mother, Sandra (Jessica Lange), Will desires to finally know the truth about his father's life. Will wants his father to admit his failures and, in the process, denounce the long-standing narrative that he has constructed as a way of presenting his life.

"All the Facts, None of the Flavor"

Ed Bloom is a storyteller. He has authored his life around a series of tales, and it is through the retelling of his fantastic tales that he understands and posits the significant moments of his life. He answers the various questions that life poses him with a story, a story in which he is the main character, but one that also includes his son in the long-running narrative. As a boy, Will

(Grayson Stone) enjoyed his father's bedtime stories, but he has outgrown them. He refers to them as "lies" and he is embarrassed that his father continuously tells these tales. Will now seeks the "true versions of things, . . . of stories" related to his father's past. He believes his father lived a "second life" with another family. Will suspects his father cheated in his marriage and that he was too preoccupied with himself to be honest with Will. Will claims to not know his father, and this distance troubles him. As Will puts it, "We never talked about not talking." Frustrated, Will believes he is merely a "footnote" in his father's story. The "truth is," he claims, "I didn't see anything of myself in my father, and I don't think he saw anything of himself in me. We were like strangers who knew each other very well."

Ed is aware that he is a storyteller, and apparently he is aware that the presentation of himself through story is his own construct: "That's what I do. I tell stories," he asserts to his imploring son. Certainly he has learned to see himself as unique and presents himself accordingly. The central story of the film is the story of a giant catfish that eats Ed's wedding ring on the day of Will's birth. Along with the story of his marriage, these are the two most prominent of many fantastic tales that Ed often retells. As his death looms, he wishes to retell to his son's wife, Josephine (Marion Cotillard), the story of his marriage, grumbling that Will would have "told it [to her] wrong anyway—all the facts, none of the flavor." The negotiation of ritual passages throughout Ed's life—important events such as high school heroics, leaving home, getting a first job, serving in the military (and mistakenly being thought to have been killed in action), establishing a professional identity, getting married, and of course, becoming a father are all told and retold with customary flavor. But now Will wants truth, not tales. He tells his father, "I believed your stories. . . . I felt like a fool to have trusted you. You're like Santa Claus and the Easter Bunny combined—just as charming and just as fake." Defending himself, Ed angrily responds, "I've been nothing but myself since the day I was born and if you can't see that it's your failing, not mine."

In this tender plot, accented with colorful flashback scenes featuring a young Ed Bloom (Ewan McGregor), Will confronts his father's characteristic obstinacy while attempting to investigate the facts of his father's life. His search brings surprising results, which are finally confirmed when the family doctor (Robert Guillaume), who was present at Will's birth, announces the ordinary circumstances of Will's origin and in the process absolves any lingering misperceptions concerning Ed's apparent failures. Dr. Bennett brings

Will to a point of recognition and confirms for the audience the harmless, even necessary manner and motive of Ed's colorful identity.

In *Big Fish* storytelling is highlighted as a means of discourse. Though Will is a successful journalist, his investigative manner proves limited and pales when matched with his father's colorful narrative. Interestingly, both father and son are aware of their preferred narrative styles: "We're storytellers, both of us," Ed tells his agitated son. "I speak mine out. You write yours down—same thing." Clearly, the identity of both characters is vitally linked to their narratives, and as such the film offers a rich opportunity to discuss foundational philosophical issues concerning personal identity and the nature of the self. I shall focus on narrative accounts of identity, or what may be referred to as intersubjective accounts of the self. Proponents of these accounts maintain that self-identity is constructed as a narrative within a dynamic process of social and linguistic interaction, and they support the view of the self as a product of storytelling. After discussing the ways in which Ed Bloom's storytelling persona illustrates more abstract philosophical accounts of the self, I shall also comment on the role of storytelling in societal discourse as exemplified in the happy ending of *Big Fish.*

Society and Self-Construction

Burton's film suggests the importance of understanding narrative identity. In particular, it indicates that identity is best understood as an intersubjective construct. By *intersubjective* I mean the sharing of subjective states that affect human development. Through encounters with others sharing material space, physical interaction, and language, we develop the idea of the self, namely, a sense of who we are. Indeed, many modern philosophers would suggest that our identity is being formed before we ever reflect upon or conceptualize our own unique sense of self. The question of the self is a prominent one in philosophy. Theories of self-development and personal identity understandably connect to the way one sees the world, how one identifies others, how one judges others, and so forth. Given this, most philosophers eventually offer some commentary relevant to discussion of the human self, and the history of philosophy would suggest various ways of understanding the self. For example, some have believed the human self to be a carbon copy of a heavenly blueprint, whereas others have posited the self as a blank tablet upon which humans write selfhood into existence as a result of experiences. Metaphysical approaches to understanding the self often emphasize its a priori nature and claim the self to be independent of experience. For example, Plato (427–347 B.C.) suggests the empirical self is a mimetic reprint of an eternal soul. On the other hand, a posteriori positions hold that the self is a product of experience. Such views are held by philosophers who reject mimetic, essentialist accounts of the self and instead suggest that the self is a product of cumulating experience. For example, David Hume (1711–1776) argues that the human self is "nothing but a bundle or collection of different perceptions. . . . The mind is a kind of theater where several perceptions successfully make their appearance, pass, repass, glide away, and mingle in an infinite variety of positions and situations." As this passage suggests, Hume denies the existence of an enduring self. Indeed, he goes so far as to refer to the self as a "fiction."[1] Considering the self as a "fiction" anticipates Ed Bloom's storied self-presentation. Importantly, it introduces the notion of the self as narrative.

Much of contemporary philosophical discussion of the self originates with Rene Descartes (1596–1650), who famously identified the self as a "thinking thing" in his formula *cogito ergo sum* (I think, therefore I am).[2] In fact, almost all modern discussions of the self in some way respond to Descartes's characterization of the cogito as an independent substance. Bertrand Russell (1872–1970) summarizes the broad-ranging Cartesian effect on modern philosophy: "There is thus, in all philosophy derived from Descartes, a tendency to subjectivism."[3] The legacy of Descartes's formula, however, is a dualistic mind/body dichotomy. While this view may have offered a sense of certainty in the seventeenth century, it is one that many modern thinkers reject, favoring instead a more holistic understanding of mind, body, and self. What modern critics suggest constitutes the self is not fully covered by the cogito.

In this chapter, I draw from several a posteriori philosophers who reject essentialist views of the self, philosophers who attempt to transcend the Cartesian formula and reject the notion of a substantive human soul or a "transcendent ego."[4] According to several prominent philosophers, the narrative account of identity posits the self as a psychosocial construct, a creation made on the part of society and the subject in and through linguistic interaction. These philosophical views recognize the interactive, reciprocal construction of what we generally call the self. The self, then, is not the discovery of an existing thing. Instead, philosophers who endorse a narrative account of the self believe that personal narratives are being written for us even before we are fully aware of the social influences that shape identity. An intersubjective account of the human self is one that sees the self as arising from human experience and language. Clearly, this view of selfhood offers an excellent basis for understanding Ed Bloom's persona. Since selfhood is developed in a social context, narrative is a primary means by which human socializing is formed and reflected. Moreover, an intersubjective construction of selfhood provides critical understanding for dramatically illustrated depictions of the self in contemporary popular culture, specifically, in Burton's *Big Fish.*

Jean-Paul Sartre: Consciousness as Prerequisite for Selfhood

When considering an intersubjective notion of human self, it is important to consider what makes selfhood possible in the first place. An important concept for understanding selfhood is found in the work of Jean-Paul Sartre (1905–1980). His major work, *Being and Nothingness,* rejects an essentialist, substantive view of human identity.[5] Here Sartre denies that the self is substantive, eternal, or intrinsic to the human animal. Instead, he asserts that individual identity is a conceptual figure that evolves through experience. Specifically, Sartre argues that the human self is constructed over time as a result of ongoing interactions with others.

Being and Nothingness asserts that humans are profoundly affected by their material and linguistic surroundings long before they become reflective and aware of their own responses to such surroundings. Indeed, Sartre makes the role of social interaction clear when he characterizes human consciousness, in itself, as a nothing. As Sartre makes plain, consciousness is not a substantive thing. Just as the eye is distinct from what it sees, human consciousness is distinct from the material and linguistic contexts that eventually shape self-consciousness. For Sartre, consciousness is the negation of substance, a blank slate upon which human identity will eventually be formed. Consciousness, then, is the prerequisite for selfhood. However, it is not synonymous with it. Humans have consciousness but not intrinsic identity, so humans may be said to arrive on the scene with consciousness but not a self. Self-consciousness develops through the experiences that humans have, even experiences that begin long before reflective responses, and long before logical decision making. Human consciousness, developed over time through social interaction, eventually evolves to self-consciousness. Social interaction prompts both the internalization of socially assigned traits and reflection on the part of the individual. The internalization that begins in the prereflective states of human development literally forms the self. Eventually the reflective process makes possible the dissociation from that identity that was written for us before we became aware of those influences. Over time we become aware of those influences and begin intentional construction of personal identity. Sartre writes, "I see *myself* because *somebody* sees me."[6] Evolving from prereflective influences, self-consciousness is necessary for one to positively construct selfhood; however, consciousness alone is not sufficient.

For Sartre, the selfhood that one eventually develops has been shaped by prereflective experiences. Eventually, a reflective human may reject or affirm prereflective influences, but that awareness is not always comfortably experienced; it does not occur naturally simply because one is human. The influence of others is vital; the prereflective influence of others is foundational. As social animals, humans are continuously being shaped; that is, one's sense of self is dynamically constructed as one grows increasingly reflective. Humans begin to shape themselves based on the stage set by prereflective influences that have first begun to form the idea of who they are. Human development, then, is contingent upon being with others. Indeed, as Sartre states, others are a "necessary condition for [one's] being-for-[him/her]self."[7] Though self is an idea, a construct, it is situated in physical, tangible contexts. Therefore, others in the physical world shape us: "The Other holds a secret—the secret of what I am."[8] Over time, human consciousness begins to reflect the influence of others as humans develop a self: "The Other teaches [us] who [we are]."[9]

Sartre's view requires the actual physical, material reciprocal interactions with others, such as the "look" and "touch."[10] In other words, even in our prereflective state, consciousness is being developed as a result of our being seen and touched by others—and our varied responses to such overtures. For example, infantile physical, nonverbal communication is foundational for eventually confirming what we are *not* as well as what we may become. In addition to visual and tactile relationships, linguistic interaction becomes increasingly significant in order for individuals to develop self-consciousness: "The Other is always there, present and experienced as the one who gives to language its meaning."[11] Individuals depend on others to perform the reciprocal role of establishing an objective reality for themselves, and thus social interaction is vital in the development of human identity: "The Other accomplishes for us a function of which we are incapable and which nevertheless is incumbent upon us: *to see ourselves as we are.*"[12]

The Sartrean emphasis on consciousness as prerequisite for selfhood is necessary for the concept of narrative identity. We write ourselves into existence, we might say, but the fact of human consciousness is the tablet upon which we write. When we consider Sartre's claims in relation to the principal characters presented in *Big Fish,* we might well conclude that the identities of Ed and his son have been shaped long before they became cognizant of this shaping. We would also understand that the identities presented in the film follow from that initial shaping. Moreover, any intentional structuring of personal identity by either Ed or Will involves the affirmation or modification of the identity established in their prereflective states.

Although the film focuses on the reunion of father and son at the time of Ed Bloom's death, it provides some clues about Ed's childhood. One of his stories suggests that he was an unwanted child and was ostensibly fatherless. We can surmise that his larger-than-life personality may in some way be a compensatory posture based on the absence he felt and endured throughout his own childhood. This compensatory pattern continues in Ed's relationship to his son. The film clearly establishes that Ed told fantastic stories to young Will, but it also makes clear that Ed was gone from the home (on the road as a traveling salesman) for much of Will's childhood, and Will has come to equate his father's stories with his absence. Not only does he now hear the stories as lies, he considers them bribes for affection—cheap compensation for his father's failures. This is especially apparent with the related stories of the "Witch" (Helena Bonham Carter) whom Will fears is his father's lover. To Will, her character is suggestive of a "second life" and the probability that his father did not want a life with him. The lasting power of this early influence is understood when, just before his father's death, Will confronts the "Witch," inquiring about his father's supposed infidelity. Even when Will learns directly from her that his father did not cheat on his mother, he still is reluctant to embrace his father's storied identity, though his own investigation has proved his father not only innocent but also generous to others. As we'll see, Will's reluctance comes not only because accepting his father will involve embracing a new narrative for him but also because it will involve writing a new narrative for himself.

George Herbert Mead: The Generalized Other and the Social Sense of Self

Sartre empties the substance out of the self, leaving consciousness as the base subjective condition of identity. Like Sartre, George Herbert Mead

(1863–1931) also emphasizes the social construction of human identity. Mead discusses the sorts of interactions that help construct the self, and in doing so he sheds light on how this entity evolves through social activity, particularly through role-playing.

Mead claims, "The self . . . is essentially a social structure, and it arises in social experience."[13] He believes human interaction is much like game playing and that, even as children, humans gain much of their identity through their discovery of established roles while playing games. In such games one understands the expected responses of others who are also playing roles. In the interaction, then, an individual's sense of self is developed within the expectations of the community with which one is involved. Mead's term for this anticipated response is the "generalized other."[14] By this he means that one's individual experience recognizes and accounts for the cumulative and organized, expected experience of the community outside oneself. In this sense, "social process influences the behavior of the individuals involved. . . . The community exercises control over the conduct of its individual members," though as I will point out, individual peculiarity remains a normal possibility.[15]

An individual's sense of self is developed by his or her particular attitudes toward other individuals, but a more generalized understanding of the attitudes of the group to which one belongs is also being confirmed through social, linguistic intercourse. Mead concludes, "A person is a personality because he belongs to a community, because he takes over the institutions of that community into his own conduct."[16] In a sense, one knows the Other before one knows (or even has) a self. One cannot develop a sense of self without the capacity to reflect. Interacting with others, particularly in the context of role-playing, helps the individual understand the concept of a self, namely, the concept of a discrete individual with specific traits as well as functions. The playing of a role implies the ability and readiness to see the self as others see it. Role-playing develops the ability to recognize the self as a construct and to adapt one's behavior to that construct. In role-playing, children are introduced to opportunities to "play" at being a person. Common childhood activities serve as rehearsals, where children learn to consider how the self is projected, how to anticipate responses, how to deal with reactions, and so on.

According to Mead, it is important to recognize the distinction between "I" and "me" when understanding the self. The "I" is the "response of the organism to the attitudes of the others while the 'me' is the organized set of attitudes of others that one assumes." The "me" functionality of a human constitutes how one understands communal perceptions of the self, a "definite organization of the community in our own attitudes." The self is a "social process going on," a dialogue of sorts between "I" and "me." In other words, "all selves" come into being by a social process and are "individual reflections" of the encountered social process.[17] Importantly, Mead's distinction is analogous to the one Sartre draws between consciousness and the conceptual figure of the self. Specifically, the "I" corresponds to consciousness whereas the "me" corresponds to the reflexive concept of the self. Whereas the "me" is determined initially and for the most part through social relations, at the same time the "I" and "me" relate to one another in a sort of feedback loop. Sartre refers to this as the circuit of selfhood.[18] Mead is attuned to this as well, and both see the interchange between the "I" of bare consciousness and its conceptual representation as the basis for individual structuring of the self.

As the foregoing suggests, the relation between individual consciousness and the individual self contributes to the potential for individuality. As both Sartre and Mead point out, while the socializing process, with its expected roles and appropriate responses, establishes a certain degree of conformity regarding selfhood, it does not deny individual personality. Mead allows that despite the socializing process, "every individual self has its own peculiar individuality, its own unique pattern," because each individual forms his or her own personal response to the community. Mead argues that an individual is "continually reacting back against" society and the "common social origin" and its "structure does not preclude wide individual differences and variations among them . . . or contradict the peculiar and more or less distinctive individuality" that each individual may possess.[19] Sartre echoes Mead's sentiment here, emphasizing that individuals each have their own facticity that makes them unique and, more importantly, possess consciousness, which, as a nothingness, can negate or change what it is given.

This emphasis on peculiarity is especially important in Burton's film when the characterization of Ed Bloom is considered. Beyond the social interaction that surrounds and shapes him in accordance with the models of Sartre and Mead, Burton's *Big Fish* celebrates a peculiar character in Will's father, one whose unique personality is a product of its social interactions and yet is anything but conformist. The film suggests that Ed was always too big for his hometown, so he set out to find a destiny that could accommodate his growing sense of self. After his military service, certainly the demands of his employment that often took him away from home, along with the desire to please and to help others he encountered—all contributed to how he has presented himself to others. His absence was troubling to Will, and despite the amusing stories of childhood, Will grew to reject his father's presentation of self. As the son of a colorful, hyperbolic storyteller, Will has failed to fulfill the dynamic possibilities of the social context he has inherited. Instead he rejects his father's identity. A flashback scene at Will's wedding shows Will reprimanding his father because Ed upstaged him by telling stories at the occasion. As a result of this argument, we are told that Will went three years without speaking to his father. Even if we allow that his father sometimes inappropriately seeks attention, the fact that Will goes three years without speaking to a man who is obviously loved and respected by Will's mother (and Will's wife, Josephine) indicates a deeper wound. It suggests that regardless of Ed's occasional lack of propriety, Will has not yet learned to navigate his own sense of self. Instead, he appears insecure, prompting him to be petty and reactive, rather than accommodating. Will's conflict suggests his own limited understanding of human development. In the terms of Mitchell Aboulafia, he may be a "circumscribed self" rather than a "mediating self."

Mitchell Aboulafia: Mediating Self or Circumscribed Self

Contemporary philosopher Mitchell Aboulafia also emphasizes the social and reflexive nature of the human self. Like Sartre and Mead, and drawing from both, Aboulafia regards the self as the product of narrative. His work is helpful when considering a mature individual who has sufficient self-consciousness to influence the construction of his or her identity.

Building on the views of Sartre and Mead, in *The Mediating Self* Aboulafia claims that individual human freedom, that is, "the capacity to decide in a purposeful fashion what one believes or what course of action to follow, is itself to be understood as integrally bound to the social."[20] Aboulafia's specific contribution to this discussion involves his concept of "the mediating self." This phrase refers to the human need to reach a normal point of self-determination. Similar to Mead's emphasis on role-playing, Aboulafia writes, "From very early on, the human being is presented with the alternative of either rejecting or identifying with the other."[21] Like Mead with his emphasis on role-playing, Aboulafia asserts that a child, in the process of determining rejection or identification, "comes to have a consciousness of object-self and alternatives to object-self," and that "only by taking the role of the other" does one develop "appreciation for the existence of alternatives."[22]

Aboulafia claims that the human self is more than "merely an object-self." This is important since Aboulafia emphasizes the goal of self-determination for a mature individual. Self-determination, however, or the ability to mediate oneself within complex social situations, must be learned and carefully negotiated. This adaptability is not innate. Instead, as he explains, "children are often startled" by responses to the external world and by their own responses, which may vary from what they had previously expected.[23] Aboulafia extends Sartre's understanding of the preconsciousness to explain that children learn "to live in a world of anticipation . . . , a world of the coming to be that is not and might not be. . . . Sociality and the internalization of the negative [any unexpected "novelty"] together produce a consciousness which, even when it does not explicitly reflect on itself, that is make of itself an object, orients itself in the world by moving toward that which it is not, and this is evident in the roles we take and live."[24]

Aboulafia's concept of a mediating self means "human beings are not simply object-selves. By interacting with others, human beings become conscious of what they are not."[25] While individuals initially tend to internalize, or take on, the identities ("object-selves") ascribed to them by others, normally, as they develop they acquire the capacity to alter their self, rather than just accept the identity that is, to a great extent, socially assigned. As Aboulafia explains, initially this ability to intentionally modify the self appears as a simple rejection of the assigned identity. Adolescent rebellion serves as a good example. However, as individuals "mature and become more aware of that which is object-self in contrast to not-self, the reflective organizing of the object-self by consciousness becomes possible." Over time, because consciousness affords us freedom and because self-consciousness yields understanding of the way the self is constructed, we can come to participate intentionally in the structuring of our own selves and participate in a way that is not merely passive (uncritical assimilation of social roles), or reactive (willful rejection of social roles), but responsive. In short, one may become a mediating self rather than a determined one.[26] One's growing awareness of self in relation to another allows one to modify one's sense of self.[27]

Of course, becoming a mediating self is a dynamic, complex process that may be limited, frustrated, and delayed by a number of negative factors in one's environment as well as one's own lack of courage. Such negative interference with human development can lead to what Aboulafia calls a determined self, or "circumscribed self." Rather than freely exercising self-determination, the "circumscribed self" descends into a subordinate position to function at the mercy of others.[28] Burton's *Big Fish,* then, posits Will at a crisis point, and he illustrates the concept of a circumscribed self. He is about to become a parent as his father, from whom he feels emotionally estranged, approaches death. Will is frustrated because his angered, three-year hiatus from his father has not changed his father at all, and on his deathbed, Ed continues to tell stories rather than grant Will a literal recounting of his life. At this crisis point, Will is faced with the Aboulafian choice: to intentionally mediate his own sense of self within the context of his father's manner, or to continue his empty quest of vainly trying to make his father be what he is not, to be what he never has been.

"What Do You Want, Will? Who Do You Want Me to Be?"

The philosophical claim that the human self is the result of interaction with others is applicable to *Big Fish.* Will falsely assumes that he knows his father. Unfortunately, he doesn't really know himself, let alone his father. Because his father is so different from himself, Will concludes that his father must be a liar or a fool, or both. Sartre says that "since I am what I am not and since I am not what I am—I can not even define myself."[29] For Sartre, Mead, and Aboulafia the self is inextricably linked to others. It is not possible, therefore, to escape the influence of others and to attempt to do so is to fail to be honest about the true nature of the self. Will, however, seems to see individuality as a vacuum untouched by the perception of others. He too easily dismisses the prereflective and other early influences that contributed to the shaping of his father's personality, as well as his own. Moreover, he seems to think his own sense of knowing the truth about his father's past will somehow establish his own sense of identity, perhaps heal a wound or even settle a score between them. Ed's stories are just too fantastic for a rational person like Will to accept. Therefore, since Ed's stories are beyond belief, Ed must be a liar withholding factual details. Will assumes that factual details, should they be presented, would somehow rectify the past and, even more important to him, happily establish his imminent future as a father. Will's identity is initially and predictably established reactively *and* passively. Rather than identify with his dad's identity, he has passively rejected it, forging a self that is the logical contrary of his dad—reporter of facts, not teller of tales. On the occasion of the film, however, since his social context seems to have validated his sense of self, Will feels empowered to assert his investigative self against his father. Whereas his father's identity is compensatory, Will's attempt to get him to tell the truth is retributive. Their continued conflict is damaging. A "win" for Will would be hollow, really, because it would merely entrench a circumscribed, reactive self rather than foster growth.

As I have indicated earlier, from the perspective of Mead, Will does not allow for the peculiarity of his father. Will demands that his father mirror the "generalized other" as he mirrors it. Will assumes a static role that a truth-telling father should embody, as well as that of a truth-seeking son. Will's inability to embrace his father's storytelling persona negatively reinforces a one-dimensional understanding of human existence—that of a prescribed role—one that Ed has decidedly rejected. Apparently, Will wants to rewrite his dad's narrative in terms acceptable to himself. Will is unable to acknowledge that narrative can be presented in colorful ways other than a presumed objective truth. While Will fails to clearly understand his father's sense of identity, he nonetheless rejects what he imagines. He contends for an alternative narrative. He favors the reporter over the storyteller. Ed's story is so troubling to Will, in part, because it is so obviously a construct. Desiring conformity rather than unique individuality, Will resents his father's social self.

Will is reluctant to allow his father the appropriate blessing of self-determination. He wants to determine his father's identity. Will stubbornly refuses to alter his horizon to recognize the dynamic roles we play when encountering the Other. Will's refusal to identify with his father, and to understand the circumstances that shape his father's self, ironically limits his own horizon. This stubborn obsession leaves him teetering on the edge of being a circumscribed self, one who fails "to embrace the [perceived] negative as [his] own."[30] Will struggles to negotiate his own sense of self because he fears the power that his father's identity presents. He intuits that to have his own unique sense of self he must accept his father's identity. Such a possibility is particularly troubling to him because, for one thing, to embody his father's manner seems foreign, even unnatural to him. For an even more important reason, Will thinks his father's manner is merely a guise for a dishonest, irresponsible life. For Will, to be like his father implies that he must also be cartoonish and dishonest. The proverb "like father, like son" is a disturbing notion to him, and as a result he resists seeing the lines of connection between himself and his father, principally that they are both storytellers.

Will is humiliated by the fact that he is biologically and socially connected to an eccentric character, and he fears that his own story has been modified in a way he does not like due to this association. As a consequence, he has distanced himself emotionally from his father, but now, at the occasion of the film, he is trying one last time to change his father rather than accept him as he is. His father's imminent death is creating the crisis in Will's character. Though he presents the crisis as a need to get the facts right before it is too late, from a psychological standpoint, it could instead be that the imminent absence of his father removes the entity against which Will has defined himself. Ed is the scapegoat for all that Will is not. Without him, Will *will* have to define himself.

The fact of social, linguistic interaction, however, does not alone explain the dynamic of Will and his father. We may recognize that Will's personality and his father's identity, like those of all humans, develop within a construct of language and reflective gestures and other feedback that human social interaction makes possible, but how are we to explain the storytelling persona that Ed has adopted? Why has his narrative identity formed in such an apparently fantastic, almost mythical manner?[31] These questions are troubling to Will, and though they are not simply answered (the film gives us *what* more than *why*), the storytelling capacity of humankind is celebrated in the film's episodes and confirmed by its conclusion. *Big Fish* is an apt illustration of the philosophical notion of narrative identity because Ed provides a hyperbolic example of the potential role and power of narrative. Though all of our identities are narrative, sometimes we do not fully appreciate that conventional discourse is also narrative and is also socially constructed. Ed's stories and Will's role as a journalist highlight this fact. News is narrative, but it is a narrative that denies itself as narrative. Will wants his dad to tell a story of himself that does not sound like a story. He wants this because he, as Ed's son, wants to be more than a character in a fiction. However, as a journalist, Will (in cooperation with the various societies he inherited and with which he interacts) is also playing a role. His life is also a narrative construct, though he fails to recognize this fact. He also fails to acknowledge the rich variety of expressive forms and roles that are possible when considering identity as narrative.

Walter Benjamin: The Decline of Storytelling

I turn now to the aspect of storytelling, which is to be seen as one means of creating narrative identity. At this point my discussion shifts a bit. Up to this point, the commentary of Sartre, Mead, and Aboulafia has assumed a social interaction within actual, that is, nonfictive, interaction. In other words, in real life, not just in created stories, humans develop their narrative identity via socialization. But reading Walter Benjamin (1892–1940) suggests the consideration of fictional contexts to comment on the manner and motive of narrative identity. *Big Fish,* after all, is fiction, so the question at hand assumes a connection between fictional representation and actual living. Some might argue that fiction is a misrepresentation of reality. In the case of *Big Fish* in particular, one could argue that Ed Bloom's representation is exaggerated (as is Will's perception of and reaction to him) and thus not to be taken as seriously as philosophers would contemplate. It's just a movie, after all, not real life, some might protest.

Certainly I disagree. I believe that fiction and actual life inform and shape each other. Two significant warrants of narrative identity include: First, and as the foregoing explains, in literal, nonfictive life, one's actual sense of self is brought into existence, shaped, and concluded very much as a story is created, extended, and concluded. Second, story, like all social interaction, occurs through the medium of language, with its various forms of expression. So if these two basic tenets are allowed, then understanding the value and methodology of storytelling seems relevant and necessary. In *Big Fish,* not only does Ed Bloom see life as a continuum of stories, but further, he comfortably finds himself starring in a plot that he did not solely create but one that is surely augmented by his dramatic persona.

In his elegiac yet stimulating essay "The Storyteller," Walter Benjamin reflects on both the method and value of storytelling. Though he laments the "remove[al of] narrative from the realm of living speech" in modern society (which, of course, reinforces the reasons to celebrate Burton's happy-ending saga of Ed and Will Bloom), Benjamin contends the supremacy of story. A storyteller is "a man who has counsel for his readers" because he provides, among other things, "wisdom . . . counsel woven into the fabric of real life is wisdom." Of course, the efficacy of storytelling assumes a society instructed in the art of listening, an attribute Will lacks. Storytelling flourishes in a society whose members appreciate that which "cannot be abbreviated."[32]

Benjamin affirms the "companionship" that is to be found in the artful process of storytelling.[33] A companionship exists between story, teller, and listener. One of the saddest facts of *Big Fish* is that the audience is fully aware that Will shares only a perfunctory relationship with his father. He is duty-bound to be alongside him at the time of death, but their companionship, until the final moments of the film, is forced, at best. Rather than invoking camaraderie and community, Ed's storytelling is an obstacle that Will feels he must overcome before he can embrace his dying father. In a way it seems that father and son are vying to control the narrative of the Bloom family. Both father and son seem to cling to a preconceived discourse that seems manageable to each—the implied fact-driven journalistic narrative represented by Will and the hyperbolic, fantastic presentation of self rendered in Ed. It is important to notice, however, that neither Ed's wife nor Will's wife, Josephine, nor the members of Ed's community share Will's preoccupation with changing his father. No one in the film but Will is put off by Ed's manner. No one but Will is suspicious of his motive. Clearly Burton sides with the storyteller when he grants his narrative greater truth than that of the journalist. In this story, the fact-seeking journalist gets the story wrong. The characters that Will assumes are fictions show up at Ed's funeral. Will discovers that reality is bigger than he thought, and that his dad was a Big Fish.

Storytellers have traditionally held a place of honor in human societies because they help us "shake off the nightmare . . . placed upon [society's] chest." In other words, Benjamin recognizes the value of lifting the burden of human experience (which is destined for death) by lightening the mood via a good story. One's authority is found not only in his "knowledge or wisdom, but above all his real life . . . the stuff that stories are made of. . . . This authority is at the very source of the story."[34] In *Big Fish,* Will is glum. Naturally, others close to Ed are saddened at his impending death, yet they are rather cheerful in spirit, even happily acknowledging the storied memories of Ed's life. In fact, at first it doesn't seem that Will's dour demeanor is a function of his dad's impending death; instead, he seems inconvenienced and irritated by it. Others close to Ed are not paralyzed by the depressing need for unnecessary, literal disclosure that Will neurotically feels. Ed knows he is dying and, far from delusional, he vigorously, if not triumphantly, plays his role. He is narrating his mediated, happy self in the plot as he understands the role that has been constructed. The film is poignant because in the end Ed needs his son to help him complete his narrative. As his energy wanes, it is harder for him to hold his narrative together. He needs Will's assistance to craft the final chapter. Their mutual assistance, their shared authorship, their combined storytelling makes for a joyous and meaningful ending.

The Uncatchable Fish: Will Bloom's Happy Ending

The looming, inescapable context of death is the source of storytelling.[35] Similar to the emphasis of dialectically embracing others (as emphasized by the philosophers referenced in this paper), storytelling is a natural, visual, dialectical process of encountering the Other, of embracing what is not us. Will's reluctance to accept the dynamic of storytelling, especially at the critical time of his father's impending death, suggests his own fear of mortality that has kept him perpetually suspicious.[36] In other areas of life, Will seems normal, happily married, successful, and responsible to his wife, mother, father, and community. Through its portrayal of Will's limited view of narrative, Burton's film argues that contemporary culture has lost the fantastic, abandoned the joy of imagination, settling instead for an arduous, joyless sense of human progress while at the same time denying the very essence of what it means to be human. Benjamin decries a decline of storytelling in the face of what he calls "the dissemination of information [that] has had a decisive share in this state of affairs."[37] Burton, like Benjamin, laments modernity's loss of story, especially the fantastic story. The devaluation of story has negative consequences for humanity since storytelling involves more than escapist entertainment. It offers a means of coping, as it presents a way of imagining and mediating the self within the structured restraints that time, society, and language impose. Through imaginative storytelling, we do not have to passively accept what is given. Granted, there are natural limits; however, fantastic stories rejuvenate our appreciation of human innovation and celebrate the creative impulse that makes life more than mindless repetition.

Professionally, Will lives and moves within a world of facts and value claims that are in constant tension. His work as a journalist suggests a pursuit of truth regarding political and social issues, but it also suggests a narrow view, a limited way of understanding human motivation and action. Will functions in a corporate world that willfully suppresses the notion that narrative constructs reality. Perhaps with the rise of self-importance in our technological age, we presumptively believe we have outgrown storytelling. If so, Will represents the impotence of a mass culture that has denuded itself with a narrow definition of truth, and in doing so cut away an important basis of human interaction. *Big Fish* suggests humans are naturally given to storytelling, and when we reduce ourselves to a story-less existence we accept a diminished reality.

The prosaic truth of Will's identity is finally revealed near the end of the film. Dr. Bennett's blunt testimony exposes the bare facts of Will's origin, ironically fulfilling Will's empty quest for truth and in the process demonstrating how Will's view of reality robs us of the joy of storytelling and dismisses the multiple layers of discovery even as it wrongly considers that his father is somehow responsible for life beyond his control. For example, both Will and the audience learn that Ed was not present at Will's birth because Will was born early, while Ed was away on business. Had the birth occurred on or near the expected date, there is reason to believe Ed would have been present.

Ironically, it could be argued that Will's dissatisfaction with his father follows from the fact that he has, on some level at least, bought into Ed's hyperbolic self-image and therefore attributes greater power to him than is necessary. Will's lingering protestation of his father's personality belies his claim that he doesn't believe Ed's narrative. Will claims that his dad should have behaved differently. It is worth considering, however, that Ed generated his hyperbolic narrative, in part, to compensate for his sense of disempowerment (maybe even guilt) at not being able to do all he wanted personally for his family because simply providing for them commanded most of his available time. In his role as a traveling salesman, gone from home several weeks at a time, he encountered many people, and apparently he soothed the pain of being away from his family by developing an outgoing, people-pleasing, entertaining persona. This personality not only enabled Ed to positively assert his will on the world he encountered, it also helped him cope and adjust to the pressing reality of his own young life, glimpses of which are visible through colorful flashback scenes—colorful but also compensatory.

Will believes his father's hyperbolic personality is covering something unreal or unnatural. He thinks his father is masking inadequacy, but such conclusions are not verified by the film. In the end, it is Ed's storied vision of life that is affirmed while Will's concerns for truth are dismissed as narrow and inconsequential. Happily, the film ends with Will accepting his father's life, and this acceptance is colorfully depicted in a fantastic portrayal of story. Beside his father's bed at the moment of death, Will fulfills his father's last wish. The roles are reversed. Will completes the saga; Will tells the ending of the story! At this critical moment, Will changes. He becomes a teller of a fantastic tale; he becomes like his dad. Will's initial panic (as his dad is literally breathing his last breaths) gives way to a glint in his eye as he tells of father and son escaping the hospital, jumping into the fire-red Charger, and speeding away to the river. The pace of the story accelerates. "The story of my life," Ed gleefully interrupts. Father and son arrive at the river. Every character from Ed's life is on the bank to "send [him] off right." Will carries his father into the immortal stream, releasing him from the bonds of mortality—bonds that Ed has challenged throughout his life with his stories.

This fantastic scene depicts the death of Ed Bloom; it triumphantly climaxes his personal epic. Most importantly, however, it is told by Will. In this critical shift, Will's telling is a spontaneous, gracious act that reunites father and son, at last, by story. The film shifts, then, to the day of the funeral. The camera silently pans Ed's many friends who have come to pay their respects. In some of these scenes, the mourners appear to be retelling stories, presumably memorable encounters with the man they loved. Burton's film ends with a future scene in which dialogue between Will and his son confirms a story about a "giant" that the son is telling to friends. Will and the boys are outside and laughter resounds. Everyone is happy. Then we hear Will's final comment: "A man tells his stories so many times that he becomes the stories; they live on after him, and in that way he becomes immortal."

It is important to recognize that Will's newfound satisfaction occurs with the help of others. His mother, his wife, Dr. Bennett, and other members of the community (along with his persistent father) all serve to bring Will to understanding and acceptance. This point makes it clear that the Will who comes to accept his father has allowed himself to be shaped by others, thereby affirming the intersubjective nature of the human self. The reciprocal involvement of others helping Will to acceptance suggests that Will Bloom will bloom (as the pun in his name implies). In the end we applaud Will's newly discovered ability to mediate his own sense of self. The happy ending of Burton's film is not simplistic nor is it merely sentimental. Burton's celebration of the storyteller is colorful, but it is also a powerful and important depiction of the formation of human identity. *Big Fish* articulates a theory of identity that is parallel to the philosophical theories discussed in this paper. Masterfully, Burton displays both negative implications and positive affirmations that can occur when considering such philosophical positions.

Notes

I am indebted to Jennifer McMahon for her helpful insight with this paper. Any shortcoming remains my responsibility. In this chapter I will generally use *self* as a comprehensive term to denote the subjective human interaction referred to by the referenced sources, though various philosophers use various distinctive terms depending upon certain contextual emphases. Terms such as *self, ego, consciousness, awareness, personality, identity,* and so on are not necessarily synonymous, though in this paper I often refer to them as indicative of human subjectivity. The epigraph is from Paul Ricoeur, *Oneself as Another* (Chicago: University of Chicago Press, 1992), 3.

1. David Hume, "A Treatise of Human Nature," in *The Essential David Hume,* ed. and intro. Robert Paul Wolff (New York: New American Library, 1969), 131–32. His use of the term *fiction* implies the self is constructed and opposes a priori metaphysical, substantive notions of "soul" or "self."

2. Rene Descartes, *Discourse on Method and Meditations,* trans. and intro. Laurence J. Lafleur (New York: Macmillan, 1960), 24–25.

3. Bertrand Russell, *A History of Western Philosophy* (New York: Simon and Schuster, 2007), 564. Russell concludes, "Modern philosophy has very largely accepted the formulation . . . from Descartes, while not accepting his solutions" (565).

4. Sartre uses the term *transcend* in *Transcendence of the Ego,* trans., anno., and intro. Forrest Williams and Robert Kirkpatrick (New York: Noonday Press, 1957), a text designed to refute the Cartesian cogito, namely, to transcend a transcendent model of the self and, in so doing, return the self to the phenomenal sphere. In a similar understanding, Mitchell Aboulafia, in *The Mediating Self: Mead, Sartre, and Self-Determination* (New Haven, CT: Yale University Press, 1986), 11, uses the phrase *transcendent ego* when referring to metaphysical positions, a phrase that subjective philosophers such as Sartre reject.

5. Jean-Paul Sartre, *Being and Nothingness,* trans. and intro. Hazel E. Barnes (New York: Washington Square Books, 1956).

6. Ibid., 349; emphasis in original.

7. Ibid., 322.

8. Ibid., 475.

9. Ibid., 366.

10. Ibid., 340, 461.

11. Ibid., 487.

12. Ibid., 463; emphasis in original.

13. George Herbert Mead, *The Social Psychology of George Herbert Mead,* ed. and intro. Anselm Strauss (Chicago: University of Chicago Press / Phoenix Books, 1956), 217.

14. Ibid., 231.

15. Ibid., 232.

16. Ibid., 235, 239.

17. Ibid., 243, 246, 247.

18. Sartre, *Being and Nothingness,* 155–58.

19. Mead, *Social Psychology,* 248, 249.

20. Aboulafia, *Mediating Self,* xvi.

21. Ibid., 92.

22. Ibid.

23. Ibid., 94.

24. Ibid., 95.

25. Ibid., 98.

26. See the Weldon chapter in this volume for further discussion of identity development, particularly as it pertains to gender.

27. Aboulafia, *Mediating Self,* 100.

28. Ibid., 126. Aboulafia relies on Hegel's master/slave dialectic, ultimately concluding, "If I have lived my life as a circumscribed object-self, whose sense of self has either not developed or been severely restricted, I will seek to nurture my object self on the limited recognition provided by those who are the leaders of society, for they symbolically embody the (generalized) other that has constituted me."

29. Sartre, *Being and Nothingness,* 348.

30. Aboulafia, *Mediating Self,* 126.

31. Ed Bloom's hyperbolic pose, in one sense, approaches the mythical, as if he is a mythic hero. Mircea Eliade, in *Myth and Reality* (New York: Harper Colophon Books, 1963), distinguishes between various definitions of myth: an invented, fictive, illusionary fable on the one hand, and a true, sacred, communal story on the other. Will Bloom's persona assumes the illusionary definition, while Ed's character seems to transcend this definition. A related study could invoke Joseph Campbell's *The Hero with a Thousand Faces* (Princeton, NJ: Princeton University Press, 1968), considering Ed as the hero who "ventures forth from the world of common day into a region of supernatural wonder: fabulous forces are there encountered and a decisive victory is won: the hero comes back from this mysterious adventure with the power to bestow boons on his fellow man"(30).

32. Walter Benjamin, "The Storyteller," in *The Novel: An Anthology of Criticism and Theory, 1900–2000,* ed. Dorothy J. Hale (Malden, MA: Blackwell, 2006), 364, 368.

33. Ibid., 372.

34. Ibid., 374, 369.

35. Ibid., 369. Benjamin writes, "Death is the sanction of everything that the storyteller can tell. He has borrowed his authority from death. In other words, it is natural history to which his stories refer back."

36. See the McMahon chapter in this volume for further discussion of how anxiety regarding mortality shapes individual experience and finds expression in the works of Tim Burton.

37. Benjamin, "The Storyteller," 365.

Catwoman and Subjectivity

Constructions of Identity and Power in Tim Burton's *Batman Returns*

Ryan Weldon

Tim Burton's films always contain a cast of interesting characters. Primarily, his character construction and interaction with the plot revolve around a critique of the normal. Normalcy, by whatever yardstick the viewer measures it, never goes unconsidered in a Tim Burton film. We see this in movies as diverse in setting and storytelling as *Edward Scissorhands* (1990) and *Sleepy Hollow* (1999). Often Burton portrays the normal people, the powerful people, and the conventionally beautiful people as possessing deep character flaws, and the entrenched systems of discourse in which they participate as pervasively corrupt. This corruption is a study in inauthenticity deriving from a subversion of individual integrity. Inauthenticity, in the existentialist sense, results from denying an important fact of our being: that we create our own values. When we are being inauthentic, we place the responsibility for our values outside of ourselves and act on those values as if they were something outside of ourselves. Burton examines the attempt to act authentically in a world in which his characters seem to have no place and no recourse to the roles legitimized by society and the power inherent in that legitimacy.

The Batman legend is an ideal field for an exploration of self, agency, power, and authenticity. The dark Gothic shadows and midcentury styling of Burton's Gotham City provide a backdrop that resonates with the internal struggles of the characters. While the deep divide between Batman's (Michael Keaton) personae—billionaire playboy and vigilante night creature—is at the core of many Batman tales, in *Batman Returns* (1992) the most interesting example of a character struggling with identity and authenticity is Catwoman/Selina Kyle (Michelle Pfeiffer).[1] As any fan of DC Comics knows,

Catwoman has a long and tangled history. From thrill-seeking socialite to tough as nails prostitute, Catwoman has been portrayed as having a variety of origins, motivations, and personalities. Although Burton's take on the character has its detractors, the Catwoman of *Batman Returns* is particularly interesting because she presents an overt representation of internal struggle. In this she is different from Batman. In the context of Burton's Gotham, we encounter Batman in medias res. He's been Batman for a while, and we are not given a window into his becoming. In contrast, we see Selina Kyle become Catwoman. Because of this, Selina Kyle/Catwoman provides an excellent subject for an examination of the interplay between Self and Other and between the individual and society, as well as how the interaction of the two construct identity and shape agency.[2] We get to watch Catwoman negotiate her identity in relation to her past as Max Shreck's meek secretary. Catwoman's journey to authenticity depends on both accepting her own alterity and integrating it into a coherent self, rather than denying it in favor of less authentic but more socially acceptable alternatives. To examine the role that authenticity and the Other play in the evolution of Catwoman in *Batman Returns,* it's useful to discuss what these terms mean from a philosophical standpoint.

Authenticity is a core idea in the existentialist philosophy of Jean-Paul Sartre (1905–1980). In "The Humanism of Existentialism," Sartre defines existentialism as "a doctrine that makes human life possible, and, in addition, declares that every truth and every action implies a human setting and a human subjectivity."[3] For Sartre, authenticity requires that we acknowledge our role in the creation of our own values and take personal responsibility for acting on those values. Authenticity, therefore, revolves around the power of choice and the tension between our *facticity* and our *transcendence.* The term *facticity* refers to the aspects of our existence over which we do not have any current say. A portion of our facticity is our environment: the circumstances and conditions into which we are born. None of us asked to be born in a particular time or place and under our particular material conditions. The other portion of our facticity springs from our past choices. We make choices in how we engage with our environment; these choices shape our lives and, in the process, the facts of our being evolve over time. As we make choices and consequences result from those choices, the multiple possibilities of our future become the inalterable facts of our past. Yet facticity is only half of the human equation.

Transcendence, on the other hand, is our ability to acquire freedom from this facticity and move beyond it through the power of our own choices. For Sartre, any denial of our capacity to transcend the facticity of our past by making choices means that we abdicate the responsibility for our choices in the creation of our lives (e.g., through determining our values and then acting on them). To act authentically, human beings must, among other things, acknowledge the responsibility of choice that comes with our consciousness. Our consciousness gives us the power to appreciate our situation and how we relate to it. Inauthenticity comes from refusing this sort of self-awareness.

In *Being and Nothingness,* Sartre illustrates this inauthenticity through observing a waiter. Sartre notes, after close observation, that "the waiter in the café plays with his condition in order to *realize* it." His *waiter-ness* is not an authentic extension of who he is but rather what the waiter feels he must be in the context of his role. He is playing a game, a game wherein his own self-consciousness places the responsibility for his behavior outside himself. Rather than be himself waiting tables, the waiter is adopting an idea of what it means to be a waiter and then performing it. The person the waiter is expected to be is undetermined by the waiter himself, and in this respect it is at odds with his authentic self. The authentic self is not merely the self that makes choices, however. It is the self that recognizes that its choices are not unlimited, but that choices proceed from a past that limits them. The waiter's performance is an example of inauthenticity, or what Sartre calls "bad faith." A bad faith performance is this sort of alienating performance, where our self-awareness abstracts the roles and performances we take on as something we do not choose to do and as if there were no possibility of rejecting them. It's not that one is necessarily acting in bad faith when performing the role of a waiter, but it is bad faith to not acknowledge this participation as a choice that will condition one's being. Failing to acknowledge his power of choice places the waiter in a state of *alterity,* where he is alienated from the facticity of his past identity and his responsibility for choices made in that past as well as from the transcendence that is possible through recognition of the role of his choice in establishing possible future identities.[4]

Feeling alienated from one's own agency, however, is not always a condition that derives from a chosen performance. The weight of facticity that's based on the conditions and circumstances of our birth is not necessarily equal between all kinds of people. Simone de Beauvoir (1908–1986) explores this alienation as a matter of systemic privilege in *The Second Sex.* Beauvoir, an existentialist and Sartre's long-term romantic partner, describes this alienation as part of being *Other.* According to Beauvoir, "no group sets itself up as the One [the Self, the normal], without at once setting up the Other over and against itself." It's a "them versus us" mentality. Beauvoir gives us a couple examples of this. She writes, "If three travelers happen to occupy the same compartment, that is enough to make vaguely hostile 'others' out of all the rest of the passengers on the train. In small-town eyes all persons not belonging to the village are 'strangers' and suspect; to the native of a country, all who inhabit other countries are 'foreigners'; Jews are 'different' to the anti-Semite, Negroes are inferior to the American racists, aborigines are 'natives' for colonists, proletarians are the 'lower class' for the privileged." Thus, to be Other (the "them") is to be objectified because those people who occupy the category of the Other never define themselves that way, but are instead defined by those who occupy the category of the One (the "us"). The Other is always the alternative and never the essential.

While Beauvoir acknowledges that the Other shows up in arenas other than gender, women as Other are her primary concern; as she sees it, our society privileges men. Men are assigned more value and are set as the norm against which women are measured. This makes women an alternative rather than just a normal part of humanity in and of themselves. For Beauvoir, this condition of being Other, and therefore an object, places women in an untenable crisis where they are doubly alienated. She writes, "Evidently to play at being a man will be for her [woman] a source of frustration; but to play at being a woman is also a delusion: to be a woman would mean to be the object, the *Other*—and the Other nevertheless remains subject in the midst of her resignation."

In this way, Beauvoir describes a condition of inauthenticity through performance, much in the same way that Sartre describes with his waiter. Unlike the waiter, however, the issue of bad faith performance in Beauvoir's discussion of women goes beyond the enacting of a professional role. If women are the Other, the objectified, then their facticity is not entirely on par with men's as an issue of choice; it doesn't have the same weight. In the terms discussed previously, they are neither recognized as having nor socially sanctioned to have the same opportunities for transcendence as their male counterparts. Instead, inauthentic performance is thrust upon them through their societal objectification. As the "alternative," they are defined by—and in relation to—the "normal" (men) and are expected to behave according to that comparative definition rather than according to their own desires, based on their own experiences.[5]

From this perspective, then, Burton's Selina Kyle is logically of a different sort than previous versions of the character. Mousey, unassuming, nervously clumsy, she possesses no wealth, power, charisma, or streetwise moxie. She is at the mercy of her environment: the context of her being is defined by her place in society. That place is in turn determined by numerous social factors, both economic and sexual. Much like Sartre's waiter, she is engaged in a particular servile performance: the role of secretary. Unlike Sartre's waiter, however, she is not a servant by choice only. When the audience first meets her, she occupies the position of the abject Other in relation to those around her. This is evident in how others treat her and interact—or in many ways fail to interact—with her. When Selina haltingly attempts to contribute an idea in a business meeting, her boss, Max Shreck (Christopher Walken), says, "Well it appears we haven't properly housebroken Ms. Kyle yet. But on the plus column, she makes one hell of a cup of coffee." The implication is that Selina exists to serve, not to contribute. She does not have any ideas worth hearing. Her failure to engage a room of powerful men illustrates her status as an outsider to the decisions of the powerful. Rather than an actor, she is the acted upon. Furthermore, Shreck's use of the term "housebroken" implies that Selina isn't human in the same way as the other occupants of the room and therefore does not deserve respect or acknowledgment.[6]

This determination, however, is not solely the result of the contemptuous gaze of powerful men. Burton illustrates the other factors that restrict Selina from being an authentic subject. Selina's apartment and her dialogue with her answering machine further illuminate the societal forces that have shaped her character. Her small apartment is painted a girlish shade of pink and festooned with decorations and curios that could only be charitably described as ingenuous, and uncharitably described as cutesy. Drawing from Beauvoir, the stereotypical femininity of her apartment also demonstrates a lack of opportunities for authentic social development and may represent a tension between the ideals and trappings of her youth and her goals for an independent future. This is in keeping with Selina's current status as a character. At this stage she is the stock clueless ingénue. More important than how her physical environment reinforces her personality for the audience, however, is how Selina's banter with herself illustrates her opinion about her own position in the world and how she views herself.[7]

For example, when Selina returns to her apartment, she greets it with a cheery, "Hi, Honey, I'm home!" She adds with weary self-deprecation, "Oh that's right: I'm not married," suggesting with her tone that it would be preferable if she were. She translates a plaintive meow from her cat as "What's that? How can anyone be so pathetic?" A string of telling messages on her answering machine follow this discussion. A date tells her that his therapist says he needs to not be her "appendage," a breakup she ascribes to her win at racquetball. Her mother describes her as a "lowly secretary," and an automated advertisement announces that Gotham Lady perfume "makes women feel like women, and the men have no complaints, either." Much of the dialogue in this section revolves around Selina's interaction with power, and also her interaction with men. Moreover, in those cases where she exhibits drive and initiative, the result is punishment and deprivation. Therefore, the film not only provides commentary on the development of self but also reinforces Beauvoir's position on the treatment of women and their disproportionate disadvantage in developing an authentic self within the confines of a system that privileges men and disempowers women.

This message is reinforced in the subsequent scene when Selina returns to the office to prepare for Shreck's meeting with Bruce Wayne (Michael Keaton). Possessed of a drive to be thorough, Selina takes the initiative and breaks into Shreck's protected files. When Shreck discovers this, and her discovery of his true intentions to launder Gotham's power supply for his own personal gain, he intimidates and threatens her. He then lulls her into a false sense of relief before pushing her out of his office window to plummet to her death. Although her actions and demise are a veiled reference to the cliché curiosity killed the cat, a deeper ideology is at work here; Selina consistently finds herself at the mercy of the people and discourses that constitute her. Given both her contempt for herself and her inability to break from her pattern of subjection, how is Selina to break these bonds? The answer employs a bit of deus ex machina on the part of Burton. She dies and is mystically resurrected by a horde of cats.

It's perfectly legitimate at this point to question why Selina Kyle should require this sort of supernatural intervention in *Batman Returns,* when her other incarnations in media do not. The Catwoman of the comics is much like Batman himself: a highly skilled, intelligent, and determined individual. Her character determines her context to a large degree, in much the same way as Batman's character defines his. Selina in *Batman Returns,* however, is not that person. It is impossible for her to be that person or to become Catwoman in the same way and using the same methods that Bruce Wayne followed in becoming Batman. She is one of the rank and file, like Clark Kent, only she isn't faking it. This is due to her position as the Other. Excluded from power and agency through the discourses that formulate her identity as a matter of both economics and gender, Selina's being is located in a far different place than Bruce Wayne's. Thus, as I suggested earlier, Burton offers Catwoman as social commentary on the plight of women. As Beauvoir indicates in *The Second Sex,* if a woman is positioned as solely Other, this places her in a context of being that determines her character, rather than the other way around. As a determined and determinable object, she lacks the power of choice essential to the construction of an authentic self. As Selina is abjectly Other in the world of the movie—at least so far—it becomes necessary to change her context in order to change her character.[8]

For this reason, Selina's death and resurrection are the beginning of her journey rather than the end. Resurrected from the dead by alley cats, impelled by drives that her predemise self kept under wraps, Catwoman encounters the hidden sides of herself. This experience both delights and disturbs the character and audience. Selina's crossing of a liminal barrier (death) and subsequent transformation upon her resurrection raise issues of authenticity and the condition of being a subject; they don't necessarily resolve them. While Selina participates in alienation from subject-hood as a matter of her gender, the transformation exacerbates that otherness and in doing so throws it into sharp relief for the audience. She becomes Other to her former self and must search for an authentic self that matches her new condition.

This search for a new self is not comfortable or easy for Selina, as demonstrated by her return to her apartment. Seemingly in a semicatatonic state, she enters her apartment in the same way that she did in the earlier scene, complete with dialogue, but in a different tone. In addition to the tenor of her emotional display, her physical appearance has changed as well. Ghastly pale and glassy-eyed, Selina both looks and sounds like she has gone through a profound shift in the state of her being, and not just the identity expressed by that shift. In fact, at this point, Selina does not necessarily know what her new identity is or should be. She does know that her old identity is no longer viable.

The shock of this comes when listening to her answering machine. Again she hears an automated advertisement for Gotham Lady perfume stating, "One whiff of this at the office and your boss will be asking you to stay after work for a candlelight staff meeting for two." Considering that her boss murdered her earlier that evening, the rage of her response is equal to the circumstances. Selina begins careening through her apartment like one possessed or insane, shoving stuffed animals down the garbage disposal and attacking her pink surroundings with a can of black spray paint. Selina destroys the evidence of who she used to be and everything she doesn't like about that person. That the perfume message should be the catalyst is appropriate not only in terms of plot but in terms of the discourses that have shaped Selina's life to this point. The message is in line with Selina's experience of woman as object, as Other. It implies a world in which those in power—assumed to be heterosexual men—subjugate women, linking a hierarchy of gender and sexuality to the hierarchy of the workplace. She lived in that world, where the social affirmation of her self depended on the acceptableness of that self to the powers that be: powers that consign women to secondary and subordinate "service" roles relative to male positions of authority. She was a "good girl" according to the constraints of those discourses. Her participation in those discourses—which dictate the hierarchical relationship of men to women in the working world as a system of legitimized power—got her killed. She's done with being a "good girl." As she dons her Catwoman costume for the first time, we see the results of her smashing the neon sign on her wall. What once said "Hello There" now says "Hell here." Selina has been to hell—or the underworld, at least—and returned, and she brought some of that back with her.

It could be assumed at this point that issues of existential authenticity might no longer pertain. After all, it is a supernatural intervention that allows this transformation in Selina's character and her abilities. We see these changes from the outset. In her first act as Catwoman, she saves a woman from an attacker by engaging him in hand-to-hand combat. The old Selina Kyle certainly gave no evidence of having combat training of any kind, much less the wherewithal to use it. It would be easy to uncritically assume that these abilities result from some elemental transformation in her physical nature: resurrected by cats, she now has catlike abilities translated into a framework for a humanoid physiology. I feel, however, that I would be remiss if I did not point out a necessary refinement to this idea. In line with the evidence garnered from the movie, Selina's resurrection experience represents in many ways the amplification and expansion of her personality and abilities; it didn't simply impart to her characteristics that she didn't previously possess. The resurrection doesn't put something new into her; it sets something free. Moreover, her character seems designed to be read symbolically, as is the case with so much of Burton's work. Rather than representing a particular, individual struggle, she represents a larger picture; she is a nexus point of struggle and conflict capable of representing a broad cross-section of the human condition.

As Sartre would have it, we are flung headfirst into an existence that we do not create but must confront. The discourses and material conditions that shape our experience from the moment of our birth existed before we got here. Being human means learning to negotiate these conditions. As the context of Selina's being changes as a result of her death and resurrection, so too does her experience and relationship to it. Her situation is a hyperbolic representation of how it is possible to kill off a self and resurrect a new one. No longer bound by many of the restrictions of her previous position, she must now navigate a world in which she has more freedom and power. She must renegotiate her relationship to the discourses of her world. That this freedom and power derive from within her is indicated even before her resurrection occurs.

For instance, when the Penguin's Red Triangle Gang makes its first appearance, terrorizing Gotham's citizens at the lighting of the Christmas tree, one of the gang members attacks Selina as she attempts to make her way through the chaos, threatening her with a high-powered taser. Batman saves her, and the gang member is left unconscious in the street. Selina, kneeling down, picks up the taser, zaps the unconscious gang member with it, and giggles. This indicates that the appetite for mischief that Catwoman demonstrates later is not something alien to Selina's personality but rather that she no longer feels compelled to restrain it. This lack of restraint and freedom from her previous inhibitions further explain her problematic interchange with the woman she saves, particularly considering her experiences prior to her resurrection.

Upon saving a woman in an alley from an attacker, Catwoman shoves the victim against the wall and says, "You make it so easy, don't you? Always looking for some Batman to save you." The indictment against the victim, that she could or should have done something to predict the violence against her and was somehow culpable for it, is ethically fraught on many levels and can be read in many different ways. Catwoman now has the power and freedom to act in ways that she could not before. But while she saves the woman, she does not represent any sort of female solidarity in the face of a subjugating power structure, nor does she demonstrate empathy regarding the plight of a woman in a situation in which she could have found herself before becoming Catwoman. While Catwoman's victim blaming is not defensible, it is explicable in light of both her past attitudes toward herself and the search for existential authenticity.

As I mentioned before, Selina demonstrates a significant self-contempt for the kind of person that she was before her resurrection. Her return from death only intensifies this contempt. As she is no longer powerless, she projects this contempt outward. This projection occurs presumably because she is still suffering from self-loathing and is still incapable of accepting her former self as the foundation of her new identity. The woman in the alley could have been her at one point in time. Her indictment of the woman for being less than proactive with regard to her safety is not just an indictment of the woman in the alley but also an indictment of her former self. Catwoman demonstrates this by her reference to Batman. He saved her from the Red Triangle Gang when she was not in a position to save herself. Furthermore, this illustrates her current interaction with the discourses of her previous self. Those discourses still exist in the world. Though Catwoman acquires the impetus to challenge them, she does not have the power to destroy them, nor can she simply avoid them. As a matter of authenticity, her only choice, her only power regarding those discourses, is choosing how she negotiates them. She is reluctant to do so in a manner that resembles her previous self. The old Selina Kyle would have never said something so cold and unfeeling to someone in danger because that isn't what nice people do. If one isn't nice, then society will censure that individual in ways great or small for going off-script. In other words, by not aligning one's behavior with prevailing societal standards, one risks being ostracized by others. Of course, Selina was nice, the world was not particularly nice in return, and she wound up dead. She is, therefore, little interested in conforming to the expectations of others, whether or not others frame those expectations as virtuous or desirable.

This is illustrated in her gender performance as well. The old Selina was an ingénue. Catwoman is a femme fatale. One could argue that the latter performance is just as inauthentic as the former and still fosters an attitude of objectification in the men around her, but her relationship to her earlier gender performance has changed, even while she appears to participate in the femme fatale role. As a result of her new outlook, she changes her interaction with discourses of gender and sexuality. Rather than being a passive participant in those discourses, she actively uses the performative trappings of her gender discourse to maneuver others. Her conscious performance is evident if we take two factors into account. Postresurrection, Catwoman mocks many of the tropes of stereotypical femininity. Her contempt for damsels in distress illustrates this. Moreover, she plays to stereotypes as a means rather than an end. For example, in a fight with Batman, he strikes her to the ground and she exclaims, "How could you? I'm a *woman!*" When Batman apologizes and reaches down to help her to her feet, she takes the opportunity to go on an offensive strike. While this scene is absurd, given that they are in the midst of combat, it highlights that Catwoman refuses to be subjected by discourses. She may not be able to ignore them or destroy them, but she can certainly use them to her advantage regarding other discourse participants.

Even though Catwoman has been given a new life and a new perspective, she still runs into many of the same challenges her former self did with regard to agency and power. Her interactions with men in the story are not altogether improved under her identity as Catwoman. This is not an issue of antagonism—although that is certainly present—inasmuch as men still do not recognize her as a subject in the same way they view themselves. Despite her predilection and ability for turning discourse rules to her advantage, those discourses are polyvalent social constructions with multiple participants. That is, the roles of woman that Catwoman negotiates aren't determined by some central authority or even overtly declared. Instead they are emergent outgrowths of the behaviors and opinions of a mass of people who reinforce the rules of their roles by enacting those rules. Her opponents still participate in those structures and interact with them, even if they do not perform them. Catwoman's change is notable, and incredibly influential for her, but it does not immediately engender change in prevailing attitudes toward women. She is still objectified (by the Penguin), ridiculed and dismissed (by Max Shreck), and repeatedly thwarted (by Batman). During the course of the film, all three of them kill her at some point. Although she demonstrates a cleverness, ruthlessness, and self-possession that her old self did not, she is still acted upon in situations not of her making, sometimes leading to detrimental results. While her new style of interaction with her world points toward an attempt to construct an authentic, internally coherent identity in line with the current conditions of her being, her actions are signifiers of her process rather than ends in themselves. Catwoman's attainment of a different subject position happens at the end of the film and hinges on an assertion based not in gender or sexuality but in ethics and ethical action. In line with existentialist thought, she takes responsibility for her values and acts as her own ethical compass.

At a New Year's Eve ball, Selina and Bruce Wayne meet and dance with each other. While Bruce shows up specifically to see Selina, and tells her as much, Selina indicates that she has come to the ball for Max Shreck. Bruce interprets this as suggesting a romantic relationship, and Selina laughs, saying, "Not *me* and Max. *This* and Max." As she says this, she pulls a gun from a garter. Bruce is horrified at the sight of the gun and struggles with Selina to conceal it from the other party guests. Selina says, "Now don't give me that 'Killing Max Won't Solve Anything' speech because it will. Aren't you sick of that sanctimonious robber baron always coming out on top when he should be six feet under?" When Bruce asks her who she thinks she is, she replies that she doesn't know anymore. In subsequent conversation, each discovers the costumed identity of the other. Selina doesn't know who she is, her true authentic self, because that hinges on a decision she has yet to make: one that she must acknowledge as her sole responsibility. Becoming an authentic self rests entirely on self-aware choice and requires that we acknowledge our role in the creation of our own values and take personal responsibility for acting on those values. An authentic self is not a costume one puts on that instantiates immediate change. Instead, it is a continual process of becoming. It is an identity continually forged in and through our actions, in much the same way that the role constraints that Catwoman struggles against are forged and reinforced through action. All of her previous experimentation with her new state of being leads to that moment.

At the end of the film, Catwoman corners Max Shreck, newly free from his imprisonment by the Penguin. She is determined to kill him. Batman saves Shreck before she is able to do so. In the following interchange, Catwoman's position as a subject, one distinct from Batman's or Shreck's, becomes solidified: for the audience, the other characters, and for her. Two key statements mark this solidification. The first occurs when Batman tells Shreck he is going to jail, and Catwoman warns Batman away with her whip, saying, "Don't be naïve! The law doesn't apply to people like him, or us!" Catwoman asserts at this point the way in which she and Batman are similar: they both operate in a world outside both legitimate power and social norms. They belong in that world. They are not suited to the world of ordinary people. Batman attempts to appeal to that commonalty and offers her what he believes is the right ethical choice for both of them: take Max to jail and go home together. Catwoman rejects his offer, stating, "I would love to live with you in your castle forever, just like in a fairy tale. [She slashes his face with her claws.] I just couldn't live with myself! So don't pretend this is a happy ending!" This demonstrates Selina's final rejection of her former self in all its inauthenticity and her rejection of the standard roles available for women. Though Batman represents an extraordinary figure, he actually aligns with tradition insofar as he appears to offer Catwoman nothing new with respect to the role available to her. The heroic man is still superior and still dictating the options available to the woman. Woman is still the second sex, and Catwoman must transcend that in order to transcend the facticity of her past life. A charming prince to her fairy-tale princess is not a relationship she will accept.

Once, being swept off her feet, saved from her life and herself by a man, would have been the fulfillment of all her hopes. But she is no longer that Selina Kyle. She will not be deterred in fulfilling her desire for justice and vengeance. Justice because she deems Shreck's death to be a necessary and righteous act proceeding from her own sense of self and will. Vengeance because it could be argued that the film conveys an object lesson in the dangers of marginalizing and depersonalizing members of society—of *othering* them—insofar as virtually all the villains in the Batman series have been mistreated in some way and are reacting against their victimization by seeking revenge.[9] Whether or not her desire partakes more of justice or revenge has more to do with who is doing the defining of those concepts. Catwoman makes a choice, but the ethics upon which that choice is based are not Batman's nor the ethics of society at large. As in her comment about law, the rules of others do not apply to her; she must make her own choices about how she interacts with the world and its power structures. In doing so, she decides what she accepts or rejects from those structures and in what context.

Catwoman's journey through the film is about this process, however, and that process has implications beyond the individual. As Sartre points out, existential choices, while proceeding from the individual, may not remove the individual from a larger social context and still remain authentic. Our choices encompass our idea of humanity and project our imagination and will on a larger field than just our individual lives. Sartre writes, "To choose to be this or that is to affirm at the same time the value [of] what we choose because we can never choose evil. We always choose the good, and nothing can be good for us without being good for all."[10] Here Sartre isn't stating that what we choose is good according to prevailing social standards, but rather that we choose what we perceive to be good. In make this assertion, he puts a twist on Kant's categorical imperative: upon making our choices, we are giving implicit approval for others to make the same choices under the same circumstances. Which leaves us to wonder: What is Catwoman's state after taking Max Shreck's life?

There are numerous possibilities for the development of the character beyond the end of the film. As we make choices in reaction to and negotiation with our environment, those choices become part of our past, and we create the content of our facticity. Catwoman is no different from rank-and-file mortals in this regard. Catwoman's journey to greater authenticity as a self-determining subject depends on her acknowledgment of her choice to kill Shreck and its value as *her* choice: one for which she alone is responsible and that evolves out of her own experiences. Her rejection of Bruce Wayne and the apparent solace he attempts to offer her would indicate that she has made peace with herself. Not only must she reject any form of salvation from Batman, but she recognizes that she cannot *be* Batman; she cannot take his role, his assumed function, or the values that go with that role and function as her own. As Beauvoir points out, emulating others as a pattern for our behavior—particularly when we deny the facticity of our past experiences—dooms us to frustration and failure. Acting authentically requires that we attempt to avoid "bad faith" awareness of our choices, whether that "bad faith" results from failing to acknowledge the facticity of our own past or from denying our freedom and accepting the role we are given as destined.[11] It could be argued that killing Shreck is an authentic act for Catwoman, a choice for which she takes full responsibility, both as an act and a value, and one that proceeds from an awareness of the facticity of her own past experience and an acknowledgment that only through her own choice, claimed and owned by her, can she hope to transcend and move from those experiences in a new direction. If this is the case, then she would have at that moment moved toward transcending her facticity and her objectification as Other, defining and determining herself and her interaction with the world on her own terms.

Even if this "authenticity ending" were the state of affairs for Catwoman at the end of *Batman Returns,* I doubt it would have remained static if her story had continued under Burton's direction. Indeed, it would be impossible to do so. Catwoman is a complex character, confounding the borders of discourse power and subverting it, even while seeming to participate in it. As I examine her existential struggle, her discourse negotiations, and her choice to kill Shreck, I find her choice occupying a space outside of the androcentric power structures occupied by Batman, Max Shreck, and the Penguin. This separate space results from a divergence in the expression and obtainment of agency between the characters' context of being. These differences are rooted in the larger social context of the world the characters inhabit, and those differences are reflected in our own world. Catwoman is an outsider to constructions of legitimate power, and as such her power predicates itself on the appearance of subversion: she twists the tropes of society with regard to women, criminality, and ethics, reframing them from her own subjective position, as unclear to her as that often is. After her rejection of Batman and the normative ethical position he represents, however, I suspect that Catwoman lacks any investment in those legitimized spaces. Rather, she continually seeks legitimacy and justification according to her own awareness of the situation at hand. On her journey toward becoming an authentic subject, how closely her identity performance matches the expectations of any outside observer does not apparently concern her. Instead, she continually seeks legitimacy and justification according to her own awareness of the situation at hand. Would Catwoman have affirmed her choice to deny Batman and kill Max and the burgeoning identity that choice describes as one available to all people? We cannot know. If she did, it would indicate a more full progression toward authenticity than the current narrative describes. In this sense, she rejects the social aspect of self and choice that virtually all of the existentialists recognize and that the individual must come to terms with if he or she is going to be authentic, at least in the traditional existential sense. She represents the beginning of a process, rather than an end. Indeed, if we read her as a symbol of existential struggle, then that process would never end; the struggle for authenticity would reappear in every future circumstance.

Notes

1. I would direct the reader interested in Batman stories to Frank Miller and David Mazzucchelli, *Batman: Year One* (New York: DC Comics, 2007); and Jeph Loeb and Tim Sale, *Batman: The Long Halloween* (New York: DC Comics, 1998).

2. See the Hada chapter in this volume for further discussion of *Big Fish* and what it says about the construction of identity.

3. Jean-Paul Sartre, "The Humanism of Existentialism," *Essays in Existentialism* (New York: Citadel, 1993), 32.

4. Jean-Paul Sartre, *Being and Nothingness: An Essay on Phenomenological Ontology* (New York: Philosophical Library, 1956), 59–60, 117.

5. Simone de Beauvoir, *The Second Sex* (New York: Vintage, 1989), xxii–xxiii, 48, 51–52.

6. *Batman Returns,* directed by Tim Burton (Warner Brothers, 1992).

7. Beauvoir, *Second Sex,* 698.

8. Ibid., 52, 718.

9. See the Decker chapter in this volume for further discussion of this theme in Burton's corpus.

10. Sartre, "Humanism of Existentialism," 37.

11. Beauvoir, *Second Sex,* 52–53.

The Consolations and Dangers of Fantasy

Burton, Poe, and *Vincent*

Daniel Sullivan

> While other kids read books like *Go Jane Go,*
> Vincent's favorite author is Edgar Allan Poe.
>
> —Tim Burton, *Vincent* (1982)

The horror film genre is part of the foundation of Tim Burton's personality and body of work. His philosophy of life and film is partly shaped by the possibilities he has long seen in the realm of dark cinematic fantasy. As a child, Burton saw in horror films and writing an inventive escape from drudgery and an outlet for aggressive or antisocial tendencies. In particular, he was captivated by the work of Vincent Price and Roger Corman, who brought the stories and poems of Edgar Allan Poe to big-screen life in the 1960s. The creative potentialities Burton saw in horror films as a child have blossomed during his adult career into a long list of unforgettable films, stories, and characters marked by the macabre: *Beetlejuice* (1988), the Joker, *Edward Scissorhands* (1990), the Inventor, the Penguin, *The Nightmare Before Christmas* (1993), Jack Skellington, *Mars Attacks!* (1996), *Sleepy Hollow* (1999), *Corpse Bride* (2005), The Boy with Nails in His Eyes, *Sweeney Todd* (2007), and many more. Although it is far from the director's sole area of concentration, the horror film is certainly beloved (and has been enriched) by Tim Burton.

The horrific element in Burton's filmography is perhaps most remarkable in light of how appealing his works are to children. Preadolescents around the world have enjoyed films like *Beetlejuice* and *The Nightmare Before Christmas* for decades.[1] It is certainly Burton's intention that his works should appeal to the imaginations of children. The films continue to reflect the anxieties and wonders he often experienced as a lonely child, some of which he seems to have never outgrown. Many of the films feature child (or childlike) protagonists.[2] The young Burton was enthralled by Corman's Poe films, and in turn generations of children have grown up enchanted by Burtonian imagery. What is it about the horror genre—especially in the way that Burton channels its dark magic—that appeals to children and seems to express something fundamental about the experience of childhood?

I propose that certain aspects of the psychological experience of childhood (particularly in the cultural "modern West") explain much of the appeal of Burton's horrific fantasy to contemporary child audiences, as well as the appeal and influence of Poe and Corman on Burton's work. Specifically, childhood is often characterized by what philosophical psychiatrist R. D. Laing, in his major work *The Divided Self,* referred to as *ontological insecurity:* a state of felt alienation, loneliness, or anxiety. Obviously, the extent to which this is true of each child's experience varies. Nevertheless, many psychologists have triangulated on the notion that childhood is often marked by at least the potential for extreme experiences of ontological insecurity.[3] As the discussion below will make clear, the lives of both Burton and Poe have been associated with a tendency toward this unstable emotional condition, and as a consequence many of their characters evidence similar instability.[4] Following Laing and others, I will argue that fantasy—including the fantasy of horror—often represents a form of retreat from precarious existence and a striving for surrogate control among ontologically insecure individuals. Thus, Burton and Poe channeled their insecurities into dark fantasies, and similarly insecure children resonate with these "therapeutic" works. Burton's breakthrough short film *Vincent* (1982) will be examined as an important case study in this regard. Not only does the film explicitly acknowledge Burton's creative debt to Poe, Corman, and Vincent Price, it also reflexively examines Burton's own use of art as an escape from insecurity.

Given that both Burton and Poe are self-aware enough to understand their use of fantasy as a medium for escaping insecurity, it will also be necessary to consider how they problematize this process in their works. I will interpret this aspect of their corpora in light of Laing and Søren Kierkegaard. These thinkers see ontologically insecure persons as being in a double bind. They are most likely to rely on fantasy to escape reality, but they are also most likely to be harmed by this form of escape, as they retreat further from reality and isolate themselves even further from those around them.

In its brief running time *Vincent* also addresses the dangerous potential of fantasy; however, the theme recurs throughout many of Burton's (and Poe's) works. Having examined the theme of dialectical interaction between insecurity and fantasy in Burton and Poe, I will conclude by using this framework (supplemented by the ideas of Otto Rank) to shape a partial "meta-aesthetics" of their work.

Burton and Poe

There is little doubt that Tim Burton has cultivated a persona of partial alienation and iconoclasm in both the eyes of the public and the popular press. In interviews dating to the beginning of his successful film career, Burton has often maintained a disheveled, somewhat morose appearance, with claims of manic depression that inevitably lead back to the story of a somewhat lonely, oppressively normal childhood.[5] In many early interviews, Burton commented on the fact that he escaped the stultifying drudgery of suburban family life by venturing into the fantastic world of horror films. In particular, he has commented repeatedly on the importance of his early hero, actor Vincent Price, and the cinematic adaptations of Edgar Allan Poe works directed by Roger Corman in which Price starred. Poe was—in Burton's own words—the director's "first poet" as a child, and Burton responded to Corman's lavish and often surreal adaptations with extreme emotion: "Vincent Price, Edgar Allan Poe, those monster movies, those *spoke* to me. You see somebody going through that anguish and torture—things you identify with—and it acts as a kind of therapy, a release. You make a connection with it."[6] Indeed, Burton has gone so far as to claim that the catharsis of death awareness he experienced as a child watching the Corman Poe films ironically "helped [him] to live."[7]

Corman directed eight horror films for American International Pictures between 1960 and 1965, seven of which starred Price.[8] Although (as Antoine de Baecque has observed) Burton is a director with many influences, as well as a highly unique style, it is not difficult to find aspects of Corman's Poe films that anticipate many of Burton's later themes and imagery. Consider, for example, the dream sequence of Montresor (Peter Lorre) in *Tales of Terror* (1962). Apparently shot with a fish-eye lens to produce an extreme effect of carnivalesque distortion, this scene involves the comical tossing back and forth of Montresor's severed head by his two recent victims. The tone of the scene is characteristic of the maniacal blend of humor and horror

Burton would pursue in films like *Beetlejuice.* In another point of connection, Corman's Poe films often contain two fictitious worlds: one, a veneer of repressive, aristocratic decorum and decadence shot in straightforward color; the other, a fantastic world of nightmares shot through colored lenses and thick with atmospheric fog. Films like *Corpse Bride* present two similar worlds—the world of the living and that of the dead—although Burton often confounds audience expectation by depicting "reality" in gray, drained tones. Yet another potential point of influence may be found in Burton's continued interest in the stories of overbearing, deranged patriarchs who bring about the ruination of innocent women—a theme evident in *Corpse Bride* and *Sweeney Todd* but also in much of Poe's work and the Corman adaptations. Indeed, in *Sleepy Hollow,* Ichabod Crane's zealously religious father tortures and kills his mother with an iron maiden, just as Vincent Price's resurrected Inquisitor kills Barbara Steele's character with such a device in *The Pit and the Pendulum* (1961).[9]

Of course, the most overt sign that Burton inherited the Corman legacy is the fortunate collaboration between Burton and Price at the end of the actor's life, which left its mark on *Vincent* and *Edward Scissorhands,* the latter of which featured Price's last live-action performance in a motion picture. In *Vincent,* the first major production over which Burton was given free creative reign, the young director chose as his subject the influence that Price, Poe, and the classic horror films had exerted on his art and childhood. The roughly six-minute claymation film presents a story written by Burton (in Seuss-inspired rhyme) about the seven-year-old Vincent Malloy, who moves in and out of the mundane reality of his family home.[10] While Vincent appears on the surface to be a dutiful, if somewhat withdrawn, child, in his creative inner life he imagines himself to be Vincent Price, constructing macabre fantasies for himself and those around him that are inspired by Poe's stories and, one can infer, Corman's adaptations of them. Very appropriately, Burton was able to recruit Price himself to perform the voiceover narration. The film is in black and white and bears many marks of the characteristic claymation style that has come to be associated with later Burton films (doubtless partly due to the contribution of animator Rick Heinrichs, who has continually worked with Burton in a variety of capacities on multiple films). *Vincent* is also consistently described as having a German Expressionist style.[11]

By choosing *Vincent* for his first major work, Burton drew attention to the significance of the affinity between himself and Poe. Without romantically exaggerating the degree of overlap—if judging only by their respective longevities, Burton is clearly a better-adjusted person than Poe ever was, and his corpus is, on the whole, far more optimistic—it is nevertheless possible to point to various similarities in the lives and works of Burton and Poe. Described as a "sensitive and neurotic child" by Philip van Doren Stern, Poe lived a life marked by loneliness and a felt inability to satisfactorily connect with others, punctuated all too briefly by occasional moments of companionship or success.[12] For his part, Burton has also commented on his own "manic-depressive" personality and the alienation he experienced as a child and teenager.[13]

Both Burton and Poe turned almost obsessively to artistic output as a means of expressing themselves, driven in large part by their shared sense that they were not quite at home in the worlds around them and were rarely fully understood by the other people in those worlds. Poe channeled his depression and fears into tales of melancholy and terror and thereby fleetingly transcended the limits of an impoverished existence. As Haldeen Braddy observes, "The single large impression that emerges from the body of Poe's art is his determined flight from reality."[14] Literature was for Poe a form of escape but also of expression. Similarly, Burton has repeatedly used film as a means of simultaneously reinventing and examining himself and the world around him. But in Burton, perhaps even more than in Poe, one gets the impression that the fantastic pageantry is really a means for the author to somehow convey his inner life to the observer. As Burton has stated, "It's why you struggle as a child and you draw and want to create. There is an impulse to be seen. For yourself: what you are. It's always scary for me to show movies. I actually hate it; I feel very, very vulnerable. Because if you weren't a verbal person, you weren't this and that, you wanna let that be the thing people see you through."[15]

Importantly, Burton and Poe immersed themselves in many of the same genres in their artistic quests for self-expression and reality flight: horror, comedy, fantasy. Equally importantly, their archetypal protagonists share many features. Helena Bassil-Morozow has, in a post-Jungian framework, referred to these archetypal protagonists in Burton's works as various instantiations of the misunderstood monster who stands outside mainstream society: the child, the genius, the maniac.[16] Both Poe and Burton repeatedly construct antiheroes who exist in marginalized positions, are disfigured in some bodily or psychological sense, and are hypersensitive, asking more of their reality than it readily offers. Consider merely, from Burton, Edward

Scissorhands or Victor van Dort of *Corpse Bride*; from Poe, Hop-Frog or the narrator of "Berenice" (1835). The question of why these artists gravitated toward these genres and protagonists will be explored more fully in the following section. It is a question to which *Vincent* provides an early answer from Burton.

Ontological Insecurity and the Possibility/Necessity Dialectic

I contend that both Burton and Poe were drawn (at least initially) to horrific fantasy as a means of escape from feelings of *ontological insecurity:* a sense of alienation or loneliness arising from a deep fear that one will be misunderstood by others or overwhelmed by a malevolent reality. R. D. Laing considers this a psychological state in which the individual "cannot take the realness, aliveness, autonomy, and identity of himself and others for granted."[17] In *The Divided Self,* Laing outlines three primary fears that the ontologically insecure individual experiences: *engulfment*—the fear of losing one's own autonomy in a suffocating relationship with another person; *implosion*—the fear of everyday reality overwhelming and persecuting the self; and *petrification*—the fear that another person will depersonalize the self, treating the self as an object or a means rather than an end in itself.

Laing contends that ontological security is a continuous spectrum, rather than a qualitative state of being; we have all experienced episodes of ontological insecurity. And some child psychologists—such as J. R. Killinger—have characterized childhood as potentially a time of near-perpetual ontological insecurity. The child's emerging self is fragile, not fully developed, and, depending on environmental factors, often impinged upon and threatened from multiple sides. As Killinger has discussed in detail, many children grow to maturity in a sustained "agony of helplessness" that bears marked similarity to Laing's discussion of ontologically insecure patients.[18] The child experiences the fear of engulfment whenever her caregivers enforce arbitrary rules or punishments upon her, the purpose of which she does not yet fully comprehend. The child experiences the fear of implosion whenever a strangely oversized reality threatens or strains her relatively weak physical and cognitive capacities. And the child experiences petrification fear when adults routinely fail to acknowledge the reality of her own inner truths and perceptions: *there is nothing hiding in the closet, you cannot really be hungry, people just don't do that.* These are the fears Burton experienced as a youth when his parents and peers seemed chronically unable to understand his innermost feelings and unique perspective. These are the fears that certainly haunted the young Poe, who after separation from his mother lived in various schools and homes with and without the foster parents who raised him in a generally repressive fashion.

The psychologist Bruno Bettelheim argues that children require grim and strange fantasies—such as the classic fairy tales of European culture—as a means of projecting and safely coping with the dark fears that plague their early cognitive development.[19] Children often act out the strange fantasies they read about or have read to them, re-creating and elaborating for themselves visions of another world that—in early childhood at least—they are not so certain does not exist. Later on, in adult life, many individuals continue to rely on more personalized fantasies or daydreams as a means of escaping—however briefly—a mundane reality perceived as stultifying or constrictive.[20]

For the ontologically insecure individual, creative fantasy may serve an especially important psychological function as a means of temporarily reasserting one's autonomy or gaining control. As Laing describes the retreat of the insecure person into fantastic inner realms, "In [f]antasy, the self can be anyone, anywhere, do anything, have everything. It is thus omnipotent and completely free."[21] As long as one dwells in a world of make-believe, one can behave however one wishes without incurring the moral or social penalties that would be attendant on many actions in the real world. Expanding on these ideas, Laing identified a common characteristic of the ontologically insecure individual, namely, a kind of experiential splitting of the self. This splitting involves maintaining a constructed "outer" self to conform to what are perceived to be the normative requirements of society and close others, while concealing an iconoclastic "inner" self, rooted in escapist fantasies, that may grow increasingly antisocial.[22] In extreme cases (such as might manifest in mental illness), the "outer" self collapses and is overtaken by the disembodied, fantastic "inner" self, now largely alienated from the reality shared by most other persons.

As this analysis suggests, the use of fantasy as an escape for coping with ontological insecurity is not without its problems. No philosophical discussion of fantasy is adequate without considering Kierkegaard's discussion of selfhood in *The Sickness unto Death,* which takes both the consolations and dangers of fantasy into account.[23] In Kierkegaard's view, the self is perpetually caught in a dialectic of *possibility,* the freedom of choice and imagination, and *necessity,* the constraints of biology and history that define each individual. The self can experience existential threat when caught either in what Kierkegaard calls "necessity's despair"—feeling constrained within narrow limits of prescribed activity, perception, and emotion—or "possibility's despair"—feeling overwhelmed by an endless array of potentialities and thereby unable to take concrete action.

The ontologically insecure individual fears and feels necessity's despair. Infringed upon by the demands and misconceptions of others, threatened by a persecutory reality, a person in this state may fly toward the perception of unconstrained possibility—toward fantasy—as a relief from that which he fears. Yet as Kierkegaard points out, an individual who retreats deep into fantasy may be characterized as "an individual [who] has become unreal."[24] Without being grounded in some amount of necessity, some prescribed pattern of activity, the person succumbs to possibility's despair, a danger especially prominent for the ontologically insecure person. For the person whose grasp on the self and reality is already tenuous, ascent into uncharted realms of fantasy may take her even further afield from the concrete world of others, amplifying her alienation.

Interestingly, Kierkegaard seems to associate the condition of possibility's despair with what Laing might refer to as the ontological insecurity of childhood. At multiple points in *The Sickness unto Death,* possibility's despair is described in ways that connect it to the child's psychology and experience. For instance: "Losing oneself in possibility may be compared with a child's utterance of vowel sounds."[25] Here Kierkegaard seems to be arguing that people who have escaped reality through flight into fantastic possibility have the creative energy to attempt communication but, like the infant, lack a solid awareness of the rules of grammar and the capacity to emit a full range of controlled vocal sounds. The person lost in possibility's despair lacks any boundaries or concrete regulations against which she might define herself; this seems to match Kierkegaard's conception of childhood as a stage in which the individual has not yet developed the capacity for critical self-reflection and self-definition.[26] Like the young child, a person who has split into a fantastic inner self and an outer self displayed to others will struggle in vain to communicate effectively with others, because the boundary between self and other, fantasy and reality, babble and speech, is not clearly delineated. It is not surprising, then, that in another major work, *The Concept of Anxiety,* Kierkegaard identifies successful communication through language as a primary means of escaping the inwardness of despair.[27]

Kierkegaard describes a process of attempted self-re-creation for the person fleeing from necessity's despair that parallels Laing's analysis of self-splitting. Specifically, Kierkegaard argues that the person who escapes into fantastic realms is experiencing a "defiant" form of despair, wherein he recognizes that he does not want to be himself but would rather be an "infinitized," grandiose version of himself that knows no limits.[28] The person in defiant despair "does not want to put on his own self, does not want to see his given self as his task." To escape his necessity-burdened identity and any external figures on whom he is dependent, the defiantly despairing individual retreats inward into recurring fantasies of self-re-creation: "Severing the self from any relation to a power that has established it . . . the self in [defiant] despair wants to be the master of itself or to create itself, to make his self into the self he wants to be."[29] But Kierkegaard insists that the fantastic possible selves the defiantly despairing individual creates cannot ultimately sustain the self, and eventually collapse as empty fictions.

Vincent Malloy—the hero of Burton's early film—is a child with clear feelings of ontological insecurity that will ultimately drive him to defiant despair. Bassil-Morozow, who describes Vincent as "a typical Burtonian protagonist," points out that in his dealings with the adults around him, Vincent is "uncompromising: he wants complete and immediate acceptance, or nothing at all."[30] These words echo Laing's description of the ontologically insecure person's relational mode: "The polarity is between complete isolation or complete merging of identity."[31] Unable to establish satisfying connections with others, Vincent feels bogged down in necessity's despair: as Price narrates in the first two lines of the film, "he does what he's told." Like the insecure children described by Killinger, Vincent seems alienated from and overwhelmed by the adults around him, who are portrayed as much larger than he is (so much so that their heads remain perpetually outside of the frame, such that we never see their faces). Near the film's climax, his mother makes repeated strong denials of the validity of his odd way of perceiving the world: "These games that you play are all in your head!" Indeed, Vincent is punished (sent to his room) for behaving strangely in front of his mother.

Vincent escapes from the dreary world of necessity by inventing ever more malicious fantasies, believing himself to be Vincent Price and enacting the murderous deeds depicted in the Corman films that inspired Burton as a child. Burton himself has described *Vincent* as being primarily about the important role played by an alternate, fantastic reality in one child's mental life: "The film just goes in and out of Vincent's own reality. He identifies and believes that he's Vincent Price, and you see the world through his eyes. It clicks in and out of reality so to speak."[32] However, *Vincent* does not portray the insecure child's escape into fantasy as an unambiguous good. Rather, the film highlights the possibility/necessity dialectic described by Kierkegaard. Vincent's continual fantasies prompt his mother to perceive him as alienated. In the voice of necessity, she implores him to return to the solid ground of normative childhood experience: "I want you to go outside and have some *real* fun." But at this late point in the film, Vincent is so consumed by his fantasy life that he appears unable to escape from it.

The structure of *Vincent* highlights the dynamic of inner/outer self-splitting among ontologically insecure persons described by Laing. The film oscillates to the beat of the Seussian rhyme between the lighter world of external reality and the darker world of Vincent's inner fantasy life.[33] This schizoid pattern makes it clear that Vincent has effectively divided his self into an outer portion that conforms to his family's expectations ("He's always polite and does what he's told") and an inner portion that defies typical behavior for a person of his age. As the film continues, Vincent's inner self increasingly dominates his experience, in line with Laing's description of the progression from neurosis to psychosis (as the narrator proclaims near the end of the film, "His horrible insanity had reached its peak"). At the same time, Vincent becomes increasingly alienated from the people and reality around him (when punished by his mother, Vincent is convinced that "the years of isolation had made him quite weak").

Importantly, the nature and tone of Vincent's fantasies change over the course of the film. Initially, his daydreams and reenactments center around compensatory assertions of power. He imagines dipping a visiting aunt in wax, presumably as a means of avenging himself against the imposing, dull world of the adults around him. He further concocts a vision in which he transforms his dog into a "horrible zombie" with whom he "can go searching for victims in the London fog." Through the multiple fantasies presented in the first half of the film, Vincent is revealed to be in Kierkegaard's state of defiant despair: perpetually willing to be an alternate, omnipotent version of himself, he re-creates his life and environment over and over again. Kierkegaard could have been describing Vincent's self when he wrote, "It constantly relates itself to itself only by way of imaginary constructions. . . . At any time it can quite arbitrarily start all over again, and no matter how long one idea is pursued, the entire action is within a hypothesis."[34]

Yet gradually Vincent's visions begin to escape from his control, and they become nightmares of the very implosion of reality that the ontologically insecure person fears. The latter fantasies are Burton's reinterpretations of Poe. After being sent to his room, Vincent feels "possessed by this house," like Roderick Usher. In the film's final moments the walls of his room close in on him in a manner suggestive of "The Pit and the Pendulum" (1842). He imagines that his wife, whom he has buried alive, returns to engulf him. In sum, Vincent's fantasy life begins as a release from ontological insecurity but ends as an infliction of it. Finally unable to heed his mother's call to return to necessity and reality, Vincent collapses at the film's conclusion, lost in fantasies of persecution and possibly dead.

The events in the second half of the film illustrate what Kierkegaard saw as one possible outcome for the ontologically insecure person, namely, that her defiant despair will eventually transform into what he referred to as "demonic" despair.[35] In a state of demonic despair, the individual clings to a condition of suffering and torment and uses her very despair as a means of defining the self. In a more advanced movement of the possibility/necessity dialectic, the defiantly despairing person, lost in fantastic self-re-creation, fetishizes an event or image of the self as tormented in order to define itself, and channels all her energy into a paranoid sense of victimization. In this advanced stage of despair, it is nearly impossible to alleviate the suffering of the insecure individual. For the demonically despairing person, to remove her suffering would actually be to remove her sense of who she is.

This is exactly what happens to Vincent. First he is in defiant despair; despite his mother's insistence, "You're not Vincent Price, you're Vincent *Malloy!*" he persistently wills to be his fantastic self. Yet after he is punished by his mother, Vincent uses his punishment to sustain his fantasy. In this way, he transitions to a state of demonic despair. Just as Kierkegaard describes, Vincent will not relinquish his new self-as-victim identity—his mother rescinds his punishment and tells him, "You're not tormented, or insane," to no avail. As a final means of escaping his concrete identity, Vincent clings to a last vision of himself "limp and lifeless down on the floor." And just as Kierkegaard describes the despairing individual as unable to use language to escape her inwardness, Vincent is now able to speak only in a whisper.

A superficial reading of *Vincent* would portray it as a celebration of the dark fantasy life that preserves the insecure child, the same sort of creative mental life that kept the young Burton afloat and continues to sustain him throughout the difficulties of adult life. This reading is not entirely incorrect. Yet *Vincent* can also be taken as a warning that possibility's despair will further alienate the insecure individual who seeks solace in fantasy, potentially leading him to a state of demonic despair. The dialectic of insecurity leading to fantasy, which then generates further insecurity or torment, is also the touchstone of many Poe stories, such as "Ligeia" (1838) or "The Fall of the House of Usher" (1840), both of which were adapted into films by Corman starring Price. In both these stories, the central male character is prone to hypersensitive lapses into reverie or artistic daydream, resulting from a desire either to escape the limits of the physical, ailment-prone body (Roderick Usher) or to reconnect with a deceased, glorified individual and thereby avoid ongoing interpersonal relationships (the narrator of "Ligeia"). The predisposition of the protagonists to such melancholy fantasies results in the undoing of themselves and the people around them in both cases. Indeed, their distracted minds cause these characters to prematurely bury the women to whom they are connected, a pattern symbolic of the characteristic defensive response of the ontologically insecure person. Afraid of being constrained or petrified themselves, insecure people often reactively depersonalize others, delving into fantasy while petrifying (entombing) those who try to get close to them.

Similarly, many of Burton's films after the overtly Poe-inspired *Vincent* continue to represent the possibility/necessity dialectic. In *The Nightmare Before Christmas,* Jack Skellington becomes bored with the necessity of constantly reperforming the same Halloween rituals every year. He ventures beyond the limits of his domain and enters the fantastic world of Christmas Town, which awakens him to new possibilities of celebration and ritual. However, in his desire to re-create the enchanting possibility of Christmas Town, Jack nearly destroys the holiday and comes close to committing suicide. Likewise, in Burton's reimagination of Roald Dahl's classic, *Charlie and the Chocolate Factory* (2005), Willy Wonka escapes his own repressive childhood by isolating himself in a bizarre empire of his own creation, eventually becoming paranoid and antisocial. Indeed, in Burton's version, Wonka's fear of being engulfed or petrified by his father—or any form of family whatsoever—is so extreme that he cannot say the word "parents." Interestingly, *Charlie and the Chocolate Factory* offers a potential resolution of the possibility/necessity dialectic when, at its conclusion, Wonka is reunited with his dentist father.[36] This sort of resolution—in which the regulating, normative family unit (the Buckets) is peaceably inserted inside the epicenter of possibility, Wonka's factory—is more common in Burton's later work; it is entirely lacking in *Vincent.*

In an interesting reversal of the more typical pattern of the dialectic, the antihero of *Edward Scissorhands* is taken from the world of possibility—the Inventor's Gothic mansion—and brought into the stifling suburban world of necessity, where he is repeatedly misunderstood and forced into situations where he would rather not be. Edward embodies the double-edged nature of fantasy: enchanting, but liable to hurt those around him. Yet beyond the fact that Edward's story represents another instantiation of the possibility/necessity dialectic in Burton's oeuvre, it is important to recognize that his character may also be interpreted as anticipating a second dialectic common to the life and work of Burton and Poe.

Specifically, Edward himself represents the dynamic interplay between life and art. Edward's life is possible only because, in a sense, he *is* a work of art; furthermore, he sustains himself within the suburban community through art. Indeed, art is the only means for the misunderstood savant to safely connect with those around him. By sculpting shrubbery and pruning poodles, Edward is temporarily able to keep the community from turning against him and casting him out. In a very real way, art is Edward's life and sustenance. The timeless circle of life sustaining (and being sacrificed for) art and vice versa in the artist's biography opens up the potential for a dialectical "meta-aesthetics" of Burton and Poe—a theory of their art that rests on top of the possibility/necessity dialectic portrayed in so many of their works.

Life and Creation: The Meta-aesthetics of Burton and Poe

It is possible to apply the theoretical framework of the possibility/necessity dialectic to understanding other thematics in Burton and Poe beyond the ontologically insecure person's relationship to fantasy. Indeed, in an almost meta-aesthetical sense, I believe this dialectic can be slightly reformulated to understand the common relationship Burton and Poe experience with the artistic process itself. More specifically, Otto Rank's psychological philosophy in *Art and Artist* (1932) presents a dialectical association for the artistic personality between life and creation, and this dialectic may be drawn upon to understand the pivotal role of art in the lives of Burton, Poe, and many of their protagonists.

According to Rank, much of human behavior and thought represents an attempt to overcome the potentially crippling awareness of our own impending mortality. People seek a variety of culturally afforded means to convince themselves that despite the fact that they will die someday, an important part of them will survive this biological death and "live on," either literally or symbolically. These culturally sanctioned routes to immortality include religious belief, economic success, parenthood, and so on. For the artist in particular—especially in our modern culture, which embraces a "cult of genius" and celebrates the personality of the artist (as the present volume indeed attests)—creative work represents a means of immortalizing the self. Thus, according to Rank, the artist is constantly flying from the transience of lived experience and seeking to preserve that experience in her art.

Interestingly, however, Rank realizes that this is not a straightforward or uncomplicated solution for the artist to the problem of personal mortality. Because the artist is attempting to preserve her own unique experience of the world and insure its longevity, she must continually engage in life itself—accruing new experiences and developing her idiosyncratic personality. Otherwise, the artist would have nothing to immortalize. Yet the act of immortalization—the act of artistic creation—takes time away from actual lived experience and can preserve only that portion of the artist's life that has already been lived. Therefore, according to Rank, just as the ontologically insecure person oscillates between the extremes of necessity and possibility, of complete dependence on the Other and complete isolation, so too the artist fluctuates between actually living life—creating her personality—and attempting to immortalize life—creatively preserving her personality.[37]

What is perhaps most original about this Rankian dialectic of life and creation is that it pictures the artist as ultimately incapable of truly escaping the problem of death awareness. If the artist chooses the path of living her life, she is struggling, Sisyphus-like, to forge a personality that is ever-changing and doomed to disappear from the earth. If she chooses the path of art, however, she is turning transient, vital experience into dead, static art. For Rank, mortality waits at the end of both life and creation.

This is why the Rankian dialectic should not be interpreted as a facile equation of artistic creation with mortality. The complex metaphorical associations between life, death, and art have been the subject of a great deal of controversy and scrutiny among artists and philosophers of art.[38] While some see in artistic creation a kind of deadening retreat from existence, others see in it the capacity for attaining higher levels of lived experience. It is important to note that Rank does not necessarily see the creative act itself as representing mortality and the flight from lived experience; however, he does tend to equate the finished *product,* the completed artwork, with a kind of immobility and immortality that is opposed to lived experience.[39] Crucially, however, for Rank both everyday, lived experience and the transcendent experience of immersion in art or fantasy contain aspects of life and death, as death is the necessary companion of life. The experience of death in everyday life is one of transience; the presence of death in artwork is the inability to transform, an immobile coldness. But both are masks of death; hence the dialectic is resolved only in the artist's final passing away.

Of course, the human encounter with death is a keystone of Poe's entire corpus, as J. Gerald Kennedy has correctly observed.[40] And death—real or imagined—is a constant presence in Burton's works as well, starting with *Vincent.*[41] Both artists have been interested in the issue of death and in how art can help or hinder the individual's pursuit of immortality. Returning to *Vincent,* although in the previous section I interpreted Vincent's momentary flights from reality as examples of childhood fantasy, it is of course also possible to reconsider the film in light of Rank's life/creation dialectic. In other words, Vincent's morbid fantasies may be understood to represent a kind of art (indeed, we are informed by the narrator that Vincent "likes to paint . . . to pass some of the time"), the same sort of art that Burton created as a young man (and continues to create) in order to alleviate the pressures of alienation and an occasionally oppressive social reality. Viewed through this lens, the film becomes a short meditation on the socially isolating nature of artistic creation. Vincent, the child genius, retreats from the mundane world around him into his dark art while his mother entreats him to abandon these pursuits and engage in more communal, normative activities. The Rankian framework also calls for a reinterpretation of *Vincent*'s conclusion. The final image of Vincent collapsed on the floor suggests that he has sacrificed himself for his art. In other words, art brings about a kind of death for the individual personality, at the same time that it paradoxically immortalizes it.

Just as the possibility/necessity dialectic in *Vincent* may be understood differently in terms of the life/creation dialectic, so too may the portrayal of inner/outer self-splitting in the film be recast in Rankian terms as an exploration of the Self/Double relationship. In his writings on the different manifestations of immortality pursuit in art and culture throughout history, Rank emphasizes the common motif of the doppelganger, or Double. In particular, Rank recognizes that, in modern literature, the Double often represents the self's attempt to gain immortality through re-creation of itself; consequently, the death of the Double represents the inescapable mortality of the self.[42] Indeed, Rank highlights Poe's story "William Wilson" (1839) as a prototypic example of this motif. *Vincent* clearly also follows the Double pattern: "Vincent Price" is Vincent Malloy's Double, the re-created version of himself through which he attempts to transcend his ordinariness by adopting an immortal persona and wielding fantastic control. Similarly, the apparent death of the Double at the end of the film represents Vincent's ultimate mortality, despite his attempts to overcome his limits by self-splitting and artistic creation.

Interestingly, however, despite this possible interpretation of the film, *Vincent* is of course itself a sustained exercise in cinematic immortalization: it sustains the memory of the actual person who narrates the film, Vincent Price. While Burton has claimed that watching Price grapple with mortality in the Poe films helped him to live as a child, Price himself has said of *Vincent,* "It was immortality—better than a star on Hollywood Boulevard."[43]

In a similar way, the Rankian life/creation dialectic can also be used to understand much of Burton's creative output beyond *Vincent.* For example, this analysis can be profitably applied to *Big Fish* (2003), in which Ed Bloom, on his deathbed, alienates his son with the fantastic stories he uses to artistically reinvent his life.[44] Ultimately, however, Bloom gains symbolic immortality through these stories, as his son notes in the closing lines of the film. The dialectic also sheds light on many aspects of the idiosyncratic appearance and mise-en-scène of Burton's films, which often blur the line between art and reality. For example, the sets and cinematography of *Edward Scissorhands* often deliberately focus the viewer on the fictional nature of the "real" suburban world being portrayed.[45] Similarly, in the opening credit sequence of *Beetlejuice,* the camera pans over what appears to be the town where the film is set, but at the end of the sequence the ostensibly real town transitions seamlessly (but surprisingly) into Adam Maitland's miniature model of the town. Later in that same film, the line between art and reality is blurred even further when Denise Deetz's drab sculptures become menacingly animated. Generally, it is possible to interpret much of Burton's body of work as a meditation on the problematic border between life and fiction.

For Rank, whatever path the creative individual takes—either sculpting her own life through vital experience or preserving it in works for an assumed posterity—death is never truly vanquished. Both in terms of the perspectives provided in their art and meta-aesthetically when considering their personal histories, it is possible to raise the question of whether artistic creation can truly sustain life and help overcome death anxiety in Burton and Poe. In both Poe's work and personal life, the answer seems less clear and the outlook bleaker. In rather stark terms, Maria Antónia Lima writes of Poe's gothic aesthetic, "Every creation is contaminated with the virus of its annihilation, which led Poe to create a perverse art that was, in part, responsible for his self-destruction."[46] In Poe's prose, art and fantasy often have the power to end life. For example, in his story "The Oval Portrait" (1842), a woman slowly withers away and dies while her artist husband obsessively paints her picture. Of course, Poe might very well have had a melancholy, self-destructive existence even without his art; nevertheless, it is true that he devoted many hours and resources in a life of near-perpetual poverty to artistic creations and schemes that brought him little financial or psychological satisfaction. And yet one can never deny the immortality that Poe has won—immortality that in a sense is very real—through his creative efforts. A part of Poe lives today in Tim Burton.

As for Burton himself, both his work and his personal life present a somewhat more optimistic vision of the capacity of art and fantasy to overcome ontological insecurity and death. Although works like *Vincent* and *Edward Scissorhands* certainly bring the potential dangers of fantasy into sharp relief, films like *Big Fish* attempt to capture art's ability to free us in certain ways, however insignificant they sometimes seem, from the confines of mortality and anxiety. Burton himself has gone from a misunderstood teenager to a symbol of artistic insecurity and outsiderhood beloved by millions. In Kierkegaardian terms, his defiant despair has become for many a model of authenticity. Furthermore, in a sense, his films give us all a small dose of immortality by making us feel young again. In doing so, Burton's films do not simply remind us why we were afraid of so many things as children. They also remind us why the dark fantasies of our youth were sometimes enchanting and how innocuous they seem compared to some of the realities of our adult lives.

Notes

I dedicate this essay to my mother, Elizabeth, who fostered my childhood obsession with Burton but was somewhat wary of my simultaneous preoccupation with Poe.

1. For example, Peter M. Nichols includes two Burton films in his list of the one hundred greatest films for children in *New York Times Essential Library: Children's Movies* (New York: Macmillan, 2003).

2. See the Walling chapter in this volume for further discussion of Burton's preoccupation with childlike characters.

3. For one prominent example, see D. W. Winnicott, *The Maturational Process and the Facilitating Environment* (London: Karnac and the Institute of Psychoanalysis,

1965). Other psychologists who make similar claims and whose work will be considered in detail later in this chapter include J. R. Killinger, Bruno Bettleheim, and Otto Rank.

4. As Adrian Schober has correctly pointed out, much of Burton criticism follows a "films-as-autobiography model of auteur theory." This is also true in the case of Poe criticism. Schober does not eschew this model himself, and it seems almost unavoidable, given the consistent nature of Burton's work, themes, and protagonists, along with his public persona. In this particular essay, I follow this model primarily to the extent that it highlights important (but largely unexplored) points of connection between Burton and Poe and that it is relevant to the influence of Roger Corman (and the horror film genre in general) on Burton's aesthetics. See Schober, "Wonka, Freud, and the Child Within," in *Lost and Othered Children in Contemporary Cinema,* ed. Debbie Olson and Andrew Scahill (Plymouth, UK: Rowman and Littlefield, 2012), 67–94.

5. A prototypic summary of Burton's semitroubled childhood is provided by Antoine de Baecque in *Tim Burton* (Paris: Cahiers du Cinéma Sarl, 2011). But also see, for instance, the opening sections of M. Salisbury, ed., *Burton on Burton* (London: Faber and Faber, 2006), or David Edelstein's 1990 interview "Odd Man In" from *Burton: Interviews,* ed. K. Fraga (Jackson: University Press of Mississippi, 2005).

6. de Baecque, *Tim Burton,* 21; Salisbury, *Burton on Burton,* 17.

7. Fraga, *Burton: Interviews,* 32.

8. An excellent summary of the production and style of the AIP Poe films is provided by Ron Haydock, "Poe, Corman and Price: A Tale of Terrors," in *The Edgar Allan Poe Scrapbook,* ed. P. Haining (New York: Schocken Books, 1978), 133–37. See also Mário Jorge Torres, "The Phosphorescence of Edgar Allan Poe on Film: Roger Corman's *The Masque of the Red Death,*" *Edgar Allan Poe Review* 11, no. 1 (2010): 182–91.

9. Of course, it should be acknowledged that many other horror film series beyond the Corman films have directly influenced Burton. For example, the Hammer horror films of the 1950s and 1960s were largely the basis for Burton's reimagination of Washington Irving's story in *Sleepy Hollow.*

10. Although it is broadly acceptable to classify *Vincent* as claymation, it is perhaps more technically accurate to acknowledge that the film is really a clever wedding of stop-motion to 2-D animation, as pointed out by Alison McMahan in *The Films of Tim Burton: Animating Live Action in Contemporary Hollywood* (New York: Continuum Books, 2005).

11. See, for example, Michael Frierson, "Tim Burton's *Vincent:* A Matter of Pastiche," *Animation World Magazine* 1, no. 9 (1996), available at http://www.awn.com/mag/issue1.9/articles/frierson1.9.html; or McMahan, *Films of Tim Burton,* 83–84. In this volume, see the Decker and Jenkins chapters for further discussion of links between Burton and German Expressionism.

12. Stern's biographical introduction to *The Portable Poe* (New York: Penguin Books, 1977), xv–xxxviii, is arguably the definitive short statement concerning the unrelenting tragedy of Poe's personal life.

13. See, e.g., Edelstein, "Odd Man In," 36.

14. Haldeen Braddy, *Three-Dimensional Poe* (El Paso: University of Texas Press, 1973), 39.

15. Edelstein, "Odd Man In," 36.

16. Helena Bassil-Morozow, *Tim Burton: The Monster and the Crowd* (New York: Routledge, 2010).

17. R. D. Laing, *The Divided Self* (New York: Penguin Books, 1965), 42.

18. J. R. Killinger, *The Loneliness of Children* (New York: Vanguard Press, 1980).

19. Bruno Bettelheim, *The Uses of Enchantment* (New York: Alfred A. Knopf, 1976).

20. Stanley Cohen and Laurie Taylor, *Escape Attempts: The Theory and Practice of Resistance to Everyday Life* (New York: Penguin Books, 1978).

21. Laing, *Divided Self,* 84.

22. Andrew Collier provides a good summary of this aspect of Laing's phenomenology in the first chapter of *R. D. Laing: The Philosophy and Politics of Psychotherapy* (New York: Pantheon Books, 1977).

23. Søren Kierkegaard, *The Sickness unto Death,* in *Basic Writings of Existentialism,* ed. Gordon Marino (New York: Modern Library, 2004), 41–110.

24. Kierkegaard, *Sickness unto Death,* 66.

25. Ibid., 67.

26. Nina Christensen, "What Is a Child? Childhood and Literature for Children in Selected Texts by Søren Kierkegaard, Hans Christian Andersen, and their Contemporaries," in *Kierkegaard Studies Yearbook 2006,* ed. Niels Jørgen Cappelørn and Hermann Deuser (Berlin: Walter de Gruyter, 2006), 148–64.

27. See Arne Grøn, *The Concept of Anxiety in Søren Kierkegaard,* trans. Jeanette B. L. Knox (Macon, GA: Mercer University Press, 2008), 130–32.

28. Kierkegaard, *Sickness unto Death,* 98–105.

29. Ibid., 99.

30. Bassil-Morozow, *Tim Burton,* 65.

31. Laing, *Divided Self,* 53.

32. Salisbury, *Burton on Burton,* 17.

33. See McMahan, *Films of Tim Burton,* 82.

34. Kierkegaard, *Sickness unto Death,* 99–100.

35. Ibid., 103–5.

36. The relationship between Wonka and his father lends itself readily to psychoanalytic interpretation, especially because their discord largely stems from the issue of Wonka's teeth, which Freud believed served as a suitably repressed representation of the sexual drive in dreams. In the context of the present framework, one might say that candy represents the promise of possibility, while teeth represent the repression of fantasy and the necessity of restricting indulgence (as well as the limits of the physical body). A satisfactory resolution of the possibility/necessity dialectic is obtained when

Wonka's adult teeth pass his father's inspection, despite the fact that he has built his life around candy consumption and production. See also Schober, "Wonka, Freud, and the Child Within."

37. See Otto Rank, *The Myth of the Birth of the Hero and Other Writings* (New York: Vintage Books, 1959), 140.

38. See, for example, Richard Shiff, "Art in Life," *Critical Inquiry* 5, no. 1 (1978): 107–22.

39. Ellen Handler Spitz, "Conflict and Creativity: Reflections on Otto Rank's Psychology of Art," *Journal of Aesthetic Education* 23, no. 3 (1989): 97–109.

40. J. Gerald Kennedy, *Poe, Death, and the Life of Writing* (New Haven, CT: Yale University Press, 1987).

41. See the McMahon chapter in this volume for further discussion of Burton's artistic treatment of death.

42. For an extensive application of Rank's ideas on the Double and mortality to contemporary literature, see Daniel Sullivan and Jeff Greenberg, "Monstrous Children as Harbingers of Mortality: A Psychological Analysis of Doris Lessing's *The Fifth Child*," *Literature Interpretation Theory* 22, no. 2 (2011): 113–33.

43. Quoted in Frierson, "Tim Burton's *Vincent*," 2.

44. See the Hada chapter in this volume for further discussion of the relationship between identity and storytelling in *Big Fish*.

45. See Joshua David Bellin's discussion of the film in *Framing Monsters* (Carbondale: Southern Illinois University Press, 2005).

46. Maria Antónia Lima, "Poe and Gothic Creativity," *Edgar Allan Poe Review* 11, no. 1 (2010): 23.

Johnny Depp Is a Big Baby!

The Philosophical Significance of Tim Burton's Preoccupation with Childhood Consciousness in *Edward Scissorhands* and *Ed Wood*

Mark Walling

Ed Wood (Johnny Depp) is directing a scene in Tim Burton's biopic (*Ed Wood,* 1994) of the man voted the worst film director of all time. The film is *Bride of the Atom,* which was released as *Bride of the Monster* (1955), one of Wood's more infamous works. As he enters a room, Tor Johnson (George "The Animal" Steele), a bald-headed, hairy-shouldered professional wrestler turned actor, receives instructions from Wood to act upset. Tor grasps his rock of a head with massive hands. Wood corrects, "No, no, you're not that upset. You want to keep moving. You've got to get through that door."

Johnson heeds the advice but rams the door frame with his shoulder during his exit. The set's fabricated wall shakes. In response, speaking through a megaphone he clearly doesn't need, Wood says, "And cut. Perfect. Print it. Let's move on."

New to working with Wood, the crew is perplexed. Wood's colorblind cinematographer, Cameraman Bill (Norman Alden), voices their concern: "Don't you want to do another take, kid? Looks like big baldy had a little trouble getting through the door."

"No, it's fine. It's real," Woods explains, radiant with understanding. "You know in actuality Lobo [Johnson's character in *Bride*] would have to struggle with that problem every day."

Shrugging, surprised yet pleased, the crew moves to the next scene. And so does the audience. A scene that could have been absurd and pathetic is transformed by Burton and Depp into a comic moment of enlightenment.

Seriously.

The question is how.

A search for the answer could direct us to the aesthetic style or thematic obsessions of Burton or the acting method of Depp or the unique collaboration of two artists whose characters have rendered several variations of a type most perfectly realized in *Ed Wood.*[1] Such forays might reveal clues to the mystery, but all of these paths of inquiry ultimately lead back to a single source of explanation: childhood. Not Burton's childhood necessarily, nor Depp's. But everyone's.

Classic and Contemporary Views of Childhood

The development of Western culture's notions of childhood is a topic of dispute. Many scholars continue to support Phillipe Aries's significant contribution *Centuries of Childhood* (published in 1960; translated into English in 1962), which argues that perspectives of childhood have undergone radical change during the last half millennium. According to Aries, in the medieval world children were viewed as smaller versions of the adults they would soon become. They required discipline and training to be prepared for their transition to the public world, which could occur as early as age seven, rather than attention to their physical, emotional, and intellectual growth. Studying medieval writings on age and maturation; artistic portrayals of children, including depictions of the baby Jesus; styles of children's dress; and histories of games, Aries concludes that "in medieval society the idea of childhood did not exist."[2] However, other scholars, including Linda Pollack and Shulamith Shahar, dispute Aries's central claim. According to Shahar, academic writing and artistic depictions of children during this period reveal that childhood consisted of developmental stages and that parents were invested both materially and emotionally in their children's well-being.[3]

Though debate persists regarding the medieval position on childhood, few would question the effect Jean-Jacques Rousseau (1712–1778) has had on Western culture's understanding of childhood. Providing theoretical cornerstones for the foundation of romanticism, Rousseau continuously emphasized the need for human beings to envision themselves as natural creatures, born of a spontaneous, wild yet organically structured nature. Rousseau's declarations represented a protest against a view of childhood informed by both medieval Christianity and Renaissance culture, specifically Christianity's emphasis on a soul that exists within yet apart from the mutable body. This dualistic view insists that a separation from nature, where wildness, savagery, decay, and chaos abound, is necessary for the liberation of the human personality in order that it might see the light and serve God. Renaissance thinkers, in turn, sought to refashion society with attention to the humanistic conceits of ancient Greek and Roman cultures, locating purpose, order, and enlightenment in study of humans and their relationship to the world. Though such a transformation did wrest central authority from the church and broadened human inquiry in the arts and sciences, the effect on Renaissance views of nature were slight. Consistent with their classical forebears, such as Plato (427–347 B.C.), Renaissance peoples strove to tame the wilderness into a garden, seeing themselves as removed from the crass, and potentially evil, natural world. This desire for separation from the natural world is expressed in the period's hierarchal society, the organization of cities and landed estates, the strict insistence on social mores, the prevalent acceptance of mannered food consumption, and the use of perfumes that masked body odor and clothing that covered and contorted the natural figure.

Rousseau saw these views as preposterous on moral, social, and educational grounds. Throughout his major philosophical works, such as *The Social Contract* (1762), Rousseau continuously insists that human beings are naturally, and therefore inherently, good; their corruption is not the result of original sin but the consequence of living in a structured, artificial society.[4] His radical views on childhood and pedagogy, which are still debated by educators, are articulated most clearly in *Emile; or, Treatise on Education* (1762), a work that was met with great disdain in several cities, including threats of public burning.[5] Using novelistic techniques, Rousseau argues that children learn in direct correlation with their natural development, not in an artificially controlled environment such as a classroom. Naturally endowed with the complementary drives of self-love (preservation) and compassion (preservation of others), children, Rousseau concludes, have a natural goodness that could fully develop only in an environment that protects it from the controlling will of adults, particularly teachers. Even books should be restrained because of the domineering focus of the author.[6]

Rousseau's influence on romanticism has been well documented and his views of childhood were influential among the enlightened aristocracy and burgeoning middle classes of his time. However, for most children, Rousseau's theories hovered in the air with the clouds. Any reader of Charles Dickens (writing one hundred years later) knows that the rigid industrial model of education and the view that children were small adults in need of proper discipline and training persisted. These concepts didn't change until the field of psychology emerged in the late nineteenth century, when critical inquiry into the notion of childhood began in a more thorough and documented fashion.

Recognition of the creative reach and cognitive power of a child's consciousness was slow in coming. Lacking time-tested modes of inquiry and established methodologies, the brave, new, uncertain field of child psychology was dominated by the theoretical advancements of Sigmund Freud (1856–1939) and Jean Piaget (1896–1980). Freud argued that each stage of a child's development is sequentially connected to specific physical, often sexual, needs and demands.[7] For Piaget, a similar sequential progression developed, but one based on maturation and experience.[8] Ultimately, the work of both theorists asserts that children's perceptions are restricted to the here and now. According to this conventional wisdom, which remains widely accepted by the general populace, a child's fantasies do not suggest a multiplication of awareness or a unique rendering of the empirical world but are simply another form of present experience.

Yet as contemporary cognitive scientists, including Alison Gopnik, have recently discovered, this "conventional picture is wrong."[9] In *The Philosophical Baby: What Children's Minds Tell Us about Truth, Love, and the Meaning of Life*, Gopnik demonstrates the creative complexity of a child's mind and the far-ranging power of a child's consciousness. New research reveals that even very young children understand concepts of time, delineate between actuality and fantasy, and utilize their imaginative capacities not only to create new worlds and extend the domain of their play but also to enhance critical thinking abilities, test their problem-solving skills, and widen their grasp of the actual world and their relationship to it.

Repeated studies demonstrate that two- and three-year-old children can distinguish between pretense and actuality.[10] Cognitive scientists have discovered that giggles, exaggerated gestures, and melodramatic facial expressions signal a child's understanding of the make-believe realm. Similar to adults, children are interested in changing the world into one they wish to inhabit temporarily, yet the nature of such control, regardless of the age of the mind that inspires it, requires parallel cognizance of its artificiality. Even the youngest children know they are pretending when they nibble invisible cookies or talk to Mom on an imaginary phone. "It's not, as scientists used to think, that children can't tell the difference between the real world and the imaginary world," writes Gopnik. "It's just that they don't see any particular reason for preferring to live in the real one."[11]

The intensity of a child's emotions appears to belie this fact, especially to contemporary parents who overestimate the power of their influence and hover, like helicopters, over every sullen mood and fearful expression. Such parents believe their continual distinctions between fact and fantasy will reduce their child's dramatic pain. Children's emotions are more intense than adults' and while "to a worried parent, it may seem that the child trembling under the covers must believe that there really is a monster in the closet," the truth is they know the game they are playing just as adults know the serial killer in the horror film is not bringing the axe to their necks. "Scientific studies show that this is not because children don't understand the difference between fiction and fact. They are just more moved by both than grown-ups."[12]

Adult artists utilize many central components of a child's way of thinking. The relationship of a child to an imaginary friend is paralleled by the relationships between many writers, directors, and actors and their imaginary characters. Both the child and the adult know the pretend person is not real, yet they both regard the figure as an autonomous person. Descriptions from both children and adults in this respect bear striking similarities; they see their characters as individual people who also happen to be nonexistent in the actual world. In his preface to *The Ambassadors* Henry James observes that he always felt a little behind his character and struggled to keep up.[13] Of his composition process, William Faulkner said he followed his characters, recording what they said and did: "Once these people come to life . . . they take off and so the writer is going at a dead run behind them trying to put down what they say and do in time. . . . They have taken charge of the story. They tell it from then on."[14]

Marjorie Taylor's research suggests that the creation and care of imaginary beings (close counterfactuals, in philosophical terms) leads to a more advanced theory of mind. This does not mean artists or imaginative children are smarter or more intelligent; it simply suggests that their conscious awareness may be more alert, perceptive, and expansive than that of their peers. Such awareness may be the source of the insight and wisdom conveyed by our best-loved and best stories. In children, according to Taylor, attention to an imaginary friend does not lead to isolation and antisocial behavior, a common concern, but to their opposite. Typically, children with such imaginary friends are more sociable and better able to anticipate the actions and emotions of others than their more reality-grounded comrades.[15]

Such capacities have also been revealed by explorations into the consciousness of babies and very young children. As adults in an empirical and pragmatic world, we know the benefits of focused tasks, disciplined effort, specialized knowledge, and refined skill sets. We also know that our consciousness of objects is heightened through our studious attention. It's not just that a major league pitching coach knows about pitchers and pitching. He knows of them.

However, babies and young children and perhaps artistic adults attend to the world in significantly different ways. A child's attention is less focused yet aware of a broader field, which is curiously how adults often describe artists and mystics. Such capacities are certainly the source of a baby's phenomenal learning power and, conversely, the very reason we find adults unable to adapt as easily to new information challenges or environments. Research demonstrates that preschoolers don't become inattentionally blinded: they experience consciousness in a less-focused way than adults, broadening their visual and cognitive attention. They don't appear to recognize or share adult understanding of attention or attentional focus. When asked questions about a person staring at a framed photograph, preschoolers explain that the viewer is looking at the subject and thinking about the action depicted in the imagery. Yet they also observe that she is looking at the frame too. They understand she isn't thinking about everything, such as the chair in the next room. But they do believe all people notice and think about everything in their field of vision. If you have ever been in a rush and tried to get a three-year-old out of the house without the child noticing or touching seemingly insignificant objects along the way, you understand the findings of the aforementioned researchers. Based on these discoveries, Gopnik concludes that "babies are, at least by some measures, more conscious than we are."[16]

The Burton-Depp Collaboration

Tim Burton's oeuvre contains only two films that focus on children as the primary characters—*Charlie and the Chocolate Factory* (2005) and *Alice in Wonderland* (2010)—and they portray children who act more like adults than the adult-child characters found in other Burton-Depp films.[17] The maturity of Charlie and Alice is required so that they might navigate the bizarre, frightful, alluring, and treacherous fantasy worlds with which they must learn to cope.

However, Burton directs a more focused sense of childlike wonder and playfulness into the fabrication of several adult leads played by Johnny Depp.[18] Though all of their films explore this thematic concern, the first two films in which the duo collaborated—*Edward Scissorhands* (1990) and *Ed Wood* (1994)—depict adult characters that embody the emergent view of child consciousness articulated by researchers such as Gopnik and Taylor. In both works Depp conveys the passionate, artistic, escapist yet lucid vision of a child. Both characters are working adult artists, yet they portray numerous characteristics of childhood psychology described in recent research. They possess an encapsulating sense of wonder about the world, and their consciousness is wide, alert, inattentional, and amazingly self-conscious. As Gopnik and others emphasize, these traits are also characteristic of a child's imaginative experience; for them, it's all just art, just pretend.[19]

Because Burton and Depp's imaginative constructions enact the experience and perspective of children so pervasively, these characters evoke consistently persuasive and compelling reactions from their audiences. Depp's highly self-conscious and stylized performances educe the stagy actions of children when they explore pretend worlds. His intuitive technique mirrors the giggles, exaggerated gestures, and melodramatic facial expressions of children at play, all of which make the characters more believable and likeable. Within the Burton-Depp collection, these films rank highest in overall critical appreciation, and most reviews point to the sense of childlike wonder portrayed in the adult characters as the primary source of viewer sympathy and appreciation.[20] According to Owen Gleiberman of *Entertainment Weekly,* Burton's flipping of the Frankenstein tale in *Edward Scissorhands* would not have worked had it not been for the ingenious pairing of the deadly scissor-like hands with Depp's ability to convey "serene wonder" through his timid voice and observant eyes. In so doing, Burton was able to fashion a "portrait of himself as an artist: a wounded child converting his private darkness into outlandish pop visions."[21] Both character and artist are redeemed through the compelling creation of a childlike consciousness, and a similar effect is achieved in *Ed Wood,* where Burton embraces the passion of imagination more than its effects.[22] Depp's depiction of Wood, regarded as the ultimate failed filmmaker, as a "wide-eyed innocent" allows Burton to explore the artistic process in, as Hal Hinson of the *Washington Post* observes, a manner "so open and uncomplicated that we immediately take him [Wood] at his word." Depp's "sunny indifference to the plain facts of real life" transforms him from a failed dreamer to a flawed artist who remains "irresistibly charming."[23] Ultimately, such positive reviews emerge from delighted responses to characters who are capable of rendering a consciousness that is intrinsically childish in its creative power, inattentional focus, and enthrallment in the artistic process. From this perspective, it is no mystery why responses from both critics and viewers to these films rate the lead characters in *Edward Scissorhands* and *Ed Wood* as the most successfully accomplished in the Burton-Depp canon.

Edward Scissorhands

Edward Scissorhands opens with an elderly woman named Kim (Wynona Rider) telling her granddaughter a bedtime story about where the snow comes from. She explains that the "haunted" mansion on the mountaintop was once inhabited by an old inventor who created a man, giving him a "heart, brain, almost everything." The inventor died before he finished the man, leaving his creation "incomplete and all alone." And with scissors for hands.

The next scene opens on a bright suburban bedroom community, stunning in its conformity, with ordered floor plans and a predominance of pastel colors. However, the unsuccessful house calls of an Avon Lady, Peg Boggs (Dianne Wiest), reveal that the occupants of the neighborhood are more varied, cynical, and sordid than the crafted facades suggest. They all resist the beautification efforts of an enthusiastic, well-meaning peer. Peg's personality retains the happiness of a child in spite of her frustrations, a foreshadowing of the greater power exuded by a more genuine adult-child and a more original artist, namely, Edward Scissorhands.

Seeing the mansion in her car's mirror, Peg decides to make an unscheduled visit. The mansion's long, bleak, gargoyle-guarded drive begins at the end of a cul-de-sac. The mansion is Gothic gray stone; lifeless, dreary sculptures abound. But once Peg leaves the car and passes through the iron gateway, the fresh perspective and broadened awareness that will be revealed through Edward's consciousness becomes immediately apparent. The musical score by Danny Elfman lifts with excitement as Peg sees a panoply of fantastic shrubs cut into an assortment of huge shapes. Awe-inspiring by virtue of their size and design, the living figures, which include a benign sea serpent, a giant deer, and an open hand, transform the otherwise lifeless setting into an inviting children's museum.

In contrast to the whimsical garden sculptures found outside the mansion, the interior of the home is bleak and dingy. At the top of the stairs Peg finds an enormous room with a partial roof. Moving within shadows, Edward approaches, initially in a sinister fashion. Backed by troubling music, the blades, which form the fingers of his hands, make a menacing clipping sound. But when he appears in the light, all of the darkness, figurative as well as literal, evaporates. He walks slowly, a bit unsteadily, the movement of the blades clearly a nervous twitch of his mechanical fingers. A slight overbite and tense lips pinch an ashen face, accentuating his wide, innocent eyes. He tells Peg, "I'm not finished." Edward is newly made, a child in a man's body. Of the inventor's death, he says, "He didn't wake up." Despite the scars on his face, the wild shock of black hair, and the worn, belted, studded leather getup, he is a lonely, forgotten child, one so isolated he doesn't know how to respond when Peg asks, "Are you alone?"

Emotionally, Peg is hooked, and so is the film's audience. The inversion of the Frankenstein tale, presenting a lonely child in place of a frightening monster, forces the audience to respond to the character's innocence. Acting on the audience's behalf, Peg reaches out to Edward. She attempts to examine one of his facial scars. Reflexively, Edward shrinks away from her concern. Serving as his first mother, Peg gently yet firmly explains the need for an astringent to prevent infection. Edward goes rigid with trepidation yet allows the contact, eyeing her actions with fear and hope.

Touched, Peg invites him to her home and the boy is born. In the car Edward sports the delighted, self-satisfied smile of a child who has finally gotten his way. Seeing a boy playing on a slip-n-slide, Edward demonstrates the range of his curiosity and his inattentional focus. He points at the scene and nearly cuts Peg's cheek with his blades. He apologizes and Peg says, "No, it's okay. You have every reason to be excited."

Though Edward changes in certain respects as the plot progresses, he does not lose his childlike nature. He becomes a celebrated artist in the community and falls in love with Kim, yet he exhibits the same genuine innocence and childlike consciousness as he did in the opening scene of the film. When he accidentally pokes holes in Kim's waterbed, he covers them with a stuffed animal. When a banker denies him a loan for a salon and tells him to establish credit and get a handicap placard for his vehicle, because it will provide him a decided advantage, Edward smiles with thanks. And his unfiltered honesty emerges after Joyce (Kathy Baker) attempts to seduce him. To the Boggses, he simply says, "She took off her clothes."

In spite of his garish appearance, Edward's childlike qualities allow him to quickly win over the Boggs family, including their teenaged daughter, Kim, the narrator of the story. However, it is his shrub-clipping artistry that initially earns him the eager attention of the neighborhood. In Burton's vision, Edward becomes the consummate romantic artist. His passion and skill emerge in the manner described by Rousseau: naturally, imaginatively, and intuitively. He receives no formal training; the only discipline he requires is a shrub to shape.

The community becomes enthralled with Edward's ability and expresses greater enthusiasm when he agrees to place his talent in the service of a more consumer-driven enterprise: cutting hair. Edward, like a child who is receiving universal permission to play, is more amused by the opportunities to create than the praise or rewards offered for the products of his work. His art is his play, and through Edward's lack of concern for profit, Burton suggests that attention to the imagination is reward enough because it unites adults with their original source, the spontaneous, transformative power of a child. In addition, the film demonstrates the potential for a benevolent society devoted to beauty and art if the natural childlike tendencies of imagination, individuality, and creativity were allowed to flourish.[24]

However, not everyone is impressed. Esmeralda (O-Lan Jones), a religious fanatic, and Jim (Anthony Michael Hall), Kim's boyfriend, are gripped by the darker passions of suspicion and jealousy. They dislike Edward and intend to sabotage his success. Jim manipulates Edward's innocence by conning him into a burglary scheme for which Edward, looking like a little boy in an oversized cap, becomes the fall guy. Later, shaping an angel ice sculpture, his first act of "making snow," Edward accidentally cuts Kim's hand. The injury becomes the excuse Jim needs to attack Edward. His anger rouses the resentment of Esmeralda and the spurned Joyce; a witch hunt of the troubled mob for the helpless innocent commences.

Edward and Kim flee to the mansion on the hill. Jim pursues them, and when he attacks, Edward does not defend himself. But when Jim strikes Kim, Edward responds, stabbing and killing Jim. Edward says goodbye to Kim and retreats into the land of myth, where he becomes one with nature, forever the maker of snow.

Clearly, *Edward Scissorhands* is an allegory of corrupt society's unwillingness to be redeemed by the purity of goodness. But the conclusion allows Edward to maintain his childlike spirit in spite of the violent necessities the adult world requires of him to protect his love. With this conclusion Burton hopes to show that it is not the naïve, natural artist who needs to grow up; rather, the fault lies with a society that has matured into a world that is intolerant and vicious because it gave up the broader consciousness of trust, honesty, and make-believe exhibited by Edward.[25]

Ed Wood

Ed Wood did not present the technical challenges offered by most Burton projects, including *Edward Scissorhands.* In terms of visual fireworks and mise-en-scène complexities, *Ed Wood* is hardly recognizable as a Tim Burton film. In fact, Burton, whose auteur signature has been penned with cinematic wizardry, chose to tell the story of a director who spun special effects with the skill of a kindergarten student. Yet it is in *Ed Wood* where the Burton-Depp partnership achieves its fullest expression of the attentive power of a child's consciousness. Burton has admitted that the appeal of the script stemmed from Wood's childlike fascination with the medium that compelled his attention. Following the reviews of *Pee-wee's Big Adventure* (1985) and *Beetlejuice* (1988), which, oddly, received mainly positive responses, Burton "felt very close to that character [Ed Wood]."[26] It's also clear that, following the success of *Edward Scissorhands,* Burton felt very close to the material's thematic concerns.

Although the technical challenges of *Ed Wood* did not match the set and costume demands required by *Edward Scissorhands,* the thematic and character complications of a story about an inept filmmaker were exceedingly more severe than those presented by the tale of a child-savant visual artist. Structurally, *Edward Scissorhands* reinforces the sympathy for the childlike main character by pitting him against a communal mob that seeks to manipulate and then destroy him. Ed Wood's only nemesis is a series of producers who are reluctant to invest in his work and are then uniformly disappointed when they do. *Ed Wood* is episodic, the loosely connected scenes linked by the presence of Wood and his singular desire: to get a film made. Instead of astonishing the other characters and the audience with his natural, artistic splendor, Wood has little grasp of the demands of his art, little talent by which to summon inspiration, and little skill by which to woo sympathy for his pursuits. And, in addition, he likes to put on women's clothes, particularly cashmere sweaters.

The focus on such a character is obviously not in keeping with established studio formulas for commercial success. Shooting the story in black and white, which Burton deemed necessary to visually transmit the financial limitations of Wood's endeavors, works on an aesthetic level but conspired with the subject matter to keep mainstream audiences away. To date, the film has grossed a paltry five million dollars.[27] Yet for critics and filmgoers who have seen it, the power of Wood's appeal is unmatched, arising largely from his childlike consciousness, a state of mind that is innocent and effervescent, that sees the world as a whole and not a sum of selected parts, that maintains enthusiasm instead of casting judgment, and that understands art as a form of play, aligned closer to life through the creative process than by the production of artificial representations.

Johnny Depp based his performance on an amalgam of three personalities: Ronald Reagan, Casey Kasem, and the Tin Man from *The Wizard of Oz.*[28] A prominent personality trait of all three individuals is innocent optimism, yet in Depp's hands the youthful nature formed the core of his approach. As Depp does with Edward Scissorhands, he acts like a child, but the Ed Wood Depp plays is not a timid, fearful infant. Instead, he is an eager, imaginative child in an adult body whose life is a moment of play, both on and off the film set. For example, when he meets the famous actor Bela Lugosi (Martin Landau), whose life has descended into a well of deprivation and addiction and whose career is long over, Wood conveys the excitement of the president of a fan club who is meeting his idol for the first time. Depp expresses a sense of childlike wonder when he listens to Lugosi explain the techniques he developed to intensify the eeriness of his iconic portrayal of Count Dracula. As Lugosi affects his trademark Transylvanian accent and works his hands for hypnotic effect, Wood imitates his every movement, like a boy learning to cast shadow figures on a wall. Later, on Halloween night, Wood frightens costumed trick-or-treaters at Lugosi's door by removing his false teeth. He tells Lugosi he lost his "pearlies" in the war, meaning World War II, as if he is speaking of a bicycle accident. Prior to a fund-raising party at the Brown Derby, Wood, seated with Lugosi and The Amazing Criswell (Jeffrey Jones), literally bounces with enthusiasm in the booth.

Wood's boyish manner is most notable on film sets, where we would expect him to finally locate an adult seriousness for the great passion of his life. Yet joy in the process is clearly the motivating force for Wood's work, according to Burton and Depp. Rejection from producers doesn't trouble him, except for the interference it might pose for future endeavors. He is not oblivious to the story he is attempting to tell. He seeks the best locations and equipment he can beg or borrow, and he offers instructions to the crew and actors. However, his understanding of success is that of a child who enjoys participation in a make-believe world. The scene described in the introduction to this essay illustrates Wood's inattentional focus. A shaking set does not disturb him because it is part of a larger landscape that includes a character who would struggle with doorways. During the shooting of a scene in Wood's most infamous work, *Plan 9 from Outer Space,* the crew discovers a potentially scene-killing mistake. The motor required to manipulate the deadly octopus was left at the warehouse from which it was borrowed without permission. But in a world where play is the thing, Wood overcomes the problem by telling Lugosi to simply "thrash its arms about" and scream louder.

Whenever possible, Wood totes a megaphone, speaking through it to crew members who could easily hear his normal speaking voice. Through this prop, Burton and Depp most effectively reveal the childlike nature of Wood's consciousness. Megaphone in hand, Wood pretends to be a movie director at the very moment he is actually directing a film. Scott Alexander, one of the film's two screenwriters, has said, "He's like an eight-year-old boy who wants to be a movie director. He's seen a cartoon of what a director looks like."[29] Inhabiting a make-believe world and simultaneously recognizing the pretense of this world reveals a fundamental attribute of a young child's consciousness, a trait that makes Depp's performance captivating and lifts Burton's story about a failed artist from a documentation of his flaws to a celebration of his inherent youthful spirit, a force that, as the film shows, is the source of all art.[30]

Though they have not gone on record and stated in precise terms that the childlike perspective of Ed Wood drew them to the character, it is clear it became a primary justification for Burton and Depp's fascination. The fondness for Wood shown by other eccentric characters—namely, Lugosi, Criswell, and the irrepressible Bunny Breckinridge (Bill Murray), who wants a sex change operation—not only serves to generate more sympathy for Wood but also becomes a barometer for the approval Burton and Depp hold for him. According to Alexander, there were "a lot more moments in the script when [Ed] had self-doubts. Questioned himself." However, "Johnny and Tim grew to love Ed so much . . . it made them feel uncomfortable to give Ed those moments."[31] For an artist with a focused, adult consciousness, such scenes may have helped generate sympathy for a character struggling to produce the object of his desire. But Wood is not an adult, at least not in terms of consciousness, and moments of severe doubt would not have fit the depiction of a boy at play, one who isn't concerned with the final product. "He just wanted to make a movie . . . to experience it."[32]

Such an approach certainly resonated with Burton, who has said he hopes that "at the end of all of it I can still maintain that enthusiasm."[33] Perhaps the key is directly stated by Wood near the end of the film. Speaking to a Baptist backer who complains when a cardboard headstone falls over during the shooting of a scene in *Plan 9 from Outer Space,* Wood explains, "Filmmaking is not about the tiny details. It's about the big picture."

And as contemporary research continues to demonstrate, it takes a child's mind to apprehend this view.

Notes

1. See the Knight and McKnight chapter in this volume for further discussion of the unique nature of the collaborative relationship between Tim Burton and Johnny Depp.

2. Phillipe Aries, *Centuries of Childhood: A Social History of Family Life,* trans. Robert Baldick (New York: Knopf, 1962), 128.

3. Shulamith Shahar, *Childhood in the Middle Ages* (New York: Routledge, 1992). See also Linda A. Pollock, *Forgotten Children: Parent–Child Relations from 1500 to 1900* (Cambridge: Cambridge University Press, 1984).

4. Jean-Jacques Rousseau, *The Social Contract,* trans. Charles Frankel (New York: Hafner, 1947), particularly books 1 and 2.

5. Leo Damrosch, *Jean-Jacques Rousseau: Restless Genius* (New York: Houghton Mifflin, 2005), see chapter 18, 331–61.

6. Jean-Jacques Rousseau, *Emile; or, Treatise on Education,* trans. William H. Payne, International Education Series, vol. 20, ed. William T. Harris (New York: Appleton, 1909), see "Book Second: Emile from Five to Twelve," 41–130.

7. Sigmund Freud, *The Ego and the Id* and *Other Works,* in *The Standard Edition of the Complete Psychological Works of Sigmund Freud,* vol. 19 (1923–25) (London: Hogarth Press, 1961), 141–48.

8. Jean Piaget, *The Child's Conception of the World* (New York: Harcourt, 1929), and Piaget, *The Construction of Reality in the Child* (New York: Basic Books, 1954).

9. Alison Gopnik, *The Philosophical Baby: What Children's Minds Tell Us about Truth, Love, and the Meaning of Life* (New York: Farrar, Straus and Giroux, 2009), 20.

10. Ibid., 68–73, 133–67. See also Alan M. Leslie, "Pretense and Representation: The Origins of Theory of Mind," *Psychological Review* 94, no. 4 (October 1987): 412–26; Angeline Lillard, "Pretend Play and Cognitive Development," in *Blackwell Handbook of Childhood Cognitive Development,* ed. Usha Goswami (Malden, MA: Blackwell, 2002), 188–205; Angeline S. Lillard and David C. Witherington, "Mother's Behavior Modifi-

cations during Pretense and Their Possible Signal Value for Toddlers," *Developmental Psychology* 40, no. 1 (January 2004): 95–113.

11. Gopnik, *Philosophical Baby,* 30, 71.

12. Ibid., 31, 134–40. Gopnik specifically delineates the difference between an ability to distinguish fantasy from actuality and the creation of false memories, which can be produced in adults as easily as children. See also Elizabeth F. Loftus, "Creating False Memories," *Scientific American* 277, no. 3 (September 1997): 70–75; and Loftus, "Memories for a Past that Never Was," in "Memory as the Theater of the Past: The Psychology of False Memories," special issue, *Current Directions in Psychological Science* 6, no. 2 (June 1997): 60–65. On the tricks adult minds play to pretend that stories are "real," see Kendall L. Walton, *Mimesis as Make-Believe: On the Foundations of the Representational Arts* (Cambridge, MA: Harvard University Press, 1990).

13. Henry James, preface to *The Ambassadors* (New York: Norton, 1964), 3–4. Such notions deepened for James as he aged. See his preface to *Portrait of a Lady,* rev. ed. (New York: Norton, 1975), 3–15.

14. Frederick L. Gwynn and Joseph L. Blotner, eds., *Faulkner in the University: Class Conferences at the University of Virginia, 1957–58* (New York: Vintage, 1959), 120.

15. Marjorie Taylor, *Imaginary Companions and the Children Who Create Them* (New York: Oxford University Press, 1999), 157. See also Walton, *Mimesis as Make-Believe,* 12, 34.

16. Gopnik, *Philosophical Baby,* 110, 124.

17. Unless we count his first feature, *Pee-wee's Big Adventure* (1985), which, interestingly, depicts an adult-child character that had been created by actor Paul Reubens and launched Burton's celluloid prototype of the model that was modified and improved through his collaboration with Depp.

18. In Burton's *Sleepy Hollow* (1999) and *Dark Shadows* (2012), Depp plays characters who reveal a similar sense of childlike wonder, yet both characters possess a much more detailed understanding of their worlds. As a result, they do not produce the same sense of innocence or childlike consciousness as portrayed in *Edward Scissorhands* and *Ed Wood,* and neither film was received as well critically as *Scissorhands* and *Wood.*

19. Gopnik, *Philosophical Baby,* 47–73; Taylor, *Imaginary Companions,* 8–33, 62–85.

20. Ratings for films made by Tim Burton and Johnny Depp, according to Flixster.com: *Edward Scissorhands* (1990), critics 91 percent, audience 88 percent; *Ed Wood* (1994), critics 92 percent, audience 83 percent; *Sleepy Hollow* (1999), critics 67 percent, audience 79 percent; *Charlie and the Chocolate Factory* (2005), critics 82 percent, audience 52 percent; *Sweeney Todd: The Demon Barber of Fleet Street* (2007), critics 86 percent, audience 81 percent; *Alice in Wonderland* (2010), critics 51 percent, audience 72 percent; *Dark Shadows* (2012), critics 40 percent, audience 46 percent.

21. Owen Gleiberman, review of *Edward Scissorhands, EW.Com,* December 7, 1990, http://www.ew.com/ew/article/0,,318762,00.html.

22. See the LaRocca chapter in this volume for further discussion of Burton's *Ed Wood.*

23. Hal Hinson, review of *Ed Wood, Washingtonpost.com,* October 7, 1994, http://www.washingtonpost.com/wp-srv/style/longterm/movies/videos/edwoodrhinson_a019be.htm.

24. Rousseau argues this point in *The Social Contract.*

25. See the Decker chapter in this volume for further discussion of the social significance of the expressive outsider.

26. Tim Burton, "Audio Commentary," *Ed Wood,* special edition (Touchstone Home Entertainment, 2004).

27. "Ed Wood," Box Office Mojo, updated November 2, 2012, http://boxofficemojo.com/movies/?id=edwood.htm; "Ed Wood," Imdb.com, n.d., http://www.imdb.com/title/tt0109707/

28. Larry Karaszewski, "Audio Commentary," *Ed Wood,* special edition (Touchstone Home Entertainment, 2004).

29. Scott Alexander, "Audio Commentary," *Ed Wood,* special edition (Touchstone Home Entertainment, 2004).

30. Reviews of *Ed Wood* repeatedly point out the effectiveness of Burton and Depp's enthusiastic portrayal of the creative spirit and the artistic process. See Roger Ebert's review at RogerEbert.com, October 7, 1994, http://rogerebert.suntimes.com/apps/pbcs.dll/article?AID=/19941007/REVIEWS/410070301; and Janet Maslin's in the *New York Times,* September 23, 1994, http://movies.nytimes.com/movie/review?res=9405E0DA143AF930A1575AC0A962958260&partner=Rotten%20Tomatoes.

31. Alexander, "Audio Commentary."

32. Karaszewski, "Audio Commentary."

33. Burton, "Audio Commentary."

Part 2

Burton and Authority

Mars Attacks!

Burton, Tocqueville, and the Self-Organizing Power of the American People

Paul A. Cantor

> I am obliged to confess I should sooner live in a society governed by the first two thousand names in the Boston telephone directory than in a society governed by the two thousand faculty members of Harvard University.
>
> —William F. Buckley Jr.

Tim Burton's wacky sci-fi film *Mars Attacks!* (1996) is not considered one of the highpoints of his career. Although the movie took in over $100 million worldwide in its initial release, it was judged a box-office failure, given the fact that it was budgeted for roughly the same amount and its backers were hoping for another blockbuster from the director of *Batman* (1989). Moreover, critics generally did not review *Mars Attacks!* favorably. Speaking for many of his colleagues, Kenneth Turan of the *Los Angeles Times* wrote, "*Mars Attacks!* is not as much fun as it should be. Few of its numerous actors make a lasting impression and Burton's heart and soul is not in the humor."[1] From the moment of its conception, the movie risked falling victim to what literary critics call the fallacy of imitative form. Burton set out to re-create the cheesy flying saucer movies of the 1950s. True to his mission, he ended up with a cheesy flying saucer movie. How much could one have expected from a film that turns out to have been based on a set of bubble-gum trading cards that depicts the Earth being invaded by a particularly nasty bunch of Martians?[2]

I myself was disappointed with *Mars Attacks!* when I first saw it. At the time I was a huge Burton fan. I was particularly struck by the consistency of his achievement, having been impressed by each of his first six feature films: *Pee-wee's Big Adventure* (1985), *Beetlejuice* (1988), *Batman* (1989), *Edward Scissorhands* (1990), *Batman Returns* (1992), and *Ed Wood* (1994). For me, *Mars Attacks!* broke this streak and left me wondering whether Burton had lost his magic touch. But like a good Bordeaux—and unlike bubble gum—*Mars Attacks!* has, at least for me, improved with age. I still would grant that it has more than its share of silly moments and cheap jokes. What changed my opinion of it, however, was realizing that it has something important to say. It is not just a random exercise in re-creating 1950s flying saucer movies; it is a serious critique of the pro-government ideology they embodied.

The Federal Government to the Rescue

While Burton may seem to be following closely the formula of his cinematic models in *Mars Attacks!*, he is, in fact, inverting and deconstructing it. As products of a Cold War mentality, the 1950s flying saucer movies generally expressed a faith in the goodness of America's political, military, and scientific elites and their capacity to save the nation from all threats. By contrast, *Mars Attacks!* systematically and mercilessly debunks the elites who claim to be able to protect America. It turns instead to the country's cultural underclass, so despised by those elites, and shows that people often dismissed as "trailer trash" are capable of defending themselves.[3] Always sympathetic to the underdog and the marginalized figure—from Pee-wee to the Penguin—Burton expresses a Tocquevillian confidence in the power of ordinary Americans to associate on their own to deal with any problem. In *Mars Attacks!* all the top-down efforts by the authorities in Washington to respond to the Martian invasion fail utterly, while pockets of outcasts, misfits, and losers around the country spontaneously come together to defeat their enemies from outer space. As Bill Warren writes, "The leaders of Earth are helpless; it's up to the little people to save the day."[4] *Mars Attacks!* is Burton's tribute to American pop culture in one of its more vulgar manifestations—the flying saucer movie—and is at the same time a celebration of the power of pop culture itself to save America. In the end, the Martians are defeated, not by the combined wisdom of America's scientists and the might of its military, but by the music of Slim Whitman, a yodeling country and western singer who virtually defines lowbrow taste in America.

To appreciate the polemical thrust of *Mars Attacks!*, the most fruitful point of comparison is Fred Sears's *Earth vs. the Flying Saucers* (1956). This is the film that Burton mentions most frequently in his comments on *Mars Attacks!,* and it provides more models for the plot elements and the special effects of his movie than any other sci-fi classic of the 1950s. Moreover, it offers perhaps the purest distillation of the political ideology that informed this moment in Hollywood history. This was the height of the Cold War, when fears of communist aggression, from both the Soviet Union and the People's Republic of China, gripped America. Anxieties focused, of course, on the threat of nuclear annihilation, but Americans were also worried about real and supposed attempts to subvert their institutions from within by communist infiltrators, spies, and traitors. By the 1950s, movies had begun to reflect and capitalize on these widespread concerns. Imaginary stories of extraterrestrial aliens invading Earth became convenient vehicles for expressing fears that America might be facing real threats from foreign powers, and perhaps internal subversion as well.[5]

In Cold War ideology, the bulwark of American defense against all these threats was the government of the United States. Movie after movie—not just sci-fi films—celebrated the competence, courage, and integrity of federal officials, particularly if, like the FBI, they combated communism.[6] Perhaps at no point in American history has the federal government inspired as much confidence as it did in the 1950s. In World War II, the federal government had successfully led the battle against enemies in Europe and Asia, and the United States had emerged from the conflict as unquestionably the strongest nation in the world economically and militarily. American triumphs in World War II were attributed to many factors; one of the most important was American scientific and technological superiority. The United States' development of the atomic bomb was credited with having ended the war with Japan, and this Manhattan Project became a powerful symbol of the federal government's ability to achieve whatever it set out to do, provided it devoted enough resources to the task and was able to mobilize the nation's scientific elite behind it.

In view of all the skepticism about nuclear power today, one must make an effort to recall how widely and enthusiastically atomic energy was embraced in the 1950s as the solution to the world's problems. The "Atoms for Peace" program, touted by the federal government, promised to translate its technological triumphs in wartime into peacetime dividends.[7] The respect and, indeed, the awe with which most Americans were taught to view atomic energy in the 1950s epitomized the pro-government ideology of the day.[8] The federal government, the military, and the scientific elite had banded together to create this new power, which was supposed to lead the country into a glorious future. What these three forces had in common in the 1950s was the aura of expertise they projected. On all issues, from politics to economics to technology, the ordinary people of America were supposed to defer to experts, who knew what was best for them. Science has never enjoyed more prestige in American culture than it did in the 1950s; grandfatherly Albert Einstein had become the poster boy for the goodness of nuclear physics. The prestige of the federal government and the prestige of science fed off each other; the one endorsed the other. The federal government began to support science at unprecedented levels of peacetime funding, while scientists flocked to work for the federal government, directly or indirectly, and lent their authority as experts to government programs.

The notion that ordinary Americans have to rely for protection on a benevolent alliance of military and federal government officials with scientific experts is at the ideological heart of the 1950s flying saucer movies. These films generally present the American people as helpless in the face of an alien invasion, overwhelmed by superior technology, which renders their ordinary weapons useless, especially their firearms. In *Earth vs. the Flying Saucers,* for example, average Americans appear largely in the form of mobs, fleeing alien attacks in total panic. They seem completely incapable of organizing themselves into any kind of reasonable response to the threat. In particular, they cannot rely on any local authorities to protect them. The police, for example, do not have anything approaching the technology needed to counter the aliens. *Earth vs. the Flying Saucers* is typical in presenting an ordinary traffic cop on a motorcycle as a comically inept figure. He gets involved in the struggle with the space invaders but makes a fool of himself by thinking that his revolver will be effective against them. The aliens end up sucking out his brain, puny as it is.

Another classic of the genre, William Cameron Menzies's *Invaders from Mars* (1953), carries this denigration of local authorities to an extreme. This movie is unusual because it tells the story from the viewpoint of an adolescent boy, who witnesses an alien invasion unfold before his eyes. The lesson he must learn is to distrust all the local authorities he has been brought up to respect, including his own family. *Invaders from Mars* follows a formula later made famous by Don Siegel's *Invasion of the Body Snatchers* (1956): the aliens systematically take over the minds of human beings one by one, in this case by implants in their necks.[9] The boy watches with horror as first his father and then his mother become zombified by the aliens and turn against him. When he goes to the local police station to get help, he discovers that the police chief has been taken over by the aliens as well.[10] The boy finds that he can rely only on a social worker to protect him by making him in effect a ward of the state. As a representative of the Department of Health, this woman symbolizes the need to replace the traditional family as a source of authority with a rational bureaucracy. The woman is, after all, an expert, namely, a medical doctor who is better able to care for the child's welfare than his own mother and father. And the force that ultimately saves the boy and the whole world is the U.S. military, which manages to marshal the technological resources to defeat the Martians.[11]

Reliance on the U.S. military and federal as opposed to local authorities is almost as prominent in *Earth vs. the Flying Saucers.* The film is filled with important-sounding federal government programs and agencies, many with links to the military, such as Operation Skyhook, the Air Intelligence Command, the Hemispheric Defense Command, and the Internal Security Commission. Somehow even the Bureau of Standards and the Bureau of Meteorology get involved in fighting the space invaders. As this array of bureaucracies suggests, *Earth vs. the Flying Saucers* offers a union between science and the military as the salvation of America. The hero is a scientist named Russell Marvin (Hugh Marlowe), who is portrayed as a superior form of human being. As he himself says of his testimony as to the existence of UFOs: "There is a qualitative difference when you're a scientist."[12] Although Marvin encounters a few difficulties working with the military top brass, on the whole they form an effective alliance to defeat the aliens, and he is as militaristic as the generals. The film underscores the lesson about the dangers of appeasement learned from the run-up to World War II. Marvin says bitterly of the alien invaders, "They'll sail into Washington in broad daylight and expect us to capitulate when they land." But not in Cold War America, according to *Earth vs. the Flying Saucers.* One of the generals reassures Marvin, "When an armed and threatening power lands uninvited in our capital, we don't meet them with tea and cookies."

The film emphasizes the need to respond to the alien threat as a nation. The aliens try to make contact directly with Dr. Marvin and wish to deal with him alone. Here a general in the Pentagon draws the line: "If we are to be confronted with a hostile and unknown power, any decision to meet with them must be made at the cabinet level." Accordingly, the film tells us, the secretary of state and the secretary of defense must fly back to Washington before any action can be taken. Nevertheless, Marvin decides to go ahead and meet with the aliens on his own. In another moment that seems to denigrate the family in the name of the nation-state, his new bride chooses to report him to the government agent assigned to shadow him, telling Marvin, "But it's not your job alone." Again and again the film asks us to put our faith in Washington, D.C. Above all, it stresses the unique ability of the federal government to respond to the technological challenge posed by the alien invaders. When they succeed in shooting down U.S. satellites and destroying a missile base, the portentous voice-over narration intones, "An aroused public demanded an answer. And the federal government dedicated the strength of all its branches to the task of finding one."

The speed with which the federal government manufactures weapons to combat the aliens is reminiscent of the Manhattan Project. With the help of other scientists, Marvin comes up with the idea for an ultrasonic gun that will knock the flying saucers out of the skies. He promises, "With enough scientific and engineering help, we could construct a working model in a very short time." In the very next scene, Marvin has his prototype ready for testing. He quickly discovers that an electromagnetic gun is more practical than an ultrasonic one. As for mass producing the experimental weapon, once again the voice-over reassures us: "From all parts of the globe, under top priority, came every facility and scientific help the governments of the world could furnish." The movie's faith in government knows no bounds. My favorite moment comes again in the voice-over narration, when the federal government has less than two weeks to evacuate the citizens of Washington in the face of a planned alien attack: "Although the authorities and the military worked miracles, when the tenth day dawned more than 60 percent of the people of Washington were still in the metropolitan area." Here *Earth vs. the Flying Saucers* inadvertently supplies a more accurate appraisal of Washington's competence. It is, indeed, a miracle any time the federal government manages to accomplish as much as 40 percent of what it claims to be able to do.

Earth vs. the Flying Saucers hammers home the lesson that many political pundits were preaching in the 1950s. Technological developments during and after World War II, especially at the dawning of the Atomic Age, supposedly had altered the human condition fundamentally, to the point where ordinary human beings were said to be no longer capable of running their own lives. Scientific and technological challenges, especially of a military kind, could only be handled at the national level, and Americans were made to feel grateful that they had a federal government devoted to their welfare and protection, with the vast resources needed to promote those ends. Of course, *Earth vs. the Flying Saucers* is only one movie, and it offers a particularly rosy image of government omnicompetence and a particularly dim view of the capacities of ordinary citizens. Other alien invasion movies complicated the ideological picture. As we have seen, *Earth vs. the Flying Saucers* suggests that scientists and the military can easily form an alliance. Other 1950s sci-fi classics raise doubts about this possibility and show the two forces at odds.

For example, in *The Thing from Another World* (1951), directed by Christian Nyby and produced by Howard Hawks, when an alien being lands in the Arctic, the military leader and the scientist confronted by it differ over how to deal with the threat. The air force captain wants to protect humanity by annihilating the alien being, but the scientist views the situation as a valuable opportunity to expand human knowledge and wants to preserve the Thing and learn how to communicate with it. The scientist is convinced that the Thing is a superior life-form, free of the corrupting effects of human emotion (one hint that the alien may symbolize the threat of what then was regarded as "soulless" communism). But the scientist is proven wrong when the Thing tries to kill him, thus vindicating the military position. In the great Cold War debate—recall that *The Thing* came out during the Korean War—the movie clearly sides with the advocates of a forceful military response to communist aggression and criticizes those who sought any kind of détente with the other side.[13]

Robert Wise's *The Day the Earth Stood Still,* which came out in 1951 as well, also sets scientists at odds with the military, but this film champions the former over the latter. In this movie, a visitor arrives from another planet to warn the people of Earth about the dangers of their reckless and destructive militarism, especially now that they have developed atomic weapons. The military authorities, with their knee-jerk hostility to anything alien and their overconfidence in their own power, bring Earth to the brink of destruction. Only the scientists work toward a peaceful and productive rapprochement with the alien visitor. *The Day the Earth Stood Still* makes a strong pacifist statement and has been viewed as subversive of American Cold War ideology.[14] Considering just these three classics of the genre makes it clear that a wide range of views on central Cold War issues was available in the 1950s flying saucer movies.

Yet despite their seeming divergence in opinion, these three films—and many others from the era—converge on one point: Ordinary people cannot solve their problems on their own and must depend on some kind of higher authority to protect them, whether it be scientific or military or some combination of the two. *The Day the Earth Stood Still* rejects the blatant nationalism of the other two films, but only by offering a supranational solution to human problems. The film holds up the United Nations as an ideal, and the scientists are pointedly from all different countries, constituting an international brotherhood ready to save humanity. *The Day the Earth Stood Still* builds up to a long and tendentious speech by the alien Klaatu (Michael Rennie), who patronizingly informs humanity that intelligent life elsewhere in the universe has long since renounced violence by surrendering their sovereignty to all-powerful robots who automatically enforce peace on their planets. Whatever lesson *The Day the Earth Stood Still* teaches, it is not one of human freedom. Indeed, it seems to teach the ultimate Hobbesian lesson—avoiding violent conflict is so important that we must surrender our autonomy to a Leviathan power that will keep us all in awe. Wise's film seems to go further than any other 1950s sci-fi classic in asking Americans to bow down before the altar of a scientific elite. For all their differences, the 1950s flying saucer movies as a group reflect the way the U.S. government was able to exploit fears of communist aggression during the Cold War to increase its role in American life and to secure its hold on the American people.

Debunking the Elite

It is not surprising that Burton, with his antiestablishment impulses and his sympathy for the little guy, found the message of 1950s flying saucer movies unacceptable, and that when he came to parody them, he completely reversed their ideological polarities, championing ordinary Americans over the elites that view them with contempt. But before plunging into a serious political analysis of *Mars Attacks!,* I should acknowledge how absurd this enterprise may seem at first sight. On the face of it, *Mars Attacks!* is a very silly movie. Burton himself said of it, "On the depth chart, it's like a *Love Boat* episode."[15] In the face of this kind of statement from the film's creator, it may seem pointless to probe *Mars Attacks!* for any kind of political message. Moreover, far from sounding like a critic of 1950s flying saucer movies, Burton has professed himself a fan: "I grew up with this kind of movie. They're in my blood."[16] He especially admires the work of Ray Harryhausen, who did the special effects for *Earth vs. the Flying Saucers:* "I love the old Ray Harryhausen movies, so a lot of this [*Mars Attacks!*] draws inspiration from those."[17] As with all his films, Burton set out to create a distinctive look for *Mars Attacks!*, and for that purpose he stuck close to his 1950s models. He particularly admires Harryhausen's mastery of stop-motion animation and talks about that subject in his interviews more than he does about any message in *Mars Attacks!*. It would be easy to conclude from the interviews that, for Burton, the movie was purely an exercise in re-creating the visual style of films that he enjoyed in his childhood.

Burton has, however, made some statements that hint at a polemical thrust to *Mars Attacks!*, particularly when he mentions the specific historical-political context for the film: "It was during the Gulf War, when the media seemed to have taken it to another level—wars having titles and theme music—and I found it kind of disturbing. I felt like these characters were just a cathartic shakeup of that kind of thing."[18] This comment strongly suggests that Burton saw the nationalism and militarism of the Cold War being revived by the enthusiasm for U.S. military adventures sparked by the Gulf War, and that he wanted to take some of the wind out of the government's sails. This idea is supported by the fact that Burton's principal creative collaborator on the film was the British screenwriter Jonathan Gems. As a foreigner, Gems was well positioned to take a critical stance on American institutions, as he himself explained: "There's a certain kind of joy in the way the Martians just come and smash everything up. I was a punk in London and we always used to do pranks. So here you get the Martians taking the piss out of society."[19]

Gems identifies the antiestablishment spirit of *Mars Attacks!*, and further comments by Burton pick up the theme, particularly when he talks about the trading card series that inspired the film: "I remembered those cards from types of cards I had as a kid. I just liked the anarchistic spirit of them. Jonathan has sort of an anarchistic spirit himself, I think—being British and living in America and having an alien perspective of it, which I sort of have myself."[20] For anyone wishing to give an antigovernment reading of *Mars Attacks!*, it is encouraging to see the words *anarchistic* and *anarchic* keep coming up in Burton's comments on the film: "I was feeling really strangely about things at the time, about America—everything just seemed really off-kilter to me, and I think that was a partial dynamic of what I liked about the material. I was just feeling more anarchic, and that was the energy I liked in it—I saw that in the Martians."[21]

Burton's talk of anarchism takes us to the thematic core of *Mars Attacks!* and its fundamental difference from its 1950s models. The original flying saucer movies were the very opposite of anarchistic in spirit. Their message was that, in the face of foreign threats, Americans had to get behind their government and work together as a nation to stave off alien destruction of their institutions. By contrast, in Burton's own account, *Mars Attacks!* takes a perverse joy in portraying just that destruction: the annihilation of Congress, the humiliation and murder of the president, and a literal downsizing of the military when a particularly aggressive U.S. general is miniaturized by a Martian and then stomped underfoot. Evidently what attracted Burton to the Martians is precisely their lack of respect for American institutions.

Mars Attacks! is unrelenting in its mockery of American elites. We see the categories familiar from the 1950s sci-fi movies—the politicians, the military, and the scientists. But Burton adds one more element to the establishment—media stars—and their narcissism provides a clue to the nature of all the elites in the film. Jason Stone (Michael J. Fox), a vain news anchor for GNN (a thinly disguised CNN), is mainly concerned about how to use the Martian invasion to advance his career. He is dismayed when his girlfriend Natalie Lake (Sarah Jessica Parker) scoops him on a rival network with an interview with the government's chief scientist, Donald Kessler (Pierce Brosnan). Lake is just as vain as Stone, and even dumber. The fact that her show, *Today in Fashion,* gets to air the main interview about the Martians is the film's comment on the shallowness of media coverage in America. Everything is reduced to the level of fashion and show business, even an Earth-threatening invasion from Mars. Stone and Lake are career-conscious media celebrities, and their vanity is the key to understanding all the elites in the film. Almost all the representatives of the establishment are portrayed as vain, more interested in their own celebrity and popularity than in public service or the common good.

In the media-dominated world the film portrays, White House Press Secretary Jerry Ross (Martin Short) seems to have the status of a cabinet official. Indeed, he exercises more influence on the president than anybody else. The prominence of the press secretary reflects the corruption of politics by television. All the establishment figures are chiefly concerned with how they appear on television and how it will affect their status as celebrities. Kessler goes on Lake's daytime talk show and openly flirts with her. A high-ranking general (Paul Winfield) is thrilled to be televised greeting the Martians at their first contact with the human race. And, of course, President James Dale (Jack Nicholson) is obsessed with his television appearances, carefully orchestrating his every move with Ross's advice. He is overjoyed to be the one to announce the Martians' arrival on television: "The people are going to love it."[22] He instructs Ross to have a speech written for him that will be statesmanlike and historical and yet still ingratiate him with the American people, ordering up "Abraham Lincoln meets *Leave It to Beaver.*" The 1950s flying saucer movies built up the Washington establishment by suggesting that the leaders are knowledgeable, public-spirited, and genuinely concerned with America's welfare. *Mars Attacks!* shows them to be self-centered, devoted only to advancing their own careers, and concerned more with show than with substance.

The elites in the film generally consist of beautiful people—fashionably dressed and superficially elegant and sophisticated. The First Lady, Marsha Dale (Glenn Close) frets over redecorating the White House. Taffy Dale (Natalie Portman), the president's daughter, comes across as a spoiled brat, but no more spoiled than the rest of the establishment. They all lead a life of privilege and self-indulgence. Jerry Ross sneaks prostitutes into the White House; the fact that he takes them to what is called the Kennedy Room suggests that higher officials have followed the same path. The establishment figures present themselves as raised above the level of ordinary Americans, but the film exposes that act to be a sham. They are hypocrites, standing up for morality in public while pursuing sexual affairs in private. One of the film's most effective satirical devices is to have Jack Nicholson play both the president and a sleazy real estate developer named Art Land. Land becomes a double for Dale, and the obvious suggestion is that the president is as much of a con man as his gambling casino counterpart. At one point, Land insists to his wife, Barbara (Annette Bening), "I'm not a crook. I'm ambitious. There's a difference." But the film suggests just the opposite, and the echo of Richard Nixon in Land's statement cements the idea that ambition is indistinguishable from crookedness in the Washington establishment.

The film undercuts the idea that any form of integrity can be expected from the nation's elites, but it goes further, suggesting that to the extent that they are at all guided by principles, they are, in fact, misguided. It does an especially good job of capturing the smug, self-satisfied political correctness of the elites in Washington. *Mars Attacks!* is filled with the high-sounding rhetoric of multiculturalism.[23] The most obvious difference from the 1950s flying saucer movies is that the aliens are initially welcomed with high hopes by the establishment, instead of being treated with suspicion and hostility. In the face of some doubts about the Martians' intentions, the scientist Kessler repeatedly assures the president about the aliens: "They're peaceful. An advanced civilization is by definition not barbaric." Pierce Brosnan may have been chosen to play the scientist because, as an Englishman, he reminds us of Michael Rennie's role as the alien Klaatu in *The Day the Earth Stood Still.* Kessler makes similarly patronizing remarks about the human race in comparison to the Martians: "They're an advanced culture—therefore peaceful and enlightened. . . . The human race, on the other hand, is an aggressively dangerous species. I suspect they have more to fear from us than we from them." This way of speaking reverses the pro-Earth, pro-America chauvinism of the typical 1950s flying saucer movie, almost as if Klaatu had now moved into the White House as the president's chief science advisor. Kessler is relentless in his multicultural embrace of the Martians: "We must be open to them," "We need a welcome mat, not a row of tanks." The president uses his announcement of the Martians' arrival to pursue a similar multicultural agenda, telling the American people, "We have become one planet and soon will be one solar system."

We are so used to this kind of talk in our culture that it may be difficult to believe that the film is satirizing it, but events in the movie repeatedly undercut the apparently high-minded rhetoric of the establishment figures, who are made to look ridiculous in their blind faith in the aliens' benevolence. Even after the Martians slaughter the greeting party sent to welcome them, Kessler sticks to his claims on their behalf: "I know this seems terrible, but let's not be rash." The film emphasizes the absurdity of Kessler's position by counterpointing it with a more pragmatic response by an old-style general named Decker (Rod Steiger), who is a throwback to the trigger-happy military figures of the 1950s movies. Decker's advice to the president concerning the Martians is concise and to the point: "Let's nuke them now." His disgust with Kessler's views registers when he leaves a meeting speaking with increasing contempt of "liberals, intellectuals, peacemongers, idiots!"[24] Yet even in the face of Martian violence, Decker does not prevail, as Kessler finds a way of explaining the initial disaster by falling back on his relativism: "This could be a case of cultural misunderstanding."[25] The president seizes upon this excuse for the Martians, and when he gets a chance to speak with them he too relies on cultural relativism: "Our customs may be strange to you, but we mean no harm." The president's motives for pursuing a peace policy with the Martians soon become clear. He thinks it will be popular with the public. When the Martians make the apparently peaceful gesture of asking to be permitted to address Congress, Dale readily grants the request and proclaims, "It's a great victory for our administration."

Unfortunately, however, the Martians use the opportunity to kill everybody in Congress, thus vindicating Decker's initial hostility to them. But even with all the evidence that the Martians cannot be trusted, Dale makes one last effort to strike a deal with them when they finally break all the way into the White House situation room. His speech is quite moving, and Nicholson delivers it with conviction: "Why be enemies? Because we're different? Is that why? Think of the things we could do. Think how strong we would be. Earth and Mars together. There is nothing that we could not accomplish. Think about it. Think about it. Why destroy, when we can create? We can have it all or we can smash it all. Why can't we work out our differences? Why can't we work things out? Why can't we just all get along?" One might think that the film endorses this eloquent speech, but, once again, the context makes Dale's posturing laughable. The Martians respond by simply killing him.

Mars Attacks! portrays a political establishment so absorbed in its own ambitions that it loses sight of the public interest and so bewitched by its own multicultural rhetoric that it loses touch with reality and proves incapable of dealing with a genuine alien threat. For all the vaunted power of the American military, it can do nothing to halt the Martian invasion.[26] When a government fails at its most basic task—protecting its people—it loses its legitimacy. Dale's efforts to reclaim his authority after the disasters that happen on his watch, especially the annihilation of Congress, are pitiful, epitomized by one of the signature lines of the film: "I want the people to know that they still have two out of the three branches of government working for them, and that ain't bad." Having failed as commander in chief, Dale has to fall back on partisan politics and the tired old claims of what government does for its citizens: "I want the people to know that the schools will still be open, okay, and I want the people to know that the garbage will still be carried out, and I want a cop on every corner, which incidentally we would already have if they had listened to me last election." In the face of the threatened annihilation of humanity, routine campaign promises ring hollow. The satire of the Washington establishment in *Mars Attacks!* culminates in this image of the moral and intellectual bankruptcy of the political class in America.

Tocqueville and American Civil Society

Disgusted by the corruption he sees in Washington, Burton moves beyond the Beltway to the rest of America, to find a saving remnant. The geography of *Mars Attacks!* provides a key to understanding the film. Several scenes are set in the heartland of the United States—Kentucky and Kansas—and Burton evokes the traditional view that virtue is to be found in rural America. But he does not operate completely within the conventional paradigm that presents rural existence as superior to urban. From the beginning, *Mars Attacks!* alternates between two cities—Washington and Las Vegas—with Nicholson in his dual role presiding over both and providing a connection between the two. It is almost as if Burton is suggesting that the United States has two capitals, Washington as its political capital, Las Vegas as its entertainment capital (in fact, Vegas claims to be the entertainment capital of the world). In a reversal of normal expectations, Burton prefers the entertainment capital to the political. Las Vegas is still Sin City in the film, focused on gambling, sex shows, and rampant real estate development. But in contrast to Washington, Las Vegas comes across in *Mars Attacks!* as a genuine city of the American people. Unlike Washington, Las Vegas gives the people what they want; its purpose is, after all, to entertain them. The Vegas of *Mars Attacks!* actually has a lot in common with the American heartland and is populated by basically the same kind of people. In both places, average American people are shown working together—especially as families—and are therefore ultimately capable of defending themselves and what they value in life—especially their families. In the eyes of the cultural elite, places like Kansas and Las Vegas represent everything that is contemptible about America, epitomized by the lowbrow entertainment beloved by country bumpkins and rubes. But in Burton's view, the cultural elite are out of touch with genuine human values; it is the ordinary people in the cultural backwaters of the county who understand what really matters in life and are willing to stand up for it. That is why *Mars Attacks!* champions traditional local areas in the United States against the national government.

In this respect, *Mars Attacks!* recurs to the original conception of the United States propounded by the Founding Fathers and to the genuine spirit of federalism. The Constitution was designed precisely so that the federal government would not be all-powerful and intrude in every aspect of life in America. The document limits the powers of the federal government and reserves many governmental functions to the individual states and even smaller political units. A long-standing principle of American government is that power is better exercised at local levels, where the authorities are more in touch with and more responsive to the needs and demands of the people. Perhaps the sharpest analyst of the American regime, the Frenchman Alexis de Tocqueville, argued in *Democracy in America* that the diffusion of power and authority in the United Sates is a key to its success. If democracy is in its essence self-government, Tocqueville was, indeed, struck by the capacity of ordinary Americans to govern themselves, especially their penchant for forming associations to deal with their problems.[27] Tocqueville celebrated the vibrancy of civil society that he saw in America, the fact that many problems were dealt with outside the formal political system by people banding together voluntarily:

> Americans of all ages, all conditions, all minds constantly unite. Not only do they have commercial and industrial associations in which all take part, but they also have a thousand other kinds: religious, moral, grave, futile, very general and very particular, immense and very small; Americans use associations to give fêtes, to found seminaries, to build inns, to raise churches, to distribute books, to send missionaries to the antipodes; in this manner they create hospitals, prisons, schools. . . . Thus the most democratic country on earth is found to be, above all, the one where men in our day have most perfected the art of pursuing the object of their common desires in common.[28]

It is striking how many of the activities that Tocqueville regarded as the province of private associations in the United States are now viewed as the legitimate (and perhaps even the inevitable) responsibility of the federal government ("hospitals, prisons, schools"). Tocqueville recognized that it is a great temptation in a democracy to turn over all activities beyond the capacity of individual human beings to government authorities. But he regarded that course as leading to the loss of freedom and the emergence of tyranny:

> A government could take the place of some of the greatest American associations, and within the Union several particular states already have attempted it. But what political power would ever be in a state to suffice for the innumerable multitude of small undertakings that American citizens execute every day with the aid of an association?
>
> It is easy to foresee that the time is approaching when a man by himself alone will be less and less in a state to produce the things that are the most common and the most necessary to his life. The task of the social power will therefore constantly increase, and its very efforts will make it vaster each day. The more it puts itself in

> place of associations, the more particular persons, losing the idea of associating with each other, will need it to their aid. . . . Will the public administration in the end direct all the industries for which an isolated citizen cannot suffice? . . . Will the head of the government have to leave the helm of state to come hold the plow?[29]

I do not know whether Tocqueville would have enjoyed 1950s flying saucer movies, but it is safe to say that he would have been troubled by their implicit claim that the complexities of the Atomic Age mean that ordinary Americans are now incapable of managing their own lives and must rely instead on the wisdom of government experts. Prophetic in so many respects, Tocqueville was at his most acute in foreseeing the erosion of freedom as a result of the increasing reliance on government to solve problems:

> The morality and intelligence of a democratic people would risk no fewer dangers than its business and its industry if the government came to take the place of associations everywhere. . . .
>
> A government can no more suffice on its own to maintain and renew the civilization of sentiments and ideas in a great people than to conduct all its industrial undertakings. As soon as it tries to leave the political sphere to project itself on this new track, it will exercise an insupportable tyranny even without wishing to; for a government knows only how to dictate precise rules; it imposes the sentiments and the ideas that it favors, and it is always hard to distinguish its counsels from its orders.[30]

Here Tocqueville outlines what Friedrich Hayek was later to call the road to serfdom.[31] Anticipating Hayek, he argues that the national government, precisely by virtue of its remoteness from the people and their specific circumstances, lacks the local knowledge necessary to deal with their problems, knowledge that is—almost by definition—more likely to be available to local authorities or the people themselves. Moreover, the larger the sphere of a government's authority, the more general are the rules by which it operates, leading it to impose "one size fits all" solutions for problems when the solutions really need to be tailored to the local circumstances. Most important, Tocqueville worries what the effect of relying on the national government will be on the character of the American people. He fears that they will lose their spirit of self-reliance, which is precisely what distinguishes them among the peoples of the world. Tocqueville's analysis of the healthy tendency of Americans to form associations lays the foundation for the concluding chapters of *Democracy in America*. There he expresses his concern about the possibility of a soft despotism emerging in the United States, if the American people, in the hope of making their existence easier and happier, allow their national government to keep expanding its powers and its ability to regulate every aspect of their lives.[32]

Trusting Trailer Trash

I do not know if Burton is at all familiar with Tocqueville's writings, but *Mars Attacks!* takes a Tocquevillian view of democracy in America, grounding it in the self-reliance of the American people, not the omnicompetence of their government. To be sure, the film cannot be accused of giving an overly optimistic portrait of the common people of America. In the Kansas scenes, it focuses on an extended and somewhat dysfunctional family, who can only be described as trailer trash—indeed, they live in a trailer. They are an urban liberal's worst nightmare. "They cling to their guns, or religion, or antipathy toward people who aren't like them, or anti-immigrant sentiments," to use the words of a famous urban liberal.[33] Although they live in Kansas, they seem more like southern rednecks, a point emphasized by having Joe Don Baker, often cast as a good old boy, play the patriarch of the clan, Mr. Norris. His favorite son has the southern-sounding name of Billy-Glen (Jack Black). The son volunteers for Martian duty at his army base. When he finally goes into battle against the invaders, he is true to the redneck tradition, shouting at them, "Die, you alien shitheads." As this remark suggests, political correctness is not a hallmark of the Norris clan. They are prejudiced, with not a hint of multicultural openness to the aliens. Seeing them on television, Norris says, "Martians—funny-lookin' little critters, ain't they?" Unlike the establishment figures in the film, Norris is hostile to the aliens from the beginning: "Any of them Martians come around here, I'm going to kick their butts." The Norris clan is strongly committed to protecting their home, and they proudly lock and load their many guns to do so. They know where to take a stand against the Martians: "I tell you one thing—they ain't getting the TV." As a tight-knit family, they close ranks against the rest of the world. Although they admire the military, they have no respect for the Washington elite. When the grandmother (Sylvia Sidney) sees what the Martians do to her representatives in the Capitol building, her only response is to say "They blew up Congress" and laugh.

In sum, in *Mars Attacks!* the Washington establishment presents itself as tolerant, open-minded, cosmopolitan, and devoted to saving the world; the Norris clan is bigoted, close-minded, parochial, and devoted to saving their own family and their TV. And yet the movie seems to take the Norrises' side. For one thing, they are right about the Martians and willing to take action against them. The movie seems to suggest that there is something healthy about the ordinary human prejudice in favor of one's own. If you care about something deeply, you will know how to defend it. In *Mars Attacks!* the common men and women are concerned with protecting not their egos and their public images, but something far more basic and real, their families, and that seems to bring out the best in people. In one of the subplots, an African American ex-boxer in Las Vegas named Byron Williams (Jim Brown) is struggling to be reunited in Washington with his divorced wife (Pam Grier) and their children. At the film's climax, he becomes a hero by fighting the Martians with his bare fists in the hopes of getting back to his family. Most important, the attempt by Richie Norris (Lukas Haas) to save his grandmother from the Martians leads to the discovery that Slim Whitman's yodeling will splatter their brains. The president's effort to forge a cosmic alliance with the Martians accomplishes nothing; it is only Richie's attempt to rescue someone in his immediate family that ends up saving the world.

Mars Attacks! thus rejects the conventional opinion that the ordinary people of America would be helpless in the face of a disaster or a crisis like a Martian invasion, unable to save themselves without the vast resources of the federal government working on their behalf. In fact, the film shows, the American people are remarkably resourceful and especially good at improvising.[34] The fact that someone may be uneducated or unsophisticated does not mean that he or she is stupid, and in real-life situations common sense can often be more useful than expertise. The Washington establishment's response to the invasion is hampered by its ingrained assumptions, especially its multicultural ideology. The ordinary Americans in the film are able to think outside the box, perhaps because they are outside the establishment. No expert would ever think of using yodeling to destroy the Martians—where is the scientific proof that it works?—but Richie is quick to recognize the potential of his unconventional weapon. The motif of an unexpected means of destroying the Martians goes all the way back to the first story of interplanetary conflict, H. G. Wells's *The War of the Worlds* (1898), where the Martians, lacking immunity to terrestrial germs, are killed off by nothing more complicated than the common cold. Burton no doubt thought that Slim Whitman's music was almost as common—and as much in the air—as the cold virus, and thus it offers another case of something very ordinary preventing the Martians from conquering the Earth.

The Slim Whitman surprise ending adds another twist to Burton's championing of the common people of America against the elites who look down on them. The members of the Washington establishment we see in the film would not be caught dead listening to a Slim Whitman album. Thus they would never discover what could defeat the Martians. The film shows that the elite keep themselves entirely separate from the common people they claim to champion. With all the complicated intercutting of plots in *Mars Attacks!*, the elites and the common people almost never interact. The White House scenes show that when tourists show up, they are kept carefully cordoned off from what really happens in the building (the joke in the film is that the White House inhabitants are not allowed to interfere with the tours). The film pointedly portrays the lack of interaction between the elites and the common people when a scene between the African American mother and her children ends, and Jerry Ross pulls up in the neighborhood in a limousine. He has arrived just to pick up a prostitute, and indeed the only ordinary person in the film admitted to the inner precincts of the White House is a prostitute (Lisa Marie Smith) brought by Ross (she actually is an alien disguised as a prostitute). In *Mars Attacks!* the elites keep their distance from the common people, except when they want to exploit them.

Thus the common people in *Mars Attacks!* are forced to rely on their own resources. The trailer trash are appropriately saved by their trailer trash culture, and not just their beloved Slim Whitman albums. Much of the effective resistance to the Martians comes from members of the underclass, precisely in their stereotypical underclass roles. Byron Williams is modeled on Mohammad Ali—he is African American and a Muslim and has fought Sonny Liston. He is the stereotypical down-and-out ex-boxer, reduced to working as a greeter in a Las Vegas casino. The cultural elite in America look down on boxing as a vulgar sport, not to be mentioned in the same breath as politically correct sports in America like tennis and soccer (who ever heard of a "boxing mom"?). But Williams is able to use his fists to keep the Martians in check. Meanwhile, his adolescent sons back in Washington are presented as stereotypical streetwise youth. Coming from a broken home, they play hooky from school and use the time to play video games like Space Invaders. The establishment would frown upon their devoting themselves to video games instead of books, but it turns out that they are thereby preparing themselves for the real-life challenges they will face. Their truancy pays off when they come up against the Martians during a school field trip to the White House. Only the boys are able to pick up the Martians' ray guns and know how to use them to kill the invaders—thanks to their video game experience.

Boxing, video games, country and western music—all these mainstays of American pop culture prove to be the mainstays of the defense against the Martians. In perhaps the wackiest development of the plot, the pop singer Tom Jones, playing himself, turns up in Las Vegas and joins the coalition against the aliens. Jones's performance in the film may be the most remarkable. One might describe it as self-parody, but he really is just playing himself, and he is, of course, totally at home in Las Vegas. With the smoothness of a veteran Vegas performer, he takes everything in stride, reacting as if nothing unusual is happening, even when the world is literally crashing down around him. Perhaps it helps that his signature tune is called "It's Not Unusual" (which he sings twice in the film). Jones's unflappability symbolizes the ability of ordinary people to stay calm in a crisis. Whatever happens in America, the show must go on, especially in Las Vegas. In a telling moment that recalls hundreds of B movies, the boxer asks Jones, "You know how to fly a plane?" and he replies without missing a beat, "Sure. You got one?" There in a nutshell is the resourcefulness of the common man (if Jones is not exactly the common man, he is the quintessential common man's entertainer). The way the forces of Las Vegas band together to fight the Martians becomes emblematic of the common men and women of America associating in their own defense. They know when a threat is real and they respond to it as real people. It is perhaps the deepest irony of *Mars Attacks!* that it presents the show business world of Las Vegas as more genuine than the political world of Washington, D.C.

Still, *Mars Attacks!* does not give a flattering portrait of the American people, even though it takes their side against the Washington establishment. Burton's movie makes fun of everybody. It may show that the hawks within the military are better judges of the Martians than the doves are, but it still caricatures their hawkishness and makes General Decker look ridiculous. Similarly, Burton does not romanticize the ordinary people in *Mars Attacks!* He does not, for example, present them as hidden geniuses or especially heroic in character. In fact, he portrays them with all their foibles because the point is to show them precisely in their ordinariness. The movie is not trying to find a new elite within the American people, but merely to suggest that in their ordinariness, the people are able to muddle through, even in extraordinary circumstances. "Muddle through" is the operative term here. The triumph of the ordinary Americans over the Martians is accidental. The Washington establishment prides itself on its superior wisdom and, above all, on its ability to plan for every contingency. Time and again, the elites in effect claim to the American people, "We have a plan, and you don't. You can rely on us." *Mars Attacks!* reminds us that government plans are likely to fall apart in the face of genuine crises and disasters. The full range of contingencies is exactly what no government can ever anticipate and plan for in advance. When confronted by the inevitable chanciness of the world, it is better to rely on improvisation, and that is what ordinary Americans, with their Yankee ingenuity, have to offer.

Mars Attacks! is deeply Tocquevillian in the way that it insists that America is much more than its governing elites, that the human resources of the country are spread widely—and unpredictably—throughout its population and territory—not concentrated in Washington. The film may appear to be unrelentingly cynical and iconoclastic, but in fact it expresses a democratic faith in the basic decency and capability of the American people. Moreover, the film goes out of its way to suggest the multiethnic and multiracial character of the American people. The Washington elite may preach multiculturalism in the abstract from their remote, privileged position, but the common people actually live out multiculturalism in their lives. To be sure, the Norris clan appears to be bigoted (although mainly against Martians). But the film opens with a Filipino family living on a farm in the middle of Kentucky, who evidently get along with their mainstream American neighbors, thus suggesting that the United States has generally welcomed at least one kind of alien in its midst. A little later in the film, in an image of racial and religious harmony, Byron Williams, an African American Muslim, is being photographed with a group of white nuns. The little band that gathers toward the end of the film to fight the Martians in Las Vegas is almost as multiethnic as a platoon in a Hollywood World War II movie, including Williams, the very ethnic Danny DeVito character, and the Welshman Tom Jones.[35] Apparently, with no help from the Washington elite, different races and ethnic groups in America can get along with each other, especially when they have an enemy in common.

The different races and ethnic groups in the film come together in Las

Vegas, which is presented as a kind of melting pot, bringing exotic cultures into the American mainstream, including the giant pyramid of the Luxor hotel and casino in which Williams works, dressed up "like King Tut" in the words of the DeVito character. By the end of the film, with all the carnage, the only group left to play the U.S. national anthem at a Washington ceremony is a mariachi band, giving a peculiar ethnic twist to the occasion. American popular culture has always been multicultural in nature and has often been quicker than elite culture when it comes to assimilating foreign influences. The country-and-western star Slim Whitman was not alone in incorporating Swiss yodeling into his singing style. The multiculturalism of song, dance, and other folk arts is one reason why the film suggests that we cannot appreciate the vitality of the American people if we leave their popular culture out of the picture. Las Vegas, with its uncanny ability to assimilate and amalgamate foreign cultural elements, is as important to a full understanding of what constitutes America as Washington is. Elitism often takes a cultural form and looks down on the entertainment of the common people as vulgar. By contrast, *Mars Attacks!* is a kind of backhanded compliment to one genre of pop culture, and as we have seen, it presents pop culture as one of the great resources of the American people.

I understand why critics have generally criticized *Mars Attacks!*, but I hope that my analysis might lead some to reconsider their opinion of the film. It has a manic energy, and in its own wacky way, it is an impressive achievement. It reminds us that film genres embody ideologies, and working within a genre can be a way of subverting it and offering an alternate ideology. Thinking about *Mars Attacks!* helped me identify the pro-government ideology of 1950s flying saucer movies and to appreciate the antigovernment message in Burton's re-creation. The look of *Mars Attacks!* may have its origins in nothing more than bubble-gum cards, but the thinking behind it ultimately goes back to Tocqueville, the original spirit of American federalism, and a serious vision of the self-organizing power of the American people.[36]

Notes

My epigraph is taken from http://en.wikiquote.org/wiki/William_F._Buckley,_Jr. (consulted June 13, 2011). This quotation appears in different forms in different places: I have chosen the wording offered on Wikiquote because to me, this sounds more like Buckley than the other versions do.

1. Kenneth Turan, "*Mars Attacks!* Tim Burton's *Plan 9*," *Los Angeles Times*, Decem-

ber 13, 1996, as cited in the Wikipedia article on the film, http://en.wikipedia.org/wiki/Mars_Attacks! (consulted on June 16, 2011).

2. One can view the complete set of the fifty-five original *Mars Attacks!* trading cards, produced by the Topps Company in the early 1960s, at: http://www.flickr.com/photos/31558613@N00/sets/72157625601126001/ (consulted on June 16, 2011).

3. For additional discussion of the tension between the elite perspective and the common man and how this tension is manifest in the work of Tim Burton, see the Benton chapter in this volume.

4. Bill Warren, "Tim Burton Attacks!," in *Tim Burton: Interviews,* ed. Kristian Fraga (Jackson: University Press of Mississippi, 2005), 111.

5. For a concise overview of science fiction films and their relation to the Cold War, see Richard A. Schwartz, *Cold War Culture: Media and the Arts, 1945–1990* (New York: Checkmark, 1998), 114–15, 276–77.

6. I discuss the portrayal of the FBI in American popular culture during the Cold War in my book *Gilligan Unbound: Pop Culture in the Age of Globalization* (Lanham, MD: Rowman & Littlefield, 2001), 115–17. Elsewhere in this book, I discuss other examples of the impact of the Cold War on American pop culture, specifically in the cases of *Gilligan's Island* (1964–67) and the original *Star Trek* television series (1966–69), as well as the movie *Star Trek VI: The Undiscovered Country* (1991).

7. The program was inaugurated by President Dwight Eisenhower in his speech "Atoms for Peace," given to the United Nations General Assembly on December 8, 1953.

8. As a pupil in the New York City public school system in the 1950s, I remember being taught—incessantly—that the two greatest achievements in the history of humanity were atomic energy and the United Nations (both credited to Franklin Delano Roosevelt, incidentally). Like most baby boomers, I can still recall being shown the 1957 Disney film *Our Friend the Atom* in school.

9. This motif appears at least as early as Edgar G. Ulmer's *The Man from Planet X* (1951). The idea of aliens taking over the minds of humans reflects Cold War anxieties about the brainwashing of U.S. soldiers captured during the Korean War. See David J. Skal, *The Monster Show: A Cultural History of Horror* (New York: Faber and Faber, 2001), 251.

10. *Invaders from Mars* may be suggesting that the way the space invaders subvert the family and the police is precisely what is sinister about them. The film may be another allegory of a takeover of American institutions by communism. Still, the negative light in which it casts the family and local institutions was noted at the time by no less an authority than the Parent-Teacher Association, as Skal reports: "PTA representatives were not pleased about *Invaders from Mars.* Wrote one: 'Here, in science fiction form, is an orgy of hate and fear and futility, with no hope of escape, no constructive element whatsoever. The child with whom one is asked to identify is bereft of any security from father and mother, from constituted authorities, and the adults burst into meaningless violence' " (Skal, *Monster Show,* 251; his citation reads: "Transcript of 1953 PTA reports on *Invaders from Mars,* Billy Rose Theatre Collection, New York Public Library for the

Performing Arts at Lincoln Center"). This description of the film may sound laughably alarmist to us today, but it shows that flying saucer movies were taken seriously and read for their political meaning even when they were first released.

11. On this point, see Schwartz, *Cold War Culture,* 151.

12. I have transcribed all quotations from *Earth vs. the Flying Saucers* from the Columbia Pictures DVD (2002).

13. See Schwartz, *Cold War Culture,* 331–32.

14. Ibid., 75.

15. See Christine Spines, "Men are from Mars, Women Are from Venus," in Fraga, *Burton,* 127.

16. Warren, "Tim Burton Attacks!," in Fraga, *Burton,* 108.

17. Ibid., 109.

18. Spines, "Men are from Mars," 120.

19. Ibid.

20. Mark Salisbury, ed., *Burton on Burton* (London: Faber and Faber, 2000), 145.

21. Ibid., 146.

22. I have transcribed all quotations from *Mars Attacks!* from the Warner Home Video DVD (1997).

23. Given Burton's sympathy for marginalized figures, one might expect him to be sympathetic to multiculturalism, and, indeed, he often speaks in favor of openness to different cultures. But Burton appears to become suspicious of multiculturalism when it becomes a political ideology. As I explain later in this chapter, Burton questions multiculturalism as an abstract slogan but champions it in the practical life of the American people.

24. The film is, of course, satirizing Decker as well for his militarism, but at least his view of the Martians proves to be correct.

25. In fact, the Martians do misinterpret a human gesture of peace at the greeting ceremony—the release of a dove—as an aggressive act. Evidently, the Martians do not like birds.

26. By contrast, in the *Mars Attacks!* trading card series, the American military, although it suffers initial defeats, quickly responds to the Martian threat by invading Mars, taking the fight to the Martians, and destroying them on their home soil.

27. On this subject, see William A. Galstone, "Civil Society and the 'Art of Association,'" *Journal of Democracy* 11, no. 1 (January 2000): 64–70.

28. Alexis de Tocqueville, *Democracy in America,* trans. Harvey C. Mansfield and Delba Winthrop (Chicago: University of Chicago Press, 2000), 489–90.

29. Ibid., 491.

30. Ibid., 491–92.

31. See Friedrich Hayek, *The Road to Serfdom* (Chicago: University of Chicago Press, 1944).

32. On this subject, see Paul A. Rahe, *Soft Despotism, Democracy as Drift: Montes-*

quieu, Rousseau, Tocqueville, and the Modern Project (New Haven, CT: Yale University Press, 2009).

33. These words were spoken by then–presidential candidate Barack Obama in a fund-raising speech delivered in San Francisco on April 11, 2008; he was referring to Americans in small towns in Pennsylvania and the Midwest. The text of the speech can be found by Googling "cling to guns and religion," as, for example, at this site: http://inkslwc.wordpress.com/2008/04/12/barack-obama-bitter-pennsylvanians-cling-to-guns-or-religion/ (consulted June 16, 2011).

34. Strictly speaking, the Americans of *Mars Attacks!* do not create associations in the formal sense that Tocqueville speaks of in *Democracy in America.* They spontaneously act alone or in small groups. Nevertheless, the film does point to exactly the self-reliance in Americans that impressed Tocqueville. *Mars Attacks!* does include several scenes of ordinary Americans who panic when faced with the Martian invasion. The film does not claim that all Americans are capable of dealing with disaster; it shows only that some are, but that is enough to deflate claims for government omnicompetence.

35. For some reason, DeVito's character did not merit a name in the script; he is identified in the cast simply as "Rude Gambler."

36. For a fuller version of my argument, see chapter 4 of my book *The Invisible Hand in Popular Culture: Liberty versus Authority in American Film and TV* (Lexington: University Press of Kentucky, 2012).

"Pinioned by a Chain of Reasoning"?

Anti-intellectualism and Models of Rationality in Tim Burton's *Sleepy Hollow*

Steve Benton

In his classic study *Love and Death in the American Novel* (1960), literary critic Leslie Fiedler famously describes Washington Irving's "Rip Van Winkle" (1819) as the foundational text of American literature because the civilization-shunning character it celebrates is the "typical male protagonist of our fiction." That protagonist, Fiedler claims, is typically "a man on the run, harried into the forest and out to sea, down the river or into combat—anywhere to avoid 'civilization.' "[1] As Fiedler points out, civilization-scorners like Irving's Rip have long evoked sympathy in American readers because we are suspicious of intellectuals and other fancy-pants civilizers.

In Washington Irving's other prominent contribution to the traditional American literary canon, "The Legend of Sleepy Hollow" (1820), it is not the scorner of civilization but its advertiser, schoolteacher Ichabod Crane, who gets harried into the forest. Yet despite this role reversal, the same anti-intellectual prejudices are at play in both stories. For though Ichabod, the agent of civilization, is the protagonist of "The Legend of Sleepy Hollow," he is also cast as a vain, selfish social climber the community can do very well without. The role of the "hero of the country round," by contrast, is reserved for the teacher's nemesis and tormenter, Brom Bones, who is eager to see Ichabod and his school removed from the Sleepy Hollow landscape—a result that he happily succeeds in bringing about.[2]

If your only encounter with Sleepy Hollow comes via Tim Burton's *Sleepy Hollow*, you may be surprised by the way Irving's original short story aligns reader sympathies, for in Burton's 1999 adaptation of Irving's tale, it is the brainy Ichabod (Johnny Depp) who prevails, while brawny Brom (Casper Van Dien) gets his head chopped off. Yet just as there is something misleading in the apparent distinction between "Rip Van Winkle" (in which civilization runs the hero out of town) and "The Legend of Sleepy Hollow" (in which the hero runs "civilization" out of town), since Irving encourages readers of both stories to sympathize with those who scorn civilization, the apparent distinction between Irving's original and Burton's adaptation is not as profound as it at first appears, either. For both the film and Irving's original story suggest that science and rationality are overrated. In this sense, the film joins a long tradition of popular American fiction and film that encourages suspicion of experts, academic training, and intellectual perspectives. Thus Burton's celebration of the alienated outsider who learns to temper his faith in his intellect and to trust more in his "heart" does not challenge familiar Hollywood constructs; it ratifies them.

On the other hand, while Burton's Ichabod learns a valuable lesson about the limits of reason, he never entirely abandons it. Burton's Ichabod remains the hero of the film, his intellectual powers are ultimately affirmed, and viewers are encouraged to conclude that the nation would be better off if rational, principled people like Constable Crane were running things. Seen in this light, Burton's *Sleepy Hollow* does not encourage suspicion of all intellectuals, just those who overrate themselves. As such, Burton's *Sleepy Hollow* makes a more subtle point than Irving's "Legend," offering redemption to the arrogant intellectual who benefits from collaboration and learns to incorporate emotional intelligence into his deliberations.

The traditional philosophical concerns alluded to above—the relationship between rationality and emotion, spirituality and collaborative thought—and the treatment these relationships get in Burton's *Sleepy Hollow* are the focus of this essay. Throughout, discerning what does and does not count as anti-intellectual will be tricky business. Traditionally, anti-intellectual forces have attacked intellectuals' disregard for feeling and defended the validity of emotions and spirituality, and they have defended the wisdom of crowds when attacking intellectuals' elitism. Yet, as we will see, many prominent philosophers have also defended the intellectual value of both emotion and a model of rationality that is both collaborative and democratic. Plotting the models of rationality presented in *Sleepy Hollow* on a pro- or anti-intellectual continuum requires consideration of the differing philosophical positions on these questions, as well as the treatment these issues have been given both in mainstream Hollywood and in the canonical short story that provides the source material for Burton's film. We'll start with the last of these.

The Legend and the Adaptation: "Sleepy Hollow" and *Sleepy Hollow*

In order to get a clearer picture of what makes Burton's adaptation of "The Legend of Sleepy Hollow" unique, it will be helpful to briefly revisit Irving's original account of Ichabod's adventures in the Hudson River valley. For many readers, the most memorable element of Irving's original story is the terrifying figure of the Headless Horseman (though some, like Burton, better remember Disney's 1949 cartoon adaptation of the film, *The Adventures of Ichabod and Mr. Toad,* than they do Irving's work).[3] Less well remembered is Irving's winking assurance to his readers that the ghoul is actually a disguised Brom Bones. Yet in Irving's story, Brom dresses himself up as the Horseman in order to spook the jittery Ichabod because Ichabod has emerged—improbably, given Ichabod's unattractive physical appearance—as Brom's rival for the affections of the village belle, Katrina Van Tassel. More importantly, Ichabod is not just a threat to Brom's prospects with Katrina; Ichabod's community of scholars also represents a threat to the prestige of Brom's "gang of rough riders." Such a reading of Ichabod's status in Sleepy Hollow is affirmed by Irving's description of the wide and growing appeal the schoolteacher enjoyed in the village, where, when "school hours were over, [Ichabod] was ever the companion and playmate of the larger boys."[4] In short, Ichabod is on track to replace Brom as Sleepy Hollow's model citizen.

In order to get rid of his rival and affirm his status as alpha male, Irving's Brom exploits Ichabod's susceptibility to fantasy and the imagination by telling him fanciful tales about the Headless Horseman and ultimately dressing up as the villain in order to ambush the frightened pedagogue on a lonely forest road. The plan is a success; Ichabod hightails it out of Sleepy Hollow, which is thereby saved from civilization's encroachment, and Brom is comfortably re-ensconced both as Katrina's suitor (they later marry) and the model of manhood for the village (and, we might add, following Fiedler, the nation).

By adapting Irving's foundational classic of American literature for the cinema, Tim Burton joins a long-running conversation about American identity and the role intellectual community plays in our national drama. And at first glance, Burton's version appears to reverse the anti-intellectual dynamics in Irving's "Legend" by reconfiguring Ichabod as the drama's hero rather than a simple source of comic amusement. For while Burton's Ichabod retains some of his comic qualities—he is still vain and jittery—he also solves the mystery, defeats the Horseman, and gets the girl. Burton's Brom, meanwhile, is demoted in status to a minor, one-dimensional character who is quickly dispatched. Burton's decision to cast handsome Johnny Depp as Ichabod affirms the director's intention to redirect viewer sympathies toward Brom's rival. While Irving's Ichabod had "huge ears, large green glassy eyes, and a long snipe nose, so that it looked like a weathercock perched upon his spindle neck, to tell which way the wind blew," Depp reports that when he offered to wear a prosthetic nose for the part, Burton balked.[5] A handsome Depp—sans prosthetic—makes the film's romantic resolution one that audiences can more easily get behind.

And yet, while Burton does reimagine Ichabod as Sleepy Hollow's new hero, this reversal does not represent an unequivocal endorsement of the intellectual. It is true that Burton's Ichabod employs his rational powers to help him figure out who is pulling the Horseman's strings, and this knowledge ultimately enables him to vanquish Sleepy Hollow's enemies. But Burton's *Sleepy Hollow* also suggests that Ichabod greatly overestimates the power of the rational intellect to account for the world we live in, for Ichabod's success follows his decision to wiggle free from the vice grip of rational science and learn to trust his heart and the people he loves.

Models of Rationality: Philosopher-Kings and Democratic Republics

Although Ichabod's alliance with Katrina (Christina Ricci) and young Masbath (Marc Pickering) recommends a model of rationality rooted in the collaboration of a small, virtuous minority, *Sleepy Hollow* suggests that the prospects of collective rationality in the democratic republic at large are bleak. Unlike "The Legend of Sleepy Hollow," whose ghost tales are counterbalanced by Irving's mild, gently comic tone, Burton's *Sleepy Hollow* depicts early America as a uniformly frightening place, where greed, viciousness, and deceit are as prevalent in the most developed cities as they are in the most out-of-the-way hamlets. To the extent that *Sleepy Hollow* imagines a democratic nation that is awash in iniquity and violence, Burton's film aligns itself with philosophers, both ancient and modern, who have regarded democracy's defenders with disdain.

For their part, defenders of American democracy typically describe America's experiment in self-governance—like that of its ancient Athenian forbears—as a vote of confidence in human rationality. In their eyes, a democratic form of government affirms the capacity of human beings to deploy their rational faculties to overcome differences and defend their common interests. To depict thinkers like Ichabod as the rarest of species is, in their estimation, to unfairly restrict the appeal of rationality and its accessibility to the unwashed masses. Their model of rationality takes faith in the rationality and wisdom of the collective.

This faith dumbfounds democracy's critics. Philosophers from Plato forward—labeled elitist by their critics—have often insisted that a democratic mob is less likely to be moved by logic and the findings of rational science than it is by demagoguery and shortsighted, selfish behavior. As Plato explains in the *Republic,* the common citizens who make up the democratic mob are motivated by emotion more than reason and are therefore more vulnerable to manipulation. A model of rationality that depends on their input is doomed. Only a few, rare individuals are sufficiently educated and sufficiently virtuous to make wise choices on behalf of a nation. Until such advanced and virtuous lovers of wisdom—philosophers, Plato calls them—"become kings in our cities, or unless those who now are kings and rulers become true philosophers, so that political power and philosophic intelligence converge . . . I believe there can be no end to troubles . . . in our cities or for all mankind."[6]

While American popular culture has long scorned the notion that the common people need intellectuals to show them the way, Western philosophers have, on the whole, embraced the Platonic view of the mob's limitations.[7] Burton's *Sleepy Hollow* affirms Plato's dark view of the troubles that await any human society that trusts its governance to the mob. So does seventeenth-century English philosopher Thomas Hobbes (1588–1679), who characterizes the original state of human community as a war "of every man against every man" in which the life of any individual is normally "solitary, poore, nasty, brutish, and short."[8] Though Hobbes's suspicion of the citizenry is profound, he does trust that the rationality of the mob is at least sufficient to acknowledge the value of giving one individual among them the responsibility of protecting them from each other and enforcing the social contract that binds the members of a community to a common code of conduct.

The model of collective rationality embodied in the American democratic experiment—which seems to be failing in Burton's *Sleepy Hollow* in part because of the antipathy its citizens direct toward virtuous thinkers like Ichabod—owes its existence in part to Hobbes's conception of such a social contract that defines the rights and responsibilities of the citizenry. But Hobbes, unlike the architects of the American republic, did not believe the common citizens of any nation were capable of governing themselves unless they were guided by a mediating sovereign. Hobbes's dim view of any model of rationality that expected too much of the common people was softened by later philosophers like John Locke (1632–1704), who had a more immediate impact on the Enlightenment ideals that inspired the American Revolution. For while Hobbes hoped the common people would at least have the good sense to hand over the job of governing them to a supervising sovereign, Locke trusted them to dismiss any sovereign who failed to meet their standards. As Locke puts it in his *Second Treatise of Government* (1690), if there should ever arise a conflict between the people and their sovereign, "in a matter where the law is silent or doubtful, and the thing be of great consequence, I should think the proper *umpire* in such a case, should be the body of the people."[9] Locke's endorsement of the "body of the people" as the "proper umpire" in a controversy between people and sovereign becomes the foundational principle of the American Declaration of Independence when it affirms the right of "one people to dissolve the political bands which have connected them with another" and proclaims "by Authority of the good People of these Colonies, . . . That these united Colonies . . . are Absolved from all Allegiance to the British Crown."

By most accounts, the model of collective rationality exemplified by the American democratic experiment experienced a full mixture of success and failure over the course of the nineteenth century. Washington Irving, the nation's first literary celebrity, reinforced the notion that the American people who contributed to that experiment should be regarded with kind indulgence or, at worst, gentle amusement. Such a characterization made it easier to imagine success for a model of rationality rooted in their essential decency. The democratic project would also receive philosophical support from Utilitarians like John Stuart Mill, who advocated for a model of rationality that is strengthened, not weakened, by difference. Mill's model of rationality challenges the conventional dichotomy between the book-smart scholar and the common sense of the common man, valorizing the view of the common people not because it is superior to the view of the educated intellectual but because one complements the other. Not only does Mill make the case that diverse peoples can negotiate their intellectual differences in the name of a common cause; he claims that such a model of rationality is the best one for determining any course of action. As Mill sees it, collective deliberation and consideration of opposing viewpoints counteract the errors of subjectivism inherent in any model of rationality that depends too much on the perspective of a single individual or clique. Writing in defense of free discussion and an education system that sees diversity of opinion not as a weakness, but as a strength, Mill claims in "On Liberty" (1859) that "ninety-nine in a hundred of what are called educated men . . . have never thrown themselves into the mental position of those who think differently from them, and considered what such persons may have to say; and consequently they do not, in any proper sense of the word, know the doctrine which they themselves profess." Collective consideration of "all important truths" is so necessary to the model of rationality endorsed by Mill that without it, he claims, no "real understanding of moral and human subjects" is possible.[10]

Mill's enthusiasm for a collaborative, democratic model of rationality is shared by American pragmatist philosopher John Dewey. Dewey, like Mill, refutes traditional moral philosophies that rely on the flawed notion that "the consciousness of each person is wholly private, a self-inclosed [*sic*] continent, intrinsically independent of the ideas, wishes, purposes of everybody else." As Dewey sees it, democratic deliberation does not cloud the waters of clear thought but makes clear thought possible. "One cannot share in intercourse with others without learning," he writes in a mood of sparkling hopefulness that is totally at odds with the attitude assumed by Ichabod when he first walks into the Sleepy Hollow imagined by Burton, "without getting a broader point of view and perceiving things of which one would otherwise be ignorant."[11]

To sum up, then, while critics of democracy like Plato (and his mentor Socrates) clearly value the dialectical exchange of ideas and the collaboration of bright minds, they also warn of the dangers to society when virtuous individual philosophers—like Burton's Crane—are thwarted by the democratic mob. Their sympathies are clearly aligned with the alienated intellectual. Dewey and Mill, on the other hand, see a greater danger in the rugged individualism (embodied in physical specimens like Brom Bones) so long celebrated in American popular culture, which too often enjoys a misplaced confidence in the self-reliance of the individual. For, as Dewey puts it, the greater the feeling of "personal independence" is, the greater the likelihood that the individual will develop an attitude of "aloofness and indifference." And the more likely it is for an individual "to develop an illusion of being really able to stand and act alone—an unnamed form of insanity which is responsible for a large part of the remediable suffering of the world."[12] From the perspective of Mill and Dewey, neither the view of the isolated intellectual nor the view of the common citizenry should be privileged. Ichabod's science isn't necessarily better than Sleepy Hollow's superstition. It is, rather, the encounter between differing viewpoints that is most productive, for such encounters expose the blind spots that limit the perspective of hermetically sealed villages, hostile to outsiders, and of hermetically sealed minds, hostile to the observations of the uneducated.

"Why am I the only one who sees . . . that we must use our brains?": Constable Crane vs. the United States of America

The sunny view of democratic community articulated by Mill and Dewey, in which differing viewpoints are shared to the benefit of all, finds no friends in the Sleepy Hollow village Burton's Ichabod enters or in the New York City he leaves behind. On the contrary, Burton depicts both the urban and the rural American community in a way that affirms Plato's suspicion of the mob and the foolishness of trusting a democratic community to discover and support those best suited to lead them. In the end, Burton's *Sleepy Hollow* does recommend a model of rationality founded on the alliance of a virtuous minority represented by Ichabod, Katrina, and young Masbath, but Burton's view of democratic society as a whole much more closely resembles a Hobbesian war "of every man against every man" than it does the kind of intellectually enlightened community envisioned by Mill and Dewey. And unlike romantic philosophers such as Jean Jacques Rousseau, who held that urban society is the primary source of human corruption, or Rousseau's ally, Thomas Jefferson, who placed great faith in the virtues of the yeoman farmer, Burton's *Sleepy Hollow* makes it clear that the corruption and vice in the democratic nation is no less common in the country than it is in the city.

Burton's dim view of the institutions that govern democratic America is evident in Ichabod's interactions with the corrupt government officials that he works with. It is the kind of malfunctioning democracy that skeptics like Plato and Socrates warned their peers about. In such a democracy, Burton's virtuous Ichabod is frustrated at every turn. This is a loss for the country, for while Irving's Ichabod is a selfish schoolteacher who dreams of becoming a fat Sleepy Hollow burgher and living off the profits from his vast landholdings, Burton's Ichabod is a brave metropolitan constable. Although he is squeamish and somewhat haughty, he has high moral and intellectual ideals that contrast sharply with those of the governmental employees he works with—callous, cruel functionaries more interested in clearing the dockets than in serving justice. For example, when we first see Burton's Ichabod, he is calling for help and poking a stick at a bloated corpse he has just found in the Hudson River. When the corpse is subsequently transported by wheelbarrow to a hellish, dungeon-like city jailhouse, Ichabod's superior officer (Alun Armstrong) impassively orders that it be burned. Ichabod protests that he needs to do an autopsy to determine "by pathology whether or not he was dead before he went into the river," but the high constable turns him down offhandedly, scoffing that to "cut up the body" would be heathenish. But the shallowness of the high constable's piety is revealed moments later when two other officers drag in a bloody, semiconscious man. "What happened to him?" the high constable asks with only mild curiosity. "Nothing, sir," one of the officers replies, feigning ignorance of the man's brutalized state. The high constable shrugs, nods, and accepts the obvious lie—this is everyday business for him; his jail is full, newcomers are continually added to the heap, and the semiconscious man is, with the high constable's blessing, dumped unceremoniously into a dark pit, which might as well drop directly to hell. Or the Hudson. A wide-eyed Ichabod looks on with an expression of comic disbelief as the constable swings his keys, tosses off a lazy "good work," and returns to his affairs.

As we soon see, a willingness to send one's fellow citizens to hell is endemic in the young democracy imagined in *Sleepy Hollow.* The callous behavior of the high constable is typical of the Republican institution he serves. He's not an exception to the rule; he is the rule. This becomes clear moments later, when we see Ichabod in a courtroom, grandly refusing the high constable's command that he "stand down" from a challenge he is issuing the court. In reply, Ichabod insists with fatuous grandeur, "I stand up, for sense and justice!" and is promptly dressed down by the grave Burgomaster (Christopher Lee) who presides over the court. The Burgomaster, as unmoved by Ichabod's display as the constable was, complains that "this is a song we have heard from you more than once" and threatens to put Ichabod in jail until he "learn[s] respect for the dignity of my office." Ichabod begs the court's pardon but promptly continues in the same, indignant vein. Displaying a confidence in the uniquely rational quality of his insights that Mill might have found troubling, Ichabod proudly asks the room, "Why am I the only one who sees that to solve crimes, to detect the guilty, we must use our brains?" In response, the Burgomaster orders Ichabod to take his "experimentations" to Sleepy Hollow, "an isolated farming community" where three persons have recently been murdered—each having their head "lopped off . . . clean as dandelions." Viewers have no difficulty imagining that the Burgomaster would not mind much if Ichabod's head were the fourth to fall.

Once Ichabod relocates to Sleepy Hollow, we see that the cruelty and vice endemic in the largest city in the young democratic nation are no less prevalent in its humble, farming communities. For whereas Washington Irving depicts his Sleepy Hollow as an idyllic, inoffensive backwater, untroubled by any serious drama (including Ichabod's adventures there), the isolated farming community encountered by Burton's Ichabod is as morally corrupt as the metropolis from which he has been recently exported. The virtue of the yeoman farmer is integral to the political philosophy of architects of American democracy like Thomas Jefferson, who argues in his *Notes on the State of Virginia* that "those who labor in the earth are the chosen people of God . . . whose breasts he has made his peculiar deposit for substantial and genuine virtue."[13] But in Burton's world, the breasts of the yeoman farmers are more likely to be snake pits of vice and deceit.

In almost every respect, Burton's dystopian vision of Sleepy Hollow contrasts with Jefferson's farm utopia and Mill's description of a rationally functioning democratic community. It is also far more brutal than the bucolic American idyll imagined by Washington Irving. While the stunt performed by Irving's Brom (dressing up as the Headless Horseman) is motivated by love—he wants to scare away his only rival for Katrina's hand—Burton's Horseman is directed by self-serving greed and revenge, embodied in the desires of the vampiric Lady Van Tassel—the Horseman's master—to steal Katrina's inheritance and leave the girl destitute. And while Irving's Horseman injures no one, Burton's Horseman kills a dozen denizens of the village, including Katrina's father, Lady Van Tassel's sister, a pregnant mother, a small child, and several other innocents. As Ichabod's investigation ultimately reveals, Lady Van Tassel is behind the Horseman's rampage. But it is important to note that Burton's film does not depict Lady Van Tassel as the lone source of evil in Sleepy Hollow. For though many of Lady Van Tassel's victims are blameless, the community of Sleepy Hollow itself is not. As we learn in the film's final narrative whirlwind, Lady Van Tassel's villainy was inspired by the sins of the very democratic community she now terrorizes.

The threads of Lady Van Tassel's conspiracy are tangled in ways that are likely to escape all but the most diligent viewers of Burton's film, but I'll offer a brief rendering of them here. Lady Van Tassel (Miranda Richardson) is Katrina Van Tassel's stepmother. Her maiden name is Archer, and I'll refer to her by that name for clarity's sake. While pretending to be a nurse, Archer kills Katrina's mother and marries Katrina's father. Her motive is both greed and revenge: when Archer was a girl, her father died, and she, her sister, and her mother were evicted from their home, which was subsequently given to the Van Tassels. The heartless landlord (Martin Landau) who evicted Archer and her family had "received many years of loyal service from [Archer's] parents," but when they were of no use to him financially, he turned them out. But just as Archer herself is not the sole source of iniquity in Sleepy Hollow, neither is the landlord the sole cause of her rage. It is, rather, the heartlessness of the Sleepy Hollow *community* that is to blame, for, as Archer reports, when her grief-stricken family is turned out of their home, "no one in this God-fearing town would take us in." Because Archer's "mother was suspected of witchcraft" (a convenient excuse?), she and her girls were forced to live alone in the "western wilderness," and Archer's mother died one year later.

The corrupt values of the Sleepy Hollow community do not go away as the girls grow up. The town and its leaders continue to be motivated by greed and lust. They steal and lie in order to advance their selfish ends. And because their virtue is superficial and their cowardice enduring, they are vulnerable to blackmail. Thus, when the town elders (the mayor, the reverend, the doctor, the notary, and the magistrate, representing in turn the most prominent branches of civil society) find themselves in possession of information that might help Ichabod solve the mystery of the recent slew of murders, for selfish reasons they do not share it. Archer holds this conspiracy together by threatening to expose their various moral transgressions. For example, by having sex with the Reverend Steenwyck (Jeffrey Jones), she is able to blackmail him and thus secure him "into [her] power"; the "Doctor's silence [she] exchange[s] for [her] complicity in his fornications with the servant girl, Sarah"; and Notary Hardenbrook and "the drunken [magistrate] Philips" are kept silent from reporting the truth because they fear that she will punish them if they do.

Most viewers are unlikely to follow all the twists and turns of the narrative, or not on the first viewing (that the film is more invested in creating an emotional effect than it is in presenting a rationally apprehensible plot is a point whose significance is, perhaps, a telling indicator of its attitude toward rationality). But in spite of the narrative clutter, one point is clear: moral corruption has reached every corner of the young republic. This isolated farming village is haunted by more than a Headless Horseman and the witch who commands his movements. The village elders and yeoman farmers that Jefferson champions as the virtuous leaders of the kind of democratic nation that Plato and Socrates regarded with suspicion are depicted in Burton's *Sleepy Hollow* as vile and self-serving. Their collaborations and collective considerations do not serve the search for truth nor do they facilitate the community's efforts to plot a wise course for its advancement in the ways conceived by Mill and Dewey. Rather, their collaboration serves merely to help them cheat the most vulnerable members of the democratic community. The film's bleak opening scenes in New York City make it clear that such villainy does not limit itself to rural backwaters; the young republic is rife with it. Thus, in the enduring philosophical conversation about the model of rationality offered by democratic societies, Burton lines up with the skeptics. Along with philosophers from Plato and Socrates forward, Burton's *Sleepy Hollow* suggests that democracies are little better than mob rule.

The Limits of Science and the Power of the Spirit World

Yet whereas Plato would replace democracy with the rule of rational philosopher-kings, Burton's *Sleepy Hollow* suggests that the value of rationality and the intellect itself is not all it is cracked up to be, either. For while it is true that Burton's Ichabod eventually solves Sleepy Hollow's murder mysteries, his success comes at the expense of his unswerving faith in scientific reasoning. For unlike Washington Irving's original tale, which depicts the intellectual as a dreamer and pokes fun at Ichabod Crane's credulity and his vulnerability to tales of the fantastic, Burton's *Sleepy Hollow* depicts the intellectual as an empiricist and pokes fun at his haughty demeanor and the awkward tools he employs in his investigations. The weakness of Irving's Ichabod is that he believes in supernatural beings; the weakness of Burton's Ichabod is that he doesn't. For in Burton's *Sleepy Hollow,* ghosts are real, spells work, and witches really can order the undead to do their bidding. Thus, in Burton's *Sleepy Hollow,* it is the intellectual who puts too much faith in reason and science who is misguided, and the backwater provincials who believe in undead Hessian serial killers have a better grip on reality—a distinction that clearly separates *Sleepy Hollow*'s skepticism toward reason from Plato's endorsement of it.

Yet you don't have to argue that *Sleepy Hollow* endorses belief in such supernatural fantasies in order to see how the film encourages sympathy with Ichabod's journey from confidence in science and reason to acceptance of a world in which the authority of the scientific community is limited at best. As we have seen, in *Sleepy Hollow*'s opening scenes, Ichabod's request to cut up the bloated corpse he has discovered floating in the Hudson is rejected out of hand by his superior, who claims that such an act would be sacrilegious, the work of a "heathen." For Ichabod, the bloated corpse is nothing more than a specimen, an inert object whose value lies in its ability to yield clues about the death of its former owner. Once Ichabod arrives in Sleepy Hollow, however, his cold, scientific attitudes about the easily separated binaries of life and death, body and spirit, reality and the supernatural are challenged and, finally, upended. For as he soon discovers, despite science's confidence to the contrary, bodies that are dead and buried are not always permanently either buried or dead.

The evolution of Ichabod's growing acceptance of a model of rationality that encompasses the magical world of spells, witchcraft, and other terms he previously dismissed out of hand is illustrated through his attitude toward the book that Katrina offers him: *A Compendium of Spells, Charms, and Devices of the Spirit World.* At first Ichabod scoffs at its value, just as he turns up his nose at the Bible offered him by the Reverend Steenwyck during Ichabod's initial interview with the leaders of Sleepy Hollow. "They tell me that you've brought books and trappings of scientific investigation," the reverend intones with patronizing solemnity after Van Tassel first tells Ichabod the story of the Headless Horseman. He then drops a large, leather-bound copy of the Holy Bible on the table where Ichabod put the teacup and a saucer that had been rattling in his hand as he listened to Van Tassel's terrifying story. Steenwyck advises the young detective, "This is the only book I recommend you read." Ichabod subsequently covers the Bible with the ledger where he records his observations, offering a visual clue to his thoughts about the reverend's advice and the text Ichabod regards as the more reliable authority.

Yet near the end of the film, when Ichabod decides to leave Sleepy Hollow (he later changes his mind and comes back), the dejected detective tosses the ledger into the fire. He cannot bring himself to throw Katrina's book of spells in after it, though. On this and multiple other occasions, the value of the books of spells—both to Ichabod and in and of itself—is affirmed. First, Katrina uses one of the spells contained within it to cast a spell of protection around the church where the townspeople have gathered when the Horseman comes to kill her father. Though the spell works to keep the Horseman outside, Ichabod doesn't appreciate its protective function because Katrina's father dies after the Horseman tosses a javelin spike through a window. Later, however, Ichabod looks through the book and recognizes the design Katrina drew in pink chalk on the floor of the church. He then realizes that Katrina was trying to protect her father, not expose him to the Horseman's wrath, when he reads that it was a spell of *protection* she was casting. This information reinitiates his efforts to put together the pieces of the mysterious puzzle. And finally, the book literally saves him by deflecting a bullet Lady Van Tassel fires at his chest.

The growing value of Katrina's magical book of spells is echoed by Ichabod's acceptance of the value of the spiritual world, which he associates both with Katrina and with his mother, whose magical powers are indicated in a dream sequence. A loving, affectionate woman who, like Katrina, believed in—and successfully cast—magic spells (in one dream sequence, we see her levitating above the forest floor), Ichabod's mother is described by her son as an "innocent child of Nature." The characterization suggests an affinity between the natural world, which Ichabod observes closely through the lens of science (which also, simultaneously, distances him from it) and the magical world, which Ichabod's conscious mind refuses to take seriously. Learning to accept the natural world in all of its forms—including those that are inaccessible to science—becomes Ichabod's challenge, and his feelings for Katrina give him a much-needed nudge in this direction. Katrina awakens repressed memories of Ichabod's mother, whom he remembers blindfolded and spinning in a clearing behind a frontier home as pink blossoms fall from the trees that surround her—an image that clearly links her to Katrina, who is blindfolded, spinning, and wearing a flower-patterned bracelet when she encounters—and kisses—Ichabod upon his arrival in Sleepy Hollow.

Ichabod's magic-practicing mother was condemned, tortured, and later killed by Ichabod's cruel father, who believed in the power of sorcery and condemned it. Hyperrational Ichabod, by way of contrast, denies the existence of a magical world. But as his facial contortions, weak knees, and frequent fainting spells make clear, at a subconscious level this denial of the supernatural masks an ongoing psychic struggle that continually threatens to reveal itself in physical form. Ichabod associates emotion, spirituality, and the supernatural with his mother; memories of his mother are repressed along with expression of the others in his own life; and it is not difficult to read his hyperrationality as a self-defense mechanism rooted in powerful emotion. As a result of the trauma of his mother's death, Ichabod reports, "I lost my faith." On the one hand, the confession suggests that the boy lost faith in the Puritanical zealotry practiced by his father, whom he describes as "a Bible-Black tyrant" who hid "behind a mask of righteousness." As a consequence of this loss of faith, Ichabod embraces the secular world of science. But the trauma also produces another loss, for Ichabod also represses belief in the spiritual world he associated with his mother. Metaphorically speaking, Ichabod buried his emotional core, just as the Hessian horseman was buried without his cerebral core. And just as the Horseman's torment will not cease until his head is redelivered to him, Ichabod's psychic wounds will not be healed until he recovers his "heart."

The flawed model of rationality Ichabod subscribes to—one that insists on a clean split between head and heart, reason and emotion—is visually represented by a toy that Ichabod's mother gave to him and that he in turn gives to Katrina: a paper disk on string, with a cardinal on one side and a cage on the other. When the twisted string spins, the bird appears to be inside the cage. Ichabod uses the device to illustrate for Katrina how "magic" is little more than an optical illusion: "The eye retains each till they combine. And yet, some would call this toy magic." Yet ultimately, Burton's *Sleepy Hollow* suggests that it is Ichabod's binary thinking—separating head from heart, bird from cage, one side of the disk from the other—that is the delusion. For only a combination of emotional and intellectual faculties, imaginative and empirical—operating like the spinning of the disk—can produce the leaps of logic required to see the solution to a difficult problem.

As long as Ichabod's model of rationality excludes consideration of emotion, it serves as little more than a trap, a confining cage. Thus, when Katrina implores Ichabod to reconsider his initial conclusion that her father is to blame for the *Sleepy Hollow* murders, first urging him to consider his feelings for her and then accusing him of having "no heart," Ichabod claims that he is "pinioned by a chain of reasoning" that will not allow him to think otherwise. Given the original meaning of *pinion* (to remove a bird's wing feathers to prevent flight) and the image of the caged bird captured by the toy, the suggestion is that Ichabod's relation to reason is negative. It has not assured his autonomy, but limited it. It is only when he abandons his total faith in reason and accepts the kind of vision offered by the combination of intuitive emotion and intellect that he is liberated from reason's cage.

Ichabod is guided in this journey to expand his constricted model of rationality by Katrina, who kisses him when she is blindfolded and loves him "without sense or reason." She senses that her father is not the one pulling the Horseman's strings, feels it intuitively, but she cannot prove it rationally and relies on Ichabod to do the required "head work." Ichabod, meanwhile, cannot solve the puzzle as long as his head refuses to accept the reality of the supernatural, spiritual forces that are at work in Sleepy Hollow, forces that science cannot measure or explain.

While Burton's *Sleepy Hollow* does not condemn Ichabod's rejection of religion, represented by his murderous father, the lustful parson of Sleepy Hollow, and the "God-fearing" souls who sent the Archer family to the western wilderness, it does find fault in Ichabod's wholesale rejection of spiritual and emotional life and the intuitive forces they affirm and empower. When Katrina asks Ichabod what he believes in, he answers, "Sense and reason. Cause and consequence," and given the challenge to his belief system embodied in the Headless Horseman, he laments, "I should not have come to this place, where my rational mind is controverted by the spirit world." Though at this point in the narrative, having his beliefs "controverted" by the spirit world is not something Ichabod values, by the end of the film, when he and Katrina journey together with young Masbath into a bleached, sunlit New York in an apparently happy relationship as father, mother, and adopted child, the implication is that he has been psychically healed. For Ichabod, controverting sense and reason was, simply put, good medicine.

Birds, Cages, and Spinning Disks: Seeing *Sleepy Hollow* as Medicine or Monster

It may be argued that, gender stereotypes aside (the man thinks/the woman feels), *Sleepy Hollow*'s narrative of healing, holistic thinking, and emotional and intellectual alliances is good medicine for a technological society like ours whose models of rationality place too much confidence in our command of the facts and our power to make sense of them. Even among those philosophers who are reason's greatest champions, the intellect is not always accepted as an unconditional force for good. Some, for example, have pointed out that reason can be put in the service of the will to execute malign projects. Immanuel Kant, for example, in the first few lines of *Grounding for the Metaphysics of Morals,* praises "intelligence, wit, judgment, and whatever talents of the mind one might want to name" but adds that these qualities can "become extremely bad and harmful if the will . . . is not good."[14]

Other philosophers, meanwhile, have expressed varying degrees of skepticism about the power of the intellect to even perceive what the "right" is if the emotional and moral character of the person engaged in such a project is not well suited to the task. These philosophers do not assume, as Plato does, that if an intellect is able to perceive the form of the good it will act in accordance with its dictates—heart following head.

In the *Nicomachean Ethics,* to use another example, Aristotle concludes that, while the "special function of a human being" is "activity of the soul in accord with reason or requiring reason," to achieve the ultimate good in our lives our rational virtues must work in concert with the emotional faculties that shape our moral habits and virtues. While the intellect helps human beings achieve the goals they set for themselves, Aristotle notes, only a person's moral virtues can allow him or her to choose goals that are worthy of achieving. Aristotle characterizes these moral virtues as emotional dispositions—"feelings, capacities, and states" such as "appetite, anger, fear, confidence, envy, joy, love, hate, longing, jealousy, pity"—and explains that when experienced in sensible proportions, these emotions are not harmful to good decision making but integral to it.[15]

Martha Nussbaum is among those contemporary philosophers who have affirmed Aristotle's regard for the emotional dimension of wise insight. Criticizing conventional philosophical prose on the grounds that it favors the cold intellect and fails to incorporate the emotions, Nussbaum laments the fact that philosophy has traditionally treated emotions as "unreliable, animal, seductive." Following Aristotle, Nussbaum argues that "practical reasoning unaccompanied by emotion is not sufficient for practical wisdom" and, further, that "emotions are not only not more unreliable than intellectual calculations, but frequently are more reliable, and less deceptively seductive." Consequently, she claims, in some contexts, "the pursuit of intellectual reasoning apart from emotion will actually prevent a full rational judgment—for example by preventing an access to one's grief, or one's love, that is necessary for the full understanding of what has taken place when a loved one dies."[16]

Seen in this light, Ichabod's reasoning powers are actually empowered by his acceptance of the passions that Katrina has awakened in him. The emotional growth that follows from this acceptance allows him to recover memories that he repressed following his mother's death, and this development becomes part of the process whereby he learns to accept the reality of the spiritual forces at work in Sleepy Hollow. In this sense, it may be argued that Burton's *Sleepy Hollow* does not ratify anti-intellectualism (in keeping with Irving) but offers a skeptical account of a particular brand of rationality, one that excludes emotion, assumes science to be the only measure of reality, and depends on the genius of a solitary individual, whose logic is uncontaminated by the views of lesser intellectual lights. In order to solve the mystery of Sleepy Hollow, Burton's Ichabod needs the help of Katrina and young Masbath, a woman and a child, entities traditionally characterized as being bereft of, or lacking in, reason.

The force of this friendly interpretation of *Sleepy Hollow* depends to a significant extent on the context in which readers analyze the film. If we choose to see *Sleepy Hollow* as an attack on the emotion-disparaging models of rationality that Nussbaum targets, we may attribute special significance to the way Ichabod and Katrina work together, balancing intellect and emotion in order to solve the crime that haunts Sleepy Hollow. If, on the other hand, we choose to see *Sleepy Hollow* as an affirmation of the democracy-disparaging models of rationality targeted by Plato and his successors, we may attribute special significance to Burton's New York and his Sleepy Hollow as emblems of the dim prospects of rational and moral behavior in an American democratic society plagued by corruption, hypocrisy, and vice.

On the other hand, we might also see *Sleepy Hollow* as a response not to these philosophical conversations but to a familiar current in Hollywood films, from *Goodbye, Mr. Chips* (1939) to *A Beautiful Mind* (2001), all of which could appear above the subtitle "How the Love of Vibrant Woman Helps a Cold, Thinking Man Learn to Feel Like Normal People Do." Charting *Sleepy Hollow*'s position with respect to this cinematic tradition, it is not difficult to hear Ichabod thanking his lucky stars, as Mr. Chips did, that the grating corners of his rational mind have been softened by a gentle, loving wife. Similarly, it is not difficult to imagine an elderly version of Burton's Ichabod looking back over his life and out over an audience of admirers that includes his loyal wife and saying, as Nobel Prize–winning economist John Nash (Russell Crowe) does at the end of *A Beautiful Mind*, "I've always believed in numbers and the equations and logics that lead to reason. But after a lifetime of such pursuits, I ask, 'What truly is logic?' 'Who decides reason?' My quest has taken me through the physical, the metaphysical, the delusional—and back. And I have made the most important discovery of my career, the most important discovery of my life: It is only in the mysterious equations of love that any logic or reasons can be found." For some viewers, Nash's message—that the "mysterious equations of love" make a better foundational principle over "any logic or reasons"—can hardly be repeated enough. To those who take *civilization* to be a term often employed along with *reason* and *logic* to justify the subjugation of the less powerful, a tool that elitists (e.g., men, economists, philosophers, the middle class) deploy for selfish ends, such a reading happily aligns Burton's work with Irving's and aligns both as contributors to the resistance against the empire of stiff intellects like Burton's Ichabod before he has been healed by Katrina's love.

Burton's transgressive appeal may be less evident, however, to others who see "civilization" as the "man on the run" in American culture and Hollywood as the pursuing monster. This will be particularly true for those who see Burton not as the monster's enemy but as an agent of its power. For those who condemn Hollywood for its shallow, simplistic fascination with romantic love and dazzling visuals over analysis of other kinds of relationships and complex social problems, there may be something nauseatingly familiar in the healing journey Burton's Ichabod undergoes from maladjusted intellectual to healthy, engaged spouse, who is imbued with new optimism as he returns to New York with a submissive, true love under his arm, "just in time for a new century."

Perhaps these various ways of seeing *Sleepy Hollow* are themselves like the images of the cardinal and the cage, love and death, that appear on opposite sides of Ichabod's spinning paper disk (and together in the title of Leslie Fiedler's study of the American novel). From this perspective, *Sleepy Hollow*'s contribution to the enduring conversation about American identity and the models of rationality represented in our national drama is less an "either/or" configuration than a "both/and." The choice we make about whether to describe the film as transgressive or conservative, antidemocratic or anti-elitist, anti-intellectual or anti-isolationist, depends on the audience we are addressing and the message we think they need to hear. Or, to put it differently, it will depend on whether we think they would benefit from seeing reason as a pinion restricting the imagination, a bird caged in a culture of anti-intellectualism, or one half of a disk (on the other side: emotion) that is most profitably employed when it is spinning.

Notes

1. Leslie A. Fiedler, *Love and Death in the American Novel* (1960; repr., Champaign, IL: Dalkey Archive Press, 2003), 26.

2. Washington Irving, "The Legend of Sleepy Hollow," in *The Legend of Sleepy Hol-*

low and Other Stories; or, The Sketch Book of Geoffrey Crayon, Gent. (1820; repr., New York: Modern Library, 2001), 303.

3. Mark Salisbury, *Burton on Burton,* rev. ed. (London: Faber and Faber, 2006), 167.

4. Irving, "Legend of Sleepy Hollow," 305, 296.

5. Ibid., 295; Johnny Depp in "Cast and Crew Interviews," *Sleepy Hollow,* directed by Tim Burton (1999; Hollywood: Paramount, 2000), DVD.

6. Plato, *The Republic,* trans. Richard W. Sterling and William C. Scott (New York: Norton, 1970), 165.

7. For further discussion of the theme of American popular culture's scorn for intellectuals, see the Cantor chapter in this volume.

8. Thomas Hobbes, *Leviathan* (1651; repr., New York: Penguin, 1968), 185, 186.

9. John Locke, *Second Treatise of Government* (1690; repr., Indianapolis: Hackett, 1980), 123; emphasis in original.

10. John Stuart Mill, "On Liberty" (1859), in *J. S. Mill: "On Liberty" and Other Writings* (Cambridge: Cambridge University Press, 1989), 39.

11. John Dewey, *Democracy and Education* (1916; repr., New York: Free Press, 1997), 297, 123.

12. Ibid., 44.

13. Merrill Peterson, ed., *Thomas Jefferson: Writings* (New York: Library of America, 1984), 290.

14. Immanuel Kant, *Grounding for the Metaphysics of Morals,* 3rd ed. (1785; repr., Indianapolis: Hackett, 1993), 393.

15. Aristotle, *Nicomachean Ethics,* 2nd ed., trans. Terence Irwin (Indianapolis: Hackett, 1999), 8–9, 23.

16. Martha Nussbaum, *Love's Knowledge: Essays on Philosophy and Literature* (New York: Oxford University Press, 1990), 40.

Culture, Hermeneutics, and the Batman

Kevin S. Decker

In Tim Burton's *Batman* (1989), the Caped Crusader's arch-nemesis, the Joker (Jack Nicholson), tries to make Batman (Michael Keaton) drop his guard by claiming that the hero is responsible for creating him. But Batman—the orphaned millionaire Bruce Wayne—can make the same claim on the Joker. The Joker, formerly known as Jack Napier, murdered Wayne's parents in a Gotham City alleyway one night after the opera. Batman hisses at the Joker, "I made you? You made me first." Then he knocks the stuffing out of him.

The Joker seems to be implying that the Dark Knight has no one but himself to blame for the Clown Prince of Crime's rampage through Gotham. The implication is that evil is an unhappy and unexpected by-product of society's best efforts to do good and maintain order. Similarly, Batman suggests that crime creates the conditions for its undoing. Without the Joker, there is no Batman. Can it also be true that in the absence of a Batman, there would be no Jokers?[1]

What follows is an exercise in "philosophical hermeneutics," an inquiry into how we understand ourselves through our past and through our anticipation of the future by interpreting popular texts such as the *Batman* films. Its central presupposition is that any cultural artifact of the popular imagination with the longevity of the adventures of the Dark Knight expresses something about the collective self-consciousness of its society. Just as Jack Napier made the Batman, who made the Joker, some of our deeper presuppositions and desires are reflected in the various incarnations of the Dark Knight. Likewise, the fable of the Batman, told and retold like a latter-day *Odyssey*, informs the way in which we see ourselves both as individuals and collectively, as members of a society in which law and order and the distinction between good and bad often seem quite fragile.

The focus of this chapter will be on what the philosophical theory of understanding, or *hermeneutics*, discloses about the motivations of the Batman and his foes. I also want to emphasize some changes over time in the depiction of the impacts of heroes and villains on social order. To do this, my focus will be squarely on Burton's *Batman* and *Batman Returns* (1992), but in establishing context, a brief look at the 1966–1968 *Batman* television show on ABC will be in order. This, in turn, can shed light on how we, the Batman's audience, have changed in the expression of many of our deepest convictions. In particular, I want to suggest a historical parallel between Burton's interpretation of social and cultural order and those of the German Expressionist movement of the 1920s. This is the same time period in which philosophical hermeneutics was gaining new ground in the philosophy of an up-and-coming philosopher from Freiburg, Martin Heidegger (1889–1976). The parallels between Expressionism and Burton's unique interpretation of the Batman suggests that Burton is a type of prophet interpreting malaises of modern society. Burton's favored malaise is the plight of what I call the "expressive outsider," the lead character type in virtually all of Burton's films.

Wholly Hermeneutics, Batman!

Modern intellectual life repeatedly reinforces the lesson that critical examination of the cultures in which we live encourages greater self-understanding, educated social consensus, and individual growth. In doing this, modern arts and social sciences engage in hermeneutics. This theory of what constitutes human understanding is the basis for the logic of anthropology, sociology, political science—in short, the "human," as opposed to the "natural," sciences. The methods of the human sciences can't simply be based on passive observation of a shared culture or the creation of a value-neutral, objective theory about human motivations. This is because humans are "self-interpreting animals," in the words of philosopher Charles Taylor.[2] Being self-interpreting, we can't help creating concepts and models for describing the behavior and social practices of individuals and groups. Public dissemination of these concepts and models, in turn, creates the background conditions for the way we view ourselves and interpret our actions and those of others. Culture, as a form of human self-understanding, is an unending series of feedback loops, both *informing* and *informed by* our interpretations as well as the actions we undertake on the basis of those interpretations.

Ultimately, these insights rest on the work of a critically important twentieth-century philosopher, Martin Heidegger. Heidegger, in his monumental and cryptic *Being and Time,* claims to examine the distinctive features of the human way of existing, calling it *Dasein,* or "there-being." Heidegger's innovative approach puts aside scientific theories of the human organism in order to show how life is concretely experienced, how it is *lived.* One of Heidegger's many fundamental discoveries is the limit that exists to objectivity: we *Dasein* cannot wholly dissociate ourselves from an everyday world of meaningful languages and practices. We are "always already" living in a world that channels our possibilities. This makes it impossible for us to move to a wholly objective, neutral ground for theory despite the fact that this has often been mentioned as the whole point of doing philosophy.

We *Dasein* are distinctive for a number of reasons, among which is our "Being-towards-possibilities." We're not simply passive players on the stage of culture with roles written by others. Instead, *understanding* through the *activity of interpretation* is something we are "always already" doing in living as part of a culture. "Nor is interpretation the *acquiring of information* about what is understood," Heidegger writes. "It is rather the *working-out of possibilities* projected in understanding."[3] For Heidegger, our very conscious states and our simplest behaviors are all characterized by a background of understanding, whether filled in by memory (past understanding) or interpretation (understanding in the present). Understanding is also future directed, or "anticipatory," taking advantage of memory while being directed by expectations both conscious and unconscious.

Heidegger's work is rooted in the philology of Friedrich Nietzsche (1844–1900). Nietzsche claims, "It is precisely facts that do not exist, only interpretations."[4] For both men, interpretation pervades human experience; there is no getting behind it to catch a glimpse of "the world without us." "In interpreting," Heidegger explains, "we do not . . . throw a 'signification' over some naked thing which is present-at-hand, we do not stick a value on it; but when something within-the-world is encountered as such, the thing in question already has an involvement which is disclosed in our understanding of the world, and this involvement is one which gets laid out by the interpretation."[5] According to this Heideggerian view of understanding, we can't gain any argumentative advantages by criticizing another's view or theory as "merely an interpretation," since there exist only better or worse interpretations. The virtue of a good interpretation is that it "discloses" part of the truth of things that had formerly remained closed off or covered up, whereas a poor interpretation muddies what formerly was clear.

Building on Nietzsche's criticism of the idea of an uninterpreted world and Heidegger's thinking about the projection of possibilities, Hans-Georg Gadamer (1900–2002) explores the details of Heidegger's *hermeneutic circle* that makes all interpretation possible. To see a confused or unfamiliar text as an opportunity for interpretation, we must have some degree of familiarity with the "situation" in which we find ourselves. Being part of a situation means that the message of a text (or another person's attempt to communicate) can emerge only when we are "reading the text with particular expectations in regard to a certain meaning. Working out this *fore-projection,* which is constantly revised in terms of what emerges," we double back on our own expectations for the text, revising them through what we have discovered.[6] Our "horizon," as Gadamer names it, our "range of vision that includes everything that can be seen from a particular vantage point," begins to shift.[7] As soon as the initial meaning emerges, the interpreter "projects a meaning for the text as a whole," so that "every revision of the fore-projection is capable of projecting before itself a new projection of meaning; rival projects can emerge side by side until it becomes clear what the unity of meaning is."[8] As first and foremost a detective, the Batman should be very familiar with this process, since the complex monitoring and data-retrieval system in the Batcave requires nuanced inquiries and subtle acts of observation in order to deliver information (as opposed to mere data). Watching the staged-for-the-media emergence of the Penguin (Danny DeVito) from the sewers in *Batman Returns,* Bruce Wayne's initial reaction to the situation is one of sympathy. He sees commonalities between himself and the orphaned Oswald Cobblepot, and this fore-projection of empathy colors his judgments irretrievably.

The movement of the understanding is a *circle* for Gadamer because novelties, surprises, and disappointments as we interpret the text modify our original understanding; this frames how we interpret the rest of the text, and so on, over and again. In this respect, since we're not treading precisely the same ground with each new interpretive glance, the hermeneutic circle might better be called a *spiral.* It's also circular because our "openness" to the meaning of a person or text "always includes our situating the other meaning in relation to the whole of our own meanings or ourselves in relation to it."[9] The process must begin with our own expectations (not just an instant engagement with the text). It ends when we—or the particular interpretive community we are a part of—are satisfied that the meanings of the *parts* of the text cohere with the meaning of the *whole.* Familiarity with our own presuppositions has engaged with the strangeness of the text, and both are tempered. Two things result from this relationship of satisfaction: first, the interpretive presuppositions of the text's reader and the text itself are changed through a Gadamerian "fusion of horizons." In other words, the text is changed in the sense that we can't view it in the same way after throwing ourselves into an interpretation of it. Conversely, the person who understands the text is changed inasmuch as she is not just "in touch" with the author or the person attempting to communicate. Instead, she's achieved something much more important in "rising to a higher universality that overcomes not only [her] own particularity, but also that of the other."[10] The second, perhaps ironic result of discerning the meaning of a text is that we realize that our interpretation is only a temporary victory. Following Nietzsche, Gadamer asserts that no interpretation is definitive, so there can be no final and complete interpretation of that text. Because times change and no person's "horizon" or set of presuppositions is the same, we shouldn't expect that the next reader will derive precisely the same meaning. Nor, if we make a genuine hermeneutic effort to deal with the same text in the future, should we anticipate finding precisely what we did the first time around.

Saved by Kitty Litter

The evolution of the story of the Batman demonstrates a further hermeneutic point, namely that competing interpretations, as disclosures of truth, aren't necessarily compatible with each other. This seems contradictory, since there is supposed to be only one "truth" corresponding to the way things actually stand. But this view of truth and understanding assumes that the nature of knowledge is to represent an already-existing world, a view that we have seen Heidegger call into question. This view of knowledge also undervalues the importance of my interpretations of myself as pointing toward self-knowledge. We could merely assume that the only sense of "truth" is that of a description of reality in objective, "experience-independent" terms. This is perhaps a goal worthy of the natural sciences, but not of what Hans-Georg Gadamer calls "aesthetic consciousness."[11] In fact, any accurate depiction of a person's behavior or attitude depends upon understanding the *situation in which that person sees him- or herself as being in.* But surely something like this cannot be seen in experience-independent terms! We must take the subject's interpretation of his or her situation into account, for example, if we're to understand why Bruce Wayne has such a difficult time explaining to Vicki Vale (Kim Basinger) about his alter ego yet can wordlessly share his essential duality with Selina Kyle (Michelle Pfeiffer) with just a glance.

Burton's *Batman* and *Batman Returns* also make this point in terms of their political and social tropes. Vehicles for stories of the Dark Knight have, for the past three decades, exploited political and social tensions as sources for the self-identification of protagonists and antagonists, and in Burton's films these identities are characterized as social outsiders. In the first film, the Joker (literally, a wild card) satirizes various social roles by *playing at* them: he tries on being a mob boss, the suitor of Carl Grissom's (Jack Palance) girlfriend Alicia Hunt (Jerry Hall) and of Vicki Vale, a political populist, a manufacturer of personal hygiene products, and even an artist who "makes art until somebody dies." The Joker has no interest in the spoils of crime—unlike his earlier ABC television counterpart, played by Cesar Romero, he has no interest in loot but wants only to cause havoc. He's also intensely jealous of the attention that Batman receives from the public, and his final ploy in the film revolves around a monstrous attempt to gain the public's trust, to be repaid by their deaths when the parade balloons full of Smilex are emptied.

In *Batman Returns,* the grotesque Penguin is accepted by his public as both a child-saving hero and a candidate for mayor of Gotham. Unlike Burgess Meredith's tailored and urbane portrayal in the television *Batman,* DeVito's Penguin is a rapacious monster, if a reflective and tragic one. Meanwhile Selina Kyle, after her transformation into Catwoman, takes revenge on corrupt businessman Max Shreck (Christopher Walken) and the patriarchal system for making her life "hell here." The contrast between the way Max treats the intelligent, if scatterbrained, Selina versus his son Chip, the intended heir to the family fortune, is a jab by Burton at the injustice of capitalist modes of production relying on nepotism and connections rather than ability. Penguin also enacts this motif when he "crashes" the Gotham socialites' holiday ball and reveals his plans for their offspring: "Right now, my troops are fanning out across town, for your children! Yes—for your first-born sons! The ones you left helpless at home, so you could get juiced, dress up like jerks, and dance . . . *badly!*"

Burton's films are an important source for the thematic possibility that a hero like Batman could exist in tension with the very city and citizens he claims to defend. In *Batman* Bruce Wayne begins his career as the Bat with the newspaper headlines crying, "Winged Bat Terrorizes City!" and in the sequel Penguin tries (unsuccessfully) to frame Batman by commandeering the Batmobile for a late-night, high-speed jaunt through Gotham. Christopher Nolan has explicitly picked up this theme with the "fall" of Batman at the end of *The Dark Knight* (2008) and his redemption in *The Dark Knight Rises* (2012).

As the background to all understanding, a world is built up from the interaction of personal experience and the active effort of self-understanding. Hermeneutics takes as a real possibility the existence of multiple, coexisting worlds, since not only interpretation but also imagination must "fill in the gaps" to create a coherent vision of past history and future prospects. "Thus we speak of the Greek world or the Byzantine world," Paul Ricoeur, a French hermeneutic theorist writes. "This world can be called 'imaginary,' in the sense that it is *represented* by writing in lieu of the world *presented* by speech; but this imaginary world is itself a creation of literature."[12] "Imaginary" here does not imply a lesser degree of reality, since political and social philosophers also refer to "worlds" as spaces in which creative and symbolic identifications of individuals converge to create communities of belief and practice.

To what extent, though, can we *stand outside* of a world in this sense, to gain critical or artistic purchase on it? One notion from Nietzsche and Gadamer is key to unpacking Burton's concept of the hero as an "expressive outsider." This notion is that people are not only unwilling to shed their non-rational prejudices, they are simply *unable* to do so. Burton's protagonists are thus essentially flawed, but no more so than any of us. His complex message, as in most of his films, is that while expressive outsiders share much of the same interpretive cultural framework as the rest of us, they can utilize their *marginalization* to shed light on the pathologies of society that affect us all. Although Burton famously identifies with his leads through his own experiences, it is never clear that he is recommending that the rest of us follow their example. In both his *Batman* films, Burton presents us with flawed villains *and* heroes, suggesting that we identify with neither but chart a course between extremes that is expressive of our own individuality.

Can social marginalization give Catwoman the edge she needs to effectively criticize and change society? Nietzsche and Gadamer are divided in their opinions about the degree to which an individual can *remove* themselves (or be removed) from the "imaginary" of their society and culture.

Nietzsche names rationality itself a "prejudice," insisting that the degree of honesty with which we acknowledge our own biases and limits is more important than trying to live without them. His emphasis on overcoming the suffering of our past by affirming life and power provides support for Bruce Wayne's decision to become a vigilante hero. Gadamer has a subtly different take on prejudices. If we understand them as "prejudgments," he claims, we cannot help but use them to infuse order into an interpretation beyond the reach of the available facts or to give order necessary to make its parts fit together into a semicoherent whole. Gadamer thus wants to distinguish between the bad prejudices of overhasty judgment and the good prejudices of tradition in order to rehabilitate the authority of *traditions.* "In fact history does not belong to us," he writes, "we belong to it. Long before we understand ourselves through the process of self-examination, we understand ourselves in a self-evident way in the family, society, and state in which we live."[13] This is a much more culturally conservative perspective than Nietzsche's radical individualism.

The history of media vehicles for the Batman is also a history of the debate between consensus and order versus the outsider. Significant differences emerge between the portrayals of the Caped Crusader in the television scripts of ABC's Lorenzo Semple Jr. and in the films by directors Burton, Joel Schumacher, and Nolan. Indeed, these differences still incite Bat-fans to debate which best depicts the Batman. This is where philosophy can step in with some redirection: the differences between the fictive worlds of the Batman are not just keyed to individual taste but instead disclose exceptionally important clues about deeply held values of the cultures that produced each.

Some Days, You Just Can't Get Rid of a Bomb!

When Burton's *Batman* was released in 1989, there were two main benchmarks against which the film could be judged for mainstream audiences. These were ABC television's *Batman,* which had run for three seasons in the late 1960s, and writer-penciller Frank Miller's *Batman: The Dark Knight Returns,* a four-issue miniseries published in 1986 by DC Comics in a luxuriant "prestige format" that has since become standard for industry graphic novels. No one could confuse the two worlds of Miller's *Batman* and the TV series. The ABC show was like the original *Star Trek* in ushering in the age of color television with its hypercolorful design; it also reflected elements of the contemporary "pop art" of Andy Warhol and Roy Lichtenstein. By contrast, Miller's *The Dark Knight Returns* tells the (purported) end of the Batman story, when an older, grizzled Bruce Wayne, sick of the need to brutally combat the evils of society, finally gives up on Gotham and leaves his cowl behind to become a hermit-like survivalist.[14]

By virtue of their stark difference, it is difficult to believe that the graphic novel *The Dark Knight* emerged less than twenty years—not even one generation—after Adam West's iconic television portrayal. Was TV's *Batman* "high camp played to perfection," as Richard Carter opines? With its Shark Repellant Batspray, over-the-top villains, Robin's exclamations ("Holy Glue Pot!" or "Holy Heart Failure!"), and carefully orchestrated fight scenes overlaid with cartoon POW! and ZAP! balloons, it's hard to disagree with the camp interpretation. Not only was TV's Caped Crusader perfect family entertainment for its time, the program continues to be important today for understanding American culture of the recent past. Richard Carter elaborates: "What is it about stuff like this from the so-called "good old days"—an inanity to end all inanities—that is so appealing? . . . Perhaps we recall those times as more honest and open. More easy going and simple. More black and white and less gray."[15]

A more sophisticated alternate view of the ABC program—one that Batman Adam West himself endorses in his memoir, *Back to the Batcave*—emphasizes an understanding of the show and its 1966 film adaptation as *parody.* By 1966 the two-dimensional Batman appeared in several comics titles besides his eponymous one, including *Detective Comics* and *The Brave and the Bold.* After World War II, DC had already moved most of its titles from the depiction of hard-boiled crime fighting laced with social commentary to "lighthearted juvenile fantasy."[16] This encouraged four-color flights of fancy in which Batman's orphan-saving, gangster-busting reputation was left behind in favor of plots where the Caped Crusader was "turned into a giant, a merman, the Zebra Batman, the Invisible Batman, and Rip Van Batman. He met an alien version of himself and was even mummified."[17] Adam West's thinking about his show was that "to have done a grim Bat-and-robbers show would have been wrong for the time. Look at what happened to the played-straight *Green Hornet,* which debuted in September of '66: it was gone by July."[18] ABC's *Batman* reached the height of its reflexive self-understanding of its own tenor in its big-screen adaptation *Batman: The Movie,* which is "respectfully" dedicated to lovers of "pure escapism," of "unadulterated entertainment," and of "the ridiculous and the bizarre."[19]

Cultural hermeneutics suggests that the reason for the occasional resurgence of camp Batman or grim and violent Batman can be found in society's expectations of what makes for plausible heroes and villains. In the context of a period in which Americans understood a clear distinction between "justified" and "unjustified" violence, it is clear why the cast and producers of the television program made Batman a moral exemplar. For example, the television series never portrays the Dark Knight's violent origin story; Batman is presented to us whole cloth from the first episode, complete with support crew. With his flamboyant "rogue's gallery" of foes, he always plays the straight man.[20] It is notable, in this latter regard, that the formulaic nature of the screenplays for the *Batman* series meant that virtually any villain—Penguin, the Riddler, Catwoman—could have been plugged into nearly any given crime plot. Batman had no arch-nemesis, a role that would later be filled by the Joker courtesy of Tim Burton and the graphic novelists who inspired him. In the beginning, "the Joker started his career as a smiling killer who murdered for profit, countered by an uncomplicated, no-nonsense, vigilante Batman. In the fifties and sixties, the Joker became a relatively harmless merry prankster countered by an uncomplicated, good-natured, boy scout Batman."[21] By the time of the release of *Batman Returns,* when Penguin claims Gotham's mayor has done nothing about "the disease that turned eagle scouts into crazed clowns and happy homemakers into catwomen," he isn't making a simple comment on Batman's origins so much as a hypertextual reference to the Dark Knight's fall from cultural moral superiority in the estimation of the film's audience.

In such a context, for Batman to credibly reflect a richer (if dualistic) inner life, more Americans would have to themselves identify as products of the fragmentation of beliefs and values. His audience would have to become convinced that soldiers lauded as heroes could really have been responsible for bombings in Cambodia and the My Lai massacre, that the American political establishment could be corrupt to its highest office. They would have to find themselves prisoners of the sterile, suburban consensus culture that Richard Nixon made appeal to in his reference to the "silent majority."

Fast-forward twenty years to contrast ABC television's memorable version of the Batman myth with the vision of producers Mike Uslan and Benjamin Melniker. Turning to the big screen, Uslan said, "The film must be about the creature of the night and capture the spirit of what Batman was originally about and what the comic, by and large, has reverted to the last couple of years."[22] Burton, upon seeing the Uslan and Melniker treatment, was worried that the studio's project would mirror the 1978 Richard Donner blockbuster

Superman in many ways. Unsurprisingly, Burton claimed that he found the treatment "the most frightening thing [he'd] every read."[23] What Burton appreciated about graphic novels like *The Dark Knight* and Brian Bolland's 1988 *The Killing Joke* was the opportunity to examine the psychological structure of a man who dressed up as a bat to fight crime. The *Batman* that was released in 1989 emerged as a synthesis of Burton's creative vision and what Warner Brothers wanted—a high-concept action film that lent itself (in spring and summer 1989, with a vengeance) to a "prevalence of Bat-paraphernalia in the stores and the ubiquity of the Bat-logo on the streets."[24]

Decent People Shouldn't Live Here

Despite its commercialization and hype, *Batman* attempts in its own way to address the plight of the outsider in a consensus culture. Describing the Joker as an illustration, Burton claimed, "any character who operates on the outside of society and is deemed a freak and an outcast . . . has the freedom to do what they want."[25] Clearly, Burton errs on the side of Nietzsche's radical individualism when it comes to the debate between him and Gadamerian cultural traditionalism. Comments and jokes about the use of masks abound in his two films, illuminating Burton's belief that the outsider gains an expressive edge in society through "covering up." "When people are covered, a certain weird freedom comes to the surface," he said. "It seems that the opposite should be true, but I've found that it isn't."[26] In terms of larger cultural implications, one of the sharpest distinctions to be drawn between Burton's Caped Crusader and that of Semple and West is that "new" Batman is framed in terms of the outsider and tempted away from the constraints of morality and justice. This temptation is crystallized in a key line in the film: "You ever dance with the devil in the pale moonlight?"

The success of *Batman* and the subsequent loosening of creative dampers by Warner Brothers allowed Burton to feel as though he could explore more freely the position of the expressive outsider in *Batman Returns*. In an unusual move (for him) of directing a sequel, Burton saw his mission as working to correct the flaws of the original *Batman*. In some ways, the goal for *Batman Returns* was for Burton, an expressive outsider himself, to reclaim a project that had been ultimately defined by other interests.[27] In this outing, Oswald Cobblepot and Selina Kyle are explicitly written as social outcasts both metaphorically and literally, since the former is dropped into an icy river as a baby and the latter is defenestrated by her crooked boss,

Max Shreck. Catwoman was a natural inclusion in Burton's decisions about villains for the piece, but he saw Penguin, whom he described as "the *least* interesting character in the comic books," as more of a challenge.[28] In the hands of Burton and screenwriter Sam Hamm, Cobblepot/Penguin becomes a tragic figure who nevertheless fails to elevate himself above the status of a monster. His nature as an outsider is determined by chance: the genetic lottery made him a horror at birth. One of the central themes of Burton's second *Batman* film—that society's castoffs must still be reckoned with, as they will always come back to haunt us—is the backbone for the narrative of Penguin's emergence from a life in freak shows and sewers to become a corrupt candidate for mayor of Gotham.[29] "From bottom—the sewer, to top—the peaked roofs that tower above the city, the alienated demand mastery," film scholar Susan Bernardo explains.[30] In Burton's films, it is always the outsider who is the catalyst for change, and this is a reminder to the mainstream audience (a reminder often carried out with particularly black humor) that those we normally ignore and berate can change not only their own destinies but ours as well. This theme also figures prominently in Selina Kyle's feline resurrection and quest for revenge against Shreck. However, Penguin's insanity is fundamentally different from Catwoman's sociopathy. Penguin is the expressive outsider in extremis, his marginalization producing volatile situations while his antics point to dangers lying in those locations we refuse to see—the abandoned zoo, the sewers, the empty homes of Gotham's socialites.[31]

Little can stop the destructive "acting-out" of the expressive outsiders in Burton's movies, as Gotham turns into a playground for the freaks to commandeer the airwaves with commercials for Joker products or to blow up the housewares department of Max Shreck's department store. In Burton's portrayal of the police and citizenry of Gotham, we find a strong variance from the ABC television series. Although in the latter Commissioner Gordon (Neil Hamilton) and Chief O'Hara (Stafford Repp) seem unable to catch on to the simplest of the Riddler's clues or to find the most obvious evidence left by the latest scheme of King Tut's gang, they do at least make the effort, and more importantly they consistently stand for the consensus culture's values on the virtues of law and order. In the eyes of Adam West's Batman, the police are deserving of help and everyday Gothamites are worth saving.

Conversely, in Burton's version, Gordon's (Pat Hingle) police force is ineffectual *and* corrupt, with the only attractive thing recommending them being their smart, double-breasted leather tunics. Gotham citizens in *Bat-*

man and *Batman Returns* are effectively window-dressing, little more than blind masses following the Joker's trail of money or cheering at the free gifts tossed by enviro-gangster Max Shreck at Christmastime. The unlikely candidacy of Penguin in the second film, together with the positive public reaction to it, also strongly underscores Burton's antipathy toward the herd attitudes that characterize consensus culture. "That saviors in our time too often come in the guise of politicians," Susan Bernardo comments, "acts as an indictment of the commercialization of religious sentiment as well as of the sheep-like mentality of the populace. . . . [*Batman Returns*] certainly indicates that its events occur in a time when only the most exaggerated and grotesque can capture the attention of the people."[32] Nietzsche's interest in how the attention of the "herd" of bourgeois European society can be caught only by decadence and grotesqueries resonates in both *Batman* films.

It's important to note, however, that Burton doesn't portray these quests for revenge by alienated characters as morally preferable to the structures they overthrow, or as any sort of movement of cosmic justice. Burton's revenge scenarios provide opportunities for the subaltern to, however briefly, come into the light to express what animates them. His direction suggests that fickle crowds are always attracted to spectacle: the Joker and Penguin are public figures, and Burton enjoys putting comedic and sometimes profound turns of phrase in their mouths. The recurring motif of supervillain-turned-benefactor in his films is not only an indictment of the public's insipidity in the face of spectacle—an effect of social repression toward "normalcy" and cultural mediocrity—but is also a reminder that the engineers of these bread and circuses always have an agenda, even when they frame themselves as the heroes. The further development of Warner Brothers' *Batman* films under the direction of Joel Schumacher seemed to ironically confirm Burton's social psychology, as *Batman Forever* (1995) and *Batman and Robin* (1997) demonstrate that subtle psychological insight can replaced by over-the-top comedy and action in the effort to create a "living comic book." It's significant in this regard to note the shift here *away* from Burton's obsession with the graphic novels of Alan Moore, Frank Miller, and Brian Bolland and back toward the four-color kid's comic.

Burton, Beckmann, Batman

From a hermeneutic perspective, *Batman* and *Batman Returns* do more than merely provide an outing for Burtonian outcasts. It's possible to draw an interpretation of these films in terms of how the expressive outsider achieves authenticity in the same way as Friedrich Nietzsche's *Übermensch* (overman) who says yes to life and power. It's equally possible to illuminate the faceless, grasping crowds of Gotham as instances of Martin Heidegger's *das Man* (the "they"), an insidious social pressure demanding conformity to the standards of what is publicly acceptable. I intend to avoid these interpretations, however, and focus on a distinctive trait of Burton's contribution as a director and producer—his sense of character and set design—as providing clues to a new and fruitful interpretation of his *Batman* films as creations of an expressive outsider.

It's in the analysis and criticism of modern art (including the filmic arts), that hermeneutics really comes into its own. H. W. Janson, in his *History of Art,* gives us to understand that there are three major genres of modern art: Expressionism, Abstractionism, and Fantasy: "The first stresses the artist's emotional attitude toward himself and the world; the second, the formal structure of the work of art; the third explores the realm of the imagination, especially its spontaneous and irrational qualities. . . . The primary concern of the Expressionist is the human community; of the Abstractionist, the structure of reality; and of the artist of Fantasy, the labyrinth of the individual human mind."[33] Many appreciators of Burton's work have pointed out its fantastical elements, perhaps the most crucial of which is shedding light on the "individual human mind" of marginalized characters defined as subhuman or socially useless. Burton cultivates the fantastical in that he is one of the few well-known moviemakers who draws detailed sketches of his characters before casting or costume design occurs, a practice he has applied to all his films and shorts.[34] This seems to be an essential part of his moviemaking. Yet to understand the wider cultural implications of the *Batman* films, we must also see Burton as an *Expressionist* concerned with the community in which this marginalization occurs.

Now, the relationship of his expressive outsiders—certainly the villains, and in his own, struggling sense, Batman—to their community is complex, as we have already seen. Unlike the watchful and lawful public of ABC's TV show, Burton's Gotham is easy prey to the efforts of villains, no matter how grotesque, to charm them over to their side. The Joker appeals to the greed of the teeming masses ("At midnight, I will dump twenty million in cash on the crowd. Now don't worry about me, I've got enough") in order to "relieve . . . the little people of the burden of [their] failed and useless lives." Penguin's well-orchestrated campaign for mayor preys upon the crowd's gullibility and sympathy ("I guess when I held my Tiffany baby rattle with a shiny flipper, instead of five chubby digits . . . [my parents] freaked"). Equally, Burton's Gothamites are decadent, luxuriantly ignorant of their own state of moral and cultural decline. Two of the most understated but telling pieces of dialogue in *Batman Returns* support this interpretation. Both are throwaway lines absentmindedly voiced by Selina Kyle and Bruce Wayne after they unexpectedly meet in downtown Gotham. Nearby are racks of newspapers bearing the headlines "BATMAN BLOWS IT" and "IT'S A CAT-ASTROPHE":

> Selina: I heard on TV that Catwoman is heard to weigh 140 pounds (*scoffs*). I don't know how these hacks sleep at night.
> Bruce: It's not even accurate, "BATMAN BLOWS IT." He probably saved millions of dollars in property damage alone.

Despite the epic overtones of their clash, it seems our hero and antiheroine cannot escape the vicissitudes of tabloid journalism even in a fictional world! Gotham's decadence seems to be mirrored by Burton's own feelings about American culture's reception of the second film: "[I] found [*Batman Returns*] much less dark than the first one. It's just the cultural climate. . . . I think the culture is much more disturbed and disturbing than this movie, a lot more."[35]

The subtle messages behind the highlighting of the decadent and the grotesque are just as important a part of Burton's vision as the Batmobile or Catwoman's costume. Burton has made no secret of his distaste for the suburban sprawl and bourgeois values that germinated in late twentieth-century America. As he was making *Batman,* the Reagan era, with its slogan of "Morning in America," was winding down. It would not have been difficult to draw the conclusion from the fiscal and military excesses of the 1980s—but also from an unreflective and mimetic culture of Madonna and Milli Vanilli—that America had entered its own new age of decadence. What is particularly modern about decadence—a concept that fascinated Nietzsche and is implicitly present in much of Heidegger's work—is its transparency as a part of culture. Usually, we can see it only in hindsight, just as the public's fascination with grotesquerie can typically be pointed out only by a third party, perhaps an expressive outsider. Burton's status as a prophet of the modern malaise of decadence can be found in his penetration of this cultural transparency, particularly in the two *Batman* film projects.

Remarkably, Burton's design vision—in these and many other films—responds to the same sense of culture in decline as that of the early twentieth-century German Expressionist school of visual art, which flourished in the interregnum between the two world wars.[36] One of the key figures of that school, Max Beckmann (1884–1950), was profoundly affected in his painting and lithography by the catastrophic defeat of Wilhelmine Germany in the First World War, and even more so by the chaos in the streets of major German cities as the former proud central European power attempted reconstruction. Echoing Burton's struggle to revisit what it means to be a hero in a decadent society, H. W. Janson asks of Beckmann's art, "How indeed could Beckmann have expressed the chaos in Germany after the war with the worn-out language of traditional symbols? 'These are the creatures that haunt my imagination,' he seems to say. 'They show the true nature of modern man—how weak we are, how helpless against ourselves in this proud era of so-called progress.'"[37]

Just as Burton's films point to the hidden corrosion of middle-class American culture, Beckmann's Berlin shows itself in explicit cultural decay. In early 1919 Beckmann was in residence in Berlin. January of that year saw the bloody Spartacus Uprising, an unsuccessful communist revolt that occurred in the shadow of the October Revolution in Russia and that claimed the lives of Spartacist leaders Rosa Luxemburg and Karl Liebknecht. Blood was quite literally flowing in the gutters. The violence and alienation Beckmann experienced there was translated into eleven lithographs that were exhibited that same year under the title *Hell.* Beckmann's experiences in wartime and postwar Germany changed his artistic style dramatically. In the view of Matthew Drutt, Beckmann's "rendering of space took on a vaguely Cubist orientation, with figures compressed into torturous settings and angular forms tilting precariously toward the picture plane. His works became a mosaic of contemporary social criticism and religious or mythical themes, and he increasingly used masked or costumed circus characters as allegorical figures, a practice that became a hallmark of his art."[38] The *Hell* exhibit startled critics with its grotesque depictions of German musicians, businessmen, and street people intertwined with each other in unnatural ways. A contemporary critic, Paul F. Schmidt, said of it, "We live in such a hell, but we do not sense it: we have shifted all the torment and despair of our condition onto the conscience of the artist; as the prophet and soothsayer of the times he carries our burden, he expresses that which the logic and madness of everyday life keeps hidden in our hearts."[39] These words echo the tragic sensibilities of the Burtonian expressive outsider.

Schmidt's review might just as well have been about a major character in both *Batman* movies we've spent little time discussing—Gotham City itself.

Burton claims, "I like it when the set [is] a character and not just a set."[40] Reminiscent of a decayed version of the city in the classic science fiction film *Metropolis* (1927), Burton's "magical realist" Gotham was designed by Anton Furst according to script direction in which the city looks as "if hell had sprung up through the pavements and kept on going." Vincent Canby of the *New York Times* pointed to the design as "an expressionist world."[41] Schmidt's review of *Hell* could easily have been referring to Furst's densely thicketed steel beams and gargoyles, or to Burton's signature, quick camera pans from sewers to rooftops: they both "connect the utmost reality in the details from an apparitional deviation from reality in the whole." Burton's Gotham and Beckmann's Berlin are both "the means of dreams, of nightmares," in which "events are distorted by a seemingly altogether arbitrary perspective and distortion of all proportions." They are artificial and decadent settings where "the individual [is] exaggerated to the grotesque and the naturalness of space and surroundings exploded in all directions: thus is created the monstrousness, the shocking immediacy of the events, the impression of an attack on our defenseless nerves."[42]

Now, there is no evidence that Burton was influenced by Beckmann, and any attribution of influence would be purely speculative. Nonetheless, the commonalities between both the visions and the critical receptions of director and artist converge in such a way that understanding Burton as an Expressionist, and not merely a fantasist, seems fruitful for our interpretation of the *Batman* films and all his other work. Of course, such an interpretation goes well beyond what I can hope to accomplish in this chapter, but what's clear is that as a "black sheep" of the movie industry, Burton's identification with creative social pariahs—from Edward Scissorhands to Barnabas Collins—positions him as modern-day prophetic voice preaching nonconformity to a howling wasteland of American popular culture.

And yet a question remains. Even if we are to interpret the world of Burton's Batman and Beckmann's Berlin as nightmare landscapes, poisoned by decadence and grotesquerie, what philosophical significance does this have? And what hope does the expressive outsider have in such a world?

Finding Ourselves

One answer to this question is that the expressive outsider, the marginalized freak in a Batsuit, is a species doomed to extinction. Little has happened in the development of new filmic Bat-worlds to suggest otherwise. Joel Schumacher's follow-ups to Burton's duet were little more than camp pastiches of their predecessors. These films, though popular at the box office, had little cinematic value or depth of characterization and effectively killed the franchise. Resurrection followed in 2005 with Christopher Nolan's trilogy *Batman Begins, The Dark Knight,* and *The Dark Knight Rises.* While the realism in the acting and cinematography of these films appeals to an older, more hardened, post-9/11 generation than Schumacher's audience represented, the nihilism in Nolan's vision is bleak. Burtonian comic book action has been replaced by intense violence, and major characters are killed off. Abused by his father as a child, the Joker is not even a hate-worthy character anymore, and the Batman is treated as a criminal in the mind-set of Gothamites as *The Dark Knight* ends. The steady erosion of values that the Batman might stand for in these films echoes the social need to be filled by philosophy in Gadamer's thoughts: "What man needs is not just the persistent posing of ultimate questions, but the sense of what is feasible, what is possible, what is correct, here and now. The philosopher, of all people, must, I think, be aware of the tension between what he claims to achieve and the reality in which he finds himself."[43] Nolan's Batman films have reopened all the questions put to audiences of the Batman.

A simple lesson about virtue and courage from *Batman Begins* also should be of interest to those of us who would take something from Burton's Expressionist *Batman* films. "Why do we fall, sir?" Alfred the butler asks, invoking Bruce Wayne's father's advice. The answer: "So that we can learn to pick ourselves up." Although heroes and villains are more unremitting in Nolan's Gotham, they share the Burtonian understanding that expressive outsiders must quit their reliance on cosmic forces of justice to right the balance of good and evil and so be constantly ready to soldier on past tragedy. Burton's unique contribution shows how individuality and imagination can assist us in considering the place of both heroes and villains, given their cultural marginalization. Burton's reliance on artistic modes characteristic of German Expressionism and his flair for characterization and set design appeal to those of us who believe that there are alternative traditions to Hollywood bang and bluster that can be profitably reclaimed. In thinking about the philosophy of Tim Burton, we should consider the transformative and even transgressive power of the artistic imagination, and how it could be inspired among a wider cross-section of Burton's audience.

Notes

1. For further discussion regarding how social relations affect the consolidation of personal identity, see the Hada and Weldon chapters in this volume.

2. Charles Taylor, "Self-Interpreting Animals," in *Human Agency and Language: Philosophical Papers,* vol. 1 (New York: Cambridge University Press, 1985), 45.

3. Martin Heidegger, *Being and Time,* trans. John MacQuarrie and Edward Robinson (New York: Harper and Row, 1962), 188–89; italics added.

4. Friedrich Nietzsche, "Notes: 1888," in *The Portable Nietzsche,* trans. Walter Kaufmann (New York: Penguin, 1954), 458.

5. Heidegger, *Being and Time,* 190–91.

6. Hans-Georg Gadamer, *Truth and Method,* 2nd rev. ed., trans. Joel Weinsheimer and Donald G. Marshall (New York: Continuum, 2004), 269; italics added.

7. Ibid., 301.

8. Ibid., 296.

9. Ibid., 271.

10. Ibid., 304.

11. Ibid., 102.

12. Paul Ricoeur, *Hermeneutics and the Human Sciences,* trans. John B. Thompson (New York: Cambridge University Press / Editions de la Maison des Sciences de l'Homme, 1981), 149; italics in original.

13. Gadamer, *Truth and Method,* 278.

14. He returns courtesy of Frank Miller's pen in 2002's *Batman: The Dark Knight Strikes Again;* see Kim Newman, "Cape Fear," *Sight & Sound* 15, no. 6 (July 2005): 21.

15. Richard G. Carter, "TV's *Batman* Outshines Later Movies," *Television Quarterly* 34, no. 1 (Fall 2003): 54.

16. Bradford Wright, *Comic Book Nation: The Transformation of Youth Culture in America* (Baltimore: Johns Hopkins University Press, 2001), 59.

17. Adam West with Jeff Rovin, *Back to the Batcave* (New York: Berkeley Books, 1994), 100.

18. Ibid., 102–3.

19. *Batman: The Movie,* directed by Leslie H. Martinson (Twentieth Century Fox, 1966).

20. West, *Back to the Batcave,* 59–60.

21. William Ulricchio and Roberta E. Pearson, "I'm Not Fooled by That Cheap Disguise," in *The Many Lives of the Batman: Critical Approaches to a Superhero and His Media,* ed. Pearson and Ulricchio (New York: Routledge, 1991), 199.

22. Uslan, cited in an interview with Tim Burton by Alan Jones (1989) reprinted in *Tim Burton: Interviews,* ed. Kristian Fraga (Jackson: University Press of Mississippi, 2005), 17; for the original, see *Cinemafantastique* 20, nos. 1 and 2 (1989): 48ff.

23. Burton, cited in Mark Salisbury, ed., *Burton on Burton* (London: Faber and Faber, 2006), 75.

24. Eileen R. Meehan, "'Holy Commodity Fetish, Batman!': The Political Economy of a Commercial Intertext," in Pearson and Ulricchio, *Many Lives of the Batman,* 48.

25. Burton, cited in Salisbury, *Burton on Burton,* 80.

26. Ibid., 106.

27. Burton, cited in an interview with Marc Shapiro (1992) reprinted in Fraga, *Tim Burton: Interviews,* 94; for the original, see *Starlog* 180 (July 1992): 40–45, 75.

28. Ibid., 90–91.

29. See Susan M. Bernardo, "Recycling Victims and Villains in *Batman Returns,*" *Literature Film Quarterly* 22, no. 1 (1994): 16–20.

30. Ibid., 18.

31. Thanks to Jennifer McMahon for pointing out this important psychological theme.

32. Bernardo, "Recycling Victims and Villains," 17.

33. H. W. Janson, *History of Art,* 3rd ed. (New York: Harry N. Abrams, 1986), 666.

34. See Leah Gallo, ed., *The Art of Tim Burton* (Los Angeles: Steeles Publishing, 2010).

35. Burton, cited in Salisbury, *Burton on Burton,* 113.

36. This connection has been confirmed by Eva Green, the French actress who played Angelique Bouchard in Burton's 2012 adaptation of *Dark Shadows;* John Anderson, "Light 'Shadows,'" review of *Dark Shadows, Spokane (WA) Spokesman-Review,* May 11, 2012, accessed 5/27/2012, http://www.spokesman.com/stories/2012/may/11/light-shadows/.

37. Janson, *History of Art,* 670.

38. Matthew Drutt, introduction to *Max Beckmann in Exile* (New York: Solomon R. Guggenheim Museum, 1997), exhibition catalog, accessed at http://www.artchive.com/artchive/B/beckmann.html.

39. Paul F. Schmidt, "Max Beckmann's *Hell,*" in *German Expressionism: Documents from the End of the Wilhelmine Empire to the Rise of National Socialism,* ed. Rose-Carol Washton Long and Ida Katherine Rigby (New York: G. K. Hall, 1993), 152.

40. Burton, cited in Alison McMahan, *The Films of Tim Burton: Animating Live Action in Contemporary Hollywood* (New York: Continuum Books, 2005), 127.

41. Edwin Page, *Gothic Fantasy: The Films of Tim Burton* (New York: Marion Boyars, 2007), 71.

42. Schmidt, "Max Beckmann's *Hell,*" 152–53.

43. Gadamer, *Truth and Method,* xxxiv.

Burtonology

Metaphysics, Epistemology, Essences, Christmas, and Vincent Price

Kimberly Baltzer-Jaray

> What's this?!
> The monsters are all missing and the nightmares can't be found
> And in their place there seems to be good feeling all around.
> Instead of screams I swear I can hear music in the air,
> The smell of cakes and pies are absolutely everywhere.
> The sights!
> The sounds!
> They're everywhere and all around
> I've never felt so good before, this empty place inside of me is filling up,
> I simply cannot get enough
> I want it, oh, I want it, oh, I want it for my own.
> I've got to know, I've got to know, what is this place that I have found.
> WHAT IS THIS?
> . . . Christmas Town . . .? Hmmmm . . .
>
> —Jack Skellington in *The Nightmare Before Christmas*

Metaphysics can be described as the branch of philosophy that deals with the nature of being, existence, and reality. Epistemology, another fundamental branch of philosophy, is intimately tied to metaphysics because it deals with the nature of knowledge: to talk about what is, one must speak of knowing what is, just as one cannot know something is without also positing that it is. The central questions of metaphysics are, What is it? and How is it? and they necessarily involve, How do I know this? or Can I know that? So when

Jack Skellington repeatedly asks, "What is this?" after his accidental arrival in Christmas Town, he is embarking on a metaphysical investigation into the nature of Christmas, and he is making a common assumption with that very question: I can know what I seek. In a similar fashion, when seven-year-old Vincent Malloy describes his most passionate wish to be just like Vincent Price, he too ventures into metaphysics and epistemology:

Vincent Malloy is seven years old
He's always polite and does what he's told
For a boy his age, he's considerate and nice
But he wants to be just like Vincent Price

He doesn't mind living with his sister, dog and cats
Though he'd rather share a home with spiders and bats
There he could reflect on the horrors he's invented
And wander dark hallways, alone and tormented

Vincent is nice when his aunt comes to see him
But imagines dipping her in wax for his wax museum . . .[1]

Metaphysical and epistemological questions are difficult to answer with any success, and for Immanuel Kant (1724–1804) the biggest obstacle on our path to answers is ourselves: our cognitive equipment (i.e., the mind) sets the boundaries for what we can know, observe, and understand, and thus how things appear to us may be different than how they are in themselves. Kant calls the two aspects of this split *phenomena* and *noumena,* or what we could call subjective and objective versions of reality, respectively. These terms are mainly epistemological in nature but have ontological consequences. Specifically, they have to do with what it means to know something, but they also reflect an understanding of the nature of reality. Kant, of course, was not the first to see the world as divided between perception and reality; many Greek philosophers did too, the most noteworthy being Plato (429–347 B.C.E.), and it is obvious that Kant's work took cues from the great ancient Greeks. However, Kant was the first to frame the problem purely cognitively rather than to attribute the distinction between subjective and objective aspects to ignorance, or the nature of the soul, or the Gods. For Kant, there is a distinction between perception and reality because our brain is hardwired or constructed in a particular way, and no change in attitude or awareness can produce a different result. Specifically, the mind is outfitted with categories, most notably space and time, that shape the objects of perception in such a way as to make them comprehensible yet render our perceptions inescapably subjective by virtue of that alteration. But where does this leave us concerning metaphysical inquiries, particularly the ones encountered by Tim Burton's characters? Can Jack ever *know* what the essence of Christmas is? Can Vincent ever fully *know* what it is like *to be* Vincent Price?

To begin to address these queries, I will use the philosophy of Kant, with a touch of Plato and Thomas Nagel (1937–), to discuss the issues presented by the phenomenal and noumenal aspects of reality and explain how these philosophies are illustrated by Burton's *The Nightmare Before Christmas* and *Vincent.* When possible, I will offer up relevant critiques of Kant, as well as potential practical solutions to the problems he left to us. After all, though we may conclude that we cannot have it, we want that happy ending (or something like it) when it comes to knowledge. Likewise, we'd like Jack to *know* the true nature and spirit of Christmas and Vincent Malloy to *know what it is to be* Vincent Price.

Adventures in Greektown

The ancient Greek philosopher Plato is one of the most prolific writers on the topic of the gap between objective and subjective reality. With the introduction of his well-known "forms," humanity's ability to know reality was violently cast into doubt, and philosophers for centuries were given a problem to ponder. For Plato, the forms were the immaterial, unchanging, perfect, absolute, eternal entities that all physical things are examples of: material things in the world participate in or mimic these forms in varying degrees. For example, Vincent's dog, Abercrombie, and Jack's dog, Zero, both participate in the form "dogness," albeit in different ways. One is alive and one is dead, but both are recognizably dogs. The form "dogness" would not only be perfect in that it contains every essential quality of a dog, but also it would never cease to be or change whatsoever. A similar relationship is also described theologically in that people of the earth are said to be mortal examples of the gods. For Plato, there is a form for every object or quality in reality, and the forms are sometimes described as occupying some kind of special realm or heaven. These forms are considered to be the highest form of reality, so what we see in the material world is not the whole picture of truth.

So how does Plato believe one comes to know or be acquainted with the forms? One of the best illustrations he provides comes by way of a dialogue titled *Symposium*, where several philosophers gathered for a party, drank a lot of wine, and performed speeches about love.[2] In Socrates's speech we are introduced to Priestess Diotima, who puts him straight about the nature of love. Love, she says, is the desire to have the form of the good forever:

> "Then," she said, "Let me put the word *good* in the place of the beautiful, and repeat the question once more: If he who loves good, what is it then that he loves?" "The possession of the good," I said. "And what does he gain who possesses the good?" "Happiness," I replied . . . "Certainly, I should say, that there is nothing." "Then," she said, "the simple truth is, that men love the good." "Yes," I said. "To which must be added that they love the possession of the good?" "Yes, that must be added." "And not only the possession, but the everlasting possession of the good?" "That must be added too." "Then love," she said, "may be described generally as the love of the everlasting possession of the good?" "That is most true."[3]

The good is the highest of all the forms: it provides being to all forms, makes all qualities or characteristics intelligible, and is an absolute measure of justice. Love does not refer fundamentally to beautiful objects or good things; instead, love refers to wisdom. Thus, for Plato, the true lover is the lover of wisdom: "For wisdom is a most beautiful thing, and Love is of the beautiful; and therefore Love is also a philosopher: or lover of wisdom, and being a lover of wisdom is in a mean between the wise and the ignorant."[4] Now, this may seem like a rather odd definition of a lover; the leading man in a romance novel or film usually isn't found snuggling with wisdom between the sheets or reading poems to it from below the windowsill. The kind of lover Diotima is describing here is a philosopher, and *philosophy* literally means love of wisdom. How convenient for Plato, to have a priestess who knows all about love describe the philosopher as the best lover of all.

The object of love, namely the ascent to this highest mystery, the form of the good, is a long, time-consuming, and arduous undertaking. Plato contends that the philosopher is the one most suited for the journey by virtue of the strength of his intellect and his reduced susceptibility to desire. As the speech indicates, the ascent to awareness of the ethereal forms begins with the encounter of material bodies, particularly material modes that manifest ideal properties, such as beauty. As Plato explains, one first notices the beauty of one's own body and from this realizes that others have similar bodies, some more beautiful than others; after this focus of attraction on physical bodies, one next takes notice of beautiful minds and can even love a person who has a more beautiful mind than body; from this one learns of many kinds of beauty in general, learning to love all kinds of beauty, including beautiful ideas and knowledge; in becoming the lover of knowledge and wisdom, one sees that all beautiful things share in the forms of beauty, love, and ultimately the good. This ascent is one from beauty in particular, material things to the eternal source of all beauty whatsoever. According to Diotima, the one who becomes the lover of knowledge, the person who seeks to see the forms and know the highest reality, lives the best life because one is able to be virtuous and hence will be loved by the gods. So seeking the eternal truths has many benefits beyond just knowledge.

Jack and Vincent both exemplify Diotima's approach in their search for their respective essences: Jack looks at wrapped presents, snowflakes, the elves, and other Christmas items and traditional activities in order to discover what the essence of Christmas is, and Vincent watches Price's Edgar Allan Poe films, reenacts them, and attempts to think and act just like the characters, all in order to find out what it is to *be* Vincent Price. In other words, both begin their journey in the real world, with the particular objects or evidence in front of them, and attempt to ascend from those earthly things to the form or essence, whether it be Christmas or Vincent Price.

This all seems logical and even achievable, but for Plato reaching the realm of the forms is a task for pretty much only the philosopher (that lover of wisdom) and not something an ordinary person can really do, largely due to ignorance and a lack of extensive training. The philosopher is taught about the existence of the forms and trained in how to ascend to them successfully and see "real" reality; knowledge is, for Plato, about the forms and not about perceptions of the material world, and a wise philosopher knows it all. In return for this special training, it is also the philosopher's responsibility to share what he has learned—that is, to attempt to enlighten others about reality and truth. Well, attempt to enlighten them or die trying, like Socrates did—I guess the people who charged him with corrupting the youth and sentenced him to death just weren't enlightened enough yet. So unless Jack and Vincent have philosophical training, unless Jack and Vincent are lovers of wisdom who seek the highest reality through ascent, they won't ever gain the essential knowledge required for their tasks concerning the true nature of Christmas and being Vincent Price: a rather unsettling conclusion that is most unhelpful to both.

However, all is not lost because what Diotima's speech illustrates is that even having an awareness of the forms and the fact that material things of the temporal world participate in them, spring forth from them in less perfect ways, is in itself an understanding of how the ideal and material worlds interact as well as of the true nature of material objects. This understanding, while not knowledge by Diotima or Plato's definition, is still better than blind ignorance; it might be the most complete understanding some people can possibly have. What becomes clear from the speech is that the pursuit of knowledge has practical benefits; it is not just an esoteric exercise for the academic.

This Is Königsburg! This Is Königsburg! Prussians Philosophize in the Dead of Night

Kant, like Jack Skellington, had grown tired of the same old things in metaphysics. In the eighteenth century battles raged between the rationalists, or those who appealed to innate faculties and the abilities of reason as the source or justification for knowledge, and the empiricists, or those who appealed to sensory experience as the source and justification for knowledge. Generally speaking, rationalists anchor knowledge largely inside the skull, whereas empiricists look largely outside it. Then the skeptic David Hume came along and cast doubt on everyone's positions in a way that left knowledge of the physical world and metaphysics terribly uncertain. However, this very act woke Kant up and inspired him to write his magnum opus, *The Critique of Pure Reason.* Just as the act of falling into Christmas Town inspired Jack and removed the emptiness and boredom he felt, Kant was inspired by Hume's skepticism to put philosophy back on a "secure path."[5] Kant, taking cues from Hume's skeptical comments, sought to show that a merger between rationalism and empiricism was the best road for philosophy. He sought to explain how coming to an understanding of how the external world affects our senses and how our mind shapes the sensory content it receives could help clarify what we can know. Most importantly, investigating in this way could go a long way toward proving whether metaphysics—namely, inquiries into things that are beyond tangible experience, like God, freedom, the soul, and immortality—could be a science at all.

One of the most significant and controversial notions Kant introduced is the distinction between phenomena and noumena: the concept of a gap between how something appears to a person and how it is in itself, or to put it another way, the idea that how the mind assembles the cognition of an object from the sense data provided could differ from how the object actually is in the world.[6] For example, Kant thought that objects must be perceived in space and time and that space and time are fundamental for experience. Hence, space and time are not only psychologically but also logically prior to experience. According to Kant, humans have pure forms of space and time hardwired in their minds, in the faculty of sensibility, and so all sensory stimuli are processed through them. What this means, in the simplest of terms, is that when experience begins, the first intuitions are that there are things outside of oneself (a primal distinction between me and not me, or embodiment) and that one can feel one's conscious mind process data sequentially (I feel my mind being aware over a period of time rather than as some chaotic mass). The extension of this notion is that Kant recognized that objects themselves do not necessarily exist in space and in time in the way we perceive them, or at all. He also acknowledged that it is highly possible that things in the world exist in dimensions we cannot perceive, have colors our eyes cannot distinguish, are made of textures our touch cannot sense, and have tastes for which we have no receptors. Kant's point is that we have to accept that our experience of the world is limited to the capacities we have. We have to admit that objects may have more intrinsic features than we can perceive and these are aspects we simply cannot know. This is where we see a clear difference between Kant and Plato: for Kant, the noumena will never be seen, no matter the amount of training in philosophy you have or how hard to you analyze all the phenomena central to a thing. It's simply an issue of cognitive and biological limitations.

The beauty of this distinction is that it is largely epistemological in nature; it speaks to what we can know using the faculties we possess. However, it does have ontological consequences in that objects themselves retain the possibility of having qualities we cannot sense or know. The phenomena/noumena distinction also allows for perceptual differences between people, because the appearance is what our mind assembles and is what we judge or make knowledge claims about, and so there is no value judgment attached to difference. For instance, things appear to someone who is color-blind or deaf in a specific way, and so they too, like those with all faculties intact, have ways of knowing their world legitimately and validly. The distinction also can account for human perceptual error while leaving the objective nature of an object untouched. For Kant, metaphysics cannot be a science because what metaphysics seeks to discover and describe cannot be experienced with our senses. Thus we cannot ever *know* in the strictest sense the true nature of things like God, freedom, the soul, and immortality. However, Kant does think that our reason gives us sufficient evidence to believe in all three.

Kant's ideas did not go unchallenged; many of his contemporaries felt his phenomena/noumena distinction reinstated a Platonic or dualistic framework, in which people mentally construct their own reality and thus have no ability to have any real objective knowledge of the world around them.[7] For some critics, the difference between the phenomenal world and the noumenal world was as distinct and separate as Halloween Town and Christmas Town.

Many modern commentators, including myself, see Kant as espousing a one-world theory rather than a two-world theory. A one-world reading interprets Kant's distinction between phenomena and noumena as denoting not two different worlds but rather two aspects of the same world, just as a single coin has two sides. This seems to solve many problems (but not all) and to be a more reasonable way of interpreting Kant. It also sheds light on the distinction between perception and reality in Burton.

"It's as real as my skull and it does exist!": Jack Skellington

Can Jack come to know the essence of Christmas just by looking at presents and snowflakes, and performing the duties of Santa Claus? For Kant, the answer here would be no; just as the Grinch found out when he attempted to stop Christmas for the Whos in Whoville by taking away all the decorations, food, and gifts, the essence or spirit of Christmas is not a physical object and it is not exhausted by the physical things associated with it. This essence is not something you experience with the five senses; the essence of Christmas is intangible, immaterial, eternal, and ultimately metaphysical. Without any experiential data, the mind has nothing to mold and process, and so knowledge (in the strictest Kantian conception) cannot occur.[8] In this situation one's faculty of reason either is allowed to speculate and get into trouble, for example, by convincing itself it can know essences or abstract notions without evidence, or it must be reined in and kept within cognitive boundaries. For the sake of certainty and truth in the sciences, Kant voted for the latter. He would tell Jack to do the same, since what he is looking for can't be empirically found.

In "Jack's Obsession," Jack sings about the problems that confront him:

These dolls and toys confuse me so,
confound it all, I love it though.
Simple objects, nothing more,
but something's hidden through a door,
though I do not have the key.
Something's here I cannot see.

In this scene Jack has borrowed lab equipment from Dr. Finklestein in hopes of using the scientific method on Christmas items, thus deducing the essence of Christmas and solidifying his knowledge of what it is. The scientific method, like one's senses, requires empirical data. But alas, what Jack is looking for is not to be empirically found in the items he has collected; it is something elusive and ethereal:

It's simple really, very clear, like music drifting in the air.
Invisible, but everywhere.
Just because I cannot see it doesn't mean I can't believe it.

The key for Kant here would be "belief," and he would have no issues with Jack believing in the essence or spirit of Christmas. In his *Critique,* Kant distinguished between knowledge and faith: faith, or belief, is holding a judgment with subjective sufficiency only (something that holds for myself but not everyone), whereas knowledge is being able to hold a judgment with both objective and subjective sufficiency (something that holds for everyone). It's perfectly okay to believe in something, whether it be the spirit of Christmas, ghosts, or the monster in the closet, but just don't confuse your belief with knowledge, because it often lacks sufficient objective evidence and might possibly not accord with the experiences of everyone. Kant would most certainly tell Jack that it is impossible to *know* the essence of Christmas in the strictest sense, no matter what equipment or method he tries, but it is entirely acceptable to believe in it, enjoy it, and have some fun around the lighted tree. However, without certainty, one would be encouraged to be cautious when attempting to improve on something. Too bad Kant wasn't there to express this sentiment to Jack. If he had been he might have prevented the spread of mutant toys and large snakes and the chaos that ensued after Jack attempted to mimic as well as improve Christmas.

And what of Vincent Malloy, can he have better luck than Jack with knowing what it is to *be* Vincent Price? In many ways Malloy illustrates the ideas behind Kant's philosophical distinction of phenomena/noumena. If your experience is filtered in a certain way, such as knowing Price only through his horror movie acting career, then that is what your idea is founded on and what your knowledge of him will be based on. There will no doubt be things you cannot experience or know, and this fact indicates only your limitations, not any limitations with the thing itself. Allow me to elaborate.

Vincent Malloy is attempting to understand the essence of Vincent Price through the movies he has acted in, which most likely do not reflect Price himself as a person but rather only the characters he has played and his ability to portray them successfully. Vincent Price the real person may be nothing like Prince Prospero from *The Mask of the Red Death* or Professor Henry Jarrod in *House of Wax.* At best, watching Price's films would give Vincent Malloy an idea of what movie roles appealed to Price or what directors he preferred to work with. But this way of going about understanding essence is limited and highly susceptible to flaws. For example, Price acted in other types of movies, like a frontier film titled *Brigham Young,* a drama titled *Wilson* about Woodrow Wilson, and the drama *The Keys to the Kingdom.* Also, limiting Price to his role as a film actor does him no justice because he had a successful stage career for much of his life, he appeared on TV numerous times in person or as a voice-over narrator (e.g., *Batman, The Muppet Show, Scooby-Doo, The Brady Bunch, The Hilarious House of Frightenstein*), and he made some appearances in the music industry, lending his persona to albums, videos, and specials (e.g., Michael Jackson, Alice Cooper). And let's not forget he had a successful radio career as well.[9]

However, we return to Kant's point again: the things Malloy can know about Price are the things made available to the five senses, but this constitutes only the phenomenal side of Price, not the actual essence. Moreover, if one knows Price only from his films then the phenomenal side one knows is really a mere fragment. The essence or noumenal side of Vincent Price is intangible and immaterial, even though he is a living person and not a holiday or spirit. Thus Vincent Malloy, according to Kant, has only a restricted phenomenal knowledge of Vincent Price, and this knowledge is not of the essence but only of some phenomenal qualities. Malloy's idea of what it is to *be* Price is composed of what he has been able to sensually perceive, in this case the roles Price has played in movies and TV shows that Malloy has watched, and nothing more. There is no mention of Price as the loving father and husband, the art historian and collector, the gourmet cook, and so on—all the aspects of Price that made him the man he was.

I think, though, that we must not neglect the fact that Vincent Malloy is a young boy and thus has a sense of naïveté about him: he doesn't understand the difference between Price the man and Price the actor. The essence he has formed is of the kitschy cinematic Vincent Price, at best: the Roger-Corman-directed-Poe-role-playing-Vincent-Price, if you will. However, this point hints at a unique factor Vincent Price has, one that adds further complications: he's an actor. As a fan, can you really know an actor? What I do think we can highlight from Malloy's efforts here is that he is attempting to follow the method Diotima described to Socrates, and that is something positive: he is analyzing the qualities perceptually available to him and attempting to build on them to gain a deeper understanding of essence. Maybe one day Vincent Malloy will be a philosopher and come to understand essences and the challenges of coming to know them more thoroughly.

However, all things considered with Jack and Vincent, one must ask, can one ever know what it is *to be* someone or something else? Is this a kind of knowledge we are capable of even having? That's a tough one, like finding a white cane in a closet full of skeletons.

"These games that you play are all in your head": Vincent's Mother

Thomas Nagel, in "What Is It Like to Be a Bat?," argues that consciousness has an essential and necessary subjective character, an aspect of what it is like to *be* that person or know what something is like *for* that person.[10] That a person has conscious experience at all means that there is something to *be* that person. Nagel points out that the objective strategies of the physical sciences cannot account for this subjective point of view that conscious creatures have, and yet to leave it out is to render the scientific approach incomplete or to pose the problem falsely. The human mind is something physical and something phenomenal, or in simple terms, the mind has objective and subjective aspects: there is physical behavior, brain states, chemical interactions, and so on, and there is also the way something feels, one's deepest inner thoughts about one's identity, preferences and biases, and so on. This subjective side of experience cannot be reduced or deduced from behavior, mental states, or events, and so it is difficult to explain or show. To demonstrate the importance of this subjective point of view of consciousness, and to highlight the difference between the objective and subjective approach, Nagel embarks on a discussion about the consciousness of bats.

It is safe to assume bats have experience. At the same time, it is evident that this experience is nothing like anything humans undergo. Thus Nagel draws an imaginative analogy that is rather difficult, if not impossible, to envision, and with this example he offers a powerful illustration of the problem of other minds. As Nagel explains, bats perceive the world primarily with sonar or echolocation. Specifically, they emit waves and these waves bounce off of things around them, enabling them to understand the size, shape, distance, motion, and texture of objects in their perceptual field. As Nagel explains, if we try to use our own experience to imagine what this is like, we run into issues because we imagine what it is like for *us* to behave *as a* bat, not what it is like for a bat to *be* a bat: "I want to know what it is like for a *bat* to be a bat. Yet if I try to imagine this, I am restricted to the resources of my own mind, and those resources are inadequate to the task. I cannot perform it either by imagining additions to my present experience, or by imagining segments gradually subtracted from it, or by imagining some combination of additions, subtractions, and modifications."[11] The best evidence is the experience of bats themselves, namely, the embodied conscious bat, and we don't have access to that since we are humans, not bats.

As Nagel's example illustrates, there is something in bat consciousness well beyond our conceptual abilities and linguistic descriptions. Physical descriptions are completely useless. This subjective viewpoint of consciousness, this "to *be*," is not reducible from the bat's behavior or physiology either, and so we cannot really know what it means to *be* a bat. By extension, we know only what it is to be who each one of us is (i.e., to be Jack, or Vincent, or Sally, etc.). So no matter what method we try, no matter what instrument of objective science we use, we will gain no ground in knowing what it is to be something we are not. We cannot know what it is to *be* a duck, *be* the Loch Ness Monster, or *be* a zombie dog.

Though less obvious, the problem persists between beings of the same species. I know my personal subjective viewpoint, but I cannot *know* what it is to *be* Tim Burton. If I am provided with details of his life and activities, I can imagine what it would be like to be Burton, but as Nagel points out, what is actually occurring when I do this is I am imagining what it would be like for me to be Tim Burton. Ultimately I lack that first-person perspective and subjective conscious experience essential to knowing what it is to *be* him.

This, of course, does not bode well for Vincent Malloy. As much as both he and Vincent Price are humans, their subjective points of view are very different. The best Vincent Malloy can have is to know what it is like for him to behave like Vincent Price, but he cannot really know what it is to *be* Vincent Price because he lacks full knowledge of the subjective point of view that Vincent Price had as a conscious creature. Malloy also lacks, as was pointed out earlier, knowledge of Price outside of his horror film career, and this further compounds the problem of knowing what it is even to behave like Price. If you know how he behaves only in a certain context, like acting in Corman horror movies, that means you don't have the entire behavioral set belonging to the person. Malloy lacks Price's conscious and experiential baggage of life, as well as his core character outside of acting.

But for a seven-year-old boy like Vincent Malloy, is this really a problem? Is he doing rigorous science or philosophy? I highly doubt it. Specifically, it is also doubtful that he is really trying (or claiming) to know what it is like to *be* Vincent Price. A young boy like Vincent Malloy is pretending to be Vincent Price, and when one pretends to be someone else the crucial things to adopt and mimic are the behaviors or physical traits of that person, not their essence or noumenal self. I think we need to call attention to the distinction between the intentions involved in "being like" someone and in "being" someone: one is an imitation of behavior and mannerisms, maybe a high level of admiration close to obsession, and the other is the impossible task of taking on another person's subjective, conscious viewpoint. To pretend to be Vincent Price, to admire him and imitate him, even as a villainous horror movie icon, is an escape from the everyday humdrum. It's a lot of fun to reenact film scenes or create new scenarios for a character. One gets the feeling from the poem that Vincent is bored, or rather dissatisfied with his life at the present moment; he clearly yearns for excitement, drama, and a level of control over his life (and the lives of a few others). Some might say that in life his own self is not being validated, that this wanting to be Vincent Price is a result of his own subjective experience of discontent and unhappiness. And while that might be true on some level, I think we must remember that Vincent Malloy is seven years old, an age when one does grow tired of being told constantly what to do and when to do it by adults.[12] It's also an age of self-discovery and character development, and these require imitation. It is natural to pretend to be an adult, after all they have all the power and freedom, and this person could be a parent, a rock star, or an actor like Vincent Price. At Vincent's age I pretended to be Darth Vader as well as Vincent Price, and this was all in good fun and not the result of depression from lack of self-validation. And I turned out all right. I think.

Playing pretend is the stuff of which childhood is made. In fact, philosophers such as George Herbert Mead suggest that imitation is how we learn a lot about things.[13] Role-playing teaches us about ourselves as well as about things that are foreign to ourselves. In kindergarten, children are taught the noises and behaviors of animals and told to imitate an animal as a way to learn about it. Likewise, much of our comedy or displays of irony is based in the imitation of someone else, a consciousness foreign to oneself, and the concept of empathy is demonstrated to children by telling them to put themselves in another's shoes to see how they would feel in that situation.

Nagel's position also does not bode well for Jack Skellington's effort to be Santa Claus. Because Jack is restricted to his own subjective viewpoint, he cannot know what it is to *be* Santa Claus; he can only know what it is like (as Jack) to behave like him (to behave as Santa Claus does). And knowing the behavior of someone or something is no guarantee of true understanding or certain knowledge, as evidenced by Jack making a mess out of Christmas while attempting to act like Santa Claus. Jack projects his own subjective point of view onto Santa Claus, whether intentionally or not, when he calls him "Sandy Claws" and describes him as "a fearsome king with a deep mighty voice" who is "like a lobster, huge and red . . . with big great arms."[14] Furthermore, the gifts that Jack hands out to the children in Christmas Town, made by the Halloween Town folks, are things typical of Halloween Town—snakes, vampire toys, a killer duck, a shrunken head, and so on—indicating that Jack and the others do not have the same subjective consciousness as Santa Claus or the people of Christmas Town.

Jack tries to become Sandy Claws because he is bored and dissatisfied with his life.[15] But instead of pretending to be Santa, Jack kidnaps Santa and really tries to assume his identity for that one special night. In his case we clearly see that the drive to know or experience other minds is frequently motivated not so much by the desire to apprehend their experience but in order to escape the monotony or pain of our own. Sometimes we're just bored or unhappy, and we assume someone else's life is better. The mind of another represents, from a psychological standpoint, the reprieve of another world. Burton and Nagel both demonstrate the failed logic of this idea.

It is interesting to note here that Nagel and Burton seem to share a respect for the unique otherness each one of us possesses. In his article presented here, we can read Nagel as saying that to attempt to transpose oneself into the consciousness of another is ultimately to replace that person's (or bat's) unique subjective perspective with our own. It is naïve to think we can place ourselves in someone else's mind and not monopolize it completely; in other words, we cannot have our own and their own viewpoint at the same time. By highlighting the incommensurable nature of subjective consciousness, Nagel effectively preserves the boundary between minds and makes communication, not imagination, the proper vehicle for coming to an understanding of the other. We must speak to each other as unique, different individuals and find a common ground of understanding in our communication. Burton often writes about socially marginalized characters, individuals who just don't think like their peers and thus are relegated to the fringe or mocked, and he does so in a sympathetic way that enables the audience to respect and value otherness rather than reducing it. In many films Burton also shows the damaging effects or consequences of forced conformity on an individual or his society. He, too, uses communication as a vehicle for understanding, with the help of analogy and allegory, and to exemplify the need to embrace difference rather than eradicate it. In this way, both Burton and Nagel are concerned with the problem of other minds: how to understand each other and celebrate otherness.

"And my soul from out that shadow that lies floating on the floor shall be lifted? Nevermore!": Edgar Allan Poe's "The Raven," as Quoted by Vincent

Not exactly the happy ending we were looking for. To recap, according to Plato, Jack Skellington and Vincent Malloy would need to be philosophers or have some kind of philosophical training in order to be able to ascend to the realm of the forms, what Plato calls the highest reality. However, to reach the understanding that the material world around us participates in the forms, albeit to an imperfect degree, is at least advancement on the road to "knowledge," in Plato's sense. For Kant, knowing the essence of Christmas or Vincent Price, or what he would call the noumenal aspect, is impossible because these lie outside the boundaries of our experience. The best Jack and Vincent Malloy can have with Kantian epistemology is belief in the essences of Christmas and Vincent Price, belief that these essences exist, but never knowledge about them because they are noumena rather than phenomena. With Nagel, the story is similar: because Jack and Vincent Malloy lack the subjective, conscious viewpoint required to know what it is to *be* Santa Claus or the spirit of Christmas or Vincent Price, they can only mimic these things or know how to behave like Santa Claus or Vincent Price might. Jack and Vincent Malloy can never know what it is like to *be* someone or something else, and that's perfectly okay. If we have learned anything from Burton and Nagel it is to celebrate our unique differences, respect them wholeheartedly, and put our efforts into understanding someone else through communication rather than attempting or wanting to *be* them. It's natural for children to pretend to be their heroes; it helps them discover themselves and have a little fun along the way. But at the end of the day the lesson learned is this: be who you are, celebrate otherness and diversity, and let others be themselves too. If we follow this, Christmas is safe and so are the flowerbeds. Maybe this is a sort of happy ending, or as close as we get.

Philosophy would say Jack learned another lesson: knowing the essence of something or someone, that intangible and ethereal sense of being, is a most difficult and yet noble task. It's the stuff of lovers—wisdom lovers, that is. The history of philosophy is littered with the creative yet failed quests of others for these very kinds of essences, and if Jack had picked up a history of philosophy text rather than one on scientific method, he might have avoided delivering scary, ghoulish gifts to the kids of Christmas Town. But then again, ghoulish toys made in Halloween Town must be more exciting and entertaining than socks and underwear.

Notes

Epigraph taken from "What's This," sung by Jack Skellington, in *The Nightmare Before Christmas,* directed by Tim Burton (Touchstone Pictures, 1993).

1. *Vincent,* directed by Tim Burton (Walt Disney Productions, 1982).

2. Plato, *Symposium,* trans. Benjamin Jowett, Internet Classics Archive, http://classics.mit.edu/Plato/symposium.html.

3. Plato, *Symposium.*

4. Plato, *Symposium.*

5. Immanuel Kant, *The Critique of Pure Reason,* trans. Werner S. Pluhar (Indianapolis: Hackett, 1993), B xiv–xv, 20.

6. Kant, *Critique of Pure Reason,* B 295–315; A 235–60, 303–22.

7. Kant's theory was highly and hotly debated because other philosophers (mainly empiricists) felt that Kant was telling them that we didn't have access to reality, inasmuch as he asserts that noumena affect our senses but remain completely out of our reach. Some even suggested that noumena occupy a different world. They saw Kant as saying that noumena existed but that we couldn't know they did, which is a complete

contradiction and quite ridiculous sounding. They also did not like the idea of faculties or intuitions being innate in the mind, that dreadful term *a priori,* because empiricists, like John Locke, saw the mind as a blank slate imprinted upon and shaped by experience. For Kant, much of what shapes experience enables experience to happen at all, and the way we have it, some things, like faculties, pure intuitions, pure concepts, and so on, must be logically and necessarily in the mind prior to experience. These a priori entities in the mind are, however, meaningless without the data provided to them by experience; without sensory information they have nothing to work with, nothing to process, nothing to do. Cognition, then, is a beautiful handshake between the external world and the internal workings of the mind—a merger between the empiricist and rationalist views—at least on the epistemological side of things. Because cognition can only be of experiential things, knowledge bears the same boundary: we can *know* something only if we can empirically experience it (i.e., if sensory data are provided to our mind to process).

8. I do acknowledge that some will argue that we have knowledge of things like the moral law, even though it does not derive from the realm of experience. Granted, that knowledge is purely formal, not material; however, it indicates the possibility of innate knowledge and limited knowledge of noumena. However, I would like to note that my analysis is strictly of Kant's first *Critique,* and it is here he is most stringent about experience being the criteria for knowledge ("Wissen," in the strictest sense). In the end of division 1 (B 196; A 157) he makes this conclusion, and throughout the whole division he repeats it. I can also mention here that in the first *Critique* Kant speaks of God as a regulative principle, and the moral world is not quite the same as the moral law in the second *Critique.* The moral world has practical application only; it has influence over the world of sense and this object of sense is an object of pure reason in its practical use, as a "mystical object" of rational beings. This kind of knowledge is not the same as what Kant speaks of earlier. It is the practical use of reason, as opposed to pure reason, and the use of the other cognitive faculties in building knowledge.

9. These are just some of the aspects of Price's life and career, and by no means should this be considered an exhaustive list.

10. Thomas Nagel, "What Is It Like to Be a Bat?," *Philosophical Review* 83, no. 4 (October 1974): 435–50, available at http://instruct.westvalley.edu/lafave/nagel_nice.html.

11. Nagel, "What Is It Like to Be a Bat?"

12. See the Walling chapter in this volume for further discussion of the unique nature of child consciousness and Tim Burton's fascination with it.

13. See the Hada chapter in this volume for further discussion of Mead's theory of role-playing.

14. Burton, *Nightmare Before Christmas.*

15. See the Sullivan chapter in this volume for further discussion of the consolations of fantasy.

Part 3

Burton and Aesthetics

A SYMPHONY OF HORROR

The Sublime Synesthesia of *Sweeney Todd*

Jennifer L. Jenkins

> Thus, the distinctive quality of food consists in its ability to submit to animal assimilation.
>
> —Jean Anthelme Brillat-Savarin, *The Physiology of Taste*

Sweeney Todd (2007) marks a significant deviation for Tim Burton in terms of his prior work and practice.[1] While he had already worked on musicals (*The Nightmare Before Christmas* [1993], *Corpse Bride* [2005]) and literary adaptations (*Sleepy Hollow* [1999], *Planet of the Apes* [2001], *Big Fish* [2004], *Charlie and the Chocolate Factory* [2005]), *Sweeney* differs by being an adaptation of an existing stage musical with a long provenance. Nor is it scored by Burton's longtime collaborator Danny Elfman. It shares with his other adapted works a firm grounding in the American literary canon, Stephen Sondheim being the touted scion of the American songbook. And, although Burton's *Sweeney* evokes the German Expressionist visual style, it does so through the filter of 1930s Universal horror films, which themselves repurposed German silent tropes for emergent U.S. sound film.[2] Burton thematically and aesthetically honors his film's antecedents in silent horror, most notably F. W. Murnau's *Nosferatu* (1922), a visual and visceral "symphony of horror" that explores unquenchable hunger and unproductive ingestion as sublime excess. Yet he does so through visual borrowings from James Whale's iconic Frankenstein films, themselves texts preoccupied with hunger and consumption. With characteristic Burtonian counterintuition, he invokes this *silent* film aesthetic to adapt the work of the United States' most *symphonic* musical theater composer, forcing a confrontation between silent-era visual conventions and Sondheim's complex polyphonic soundscape. Sondheim's own 1979 musical adaptation of the Grand Guignol story of the Demon Barber of Fleet Street had shifted the locus of horror from visual spectacle to Brechtian sonic extravaganza.[3] In turn, Burton's 2007 film blends sight, sound, and representations of taste: Burton's Sweeney experiences and eventually comes to personify the sublime as a result of his drive to *see* vengeance done, while all Fleet Street unwittingly *tastes* the horrific sublime in Mrs. Lovett's pies. Burton's revisioning of *Sweeney Todd* compellingly illustrates aspects of Burke's theory of the sublime through adaptive use of silent film aesthetics and notions of synesthesia.

Edmund Burke posits the sublime in binary opposition to beauty. Excess, spectacle, and sensory overload mark the sublime. Though not its exclusive catalyst, the natural world frequently provokes a sublime response: the untamed, unknowable entity that reminds humans of their small, insignificant place in the universe. Regardless of the cause, Burke maintains that the sublime inspires awe through the combination of enjoyable compulsion and uncomfortable horror. Indeed, he initially defines the sublime in terms of pain: "Whatever is fitted in any sort to excite the ideas of pain, and danger, that is to say, whatever is in any sort terrible, or is conversant about terrible objects, or operated in a manner analogous to terror, is a source of the *Sublime;* that is, it is productive of the strongest emotion which the mind is capable of feeling."[4] Such excitations provoke a sense of the sublime—as opposed to terror—precisely because one avoids actual pain (or imminent danger) and enjoys instead the relief of a near miss.[5] Burke adds that "terror is a passion which always produces delight when it does not press too close."[6] Terror and the sublime are not synonymous for Burke but rather are degrees of emotional response to awesome stimuli. Terror's basis in delight depends upon distance from the cause and therefore a fundamental sense of security; the sublime removes that distance, forces the individual to confront the terror, and thus produces the "uneasiness" that can present as nausea, cold sweats, and other physiological symptoms of a psychological experience. Clearly the story of Sweeney Todd was designed to "excite" such ideas, from its source material in the penny press story "The String of Pearls: A Romance" onward.[7]

To oversimplify, then, the eighteenth century located "pain," "danger," and "terrible objects," as Burke termed them, in nature and its irrational forces; however, by the nineteenth century western European culture was in the throes of industrialization and concomitant poverty. Child labor, workhouses, and slums presented new terrors. Consequently, the city—rather than nature—came to "excite the ideas of pain and danger" that shape the sublime. Burke's philosophy accommodates this cultural shift by placing the experience of the sublime not in a specific locus but in the individual's response to his or her immediate sensory environment. Thus, when the man-made city replaces nature as a locus of pain and danger, it carries with it the giddy-horror frisson of "man devouring man, my dear."[8] A far greater threat to modern humanity than nature, the city—precisely because it is man-made—creates a sublime space of external *and* internal terror. While Burke argues that the sublime takes its power from the blending of terror and delight, that emotion does not presume altruism. Indeed, Burke is quick to note that "there is no spectacle we so eagerly pursue" as that of "calamity" befalling our fellow humans, but he primly adds that "this is not an unmixed delight, but blended with no small uneasiness."[9] The appeal of queasy delight is that of escaping a similar fate while at the same time gazing into the abyss: *this could happen to you,* but it didn't—this time. The city thrives on the anonymous, emotionless, often automated "calamity" of consumption, while individuals consume themselves in response. The spectacle of such calamity allows distance from the crowd but terror for the individual. It is poignant, indeed, that Toby and Mrs. Lovett's intimate duet of love and family, "Not While I'm Around," is the penultimate scene before Sweeney claims his urban family and fully enacts the urban sublime.

Katherine Newey's work on the city in Victorian theater reveals that "the urban theatrical setting deals with the city as . . . an active and villainous character in the melodramatic struggle between the forces of good and evil."[10] The Sweeney legend, with its Victorian provenance, was part and parcel of the performance context that proffered the city as sublime, indeed, gothic sublime.[11] Moreover, the subject matter of the Sweeney narrative was tailor-made for the emerging Grand Guignol shock theater of the late Victorian era, itself a product of and answer to urban squalor.[12] Consumption defines the city in the Sweeney narrative, represented by a series of machines: the commodity-producing factories (Sondheim's stage play begins with the shriek of a factory whistle); the corpse-producing barber chair; and the meat grinder. All are machines of ingestion and degustation. As Benjamin Poore and Kelly Jones determined during the 2008 *Sweeney Todd* Symposium at the University of Lincoln (U.K.), "the legend plays on our continued wariness of the city as a place where identities become disturbingly changeable, where loved ones can be 'lost'—or lose themselves—and where the concentration of people leads to arbitrary choices (to visit one barber's shop rather than another) with potentially deadly consequences."[13] Thus the man-made hell of the industrial age is both cause and effect of this shift of the sublime from nature to city. Clearly Sondheim saw an analogy to the crime-ridden, collapsing New York of the 1970s; Burton updates the transatlantic analogy with the sense and sensibility of millennial goth design verging on steampunk and reveling in the beauty of decay.

Thus Burton finds a congenial tone in Sondheim's masterwork through the very elements we recognize in Burke's aesthetics. In his filmic adaptation, Burton establishes the urban sublime in broad strokes through production design, mise-en-scène, and costuming of the supporting cast, then uses synesthetic devices to extrude the interiority of the primary characters and shape the corresponding audience experience of that sense of confusion. In fact, the editorial reduction of dialogue and recitative in the final cut of the film seems calculated to make Sweeney himself a physical incarnation of the sublime.[14]

Adaptation: Cannibalism or Transubstantiation?

One of the challenges in parsing the philosophy of Tim Burton in *Sweeney Todd* is the necessity of distinguishing Burton's creative ethos from Sondheim's. In any instance of adapted material, one faces an anxiety of influence. With the transition from staged production to screen—rather than simply from page to screen—the adaptation process moves through two full iterations of performance and design, beginning with the book, then the stage production, and then the cinematic spectacle. This complex relation between source text, the *hypotexte,* and the adaptation, or *hypertexte,* is one that Gérard Genette identifies as transplanted (*se greffer*), absent the priority of temporality.[15] The *texte au second degré,* which carries the sense of "once removed," is for Genette both a contingent and an autonomous text. The creative team on Burton's *Sweeney Todd,* from Sondheim on down, all insisted that the film be a wholly new conceptualization of the material—not a filmed stage performance. That distinction is clearly achieved, with 360-degree camera movement, cinematic shot selection, filmic mise-en-scène, and the absence of distinctively stagey production numbers that pause the narrative action. The decision to eliminate chorus numbers ("The Ballad of Sweeney Todd") and reduce chorus melodies to instrumental underscore ("God, That's Good")—made in full consultation with and approval of Sondheim—allows for a more integrated musical narrative and, as the effects team note repeatedly, "full blood."[16] As such, the adaptation both follows and anticipates, is both consequent and antecedent to, the Sondheim stage musical, the Christopher Bond stage play, and the tabloid story "The String of Pearls." Burton's London is both more and less authentic than Sondheim's, and the film's imaginary is read through plural filmic, textual, and musical milieux. This intertextuality enhances the sensory confusion of synesthesia and the associated pain or anxiety of the sublime.[17] These different levels of audiovisual, cultural, and textual references create a rich stew for audience delectation, one laced with "no small uneasiness" in nearly every bite.

What, then, is Burton's cinematic ethos in this film? Sondheim reports wanting the 1979 theater piece to achieve a conflict of emotions: he sought to "scare an audience, and see if you could do it while people were singing."[18] This statement captures the very aesthetic paradox that Burton also found compelling: "When I first saw the show the imagery, which was quite dark and harsh, set with the music, which was quite lush and beautiful, was something I'd never seen before and was the reason I wanted to do it."[19] Burton's identification here of Sondheim's synthesis of "harsh" and "beautiful" harkens back to Burke's binary configuration of the sublime as derived from the juxtaposition of just those sensations: "Sublime objects are vast in their dimensions, beautiful ones comparatively small; . . . the great in many cases loves the right line, and when it deviates, it often makes a strong deviation; *beauty should not be obscure;* the great ought to be *dark and gloomy;* beauty should be light and delicate; the great ought to be solid, and even massive. *They are indeed ideas of a very different nature, one being founded on pain, the other on pleasure.*"[20] Burton, who saw the 1980 London production multiple times, spoke at press junkets about wanting to make an old-fashioned horror movie, a "silent movie with music."[21] This intentional pairing of sight and sound again evokes the Burkean dialectic of sublime and beautiful. At first viewing, one might presume that Sondheim divided beauty and the sublime musically into lilting and dark melodies, respectively, and that Burton simply followed those melodic cues. Yet some of Sondheim's most stirring and beautiful melodies accompany or segue into the grisliest scenes of Burton's film, such as "My Friends," the reprise of "Johanna," and "Not While I'm Around."

Rather than a balanced pairing, then, Burton places beauty and the sublime in tension, then shows the historical process by which, in the Sweeney narrative, beauty is tainted by, falls to, and is ultimately consumed by the urban sublime over the course of the film. Through his use of color palette and temperature, Burton draws a stark distinction between the past beauty of Sweeney's life with Lucy and the infant Johanna and the hideous but compelling present sublime of Sweeney's return.[22] He pointedly places the Barker family in a flower market, linking the idealized past to nature. The fully desaturated palette and low-angle shots in the narrative's present time complement Sweeney's vengeance quest and the darker melodies of Sondheim's score and create the "dark and gloomy" urban sublime in numbers like "My Friends" and "Epiphany." In stark contrast, color-saturated memory and fantasy eye-level shot sequences offer "light and delicate" instances of idealized beauty—beauty that is utterly lost to Sweeney, in "No Place Like London" and "Poor Thing," and utterly unobtainable to Mrs. Lovett, in "By the Sea." The transition from beautiful to sublime that occurs as Lucy leaves her bower to fall prey to Judge Turpin is, of course, inaugurated by a symbol of poisoned nature ("every day he sent her a flower / but would she come down from her bower"). A figure of institutionalized voracity, Judge Turpin drives the shift from beautiful to sublime: as the city closes around poor Lucy, the color temperature cools, and she is consumed by the dark and gloom of Turpin's London. This filmic contrast underscores Sweeney's contention that all color and light, indeed all beauty, is illusory: "There's a hole the world like a great, black pit / And it's filled with people who are filled with shit / And the vermin of the world inhabit it."[23] In Burton's film, beauty and the sublime stand in stark contrast with no possibility of synthesis, and the sobering message of Sweeney's quest is that the city consumes all beauty and offers no hope of natural redemption.

Since Burton's dominant filmic signature is visual style, it is important to see that style's foundation in earlier traditions. Like Sondheim reaching back to nineteenth-century melodrama for his musical, Burton looks back to German Expressionism, a style that has marked his work from *Vincent* (1982) and *Frankenweenie* (1984) forward. James Whale's adoption of the Weimar silent aesthetic in his Frankenstein films clearly influenced Burton's (sometimes) camp refiguring of those post–World War I issues and themes. While such a style might seem anachronistic in the Victorian milieu of *Sweeney Todd,* Burton's art team, led by scenic designer Dante Ferretti and costumer Colleen Atwood, constructed a hybrid imaginary that blends Victorian streetscapes and costumes with Weimar interiors and makeup. Sweeney Todd's and Mrs. Lovett's costuming, makeup, and placement in frame demarcate them as denizens of the city of endless night that is Fleet Street and St. Dunstan's Parish.[24] From Sweeney's Bride of Frankenstein wig to his hobnailed razor holsters and Mrs. Lovett's modified saloon-girl ensembles to the retrofitted design of the barber chair itself, Burton enlists the classical Hollywood horror visual vocabulary adapted from German Expressionism and its deliberate confusion of the senses. Burton himself hailed this period ambiguity, dubbing it "horror movie London," a chronotope shaped less by reality than by historical cinema and visual style.[25] Thus we have a cinematic gallimaufry of genre references, textual allusions, visual quotations, and puns that shows Burton's skill at synthesis of disparate elements and his appetite for aesthetic accumulation.[26]

The Skin of the Nightmare: Synesthesia

In both style and content, Burton's *Sweeney Todd* embraces Burke's sublime by way of the aesthetic device of synesthesia. Popularized in cinema by the German Expressionists, synesthesia is a perceptual substitution of one sensory experience for another, as in hearing color or smelling sounds. Often considered an adjunct of abstraction in art and literature, synesthesia also has a history within narrative film, as Joshua Yumibe has shown in his study of early color film and modernism: "The redness of a fire was not only indicative of the fire's nature, but also it stimulated the audience's sensual and emotional reactions. This was, broadly construed, a synaesthetic understanding of color's influence: that is, color can cross sensory nerves, making one hear sounds, feel new emotions, and transcend spiritual heights."[27] Thus, early filmmakers sought ways to convey visceral human experience through visual and, later, audiovisual stimuli. Robert Wiene's iconic *Das Kabinet des Dr. Caligari* (1920) experiments, in both story and aesthetic, with the confusion of senses. In addition to canted, antinaturalist sets and art design, the film is tinted in sequences to convey atmospheric conditions such as day and night, as well as the projected emotional states of the protagonists. In this story about hypnosis and somnambulist mind-control, Wiene also interpolated cut-out text in frame to represent the thoughts of the crazed asylum director. All of these devices were meant to serve the dreamscape narrative of a tale told by (it turns out) a madman. Today, *Caligari* is best known for its distorted and canted visuals—a distinctive look that defines German Expressionism. Siegfried Kracauer notes that production designer Hermann Warm's "formula" was, "Films must be drawings brought to life"—a sentiment closely mirrored in Burton's own cinematic practice.[28] Of course, Caligari's visual influence on Burton's body of work is unmistakable. In the same vein, Murnau's *Nosferatu,* subtitled "eine Symphonie des Grauens" (A symphony of horror), signals this sense-mixing by blending the auditory metaphor of symphony with visceral horror. By invoking German Expressionism as the aesthetic of *Sweeney Todd,* Burton also taps into its heady zeitgeist of intellectual and cultural obsessions with psychoanalysis, dream theory, and epistemologies of sense impression. This expression of sensory ambiguity explores—and, in Burton's cinema, exploits—human understanding of one sense in terms of another.[29] Burton's interest in the confusion or mixing of senses has colored and shaped the mise-en-scène of most of his films and defined the style that we have come to know as distinctively Burton-ian. Indeed, the 2010 Burton retrospective at the Museum of Modern Art (MOMA) in New York was constructed to confuse the senses and startle visitor expectations of visual and tactile impressions. Throughout Burton's oeuvre we find the sublime expressed through the devices of synesthesia, and nowhere more than in his adaptation of Sondheim's *Sweeney Todd.*

Dropping In

Sweeney Todd's compelling credit sequence, designed by Richard Morrison, establishes the visual and narrative tone for the film to follow and anchors the film within the urban sublime. "The Ballad of Sweeney Todd," a company number in the stage play, now functions as an instrumental overture and underscores this visual prologue to the film. In contrast to the public and populist voice of the ballad in the prologue, Morrison and Burton establish an intimate and individual perspective more in keeping with Burton's invocation of the sublime, as noted above.

Sondheim's score denotes the prelude for the organ "*largo e maestoso*" (loud and majestic), signaling his own invocation of the sublime. Importantly, Burke identifies loudness and sonorousness as qualities that contribute to a sensation of the sublime, noting in particular the difference between visual and auditory stimuli: "The eye is not the only organ of sensation, by which a sublime passion may be produced. Sounds have a great power in these as in most other passions. . . . Excessive loudness alone is sufficient to overpower the soul, to suspend its action, and to fill it with terror. The noise of vast cataracts, raging storms, thunder, or artillery, awakes a great and awful sensation in the mind, though we can observe no nicety or artifice in those sorts of music."[30] Sondheim's theme does evoke cataracts, storms, thunder: the loudness of nature. But in Sweeney's case it is *human* nature that roils the atmosphere in a kind of sonic pathetic fallacy. For Burton and his credit designer Richard Morrison, the sublime resides not, as for Burke, in the majesty of nature but in the "great and awful" cityscape. After establishing the city as horror and nature as beauty, the credit sequence then merges the two by effecting a transformation from raindrop to blood-drop. What is initially understood as a gentle rain becomes a cascade of blood, evidence of life taken rather than given. Grand Guignol's effects—though not its means—appear from the first frame, then, as Burton visually quotes the earliest of sensationalist stage-to-screen mechanisms.

Cleft Palettes: Black and White and Red All Over

The animated credit sequence is worth examining closely, as it establishes Burton's distinctive filmic ethos and aesthetic perspective on Sondheim's *hypotexte*. The credit sequence opens with a pan right across a crescent moon reflected in a body of water; a single raindrop disturbs the image of the moon, at which point the camera tilts up to the crescent in the sky with a boy fishing off the horn. Thus disturbance is established from before the very first frame of the film proper. As the crescent moon turns into a letter *D* (for distributor Dreamworks), the camera begins to crab right at cloud level, and Sondheim's prelude commences, "*largo e maestoso,*" as noted. The prelude echoes the tone and timbre of *The Phantom of the Opera* and clearly signals that any dream work to follow will not be therapeutic. Fittingly, the organ hits a nightmarish crescendo just as the Dreamworks logo appears full-frame against a cloudy night sky. Strains of the prelude rise and resolve as the Warner Bros. logo appears, then fades to black (00:00:39). Within ten seconds, the scene has returned to the blue-black night sky, while intermittent raindrops fall vertically, lit from behind by occasional lightning flashes in the clouds. The camera cranes down and right, as producer credits appear and the strains of the prologue rise. A single red droplet falls amid the rain, barely noticeable on a conscious level (00:00:54). Second and third drops fall four seconds later, while chimney tops move into frame and out at eye line as the camera trucks right to pause on a rooftop. In a visual nod to both Murnau and Hitchcock, the camera approaches a slanted atelier window and tilts down to an extreme high angle through the murky panes to a chair positioned in a circle of moonlight. Just before the camera passes "through" the windowpane, metaphorically entering the story world, a blood spray hits the upper left pane with a barely audible splat. At the same instant, "A

Tim Burton Film" appears center frame, superimposed over the chair. The first three notes of "The Ballad of Sweeney Todd" play. The first edit in this title sequence is a cut to an interior, the frame vertically divided by a blood-drenched shadow portrait on a wall, right, and the actor credit for Johnny Depp on the left (00:01:15). An emblematic piece of set-dressing in British film and television heritage dramatizations of literature from Austen and the Brontës through Dickens, the shadow portrait signals both the domestic nature of the tale to come and, in this context, its utter corruption—the awful and painful dimension of the sublime.

As a piccolo introduces the melody, the credit "Helena Bonham Carter" appears beneath the female shadow portrait. With this, Morrison establishes a subtle association between the amount of blood in frame and the various character roles, these visuals timed to the melody as well. The camera pulls back and tilts down to follow a thin blood trickle that grows thicker as it flows over the back of the iconic barber chair, down the arm, and past a lion's-head seat support onto the chair's own tilt mechanism. Alan Rickman's name appears opposite the lion's-head carving, denoting his role as royally sanctioned Judge Turpin; this placement also signals Judge Turpin's role as the object and impetus of Sweeney's bloody quest. The second cut (00:01:33) is from the chair to a horizontal cogwheel: the bloodstream drips, pools, and stripes as the wheel begins to move counterclockwise toward the camera, accompanied by the sound of gears turning and blood dropping and squishing over the melody. Viscous red breaks the monochromatic palette and traces a serrated path across the screen in a vertical shot of interlocking spur gears with bright red blood between the teeth. In this sequence leading to the title, the camera moves up, across, then down, down, down, sketching both the character arc and the melodramatic plotline.

The title itself is ushered into frame by streams of blood or threads of ground meat slithering toward a trapdoor that opens into background darkness. In red letters, "SWEENEY TODD" falls into frame like the blood drops, underscored by "The Demon Barber of Fleet Street" in white—all well before the twenty-fourth measure of the ballad, when this identifying epithet would be voiced in the stage version.

On the first phrase of the (unsung) chorus ("Swing your razor wide, Sweeney / Hold it to the skies!"), the image cuts from black to a head-on shot of the meat-grinder mechanism.[31] The tendrils of ground meat ("Timothy Spall") reach out toward the audience, dissolve into blood drops, and fall into an underground stream of bloody water that swirls into an iconic Burtonian spiral ("Sacha Baron Cohen"), red on black in an overhead shot. Flames backlight a tray of pies; as the camera pulls back, a pool of blood on the oven rack begins to bubble and drip over the side ("Music and Lyrics by Stephen Sondheim"). This shift from darkness to firelight briefly introduces color and savory-looking pies—Burkean beauty—into the sequence, the better to offset the loud, dark, monochromatic sublime. The fact that the casting director and the composer alone share the golden glow underscores the dialectic of sublime and beautiful in this visual introduction to the film.

Jump cut to the oven door, which slams closed as the camera pans down left to lead a new bloodstream that cuts diagonally right to left across frame in the cellar gutter to a drain. This composition mirrors the iconic framing of Auguste and Louis Lumière's *L'arrivée du train à La Ciotat* and hints at Katherine Newey's observation that in Victorian "sensation melodramas . . . the latest technology was used to represent the drama of modern city life."[32] Combined with the chair gears, the oven, and the pathways of drainage for the blood, this abattoir sequence well illustrates the mechanisms of death and vengeance that the tale to come will engage.

In the final section of the credit sequence, the scene shifts to inside the drain, with the blood drip falling vertically frame right as the camera tilts down to the sewer and red-tinged outflow. The camera trucks back, pulling away from the churning water, backing out through the sewer grate and into the river. The blue-black water reflects the night sky, returning to the opening image of the sequence; foggy miasma fills the frame as the director credit appears. This stillness is pierced by the stem of the *Bountiful*, the ship that returns Sweeney and Anthony to London and introduces the establishing number, "No Place Like London."

While this close reading may seem laborious and detail-obsessed, the credit sequence fulfills the function of an overture and a prologue and schools spectators in the parameters of this visual narrative. As one of two powerful animated sequences in the film, Morrison's credit sequence sets the stage for the film's exploration of the urban sublime and its consumption of its paired opposite, beauty.

In the Belly of the Beast

The most distinct early juxtaposition of sublime and beautiful occurs as Anthony (Jamie Campbell Bower) and Sweeney (Johnny Depp) part ways at dockside. Not only are the two paired as opposites from the first refrain of the opening song, but Anthony's youthful optimism, indeed beauty, and Sweeney's world-weary cynicism appear in the casting and makeup of the two characters. Thus the binaries of character reflect the binaries of the beautiful and sublime. Like Starbuck and Ahab, Anthony and Sweeney are divided by age, demeanor, experience, and view of the world.[33] Their nighttime disembarkation into the gaslit streets of London amid a threatening storm, thunder on the horizon, and intermittent lightning is an entry into hell.

Burton reveals the city to be precisely the place of horror and distaste that Sweeney Todd's song and Burke's aesthetic both define. On the point of leave-taking, Sweeney recounts to Anthony the history of his abduction and transport by Judge Turpin. In warm sepia and pastel flashback, Sweeney's domestic memories of Lucy and Johanna illustrate Burke's notion of beauty, even as the sequence is offset by the dark and foreboding city and Sweeney's mournful voiceover ballad ("There was a barber and his wife"). The interlude that follows hard upon this watercolor memory depicts the city as sublime, based on Sondheim's music in 12/16 time and carried by Burton's high-speed composite animation and live-action trajectory along the labyrinthine path from the docks to Fleet Street. Resembling a funhouse ride in its pace and interruption by dark figures that lean in from left and right, spin around, and bar the path, this near-montage carries the narrative and the aesthetic into the heart of the labyrinth—Fleet Street—with all the monstrous implications that it implies. The sensory overload induced by this high-speed sequence mixes visual and audio to confound the senses in a synesthetic sensation of "no small uneasiness." We arrive in Fleet Street disoriented, dislocated, and slightly queasy: a likely condition in which to meet Mrs. Lovett.

Bon Appetit

Mrs. Lovett's pie shop is ground zero of the collision of violence and domesticity, sublime and beauty, dark and light, evil and good, cannibalism and feasting. That these binaries merge over food is significant, as it underscores the visceral nature of survival in London. Mrs. Lovett's first number, "The Worst Pies in London," carries a staggering provenance for anyone attempting the role. Just as Burton needed to make the libretto of the musical his own, so Helena Bonham Carter needed to register a performance distinct from those of Broadway doyennes Angela Lansbury and Patti Lupone.

Together, Burton and Carter construct Mrs. Lovett as a working woman with cash flow and marketing concerns rather than the frowsy music-hall stock character of Broadway.

In a clever nod to popular culture, Burton shoots this song sequence using the visual vocabulary and tropes of twenty-first-century television cooking shows. Mrs. Lovett addresses the camera in medium shot across a cooking island as she makes the eponymously worst pies in London, interspersing her explanation of ingredients and technique with comments to the in-studio audience of Sweeney Todd. Utensils and bowls are laid out in recognizable foreground mise-en-place; the oven, cooktop, and (filthy) prep station fill the rear wall. Close-ups of the pies intercut with exposition head shots. Rolling out "crusting" on the beat, Mrs. Lovett exudes the technical precision of Giada De Laurentiis and the feisty determination of Rachel Ray—without the smile. While the song is wholly Sondheim, the staging is pure Burton.[34] The synesthetic merger of visual and olfactory in the pie shop reflects and reinforces sensory confusion as well as engendering revulsion at the "greasy and gritty" pies, with insects crawling out from beneath the pastry. Little wonder that "no-one comes in even to inhale."

The cutaway to Anthony's wanderings and his discovery of Johanna (Jayne Wisener) functions as a companion piece to the Todd-Lovett meeting and counters "The Worst Pies" on every level. In contrast to the straight-on, eye-level framing of Mrs. Lovett in her murky, low-light pie shop, Johanna is introduced as a figure of absolute and nearly unattainable beauty, not unlike the barber's wife in Sweeney's flashback. She looks and sounds ethereal in low-angle shots of her in a high window, her highly operatic caged-bird song establishing her as utterly apart from all other characters in the film. The desaturated blue filter emphasizes actor Jayne Wisener's nearly transparent paleness and emphasizes her delicate features—without what Carter calls the "insomniac" eye makeup of Todd and Lovett. Her blue costume enhances this construction of beauty, and the fact that she is engaged in embroidery at her window evokes Tennyson's Lady of Shallot, also a figure of mythic and unattainable beauty. Johanna thus exemplifies the antithesis of Burke's sublime: she is small, light, and delicate. Her single high-pitched, twittering song lands on the ear an octave above Mrs. Lovett's sales pitch, again setting her apart and above the sublime fray of London. Like her mother, Johanna is insulated from the urban sublime by her beauty; also like her mother, she is imperiled by Judge Turpin, the authorized agent of contamination.

Comic Sublime: Pirelli

The Pirelli sequence, which commences the rising action in the plot, inserts a comic note into Burton's narrative of the urban sublime. Presented as spectacle within the grand, monochromatic cornucopia of St. Dunstan's Market, Pirelli's contest with Todd seems at first stroke to be mere comic interlude. Pirelli (Sacha Baron Cohen) appears on-screen as a commedia dell'arte Scaramouche: the conceited, dandified, sly figure who often disguises himself as a foreigner. Sondheim's Pirelli is a Black Irish thug hawking an Italian ethnic stereotype no more sophisticated than himself. Burton chose a skilled postmodern cultural mimic and chameleon of stereotypes in casting Sacha Baron Cohen. His Pirelli, played as a classical Scaramouche, emphasizes the duplicity and menace simmering in the preening, posturing Barber of Kings and employs the stage violence and petit Guignol Punch and Judy puppet-bashing that would be taken to excess in Grand Guignol. His entrance is greeted by a smooth crane-in from longshot to close-up, ending just below eye level. Pirelli is framed consistently from a low angle, emphasizing his "panache" and visual control of the scene as well as the menacing undertone of his condescension. His electric-blue costume provides the only color in the scene: he embodies the cruel, illusory beauty of the urban sublime—in distinct contrast to Johanna's ethereal blue gown and heavenly beauty.[35] The shot sequence alternates between low-angle shots of Pirelli singing and high-angle, over-the-shoulder reaction shots of the crowd, Sweeney and Mrs. Lovett, and Toby (Ed Sanders). The true urban sublime emerges as Pirelli strops his razor, hitting Toby's knuckles with every stroke. This offhand sadism, subordinate to his performance of self, illustrates Pirelli's nature as grounded in the creation of pain, danger, and terror—the troika of sensation that Burke credits to the sublime. That this terrorizing takes place as part of Pirelli's public performance of skill and ego reinforces all the more the threatening sublime lurking in humans under the guise of purported beauty. Only during the contest itself do the two barbers appear in frame together, separated by rack focus as camera-directed attention shifts from foreground to background, alternating between sublime and ridiculous.

The subsequent murder of Pirelli in Sweeney's "tonsorial parlor" inaugurates the Grand Guignol turn of the film and foregrounds the power of the urban sublime in this environment. Burton's Sweeney beats Pirelli to pulpy unconsciousness with a cast-iron teakettle, signaling the marriage of violence and domesticity that will reign over the remainder of the film.[36] The assault occurs in tight close-up, making the violence personal and immediate; an overhead shot reveals the pooling blood once the body stops moving. Literally and figuratively visceral, this attack forces synesthesia upon the viewer through both instrument and outcome. The filmic choice of teakettle as weapon ties this murder to the culinary arena downstairs and serves as a predictive metonym of Mrs. Lovett's locavore dream of "all them pies." With Pirelli's murder, the production line of barber chair to abattoir to oven to pie shop establishes a literal devolution from beauty industry to cannibalism as the ultimate expression of the urban sublime. In this world beauty—in whatever form—exists only to be consumed, either by the gaze, exemplified by Judge Turpin's peephole and Anthony's alleged "gandering," or by the machinery of the urban sublime that turns people into pies and customers into cannibals. Anything or anyone not of the city, as beauty clearly is not, will be consumed by it or consigned to an offal fate.

In response to the interruption of his planned assault on the judge, Sweeney's "Epiphany" projects his thwarted obsession outward, into the necropolis of his imagined London. This most traditionally staged musical number in Burton's film contains a nonsinging company who function as a crowd of potential client-victims to amplify the urban sublime. In his discussion of the passions belonging to society, Burke notes that "the passions belonging to the preservation of the individual turn wholly on pain and danger. . . . When men have suffered their imaginations to be long affected with any idea, it so wholly engrosses them as to shut out by degrees almost every other, and to break down every partition of the mind which would confine it."[37] As Sweeney articulates his vengeance quest, the montage follows him out of his shop to the dank and rainy streetscape, where his "engrossing" grief and anger seem to color the very environment. Burton's camera work fluidly moves around, above, and among the buildings as Sweeney asserts that "Not one man, no, / Nor ten men / Nor a hundred / Can assuage me." The blocking of this sequence retraces the animated labyrinthine traverse from dockside to Fleet Street; Burton employs this kind of visual quoting between early and late scenes throughout the film, suggesting an eternal recurrence of the same that grows ever more constricting. True to Burkean predictions, the obsession carries its own reward: "But the work waits / I'm alive at last / And I'm full of joy." His epiphany is one of blood lust, and the revelation is that he fully embraces the "work." This insight into the birth of a serial killer does not prompt parallel joy in most audiences, despite the triumphant ring of Sondheim's score. Sweeney ends on F-natural in the key of G, providing a tonal correlative to his queasiness-inducing sentiment. The visual sequence concludes with Sweeney coming to in the shop, suggesting that the "Epiphany" montage was a dream, fantasy, or seizure of sorts—most likely the latter, as the dream and fantasy sequences in the film occur in pastel or fully saturated color. Sweeney's revelation of his schadenfreude, made amid a real or imagined crowd, signals his declaration of war on the world. Thus the narrative shifts from pathos to terror as Sweeney shifts from object of audience sympathy to agent of the urban sublime. That we delight in this shift is testament to Burke's insights into the human condition.

Plenty of Flavors

Mrs. Lovett's own moment of entrepreneurial insight demands a corresponding scene of music and dance. These two paired scenes illustrate the embedded shift from seeing vengeance done to revenge served cold in a tasty pie—Burton's insertion of synesthesia as a means of justifying their "desperate measures." Both Sweeney's quest for justice and Mrs. Lovett's quest for profit are the kind of obsessions that Burke describes—forsaking all others and shirking all restraints. Utterly consuming.

Burton shoots "A Little Priest" on the pie-shop set, emphasizing Mrs. Lovett's practical solution to Sweeney's customer service problem. By returning to the culinary arena, the dark comedy of Sondheim's lyrics blends with the couple's survey of the available local ingredients (priest, poet, lawyer, grocer, Royal Marine, actor, fop, shepherd, politician, friar, actor). Sweeney and Mrs. Lovett commit to each other and their new enterprise as the idea grows measure by measure, while the twinning of Depp and Carter in looks, stature, and makeup allows for an uncanny doubling that reveals both their pleasure and the true horror of their plan. Curiously, Burke identifies just such a condition as "the effects of sympathy in the distresses of others": "Whenever we are formed by nature to any active purpose, the passion which animates us to it, is attended with delight, or a pleasure of some kind, let the subject matter be what it will; and as our Creator has designed we should be united by the bond of sympathy, he has strengthened that bond by a proportionable delight; and there most where our sympathy is most wanted, in the distresses of others . . . there is no spectacle we so eagerly pursue, as that of some uncommon and grievous calamity."[38] This sequence truly demonstrates what film can do that stage production cannot: the masterful editing by longtime Burton collaborator Chris Lebenzon tracks Mrs.

Lovett's stream of consciousness and Sweeney's slower uptake. In developing the business plan, Mrs. Lovett paces about the kitchen, met with head-on and tail-on shots that cut each time she has a new thought ("With the price of meat what it is / When you get / If you get it"). When Sweeney catches on ("Good, you got it") he moves into foreground framing, and they begin to finish each other's phrases and thoughts in a shot–reverse shot sequence. The 3/4 time denotes the circularity of this in-house food chain. The point of view cuts between interior and exterior positions with the multipaned window framing Sweeney and Mrs. Lovett inside the shop and wavy period glass distorting life outside on Fleet Street, respectively. As the recipe for Mrs. Lovett's gallimaufry grows, the pair take up metonymic utensils: a rolling pin for her, a cleaver for him in this *valse macabre*. The sequence ends with an eye-level exterior pullaway across the streetscape crowd that frames the couple and their devices (and desires) in the window like a sublime neo-capitalist coat of arms.

Synesthesia dominates the remainder of the story, as the sights and smells of the boutique-barber-bakeshop blend and mix with the sounds of Sondheim's score. Sensory muddling culminates in the duet reprise of "Johanna / City on Fire," in which Anthony's refrain, "I feel you . . . and one day I'll steal you," intercuts with Sweeney's bleak and sentimental dreams of his daughter. Burton crosscuts between Sweeney slicing throat after throat and Anthony wandering through the meatpacking district, graveyards, and docksides, marking a darkly comic connection between the two men's entrenchment in the urban sublime and contrast to their transcendent imaginings of Johanna's beauty. Within this montage of male desire and nostalgia, Mrs. Lovett and the Old Woman offer a dose of practicality and realism, respectively, the former marching up and down stairs to the cellar oven and the crone warning, Cassandra-like, of the "mischief" afoot in the smoky, evil-smelling city on fire. Thus sight, touch, smell, and taste converge in this audibly sentimental but visually distorted sequence shared by the principals, who will also converge in tragedy. Burton's decision to make these characters' visual narratives coterminous by intercutting, rather than successive as theater staging would demand, allows for sense mixing within and among the characters—and a sensory overload for spectators. One of the most powerful moments in the sequence, for example, occurs midway through the "Johanna" duet, as Sweeney absently cuts throats as he sings, "You stay, Johanna— / The way I've dreamed you are." Just at the rhyme "Oh, look, Johanna— / A star! / A shooting star!" jugular spray splatters the atelier window, creating a red starburst and linking the beauty of the melody to the pattern of the spray from a hideous killing. How are we to feel about this combination of visual and audio cues? Cinema audiences have been heard to gasp, students to chuckle, and bloggers to crow with delight. Clearly the counterintuitive blending of sensory stimuli, the collapsing of sublime and beautiful, is meant to unsettle us during what is arguably Sondheim's most beautiful blending of voices and melodies.[39]

Darkness at the End of the World

Just as Sondheim echoes act 1 songs in act 2 reprises, so Burton quotes himself through revisiting visual sequences and settings, changing only the dominant sense impression. The final number, which musically blends reprises of "Poor Thing" and "A Little Priest," takes place in a space recognizable as the oven room, which is laid out as a copy of the pie shop directly above it. The spatial orientation mirrors the two most-used interiors, Mrs. Lovett's shop and Sweeney's parlor, with the windows or oven occupying the back wall of each, respectively. The action has fallen to the lowest level, as the credit sequence predicted. The palette has darkened to extreme degrees, and the action occurs only by the chiaroscuro light of the bakery oven. As Mrs. Lovett explains about Lucy, and Sweeney realizes that he has murdered his beloved wife, the shot sequence follows that of the "Priest" number, relocated to the cellar. Dancing in front of the hell-mouth oven instead of the pie-shop window-on-the-world upstairs, Sweeney and Mrs. Lovett's waltz now truly becomes a *danse macabre.* The earlier "coat of arms" shot, with chopper and rolling pin as devices, now is answered by the gruesome image of the immolated Mrs. Lovett, framed by the oven door. Her auto-da-fé and its Grand Guignol effects reference the creation scene in the 1910 Edison *Frankenstein,* thus tying the visual narrative back to roots in the silent era in the penultimate scene.[40] Sweeney finds Lucy, is dispatched by Toby, and bleeds out in a pietà that fully embodies the qualities of Burke's sublime: "United by the bond of sympathy . . . there is no spectacle we so eagerly pursue, as that of some uncommon and grievous calamity." After this, the rest is silence.

Burton foregoes the overtly moralizing epilogue with which Sondheim closed the stage production. That is not to say that Burton's filmic construct is amoral. Rather, he ends with a fade to black that underscores the message that consuming passions, whether expressed as personal revenge or as cultural ravening, ultimately consume themselves. The black screen, held for a full twelve seconds before the credits roll, denotes the removal of sensory stimuli and the cessation of the synesthetic tumult that is the film. In the Renaissance, the confusion of senses resulted in the baroque, a polysemic, polyphonic celebration of human endeavor. By the nineteenth century of *Sweeney*'s setting, the late twentieth century of Sondheim's stage play and the twenty-first century of Burton's film, such ordered chaos would be regarded as ostentatious and self-indulgent. The sum of its provenance, Burton's *Sweeney Todd* ends in nothingness, without even a reassuring glimpse of Anthony and Johanna's escape. This refusal to allow beauty to reappear at the end the film offers a resolution that rests firmly on—and bows to—the nihilistic, fearful, awe-filled sublime. There is no near-miss to assuage our fears, no sneak peek at the future as in *Edward Scissorhands,* no Ed Wood to claim, "The next one will be better," no new century of light and color away from *Sleepy Hollow.* There is only Burkean darkness, "terrible in its own nature."

Notes

1. *Sweeney Todd: The Demon Barber of Fleet Street,* directed by Tim Burton, story by Christopher Bond, playscript and score by Stephen Sondheim and Harold Prince, screenplay by John Logan, performances by Johnny Depp, Helena Bonham Carter, Alan Rickman, Timothy Spall, Sacha Baron Cohen (Burbank, CA: Warner Bros., 2007; Dreamworks, 2008), DVD and extras.

2. See the Decker chapter in this volume for further discussion of Tim Burton's invocation of the German Expressionist style.

3. Scott McMillin, "Brecht and Sondheim: An Unholy Alliance," *The Brecht Yearbook* 30 (Pittsburgh: International Brecht Society, 2005), 232–332.

4. Edmund Burke, *A Philosophical Enquiry into the Origin of Our Ideas of the Sublime and Beautiful,* ed. Adam Phillips (New York: Oxford University Press, 1990), pt. 1, sec. 7, p. 36.

5. In this avoidance impulse, Burke anticipates to some degree Freud's pleasure principle.

6. Burke, *Philosophical Enquiry,* pt. 1, sec. 14, p. 42.

7. In conjunction with Burton's film release in 2007, Robert L. Mack edited and provided a useful introduction to this text. See Robert L. Mack, ed. and intro, *Sweeney Todd: The Demon Barber of Fleet Street* (New York: Oxford University Press, 2007); reprint of "The String of Pearls: A Romance," *People's Periodical and Family Library* (London) 7, no. 1 (1846). See also the thorough account of the story's genealogy in Benjamin Poore

and Kelly Jones, "Introduction to 'Swing Your Razor Wide . . . ': Sweeney Todd and Other (Neo-)Victorian Criminalities," *Neo-Victorian Studies* 2, no. 1 (Winter 2008/2009): 1–2.

8. Stephen Sondheim, "A Little Priest," in *Sweeney Todd, the Demon Barber of Fleet Street: A Musical Thriller,* piano/vocal score, rev. ed. (1997; repr., New York: Rilting Music and Warner Brothers Publications, 1999), 186. Song lyrics are drawn from this text rather than the publically available John Logan shooting script (December 21, 2006) for ease of documentation.

9. Burke, *Philosophical Enquiry,* pt. 1, sec. 15, p. 43.

10. Katherine Newey, "Attic Windows and Street Scenes: Victorian Images of the City on the Stage," *Victorian Literature and Culture* 25 no. 2 (1997): 253–56, quote on 254.

11. Vijay Mishra, *The Gothic Sublime* (Albany: State University of New York Press, 1994), and Jack Voller, *The Supernatural Sublime: The Metaphysics of Terror in Anglo-American Romanticism* (DeKalb: Northern Illinois University Press, 1994) were at the vanguard of a millennial surge in work on the sublime, the gothic, and intersections between the two. Both nostalgic and apocalyptic in tone, this trend sought to compare the respective fin de siècle conditions of social dis-ease and terror.

12. Richard J. Hand and Michael Wilson trace Grand Guignol theatrical spectacle to the opening of André Antoine's Théâtre Libre in the Pigalle district of Paris in 1887. Dedicated to dramatic naturalism, and drawing material directly from police files, Guignol dramas moved to an eponymous theater in 1897, where they were staged in an olio program ranging from "erotic drama to sex farce" with liberal doses of onstage horror-show amputations, gougings, slashings, acid burns, and decapitations. While the popularity of the form waned after World War II, the theater remained in business until 1961. See Hand and Wilson, *Grand Guignol: The French Theatre of Horror* (Exeter: University of Exeter Press, 2002), chap. 1.

13. Poore and Jones, "Introduction to 'Swing Your Razor Wide . . . ,'" 6.

14. John Logan's shooting script contains the plural characters of the company in the prologue and dialogue that was omitted in the final cut of the film.

15. Gérard Genette, *Palimpsestes: La littérature au second degré* (Paris: Seuil, 1982), 13.

16. "A Bloody Business," in *Sweeney Todd,* directed by Burton, DVD 2.

17. Such intertextuality within this provenance may define *Sweeney Todd* as a "pataphysical" film, as Alison McMahan has defined the strain she perceives in Burton's work prior to 2005. While *Sweeney* does share an "antiestablishment message" with much of his other work, that message is embedded in the paratext. A case could be made for the antiestablishment treatment of the conventions of the stage musical, along with the excesses of special effects in the "full blood" production. See McMahan, *The Films of Tim Burton* (New York: Continuum, 2005), 15–16.

18. "Musical Mayhem: Stephen Sondheim's *Sweeney Todd,*" supplementary visual essay, produced by Eric Young, edited by Paul Baker, in *Sweeney Todd,* directed by Burton, DVD 2.

19. "Press Conference," with Richard Zanuck, Timothy Spall, Tim Burton, Johnny

Depp, Helena Bonham Carter, and Alan Rickman, in *Sweeney Todd,* directed by Burton, DVD 2.

20. Burke, *Philosophical Enquiry,* pt. 3, sec. 27, p. 113; emphasis mine.

21. "Burton+Depp+Carter=Todd," DVD special feature, in *Sweeney Todd,* directed by Burton, DVD.

22. See the Olson chapter in this volume for further discussion of the symbolism and effects of Burton's use of color.

23. Sondheim, "No Place Like London," in *Sweeney Todd,* piano/vocal score, 31.

24. Kim Philpotts, writing in the *Sondheim Review,* notes that the world of the film has "a graphic quality rather like a three-dimensional Edward Gorey illustration." Philpotts, "His Dark Material: Tim Burton Remakes *Sweeney Todd* According to His Own Vision," *Sondheim Review* 14, no. 4 (Summer 2008): 15. Paul Puccio finds "images that evoke the moody paintings of John Atkinson Grimshaw and the chiaroscuro illustrations in late Dickens novels" in Ferretti's vision of London, the "city that launched a thousand horror movies." Puccio, "Ghosts of *Sweeney Todd:* Hauntings on Stage and Screen," *Sondheim Review* 15, no. 3 (Spring 2009): 13.

25. "Burton+Depp+Carter=Todd."

26. Peter Lowentrout makes a similar claim about Burton's construction of Gotham as a mélange of twentieth-century styles and references in the first *Batman* film. Lowentrout, "*Batman:* Winging through the Ruins of the American Baroque," *Extrapolation* 33, no. 1 (1992): 24–31.

27. Joshua Yumibe, *Moving Color: Early Film, Mass Culture, Modernism* (New Brunswick, NJ: Rutgers University Press, 2012), 137.

28. Siegfried Kracauer, *From Caligari to Hitler: A Psychological History of German Film,* ed. and intro. Leonardo Quaresima, rev. ed. (1947; repr., Princeton, NJ: Princeton University Press, 2004), 68.

29. Indeed, Laura U. Marks takes this episteme beyond sight and sound to smell, suggesting that "the proximal senses, touch, taste, and smell, are not only hedonic but may also be the senses of knowledge (epistemology), vehicles of beauty (aesthetics), and even media of ethics." Marks, "Thinking Multisensory Culture," *Paragraph: A Journal of Modern Critical Theory* 31, no. 2 (2008): 125. Much recent discussion of synesthesia and cinema tends toward phenomenological investigations of cinematic excess as a sensory experience among viewers. See, for example, Jennifer M. Barker, "Out of Sync, Out of Sight: Synesthesia and Film Spectacle," *Paragraph: A Journal of Modern Critical Theory* 31, no. 2 (2008): 236–51, in which she reads David Lynch's *Mulholland Drive* as "a way of being in space and time" (237). Such approaches sit on a razor's edge between philosophical analysis and emotional response.

30. Burke, *Philosophical Enquiry,* pt. 2, sec. 17, p. 75.

31. Burton's fascination with machines dates back to his earliest shorts. The cookie conveyor belt in *Edward Scissorhands* is the clearest antecedent to this machine, although the sequence also evokes the Rube Goldberg breakfast machine in *Pee-wee's Big Adven-*

ture. So many of these mechanisms facilitate disposal of obstacles (*Vincent, Beetlejuice, Sleepy Hollow*) or delivery of foodstuffs, whether edible or not (*Edward* and *Pee-wee*, as noted, as well as *Batman Returns, Nightmare Before Christmas, Charlie and the Chocolate Factory*).

32. Newey, "Attic Windows and Street Scenes," 253.

33. Poore and Jones note, however, the prettified casting of the principals to emphasize "ethereal, dark-eyed beauties with high cheekbones," and a goth/emo aesthetic familiar to Burton's fans. Poore and Jones, "Introduction to 'Swing Your Razor, High,'" 11. Carter contends that the dark, silent-cinema makeup reflects Burton's own insomniac aesthetic. Carter, "Burton+Depp+Carter=Todd."

34. Burton's body of work reveals a fascination with domestic processes and the mechanization of food preparation; this sequence joins the Rube Goldberg breakfast from *Pee-wee's Big Adventure*, the dining room scene from *Beetlejuice*, the heart-cookie machine from *Edward Scissorhands*, and the food production lines of *Charlie and the Chocolate Factory*. Taken together, these scenes suggest some issues with family dinners.

35. Colleen Atwood reports that Pirelli's costume was designed to make him look like a "rooster" by way of color and a corset. Atwood, "The Making of Sweeney Todd: The Demon Barber of Fleet Street," in *Sweeney Todd*, directed by Burton, DVD extra.

36. In Sondheim and Prince's production, Sweeney strangles Pirelli onstage.

37. Burke, *Philosophical Enquiry*, pt. 1, sec. 8, p. 37.

38. Ibid., pt. 1, sec. 14, p. 42.

39. Greg M. Smith defines such unsettling as the result of a blending of "mood-cues" that a film aesthetic delivers. Generally keyed to genre conventions, such mood-cues can trigger an emotional response in spectators; thus their mixing or counterintuitive use can provoke sense confusion not unlike synesthesia. See Smith, *Film Structure and the Emotion System* (New York: Cambridge University Press, 2003), 48–51.

40. *Frankenstein*, directed by J. Searle Dawley, produced by Thomas Edison, based on the novel by Mary Shelley (New York: Edison Manufacturing Company, 1910).

Tim Burton, Johnny Depp, and the Fantastic

Deborah Knight and George McKnight

Johnny Depp has appeared in eight films directed by Tim Burton, most recently *Dark Shadows* (2012). In this chapter we explore Burton's construction of fantastic worlds in the films that feature Depp as Burton's persona, or "second self." Our starting point is Tzvetan Todorov's conception of "the fantastic," as well as the two closely connected categories that Todorov designates as "the uncanny" and "the marvelous." We develop Todorov's ideas into an explanatory hypothesis for understanding Burton's filmmaking, especially with respect to the films starring Depp. We argue that Burton creates fictional worlds that are, in something like Todorov's sense, fantastic. The fantastic is not simply a means of expression for Burton but is deeply rooted in his thinking and is an integral part of his artistic practice. For Burton the fantastic is not a genre, as Todorov would claim, but a film mode, a mode of expression that Burton employs in conjunction with cinematic and narrative resources drawn from a variety of conventional film genres. Burton's use of the fantastic affects both his films' aesthetics and their narratives.

Central to this mode of expression are the characters performed by Depp as Burton's cinematic surrogate and persona. By drawing on Depp's mercurial acting talents, Burton raises questions about how such a persona might work as a realization and concretization of the filmmaker's vision. The Burton-Depp films often deal with characters who are artistic or skilled yet reclusive, idiosyncratic, or doubted by others. Contrasted to them are characters whose lives embody cultural norms and norms of social behavior, as well as characters in positions of authority or influence who reveal to us something of the dark underside of human psychology and self-interest. The films featuring Depp invariably involve characters whose beliefs and actions raise questions about established social practices and norms and about how we are to understand each specific fictional world and our experience of it. Burton's fantastic worlds raise questions about how our understanding is shaped as well as how our actions are limited both by what we take to be natural and by norms of individual and social behavior. In our conclusion we will suggest that certain of the Burton-Depp films exemplify what Todorov describes as "the uncanny," while some, notably *Alice in Wonderland* (2010), exemplify "the marvelous."

Todorov and the Fantastic

In *The Fantastic: A Structural Approach to a Literary Genre,* Todorov argues, "In a world which is indeed our world, the one we know, . . . there occurs an event which cannot be explained by the laws of this same familiar world. The person who experiences the event must opt for one of two possible solutions: either he is the victim of an illusion of the senses, or a product of the imagination—and the laws of the world then remain what they are; or else the event has indeed taken place; it is an integral part of reality—but then this reality is controlled by laws unknown to us."[1] Note that the world Todorov describes is "our world." For Todorov, the fantastic describes the uncertainty experienced by the reader or viewer when confronted with an apparently supernatural event. He locates the fantastic as "that median line" between what he terms "the uncanny" (an event where "the laws of the world then remain," and so one that is rationally explicable) and "the marvelous" (an event we would call supernatural because it cannot be explained by what he calls "the laws of nature").[2] For Todorov, "The fantastic occupies the duration of this uncertainty. Once we choose one answer or the other, we leave the fantastic for a neighboring genre, the uncanny or the marvelous. The fantastic is that hesitation experienced by a person who knows only the laws of nature, confronting an apparently supernatural event."[3]

According to Todorov, three conditions are required for a work to be an example of the fantastic:

> First, the text must oblige the reader to consider the world of the characters as a world of living persons and to hesitate between a natural or supernatural explanation of the events described. Second, this hesitation may also be experienced by a character; thus the reader's role is so to speak entrusted to a character, and at the same

> time the hesitation is represented, it becomes one of the themes of the work—in the case of naïve reading, the actual reader identifies himself with the character. Third, the reader must adopt a certain attitude with regard to the text: he will reject allegorical as well as "poetic" interpretations.[4]

The first condition emphasizes that the text obliges the reader or viewer to view the "world of the characters" not just as some imaginary or purely fictional construction but also as a "world of living persons" where the reader or viewer will hesitate between "a natural or supernatural explanation of the events described." Consequently, we should not discount the uncertainty or hesitation we experience as just part of a fictional world. While a character within the text may experience hesitation, that hesitation is "represented," as Todorov states in his second condition, and should be recognized as significant and not simply dismissed. Todorov makes a crucial distinction between the naïve reader who would identify with the character and the reader who should recognize the representation of a character's uncertainty or hesitation as one of the "themes" of the work. As he states, "*The reader's hesitation* is therefore the first condition of the fantastic."[5] The first two conditions are reiterated by the third, which insists we "reject" both allegorical and "poetic" interpretations of events in the text that would allow us to dismiss the hesitancy we experience. It is clear that Todorov calls for an astute reader or viewer who does not simply identify with the character within the text but who recognizes that to hesitate between a "natural or supernatural explanation of events" is central to recognizing that "the fantastic occupies the duration of this uncertainty."[6]

As Todorov argues, "At the story's end, the reader makes a decision even if the character does not; he opts for one solution or the other, and thereby emerges from the fantastic. If he decides that the laws of reality remain intact and permit an explanation of the phenomena described, we say that the work belongs to another genre: the uncanny. If, on the contrary, he decides that new laws of nature must be entertained to account for the phenomena, we enter the genre of the marvelous."[7]

Todorov maintains, however, that "it would be wrong to claim that the fantastic can exist only in a part of the work, for there are certain texts which sustain their ambiguity to the very end, i.e., even beyond the narrative itself."[8] Our contention is that Burton creates his fantastic cinematic worlds so as to generate and, more importantly, to maintain throughout each film this hesitation and uncertainty experienced by the viewer. As viewers, we experience this uncertainty both visually and when dealing with events, dramatic situations, and characters in his films, particularly in relation to Depp's characters, for it is invariably these characters that help to establish and maintain this experience of uncertainty for us.

Burton, the Transgeneric, and the Fantastic

Burton's films never fit easily into any single generic category. They are best described as transgeneric. They combine figures, locations, plot incidents, familiar story lines, and narrative structures drawn from a range of different film genres. The films with Depp are all based on established and familiar generic stories. His films develop quite clearly along conventional lines, and their generic features and structures are often familiar and transparent. *Edward Scissorhands* (1990) interweaves generic plotlines drawn from the horror film, family melodrama, and teen romance set within the drama of American suburban family life. *Ed Wood* (1994) employs conventions from the biopic to create a paradoxical form of "celebration" of the artistic career of real-life Hollywood filmmaker Ed Wood (1924–1978), famed for being one of the worst filmmakers of all time. Additionally, *Ed Wood* references B movies such as exploitation films, horror, and science fiction films. *Sleepy Hollow* (1999) combines the historical romance and the police procedural with the horror film. There is also an element of the fantasy film genre, given the supernatural figure of the Headless Horseman. *Charlie and the Chocolate Factory* (2005) is essentially a family melodrama, although it draws on the musical and the satiric aspects of comedy. *Corpse Bride* (2005) combines elements of the fantasy film, the romantic comedy, and the musical in a stop-motion animated film. *Sweeney Todd: The Demon Barber of Fleet Street* (2007) draws on the horror film, the musical, the revenge tragedy, and family melodrama. *Alice in Wonderland* is arguably a fantasy adventure film set within a family melodrama that draws on what Northrop Frye would call the "master genre" of romance.[9] The archetypal romance narrative features a character who must come to recognize that he or she is the chosen one, the one who must fulfill the role of the hero or heroine and complete a mission such as slaying the dragon (here the Jabberwocky) and returning the kingdom to its rightful ruler. The romance narrative conventionally takes the form of a physical journey or quest that is invariably also a spiritual journey of self-recognition or self-realization for the hero or heroine. *Dark Shadows* interweaves familiar features from the horror film and family melodrama within the narrative structure of a romantic comedy.

As demonstrated, Burton draws upon conventionalized features specific to more than one particular genre in his films, which is why we describe his filmmaking practice as transgeneric. The transgeneric character of Burton's films offers both a foundation and a structure for narrative action but also a basis for Depp's creation of characters. For example, *Edward Scissorhands* includes a number of distinctive yet integrated framing devices that unite characters and locations. The film's narrative is framed by the bedtime story about where snow comes from. Within that framework, there is another framing device—the familiar horror-film story line of the scientist who creates artificial life, a monster that the community will inevitably turn against, hunt down, and try to eliminate. Burton and Depp juxtapose the horror film's scientifically created figure, Edward (Johnny Depp), with the highly stylized American suburb that embodies routine, order, conformity, and a clear sense of community. Edward's antagonist is the conventionalized figure of the jealous boyfriend from the teen romance, who both discredits him and initiates violence. Finally, there is the improbable juxtaposition of the mansion on top of the hill that resembles the Gothic castle from horror films and the adjoining idealized suburb, the two bound together by the snow from Edward's ice sculptures that we see in the film's opening and closing scenes.

Our position is that, like suspense, melodrama, and social satire, the fantastic is a cinematic mode, not a film genre. Genres help to determine what a film's story line is, what sort of characters to expect, what story arcs are likely, and what would count as an appropriate narrative conclusion. Modes help to determine how story lines are realized. Suspense, melodrama, social satire, and the fantastic govern the affective tone of a film and thus shape viewers' emotional and cognitive responses to represented actions.[10] While Todorov has proposed that we treat the fantastic as a narrative genre, we think that the themes of uncertainty and hesitancy that he draws to our attention are actually features of the fantastic as a film mode. Hence our focus on Burton's ability to create "fantastic worlds": transgeneric fictional worlds in which the uncertainty and hesitancy that Todorov emphasizes are realized cinematically.

Burton creates a distinctive fantastic world for each film through its narrative construction and visual design. His fantastic worlds are pure cinematic constructs, although they do reference and draw initially on our knowledge of iconic if not stereotypical culturally received images of locations such as mid-twentieth-century American suburbia, Hollywood B movie productions of the 1950s, rural colonial New York state, the streets of London in the nineteenth century, and English country estates. In Burton's hands, the fantastic is a conjunction of transgeneric or hybrid generic elements, a variety of visual styles, and events and actions that produce for the viewer that period of uncertainty between the uncanny and the marvelous. In each film Burton creates a hyperreal world even though it is clearly never quite our natural world. It is a world somewhere between the world we conventionally understand as the real world and a fictional world that exists only within each particular film. It is an elaborate visual conceit of our world.

Framing Devices

Burton's films are self-enclosed aesthetic structures. One aspect of Burton's use of familiar story structures involves framing devices that draw the viewer's attention to the art and artifice of storytelling. As already noted in *Edward Scissorhands,* Burton's films are constructed so that the concluding shots refer the viewer back to the film's opening. These framing devices invariably feature not only parallel actions, visual details, and occasionally, lines of dialogue, but also corresponding or inverted tracking shots, close-ups, and upward or downward camera movements.

Ed Wood begins with a precredits scene where, amid thunder and lightning, the camera moves toward a house, then through a window and across the room to reveal a coffin lid opening. Criswell (Jeffrey Jones) emerges from the coffin, addresses us directly, then lies back down as the lid closes. The film ends with brief accounts of the principal characters and concludes with Criswell, who again lies back in a coffin as the lid closes and the camera tracks back across the room. *Sleepy Hollow* begins with a camera movement that includes a close-up of the clasping of hands by an unidentified couple, a couple who will be murdered. The film ends in New York with Ichabod (Johnny Depp) clasping Katrina's (Christina Ricci) hand when he helps her down from their carriage. *Charlie and the Chocolate Factory* begins with snow falling across the credits and images of the factory's smokestacks and mechanisms as a narrator's voice introduces Charlie (Freddie Highmore). The film ends with the camera pulling back from the window of Charlie's home to reveal snow falling from three containers suspended from an apparatus above the house. Finally, the narrator (Deep Roy) appears on screen, not merely speaking in voice-over as he did at the beginning. *Corpse Bride* begins with Victor (Johnny Depp, voice) sketching a butterfly under the credits, then releasing a butterfly that flies around the village, passing many of the characters that appear in the story. The film ends with butterflies appearing to emanate from Emily's (Helena Bonham Carter, voice) clothing. She then disappears amid hundreds of butterflies flying up to the moon.

Sweeney Todd begins with blood dripping, then running down beneath the credits and ends with Sweeney Todd's (Johnny Depp) blood running down onto his wife, Lucy's (Laura Michelle Kelly), face and onto the blood-covered floor. *Alice in Wonderland* opens with a downward camera movement away from the moon to London and across rooftops to reveal the window of a house, inside which a business meeting is going on where Lord Ascot (Tim Piggot-Smith) says to Alice's father (Marton Csokas), who is proposing trading posts in Rangoon, Bangkok, and Jakarta, "Charles, you have finally lost your senses." The film ends with a business meeting between Lord Ascot and Alice (Mia Wasikowska) where she proposes extending her father's plans "all the way to China." Lord Ascot slyly responds that if others made such a proposal to him, "I'd say you've lost your senses." *Dark Shadows*'s precredit sequence establishes as its framing device the narrative arc of romantic comedy. Romantic comedy conventionally develops around the initial separation of the right romantic couple, who must overcome various obstacles posed by family or jealous rivals until they are finally reunited. The precredit sequence also puts in place the historical detail that forms the backdrop for the plot action set in 1972. In this sequence the witch Angelique (Eva Green) becomes enraged when she sees Barnabas (Johnny Depp) and Josette (Bella Heathcote) kiss. She casts a spell that results in Josette's death and turns Barnabas into a vampire. The film's conclusion repeats the scene where Angelique sees Barnabas kiss Victoria/Josette, leading again to the spell where Victoria walks toward Widow's Peak to kill herself. Romantic comedy and the horror film are brought together when the right romantic couple is finally, though ironically, united in eternal love as Barnabas saves Victoria from death by turning her into a vampire.

Counterpositioning

Burton's films featuring Depp typically counterpose different fictional worlds, values, desires, or states of being or visually different sets of characters. Counterpositioning is invariably accompanied by very visible technical features, such as swift and unexpected camera movements that are unsettling as well as visually disorienting, shifts from scenes in darkness—or where color has been all but drained from the image—to scenes in bright, sometimes vibrant colors, contrasts between distinctly different locations, or by unexpected events. The effect is to produce incongruous juxtapositions both visually and dramatically, even though there is always a clear line of plot action. A clear plotline provides the viewer with immediate access to characters' actions, while counterpositioning confronts the viewer with differences from what we assume to be natural or from the norms and expectations of everyday life. Such counterpositioning invariably establishes contrasts and conflict that initially produce the uncertainty that Todorov argues is fundamental to the fantastic.

Edward Scissorhands counterposes the Gothic mansion and the American suburb, the artificial if not supernatural creation Edward, and the seemingly natural world of everyday suburban family life that is itself, of course, highly artificial. For his location, Burton chose a suburb where the bungalows were actually repainted in a range of pastel colors, notably blue, pink, yellow, purple, olive, orange, and green, to achieve a particular color-coordinated palette. Cars and clothing are also in pastel colors. Edward is the outsider, the immediate marker of difference, as signaled by his wild black hair, pale face with dark eyes and lips, clothes that range from black to gray to white, and of course, by his steely scissor hands. Because of his appearance, he is a counterpoint to both the everyday activities and the sensibility of American suburban life. Characters dressed predominantly in pastel colors are frequently set in relation to complementary colors in their surroundings, such as a woman wearing teal-colored trousers watering the grass who is framed in shot–counter shots by houses painted robin's-egg blue and pink. The skirt of a child is color-coordinated with the color of a house she cycles past. The Avon lady (Dianne Wiest), wearing a purple outfit and carrying a blue case, approaches a green house—identical in color to the one across the street—whose hallway is blue.

Ed Wood sets the aspirations and vision of an eccentric filmmaker against those of mainstream Hollywood film production. Filmmaking is a metaphor for fabricating a cinematic world, a world that in Ed Wood's case does not correspond to the norms of Hollywood film practice. Notoriously, Ed Wood's continuity editing was awful, his sets shook, and his main actors were stiff and unintentionally artificial. That said, *Ed Wood*'s key themes include image and identity, gender and sexual norms, sexual identity, sexual difference, and sexual preference. These issues are introduced initially through the Christine Jorgenson story and Ed's first film, *Glen or Glenda. Ed Wood* is replete with characters whose identities mark them as different from the conventional or the norm. Bunny (Bill Murray), who is openly gay, wants a sex-change operation. Ed Wood, though heterosexual, initially conceals his identity as a transvestite, especially from his girlfriend Dolores (Sarah Jessica Parker). Other characters take on identities that become their public personae, such as Bela Lugosi (Martin Landau), who is inseparable from his cinematic identity as Dracula; Vampira (Lisa Marie), who is visually inseparable from her identity, whether on-screen or off; and The Amazing Criswell, a psychic and television performer who ironically does not appear to have any psychic abilities. The conventional or norm in the film is represented by the mainstream studio system, by the Baptist Church and its members, and also by Dolores, who is finally unable to accept Ed as a transvestite. It would be easy for viewers to dismiss Ed, his filmmaking, and the film's various characters as aberrations, but *Ed Wood* is a celebration of differences and of the individual's determination to live by his or her own vision and identity. The character of Orson Welles (Vincent D'Onofrio) appears to speak for Burton when Welles tells Ed, "Visions are worth fighting for. Why spend your life making someone else's dreams?" After this encounter, Ed—still in women's clothing—again confronts his financial backers, the Baptist Church, and confidently completes his film. Conventional norms and expectations remain unresolved at the film's conclusion as it celebrates the determination of a unique filmmaker and individual identity. *Ed Wood* ends following an apparently successful premier of *Plan 9 from Outer Space.* Ed and Kathy (Patricia Arquette), who accepts Ed's predilection for dressing in women's clothing, leave for Las Vegas to be married.

Sleepy Hollow counterposes the natural and the supernatural, the city and the countryside, science and spells or charms, religion and witchcraft, rationality and psychotic desire. The investigative procedures of Ichabod Crane, the constable, whose methods are grounded in "reason and deduction," are set against the "spirit world" and the figure of the Headless Horseman (Christopher Walken) who appears from beneath the Tree of Death, which the constable describes as "a gateway between two worlds." Upon finding the grave containing the skeleton missing the skull, the constable's deductions that the Horseman "takes heads until his own is restored to him" and that "someone who controls him is of flesh and blood" are correct. The constable solves the mystery and reunites the Horseman and his skull. In doing so, however, he appears finally to abandon some of his initial "scientific techniques" (evidenced in his decision to burn his notebook), acknowledges the supernatural (he now carries with him the *Compendium of Spells, Charms, and Devices from the Spirit World,* which saves his life), and departs from Sleepy Hollow with Katrina (presumably to wed a witch). Though there is an explanation for the motivation that compels the Horseman to act, there is no a rational account of either the supernatural world or the Horseman regaining human form before he carries Lady Van Tassel (Miranda Richardson) under the Tree of Death. While there might be a rational explanation for the Horseman's actions, *Sleepy Hollow* arguably maintains the uncertainty between the natural and the supernatural for the viewer because, within the film, the supernatural cannot be explained by the laws of nature.

Burton's initial films with Depp are located in seemingly natural locations, while later films, such as *Charlie and the Chocolate Factory, Corpse Bride, Sweeney Todd,* and *Alice in Wonderland,* are increasingly denaturalized. In these later films, actors provide the voices for highly stylized animated figures, act against green screens, or are part of motion capture, and the films frequently involve computer-generated special effects, particularly elaborate decor and settings. *Charlie and the Chocolate Factory* acknowledges the potentially isolated and misanthropic life of the creative individual separated from family. It sets the reclusive figure of Willy Wonka (Johnny Depp), who has no contact with his father (Christopher Lee), against the three generations living literally side by side in Charlie's house and contrasts the uniformity of automata such as the Oompa-Loompas or squirrels with the freedom of the individual to choose. Charlie's initial decision to remain with his family rather than live a reclusive life in Wonka's factory is set against the greed and self-interest of others. The world inside the factory is a visually fantastic world because of its vibrant colors, its chocolate river and waterfall, its fudge mountain, its technological innovations and monumental spaces. The room the visitors first enter, with its edible meadow, its brilliantly colored candy gourds, mushrooms, and candy-cane plants, is a stark contrast to the dark, drab world outside the factory. Yet for all its visual wonder, the world inside Wonka's factory is devoid of life. In contrast to the factory, what is real or true is the diversity of human desires and feelings among the characters, ranging from the stereotypical affection of parents and children; Willy Wonka's indifference to various situations; the controlling nature of the Wonkas, both father and son; through to the sensitivity of Charlie. While there may finally be a form of reconciliation between Willy Wonka and his father in this family melodrama, the film's final images celebrate Willy Wonka's inclusion in Charlie's family. In the final scene, as the camera withdraws from the window, as the snow falls and the narrator appears telling us that "life had never been sweeter," the viewer is confronted with the film's artifice, which reminds us that the fantastic world of the factory and Charlie's family home are ideal yet purely imaginary worlds.

While *Corpse Bride* appears initially to be constructed around polarities and differences, the conceit of the film is that these are all clearly established only to be collapsed in the end. These apparent differences include the Land of the Living as opposed to the Land of the Dead, the world "upstairs" and the world beneath, the stylized full figures of the residents of the village and the skeletal and partial figures of the dead, the muted colors among the living and the bright colors in the Land of the Dead, the church ritual of the living and the ritual potions of the dead, Pastor Gallswells (Christopher Lee, voice) of the living and Elder Gutknecht (Michael Gough, voice) of the dead, and the fear of death of the living and the joyful play of the dead in the Land of the Living. The difference between the bleak, routine life of the living and the spontaneity of the dead is captured perfectly when the Land of the Dead gives quite literal expression to familiar terms and expressions from the Land of the Living, such as *headwaiter, half-pint, secondhand shop, dead end, take my breath away, dog scraps, play dead, picking up the pieces,* and *people are dying to get down here.*

Burton's *Corpse Bride* combines highly stylized animated figures that evoke a range of emotions within the familiar plotline of uniting the right romantic couple. It subverts convention insofar as the dead are more vital and animated than the living. Characters from the Land of the Dead often express the very feelings characters from the Land of the Living lack. The collapse of these polarities is brought about by the characters' expressions of emotion and by reunions, right actions, and the potion that will finally bring about the union of both couples. In one sense the characters are neither alive nor dead, as there is no distinction between how the characters from the different lands share and express feelings and desires. This is certainly borne out in the different reunions, whether between Victor and Scraps, between the dead husband and his wife, or between grandchild and grandfather. Victor's decision to do the right thing and marry Emily is reciprocated when she is moved emotionally after seeing Victoria's (Emily Watson, voice) face at the ceremony just as Victor is about to drink from the chalice, and this enables Victor to be reunited with Victoria. While the chalice containing the potion from the Land of the Dead is the apparent means by which the "right" couples are finally aligned, this is possible only because of Emily's empathy for Victoria and Lord Barkis's (Richard E. Grant, voice) egocentricity and condescension. Though *Corpse Bride* creates its fantastic worlds through obvious visual contrasts in color and the design of the characters, it is the poignancy of emotion we experience at the film's end that remains beyond Emily's supernatural disappearance.

Sweeney Todd offers a very dark vision of power and privilege, with a love story set against a background of sexual violation, the violation of social taboos, and revenge. It is a dark film in both its appearance and its subject matter. The most obvious techniques Burton uses to create this fantastic world include the computer-generated settings of London, a self-conscious use of lighting within the shots, extremely swift camera movements, and the use of desaturated color film stock so that colors are muted and all but drained from the image. The dark brickwork and cobblestone streets of bleak, working-class London are set against the mansion of Judge Turpin (Alan Rickman) and the enclosed garden across the street. Lighting on faces is used to give further expression to a character's feelings, with the face or part of the face frequently lit so it appears isolated within the darkness of the image. Very visible camera movements, such as an extremely high-speed movement that would appear to approximate Benjamin's walk to Fleet Street or the slow zoom out and backward from the window of Sweeney's shop to a view above London, draw the viewer's attention to the techniques that produce these images. Two scenes early in the film in which past incidents are recollected set their vibrant colors in direct contrast to the darkness of the scenes that frame them. Toward the end of the film, the scene by the sea is framed by the scene in the countryside, with both scenes in full color, framed by dark scenes set in London. Songs, particularly when Sweeney or Anthony (Jamie Campbell Bower) appears in street scenes, go completely unnoticed by passers-by, although Sweeney's song is finally revealed as his imagining.

While Sweeney Todd begins as a sympathetic character, the viewer is faced with his descent into a frenzy of violence in which he unknowingly kills his wife and Mrs. Lovett (Helena Bonham Carter). The abruptness of Sweeney Todd's death and the final, lingering shot of the bodies of him and his wife just before the camera slowly tracks back leave viewers dealing with their emotional responses to the ironies of these deaths. *Sweeney Todd* evokes the viewer's emotional responses through techniques that draw attention to themselves as aspects of the film's self-conscious visual construction of a world and through Depp's creation of a character driven by the darkest of human motivations. That same self-consciousness of design and visual style is evident in *Dark Shadows.* While the film has two temporal settings, its present-day (1972) perspective is made evident by the choice of music and the film's art direction. You know you are looking at a Tim Burton film: scenic elements are a consistent part of his films. There is always a stylized color palette, as well as stylized decor and settings, period costumes, and furniture. His films are too overtly designed for any part of the visual style to be an accident.

Dark Shadows combines a clear line of plot action with incongruous juxtapositions developed around idiosyncratic characters as well as familiar film genres. Given an audience's familiarity with generic story lines and conventions, there is, perhaps, less a cultivation of expectations of originality here than a playful engagement with the film's viewing audience. We are not surprised by spells, curses, ghostly figures, a witch, a werewolf—or a vampire, who, as part of the social satire, becomes an American capitalist. Barnabas, albeit cursed, is the embodiment of both moral evil and true love. He is emblematic of the film's counterpositioning: past and present, light and shadows, human characters and the undead, the lover's kiss and the lover's bite, the duality of blood as both life taking and life giving, death and immortal existence. The supernatural exists alongside the apparently natural. Much of the comedy, both visual and verbal, is developed not simply around Barnabas confronting the unfamiliar world of 1972 but around visually different sets of characters, states of being, and cultural references. For example, Alice Cooper appears as himself, seemingly unchanged since 1972. *Dark Shadows* exemplifies Burton's increasingly self-conscious cinematic construction of fantastic worlds. In the scene of passion, the burning of the factory, and Angelique's destruction of Collingwood, there is a consciousness that these are set pieces where blood can run down walls and where period decor, furniture, objects, statuary, and portraits are film sets being destroyed as visual spectacle. The film's final shot of Dr. Hoffman (Helena Bonham Carter) playfully suggests a possible film sequel.

Persona, Film Persona, and Star Persona

The term *persona* has its origins in the mask worn by actors in ancient Greek tragedy that was thought to function as a resonating device for the actor's voice and to evoke emotions or affirm beliefs among the audience. In Latin, *persona* means a mask and later came to refer to a character played by an actor. It can be linked to the Italian *personare,* meaning to sound through. The term *persona,* then, carries the connotation of giving voice to the work of a dramatist. It is identified historically with theater and literature and as a consequence of its basis in narrative forms can be applied to discussions of other narrative media, such as filmmaking. Our use of the term, which we adapt from Wayne C. Booth's discussion of a narrator, an implied author, and a reliable narrator, is closer to the idea of "the author's second self."[11] We argue that what Booth writes about the "reliable narrator" in a work of literary fiction applies also to the relationship between Depp's characters and Burton's fictional worlds: "The art of constructing reliable narrators is largely that of mastering all of oneself in order to project the persona, the second self, that really belongs in the book."[12] Booth argues that "the 'implied author' chooses, consciously or unconsciously, what we read; we infer him as an ideal, literary version of the real man; he is the sum of his own choices."[13] Booth acknowledges the difficulties posed by a number of closely related terms when he writes about a narrator or implied author: "We have no terms either for this created 'second self' or for our relationship with him. None of our terms for the various aspects of a narrator are quite accurate. 'Persona,' 'mask,' and 'narrator' are sometimes used."[14] Referring to the idea of a detectable presence of an author in a literary work, Booth writes, "Whether we call this implied author an 'official scribe,' or adopt a term recently revived by Kathleen Tillotson—the author's 'second self'—it is clear that the picture the reader gets of this presence is one of the author's most important effects."[15]

Here we highlight the idea of this "presence" as one of "the author's most important effects," an effect brought about by a cause or agent. While this presence in a work of literature can be called an "implied author," in films there is both a filmmaker and an actor who combine to create a performance, a "presence," within the work. Writing about Booth's term *persona,* Gareth Griffiths supports the idea that "recognizing the persona is therefore central to the act of effective reading since the persona represents the sum of all the author's choices in a realized and more complete self as 'artist.'"[16]

The Depp Characters: Three Patterns

Three interrelated patterns appear across Burton's films featuring Depp. While Depp is not the central protagonist in all of these films, his recurring presence supports the argument that he functions as Burton's persona or surrogate. First, there is a distinctive feature about Depp's characters, whether central or secondary, that makes these figures unique, noticeably different, and often at odds with the world around them. They are either artistic or have a special skill—be they sculptor, filmmaker, a constable invested in the scientific investigation of a crime, the creator of chocolates, a young man who both sketches and plays the piano, a barber who is "a proper artist with a knife," or a hatter. Barnabas's distinctive feature is that he has been cursed and now exists as a vampire. In addition, most have been subject to a fate that has befallen them, such as Edward Scissorhands, Willy Wonka, Sweeney Todd, and Barnabas, and so their character and actions are often a consequence of things that have happened to them at the hands of others.

Second, these films all deal with outsiders confronting a new set of circumstances or a world different from their own where they must deal with some form of authority and/or where they face a challenge or a test where they must prove themselves. These characters, often considered oddities by those around them, are markedly different from others. While they are doubted, or their abilities are scorned, or they have been victimized, most never finally lose a unique self-confidence. Edward Scissorhands's skills set him apart from his neighbors. Ed Wood is a filmmaker who continues to make films even though his work is scorned by studio producers. Charlie enters Willy Wonka's factory in the shadow of the other, more forceful children but finally reunites Willy with his father. Constable Crane arrives at Sleepy Hollow confident about his "scientific techniques" and solves the mystery, although his methods are doubted by his superiors and by the villagers. Benjamin Barber/Sweeney Todd returns to London a victim of Turpin's authority and injustices, although finally he is the victim of his own desire for revenge. Victor Van Dort, initially shy and clumsy, is taken to the Land of the Dead but in the final scenes he is decisive and agile in his fight with Lord Barkis. Alice enters Underland uncertain whether she is the "right Alice" but finally realizes her identity as the true champion by killing the Jabberwocky and restoring the White Queen (Anne Hathaway) to her throne. Unearthed in 1972, Barnabas becomes determined to restore the family business to its former glory and to be united with Victoria/Josette. But he must again face Angelique, whom he finally rejects as someone who cannot love, saying to her, "That is your curse."

Third, these films feature some form of surrogate parental relationship that often involves either parental authority or the death or separation from a father or father figure. In this context, the idea of Depp as Burton's cinematic persona or surrogate is noteworthy in relation to Burton's ongoing concern with what he describes in an online *Dark Shadows* trailer, "Strange Family," as "the workings of the melodrama of a family."[17] Edward is separated from his father-creator, who dies before he can replace Edward's scissor hands. Ed Wood's initial inspirational figure, Bela Lugosi, dies yet remains central to *Plan 9 from Outer Space,* while Orson Welles becomes the new inspiration for Ed to complete his film. Constable Crane recalls the cruelty of his own father, who killed Ichabod's mother, yet himself becomes the father figure for young Masbath (Marc Pickering) after the Horseman kills the boy's father. Willy Wonka is estranged from his father and has withdrawn into a world of his own creation. Benjamin/Sweeney becomes a father figure both to Anthony—helping him form a plan to rescue Johanna (Jayne Wisener), self-serving as it may be—and to Toby (Ed Sanders), who will finally kill him. Victor and Victoria face authority in the form of their parents as well as Pastor Gallswells. Alice, who is unwilling to enter a marriage arranged by her mother, finally refuses the engagement. Instead, with the help of Lord Ascot, she extends her late father's dream of establishing trade routes to the Far East. Angelique kills Barnabas's parents. Victoria's parents send her away. David is deserted by his father, Roger (Jonny Lee Miller), although Barnabas fulfills the role of surrogate parent by saving him from the falling mirror ball and is rewarded when David releases him from the tomb in which Angelique had chained him.

Depp's Performances

We argue that Burton's presence is visible not only through the recurring thematic concerns and characteristic features of his cinematic style but particularly through the recurrence of Depp's performances. While Booth's "implied author" is seen as an imaginary figure distinct from the actual author (who might create different personae across different works), the collaboration between Burton and Depp and the recurrence of consistent patterns within these films support our contention that Depp functions as Burton's "second self." We take Booth's view to be that a form of reciprocal relationship between the creator and a "second self" can exist when a fictional character functions as a surrogate or voice speaking on behalf of an author. Such a persona can be a means of objectifying, within a particular work of art, the vision of a creative artist. Burton has consistently relied on

Depp's performances both to help construct and in fact to legitimate his films' distinctive fictional worlds. He has chosen to work collaboratively with Depp, allowing Depp to realize precise and idiosyncratic characters that keep viewers engaged and are always central to the film's moral framework. The irony and satire in these films are never at the expense of Depp's characters.

Consideration of Depp as persona or surrogate for Burton inevitably involves questions of artistic intention, but this should not be thought of as straightforwardly reverting to Burton's autobiography or psychology. Both Burton and Depp frequently cite their own youthful personal experiences as contributing factors in various films, beginning with *Edward Scissorhands* and running right through to *Dark Shadows*. That said, autobiographical detail does not in itself explain or account for the particular cinematic worlds realized in each film. As Griffiths says, filmic personae represent "the sum of all the author's choices," and so both Burton's films and Depp's roles must be considered as artistic and aesthetic constructs. The questions then would be, how does Depp, through the various characters he portrays, function as persona or surrogate for Burton, and how do these roles contribute to what we describe as Burton's fantastic fictional worlds, helping to concretize the vision of the filmmaker?

Our view is that Depp, certainly at this point in his career, is a star and, for better or worse, a celebrity. But he does not possess the more conventional, straightforward, and consistent public star persona of the sort we associate with George Clooney or Brad Pitt. If anything, Depp is chameleon-like in his ability to become his characters. This is the main feature of his acting style that makes him a perfect match for Burton's conception of the work. Burton is a visual artist whose art is drawn in the realm of the fantastic. His pen, his instrument, is often Depp, although Depp is an active participant. He helps Burton realize the fantastic, film by film. Depp helps sustain the uncertainty that is an essential feature of Burton's fantastic fictional worlds. At the center of these worlds are the singular characterizations developed by and around Depp. Burton's stamp on a work is expressed, in part, through Depp's characterizations. What Burton achieves by concretizing his fantastic worlds, Depp achieves through his remarkable ability to create distinctive characters across this range of films. Depp brings himself into alignment with Burton's visual design of each film by transforming himself physically through makeup, hair, costume, voice, accent, demeanor, and hand gestures. The almost unwavering optimism of Ed Wood, the seriousness and single-mindedness of Constable Crane, the dismissiveness of Willy Wonka, and the grim determination of the unsmiling Sweeney Todd are understood in large measure not only through Depp's creation of a voice for these characters but through stylized yet subtle facial expressions. Examples include the innocence and vulnerability expressed by Edward Scissorhands's eyes, the empty smile of Willy Wonka, the tilt of the head and slow closing of the eyes of Sweeney Todd, the determined smile of Ed Wood, and the certainty of Constable Crane. Through such often-minimal yet telling expressions, Depp embodies Burton's unique, dramatic, distinctive storytelling ability. This vital, creative, collaborative persona, performed by Depp, personifies and consolidates Burton's artistic vision within each film's narrative.

Depp is a realizer of the fantastic in his films with Burton. This is not to say that cinematography, settings, color, costumes, makeup, and computer-generated visual effects do not make a significant contribution. But Depp is the catalyst that brings both the technical aspects of the film and the creation and performance of a central character together as a unified whole. It doesn't matter if the character he portrays is an artificial creation such as Edward Scissorhands, a "historical" character such as Ed Wood, a rational character such as Constable Crane, an eccentric character such as Willie Wonka, a dark and violent character such as Sweeney Todd, or an extravagant character such as the Mad Hatter. Regardless of whether Depp's character is the protagonist, such as Edward Scissorhands or Ed Wood, or a major secondary character, such as the Hatter, he is the gravitational center around which these narratives orbit. His roles give the whole narrative structure not only a center but—whether for good or evil—a moral center.

Concluding Thoughts on the Fantastic, the Uncanny, and the Marvelous

As we reinterpret Todorov's main argument, the fantastic is a film mode, not a genre, and for that matter, so too are the uncanny and the marvelous. Viewers enter into a film constructed in the mode of the fantastic. As the narrative develops, the question is how, and whether, the fantastic will resolve itself into either the uncanny or the marvelous. The viewer is initially undecided as to whether depicted events can be explained rationally, which is to say, scientifically, according to recognized physical laws of cause and effect. If that uncertainty is resolved positively, then the viewer concludes that the work falls into the category of the uncanny, where, after all, the "laws of reality remain intact." If that uncertainty comes out negatively, then the work falls into the category of the marvelous, where "new laws of nature must be entertained." Todorov also admits that some fantastic narratives may not resolve one way or the other, which means that the status of the fantastic carries over even after the story has ended.

The question, then, is, how do the Burton-Depp films resolve the impasse represented by the fantastic? Several of these films do seem to resolve themselves into the category of the uncanny. As we interpret Todorov, the uncanny is not restricted to narratives where there is an obvious solution to be provided by our current understanding of science, but rather can involve a narrative resolution that can be given a scientifically plausible explanation. *Ed Wood* is probably the most obvious candidate for this category. We would add *Edward Scissorhands,* assuming we accept that the inventor (Vincent Price) could create a being such as Edward. The characters of Willie Wonka and Sweeney Todd also seem to be figures of the uncanny. Although the cinematic worlds in which they figure are fantastic, there is a plausible causal story to explain how they have come to be what they are and how they have acted as they have.

What, then, of the marvelous? Todorov argues that new laws must be entertained to account for the marvelous. We propose *Sleepy Hollow, Corpse Bride, Alice in Wonderland,* and *Dark Shadows* as examples of films that move from the fantastic to the marvelous. The most problematic is *Sleepy Hollow.* Is there a clear decision about whether or not the events presented, or the figure of the Headless Horseman, work within the bounds of any conceivable scientific explanation? While *Sleepy Hollow* initially encourages uncertainty regarding the nature of the Horseman, in the end it does seem to compel audiences to accept a view of the natural that is considerably different from the scientific one. While it is just possible to imagine something like a scientific or rational explanation of characters such as Edward Scissorhands or Sweeney Todd, characters such as the Headless Horseman, Emily, Barnabas, the Blue Caterpillar Absolem (Alan Rickman, voice), and the Hatter depart from the "laws of nature" we either know or could easily imagine.

Alice in Wonderland and the Marvelous

In *Alice,* we literally fall into the fantastic world when Alice falls down the rabbit hole. Once she reaches Underland, the question is how to persuade her that she is the real Alice. There are several major forces in Underworld, namely the Red Queen (Helena Bonham Carter), the White Queen, Alice, and the Blue Caterpillar, but more importantly, the Hatter. The Blue Caterpillar and the Hatter represent the moral center of *Alice in Wonderland* and are the key figures guiding Alice to her realization that she must become the White Queen's true champion on the Frabjous Day. While Alice is the central protagonist of the film, the Hatter is the realizer of the fantastic. There is a level of creative detail around the Hatter that contributes a wealth of visual information and a range of moods and emotions to Burton's fantastic cinematic world. These include the Hatter's wild orange hair and popping eyes; his skin color; the gap between his teeth; his changes in voice and accent, mood, and emotion; his coat; his ability to create a dress for the suddenly shrunken Alice in the teapot; the hats he creates for the Red Queen—all rejected, of course; his own hat, which seems to have its own existence; his wrist pincushion, from which he draws a pin to stab Stayne (Crispin Glover) during the battle; and of course, his dance—the "futterwacken." Burton and Depp's realization of the Hatter is both emblematic of the fantastic and a moral center of the film. The Hatter is completely aware of the moral world in which he exists. Arguably, the evil of the Red Queen has contributed to his madness. Understanding that the White Queen, the good queen, needs a champion, he volunteers, although he is not chosen. But when the Jabberwocky is killed, he does not in turn kill the Red Queen's defender, Stayne, the knave of hearts.

The White Queen would not have found her true champion except through the actions of the Hatter and Alice's attempts to defend him. Alice is, of course, the true champion, even though nearly everyone in the court of the White Queen steps forward for this deadly task on the Frabjous Day. As the Jabberwocky approaches, the Hatter gives Alice the emotional support she needs in order to take on her role as champion. She reminds herself that, like her father, she has often thought of six impossible things before breakfast. "Six impossible things. That is an excellent practice," the Hatter says to her. We see not only the Hatter's consistent concern and support for Alice but her reciprocation of that concern. Both Alice and the Hatter, who gets much clearer about his hopes and goals as the narrative progresses, discover their "true" selves. The Red Queen fails utterly to achieve any self-realization and is astonished that Stayne would try to kill her. While the White Queen is the true monarch, the Hatter is the moral compass of Underland. On the basis of the Hatter's actions, and Alice's responses to them, the proper resolution finally occurs. The Hatter, although not the champion, is the character around which the "reality" of Underland revolves. Although the Hatter suggests that Alice might remain in Underland, she must leave and return to "reality," where she declines the offer of engagement, dances her version of the Hatter's "futterwacken," and will fulfill the dream of her father—although it is not for nothing that the final person from Underland to whom Alice says goodbye is the Hatter.

We have argued that the characters performed by Johnny Depp in his various roles in Tim Burton's films serve as visual realizers of Burton's filmic persona, a persona that Depp has actively contributed to. A filmic persona differs from a literary persona when an actor collaborates with the film director to realize that role. Burton has gravitated, in his films starring Depp, toward fantastic worlds and fantastic narrative scenarios of the sort anticipated by Todorov. Todorov's notions of the fantastic, the uncanny, and the marvelous, adapted as we have suggested, provide a range of interpretative resources. So too does the idea of a narrative persona, an idea developed by Wayne C. Booth in the context of literary fiction, but one that we have adapted to apply to Depp's performance of a range of characters in the oeuvre of Burton as a filmmaker.

Notes

Particular thanks to Jennifer McMahon, who is always a pleasure to work with, for her enthusiasm for this project and her excellent suggestions about our essay.

1. Tzvetan Todorov, *The Fantastic: A Structural Approach to a Literary Genre* (Ithaca, NY: Cornell University Press, 1975), 25.

2. Ibid., 25, 51.

3. Ibid., 25.

4. Ibid., 33.

5. Ibid., 31; italics in the original.

6. Ibid., 25.

7. Ibid., 41.

8. Ibid., 43.

9. Northrop Frye, *Anatomy of Criticism* (Princeton, NJ: Princeton University Press, 1957), 33–67.

10. We are all familiar with modes in the cinema, although we may not recognize them as such. Some of the most familiar modes are suspense, romance (in the sense of romantic love), melodrama, mystery, parody, comedy (humor), and social satire. A plotline developed around the right romantic couple, for example, is a staple of most film genres. Modes contribute to the development of dominant plotlines and help to establish a film's tone and perspective, be it dramatic, comedic, or satiric. Modes are not

exclusive to a particular genre nor are they mutually exclusive within a film, as they can complement one another within a dominant generic story line. We find social satire, romance, and suspense in *Edward Scissorhands,* where suspense is developed toward the conclusion of the film around Edward's fate—but the emphasis on Edward's fate does not make this an example of the suspense thriller. Comedy is central to Burton's films featuring Depp even when the dominant generic plotline is drawn from the horror genre. Mystery is developed around the identity of the beggar woman Lucy, whose murder leads to Sweeney Todd's own murder. Burton's transgeneric films frequently involve the heightened dramatic and emotional situations characteristic of melodrama developed around relationships and conflicts within the family.

11. Wayne C. Booth, *The Rhetoric of Fiction,* 2nd ed. (Chicago: University of Chicago Press, 1983), 71.

12. Ibid, 83.

13. Ibid., 74–75.

14. Ibid., 73.

15. Ibid., 71.

16. Gareth Griffiths, "Persona," in *The Routledge Dictionary of Literary Terms,* ed. Peter Childs and Roger Fowler (London: Routledge, 2006), 170–71.

17. The trailer "Dark Shadows: The Official Strange Family Featurette" can be found at http://www.youtube.com/watch?v=xbzeqt0vBEs.

It's Uncanny

Death in Tim Burton's Corpus

Jennifer L. McMahon

For a quarter of a century, Tim Burton has captivated audiences with his offbeat creations. Known for his macabre style and predisposition for the fantastic, Burton consistently delights viewers with his strange settings and peculiar characters. As anyone acquainted with Burton's corpus is aware, his work is often characterized as macabre because it features death so prominently. Whether blatantly, through the presence of characters that personify death, or merely through a character's encounter with mortality, Burton consistently reminds audiences of their finitude. Indeed, he reinstates the long-standing artistic tradition of memento mori, the tradition of incorporating explicit symbols of mortality into works of art and literature, by having death figure so blatantly in his works. While Burton has received critical and popular acclaim for his dark arts, works of existentialism with a similar emphasis often strike general audiences as morbid and depressing. For this reason, it can be argued that Burton has had more success conveying the unpalatable truth of human finitude to the general public than some of existentialism's most notable proponents.

This essay will examine the existential theme of mortality in Burton's cinematic corpus and argue that his works help audiences toward the existential goal of authenticity, namely, honest awareness of the human condition. Burton's works foster authenticity by helping audiences achieve greater awareness of their mortality, awareness that can prompt various positive effects, including heightened existential engagement and greater moral responsibility. They produce heightened awareness of mortality largely by generating the experience of the uncanny, particularly a dislocating feeling of generalized anxiety. To the extent Burton's uncanny works can help engender existential authenticity, they serve as much more than entertaining fictions.

The Essence of the Uncanny

If Burton's principal means of promoting heightened awareness of mortality is the uncanny, then it is necessary to examine this concept in detail before engaging in an analysis of specific works in his corpus. Arguably, the most well-known account of the uncanny is found in Sigmund Freud's essay of the same name, published in 1919. Though this work has shaped the modern understanding of the uncanny, Freud admits he is moving outside his area of expertise in dealing with the concept. He states, "Only rarely does the psychologist feel impelled to engage in aesthetic investigations . . . relating to the qualities of our feeling. . . . Yet now and then . . . he has to take an interest in a particular area of aesthetics . . . [when it] has been neglected in the specialist literature. One such is the uncanny."[1] As Freud indicates, he feels compelled to investigate the uncanny because philosophers have not paid sufficient attention to it.

Freud asserts that the uncanny, or *unheimliche,* refers primarily to a type of feeling. He notes that the term is also used to refer to causes sufficient to generate the feeling and that as a result it is "not always used in a clearly definable sense." Despite inconsistent usage of the term, Freud asserts that the uncanny has "a specific affective nucleus" and "belongs to the realm of the frightening." With respect to the core components of the uncanny, Freud specifies that the uncanny "evokes fear and dread," "repulsion and distress," and also feelings of "helplessness." What distinguishes the uncanny from other species of the frightening is the element of familiarity evident in it. Indeed, Freud's etymological analysis of the term explains that *unheimliche* derives from *heimliche,* which translates to "familiar" or "related to the home." As Freud states, "The uncanny is that species of the frightening that goes back to what was once well known," continuing, "the uncanny is actually nothing new or strange, but something that was long familiar to the psyche and was estranged from it only through being repressed." Here Freud makes another important point about the uncanny. In addition to involving the familiar, the uncanny also involves repression. Freud states, "The frightening element [in the uncanny] is something that has been repressed [but] now returns."[2] Thus the uncanny is an affective response generated by the revelation of something once familiar but repressed or forgotten, and to the extent it involves awareness of repressed information, it has a cognitive component.

Freud maintains that there are a variety of catalysts for the feeling of the uncanny. They include solitude, darkness, doubles (both in the sense of duplicate individuals and in duplicated experiences), and most important for present purposes, death. These items conjure feelings of the uncanny because they refer to, and thereby prompt recollection of, one of the two basic causes Freud identifies for the uncanny: repressed complexes and surmounted beliefs.[3] Indeed, to the extent that Freud identifies two distinct causes for the uncanny, he effectively generates two distinct types of the uncanny: that generated by the revelation of repressed content and that generated by allusion to surmounted beliefs. In addition, Freud asserts that these two types of the uncanny can be generated in two different ways. Specifically, he states that we can "distinguish between the uncanny one knows from experience and the uncanny one only . . . reads about." Here Freud differentiates between experiences of the uncanny prompted by real events and those generated by fiction. He asserts that we should differentiate these different modes of uncanny experience because there is an "important and psychologically significant distinction" between the two, including the fact that authors of fiction "can intensify and multiply [the uncanny] far beyond what is feasible in normal experience." Freud also notes that the species of the uncanny generated by repressed complexes, while frequently more powerful, is also "more resistant" to generation in actual life, presumably due to psychological resistance.[4] Perhaps this is part of the reason why Freud goes on to assert that "fiction affords possibilities for a sense of the uncanny that would not be available in real life" and why he presents a literary work, Ernst Theodor Wilhelm Hoffman's "The Sandman" (1816), as his paradigmatic example of the uncanny.[5]

As Hoffman's title suggests, the central figure in the story is the fabled Sandman, whose potential appearance encourages children to go to sleep for fear that staying awake will prompt him to "tea[r] out [their] eyes." Though elements other than the Sandman serve to heighten the story's disarming effect, Freud attributes its capacity to elicit the uncanny primarily to the appearance of the "demon-optician" and his ability to symbolically represent, and thereby resurrect, readers' repressed anxiety regarding castration.[6] Perhaps not surprisingly, it is this explanation, and Freud's general tendency to associate the uncanny, among other things, with repressed sexual complexes, that has led to criticism of his account. For example, Hélène Cixous asserts that while castration anxiety is real, it is likely the case that in Hoffman's story "castration . . . refers to a secret more profound" than emasculation, namely, our primal fear of death.[7] Likewise, Nicholas Royle asserts that Freud does "strange violence" to the subject of the uncanny by attributing it to an erotic cause.[8] Diane Jonte-Pace agrees, stating, "Freud's quick substitution of sex for death [as a basis for the uncanny] stands out as a troubling distortion."[9] Interestingly, while Freud himself admits the possibility of alternative readings of Hoffman's story, readings that interpret eyes not as symbolic substitutes for the phallus but as symbols of an even more primal vulnerability, he concludes, "I would not advise . . . the contention that fear for the eyes [represents] something independent of the castration complex." Thus, while Freud acknowledges that "to many people the acme of the uncanny is represented by anything to do with death" and even confesses that there is a "link between the uncanny and death," he ultimately resists attributing the uncanny to it. While Freud's association of the uncanny principally with sexual complexes is perhaps a function of the cases he examines, it could also be expressive of his own unconscious resistance to investigating alternative objects of repression, particularly mortality. After all, Freud admits that humans are as "unreceptive as ever . . . to the idea of [their] own mortality."[10] Perhaps he too would rather leave the connection between death and the uncanny without a full autopsy.

An Alternative Account of the Uncanny

In light of Freud's limited examination of the relation between death and the uncanny, it appears that in order to fully explore this link and thereby develop a complete understanding of the uncanny, one needs to go beyond Freud. Of course, one can find important commentary on the uncanny in the works of other prominent psychological theorists, including, for example, Otto Rank (1884–1939). However, within the context of the philosophical canon, one also finds explicit discussion of the uncanny, and importantly, its connection to death, in the work of existentialist philosopher Martin Heidegger (1889–1976).[11] Though Heidegger makes reference to the uncanny in several essays, his most sustained discussion of the concept is found in his major work, *Being and Time* (1927).

Whereas the uncanny is the focus of Freud's essay of the same name, it is not the focus of *Being and Time*. Instead, Heidegger's principle objective is to articulate the nature and meaning of a broader term: being. While this term may sound indefinite or call to mind an abstract universal, Heidegger is clear that the being he is concerned with is human being, or what he calls *Da-sein*.[12] According to Heidegger, formal philosophical inquiry into the nature and meaning of human being is important because a clear understanding of the nature and meaning of human being is not immediately present in, nor readily available to, most individuals but is necessary if we seek to understand ourselves and achieve our potential.

Heidegger offers a variety of important claims regarding the nature of human being in *Being and Time*. As the title suggests, Heidegger's major point is that human being is fundamentally temporal: our being is time. Another critical assertion is that our time is finite. We are beings who die. As Heidegger explains, human being has various "constitutive factors" that comprise what he calls our "facticity." These features include not only temporality and finitude but also worldliness and sociality. Specifically, we are beings who exist in the world, in time, are fundamentally social, and ultimately die. Moreover, we are beings characterized by concern for being, or what Heidegger calls "care." What is interesting about this latter claim is the fact that while Heidegger asserts that humans are entities who care about being, he likewise asserts that we "initially and for the most part liv[e] in deficient modes of concern" or "indifference." Rather than direct themselves to the question of being, most people instead try to "fle[e] from it and . . . forge[t] it."[13]

This odd behavior invites the question, Why would a being that is concerned about its being seek to flee that being and forget about it? The answer: because the being revealed is anxiety producing. As Heidegger explains, humans have a primordial and prereflective concern for being; they are "concerned in [their] being about . . . being." We orient ourselves toward being because we know our survival depends on it. Now, to be sure, we don't initially know this in a formal sense. Instead, we understand it in what one might call an intuitive fashion. As Heidegger explains, humans initially understand themselves, others, and the context in which they find themselves in a prereflective manner and primarily through emotion. Heidegger describes this phenomenon as "attunement" and explains that our attunement, or "mood," reflects our primordial understanding of being. Importantly, he identifies anxiety, or "angst," as our "fundamental mode of being-in-the-world." As such, he identifies anxiety as our primary emotion and the ontological anchor for care. Although anxiety is primarily about each individual's own being, it prompts care not just about that being but also about existence generally because it reveals that the individual's being depends upon people and things that lie outside it. Heidegger asserts that all other moods derive from anxiety; for example, all fears of specific things are grounded in anxiety to the extent that things can become fearful to an entity only if that entity is, at some level, cognizant of its own vulnerability. Speaking of cognizance, Heidegger asserts that existential anxiety appears "before all [formal] cognition" and serves as its necessary condition. Indeed, setting the stage for contemporary theorists such as Martha Nussbaum, Amelie Rorty, Jenefer Robinson, and Ronald de Sousa, Heidegger links emotion to understanding and maintains that cognition develops as moods disclose a "deficiency of having to do with the world," namely, when an individual's productive engagement with the world is interrupted and concern regarding her ability to obtain material that is necessary to her being is heightened.[14] This heightened concern motivates formal reflection and cognitive effort to understand the situation better so as to restore continuity and diminish anxiety. Interestingly, though Heidegger asserts that emotions motivate conscious awareness, he also notes that individuals do not always "allow [themselves] to confront what [their moods] ha[ve] disclosed," particularly when they encourage recognition of life's more "burdensome" aspects, namely, things they might prefer not to know.[15]

While various aspects of our being have troublesome qualities, none is more troubling to us than our mortality. It is for this reason that Heidegger pays special attention to "being-toward-death" in *Being and Time.* As Heidegger explains, anxiety fundamentally concerns, provides affective awareness of, and ultimately motivates formal consciousness of our "being-toward-death." Anxiety reveals that our "being lies between birth and death" and that death is something that we are "unable to bypass," regardless of any desire we have to do so. As Heidegger makes clear, though we frequently try to envision it as such, death is not something that lies outside of and awaits the individual; instead it is something inscribed in her being. As he states, whether the individual acknowledges it or not, she is "always already [her] end" because "death is a way to be that *Da-sein* takes over as soon as it is."[16] Anxiety discloses the fact that an irrevocable danger exists for the individual, namely, a threat to her being that cannot be surmounted because it is part of her being: finitude.

As Heidegger explains, because it discloses a threat that lies close to home, anxiety arouses the feeling of the uncanny. He states, "Uncanniness reveals itself . . . in the fundamental attunement of angst." In effect, uncanniness is the felt quality of angst. The feeling of the uncanny makes the individual profoundly uncomfortable, uncomfortable in her own skin; it makes her feel "not . . . at home" primarily because it reveals her "undisguised nullity," or imminent nonbeing. Due to the discomfort the uncanny causes, Heidegger maintains that most people try to flee anxiety, suppress the uncanny, and "cove[r] over [their] own most being-toward-death." Instead, individuals seek "constant tranquillization about death" and "evasion of death . . . dominates."[17]

According to Heidegger, anxiety, and the discomfort caused by its concomitant feeling, the uncanny, prompts the majority of people to try and disguise the truth of the human condition and engenders the "inclination to be entangled in the world." Indeed, Heidegger goes so far as to assert that "flight from uncanniness" motivates one of the two modes of human being that Heidegger identifies: inauthenticity. Whereas being authentic involves honest awareness of the human condition, being inauthentic denies or suppresses this lucidity. According to Heidegger, the feeling of the uncanny initially and for the most part motivates individuals to engage in the various forms of inauthentic being that he enumerates: "idle talk," "curiosity," and "ambiguity." As Heidegger explains, society attempts to inoculate individuals against anxiety and the uncanny feelings and frightening thoughts it brings about through indoctrination that encourages (a) preoccupation with superficial matters and communication; (b) fixation on, and relentless pursuit of, "entertaining incidentals"; and (c) reluctance to acknowledge important existential truths, including and most obviously, mortality. Together, these techniques allow most people to keep their attention away from their being and to thereby suppress feelings of anxiety, namely, feelings of uncanniness, as well as consequential thought about death. "Lostness in [society]," Heidegger states, "reveal[s] itself . . . as flight from death."[18]

Importantly, Heidegger's claims regarding the prevalence of the denial of death have been corroborated by contemporary social psychologists such as Ernest Becker and his theoretical successors, the proponents of Terror Management Theory (TMT).[19] Becker and advocates of TMT maintain that culture is motivated by and serves to insulate individuals against the terror brought on by awareness of death. They assert that human activity is "designed largely to avoid the fatality of death" and that denial, repression, and redirection keep formal thought of death at bay for most people.[20]

Though Heidegger maintains that the primordial experience of the uncanny drives most people into inauthenticity and being inauthentic successfully forestalls most thought about death for them, he is clear that it does not preclude bouts of anxiety or experiences of the uncanny and that it is not without adverse consequences. It is for this reason that Heidegger recommends authenticity, and interestingly, he links the uncanny to this mode of being as well. As Heidegger maintains, and advocates of TMT elaborate, individuals suppress anxiety, feelings of the uncanny, and thoughts about death by subscribing to belief systems that deny death and by redirecting their attention to superficial matters, namely, the worldly interests and occupations that their cultures identify as appropriate targets of concern. In effect, in the inauthentic state of being that Heidegger describes as "everydayness," basic ontological concern, which is anchored in the anxious experience of the uncanny, is sublimated or transferred into specific worldly concerns, concerns that remain motivated by existential anxiety and whose energy and urgency derive from it but that are willfully unconscious of this connection. Because inauthenticity requires the suppression of one's core emotion and the "knowledge of [self]" that such suppression brings, Heidegger asserts that inauthenticity "estranges" the individual from her being, limits her engagement with others, motivates indifference, and limits her possibilities. As Heidegger makes clear, individuals who are inauthentic are effectively on the run from being. While our mortal nature can be kept from consciousness to a great extent, its being cannot be denied because existence offers reminders of it, and for this reason, anxiety and the uncanny can never be eliminated. Thus, the implicit goal of inauthenticity, escape, is unattainable. Rather, "uncanniness pursues [the individual] and threatens [her] self-forgetful lostness," and one who "flees death is pursued by it even as one evades it." For Heidegger, inauthenticity, though prevalent, is simultaneously perilous. It is ever vulnerable to the return of the repressed, and he sees this return, though disturbing, as an epistemological and ontological opportunity. Anxiety and its herald, the uncanny, constitute the core of what Heidegger defines as "conscience"; they serve as reminders of mortality that call the individual back to being, and in doing so extend to her the invitation to authenticity.[21]

As the foregoing suggests, there is a fundamental link between death, anxiety, and the uncanny. Anxiety is fundamentally about death and engenders the experience of the uncanny. Though the discomfort associated with the uncanny frequently compels the desire to evade it and thereby promotes inauthenticity, Heidegger asserts that the call of conscience, the call to authenticity, also comes "out of uncanniness." Thus, what originally promotes inauthenticity is simultaneously what can rescue us from it. It can do so because the experience of the uncanny is a turning point. It marks "neither an evasive forgetting . . . nor a[n] [explicit] remembering"; instead, it can occasion either one. The uncanny is as instrumental in engendering authenticity as inauthenticity because it promotes a sense of anxious dislocation, an affective response that makes it difficult for the individual to "lose [herself]" in normal preoccupations, and thereby upsets the standard somnambulism of inauthenticity.[22] As Susan Bernstein notes, "For Heidegger, the uncanny happening or event disrupts [the normal] circle, breaks it apart, and creates the possibility of an openness toward something other."[23] In particular, the uncanny prompts "the disruption of . . . [the individual's conventional] understanding," an "understanding" in which certain information, particularly awareness of mortality, is repressed.[24] Curtis Bowman agrees, stating that for Heidegger, "uncanniness forces us to . . . reject accustomed ways of thinking and . . . [thereby helps us] make some small step toward authenticity."[25] In particular, the uncanny fosters authenticity by urging us, with a characteristic and disarming "jolt," to an honest admission of our mortality.[26] Importantly, this is neither a morbid preoccupation with nor a "brooding over death," but rather a forthright and resolute acknowledgment of finitude that "brings the individual face to face with the possibility to be [her]self." Authenticity frees the individual from "null possibilities," namely, "the endless multiplicity of possibilities offering themselves nearest by" and the anonymous possibilities that "circulate in the public." Instead, it helps the individual, in admitting her finite time, to at once become "free of illusion" and cognizant of her "higher power, the power of finite freedom," a power that gives her the opportunity to "tak[e] over [her] thrownness and [exist fully] in the Moment for [her] time." In effect, Heidegger describes an ironic dialectic of the uncanny, a situation wherein the feeling that initially motivates ideological escapism and social conformity can eventually serve as the principle of emancipation from those same structures and can, by virtue of the way it reminds us of our mortality, disclose the urgency of our existential situation in such a way as to drive the individual to "being together with things at hand, [motivate her to] actually take care of them, and . . . pus[h] [her] toward concerned being-with-others."[27]

Memories of Death: Classic Catalysts of the Uncanny

Ultimately, Heidegger's recommendation that individuals acknowledge their mortality is not altogether new in western intellectual history. Indeed, it echoes the classical tradition of memento mori, or the inclusion of reminders of death in literary and artistic works for the purpose of moral improvement. As Harry Morris states, works that incorporate memento mori "present in imagery or diction . . . [a] reminder of death, most often a fleshless skull but sometimes other imagery the purpose of which is to remind the [individual] of the . . . end of his body . . . [the goal of which] is either the intended reformation of the [character] or an exhortation to the [audience]."[28] Importantly, use of memento mori differs notably from more generic appearances of death and dying that are commonplace in artistic and literary works. Whereas countless works feature death, using it as a means to move the plot forward or deliver poetic justice, works that employ memento mori make death itself a focal point by incorporating blatant symbols of death (e.g., skulls, corpses) that draw the viewer's attention. Though the tradition of memento mori originated in ancient times, it has persisted, finding popularity at various points in history, including the Renaissance and Victorian eras. For example, as Bruce Redwine notes in his examination of memento mori in *Vanity Fair,* while the classical use of memento mori differs from later Christian applications, works that utilize memento mori are united in their efforts to employ "the appearance of death. . . . [in order to] make us want to change our values."[29] He states that the effective use of memento mori "humbles and humanizes . . . and we in turn find our attitudes being changed. . . . based upon the recognition of human mortality." In particular, he notes a shift from "contempt to sympathy" with respect to our association with others as well as the development of a deeper appreciation of life and the opportunities it presents.[30] Importantly for present purposes, theorists concur that the mechanism for this change is emotional. Works in this tradition invoke "grisly images. . . . [of] the terrors of the grave" in order to generate sufficient "disquietude" to prompt reflection, and potentially reformation.[31] This disquietude, arguably an effective synonym for the uncanny, disrupts the individual's normal and largely evasive preoccupations and forces her to think more definitively about life as a result of a reminder of death.

Burton's Uncanny Corpus: Contemporary Examples of Memento Mori

Now, finally, we arrive back at the works of Tim Burton. Certainly no other contemporary American director has as obvious a preoccupation with death or as disarming a knack for the uncanny. Death is literally everywhere in his works, and it is presented in such a way as to readily engender the experience of the uncanny. Continuing the tradition of memento mori, Burton populates his works with personifications of death and other reminders of our mortality, presumably in hopes of modifying not only his audience's relationship to death but also their engagement with life. As critics of Burton's work attest, his films "often play on cultural anxieties" as well as "personal" anxieties that are "widely felt but rarely acknowledged," and "death" is a particular focal point.[32] Burton himself indicates that "everything I've done . . . mean[s] something; even if it's not clear-cut" and that one of the things he is trying to do is reproduce the "therap[eutic]" effect that movies had on him, that is, to "tap into [viewers'] dreams and subconscious" and thereby help them manage their greatest fears and achieve their finest aspirations.[33] As Edwin Page states, Burton's works are "like fairy tales, communicating to us on a symbolic level, speaking of things far deeper in our conscious and subconscious minds than most films would dare to delve."[34] Most important for present purposes, through their explicit focus on death, they remind us of, and thereby can help us come to grips with, our own mortality. And Burton's morbidity is no accident; he recognizes his fascination with death. He states, "I just love those skeletons." He notes that while he "came from a sort of Puritanical suburban existence where death was thought of as dark and negative," at the same time, "it happens to everybody, and I always responded to cultures that made death feel more a part of life."[35] Ultimately, by "juxtaposing . . . horror and humour," Burton's films succeed not only in reminding viewers of death but also in assuaging some of their anxiety by showing them that death is part of life.[36] With their plethora of skulls and bones, coffins and cadavers, and graveyards as "staple locations," Burton's works stand as modern examples of memento mori, works that feature death prominently in order to call us out of denial.[37]

As intimated earlier, one finds symbols of death (and therefore the capacity to elicit the uncanny) in virtually all of Burton's works. Works such as *Sleepy Hollow* (1999) and *Sweeney Todd* (2007) offer hyperbolic personifications of death in the form of the Hessian Horseman (Christopher Walken) and Sweeney Todd (Johnny Depp). The heads that roll from the Horseman and cascades of blood that flow from the demon barber excite not merely horror but also a sense of the uncanny by virtue of the way in which they remind us of the mortal dangers that lie close to home. *Beetlejuice* (1988) has a similarly blatant preoccupation with death; however, it foregrounds mortality in a more comic fashion, with the spirited spirit Beetlejuice (Michael Keaton) helping Barbara and Adam Maitland (Gina Davis and Alec Baldwin) come to grips with being "newlydeads." Likewise, Burton's famous animated short, now turned 3-D feature, *Frankenweenie* (1984, 2012) takes a comic look at the liminal barrier between life and death when its protagonist, Victor (Charlie Tahan, voice), rescues his beloved dog, Sparky, from the grips of death, with some unintended consequences. Other works are less obvious in their invocation of death. For example, *Big Fish* (2003) presents death in a less flamboyant but no less powerful manner, examining in a rather poignant fashion how individuals negotiate their imminent death, and the death of loved ones, in more and less productive ways. Even works that don't seem to focus on death often have it in the wings. For example, the ominous atmosphere in *Batman* (1989), the threat of extinction in *Planet of the Apes* (2001), and the precarious existence of the Buckets in *Charlie and the Chocolate Factory* (2005) also allude, with varying degrees of explicitness, to the perennial vulnerability of being, the ever-present risk of death, and the way in which awareness of mortality undercuts naïve feelings of security and arouses, instead, the uncanny.

Given that so many of Burton's works foreground death and elicit the uncanny, the focus here will be on three works in which the focus on death and the uncanny is unprecedented and that also demonstrate clear continuity with the classical tradition of memento mori: *The Nightmare Before Christmas* (1993), *Corpse Bride* (2005), and *Dark Shadows* (2012). As mentioned previously, works that employ memento mori have certain common features. First, they engender an explicit focus on mortality through the integration and foregrounding of symbols of death. For example, they normally include symbols such as a "grinning skull" or "draped skeleton"; skeletons are frequently "animated" and there is a tradition of presenting them in a "long row" doing the "Dance of Death."[38] Finally, these images of death are commonly made even more provocative through juxtaposition with recognizable symbols of life, such as food and sex. For example, prominent in the tradition are works that place death at a "banquet" or relate love and death by featuring a beautiful maiden together with a personification of death.[39] Sounds like Burton, right?

Clearly, Burton's animated feature *The Nightmare Before Christmas* qualifies as a contemporary and wonderfully uncanny work of memento mori by virtue of its self-conscious focus on death, evident most notably in the main character, Jack Skellington (Chris Sarandon, voice). As those familiar with the film are aware, Jack draws audience attention to death not primarily by virtue of his name but because he actually has only a skull for a head and no flesh on his bones. Reminiscent of Edward Gorey's macabre drawings, Jack, born of Burton's own hand, exemplifies the animated skeleton seen in classical works of memento mori.[40] Additionally, as the pumpkin king of Halloween Town, Jack is, in effect, lord of the dead. Moreover, as he vies with Santa Claus for control of Christmas, Jack is not merely juxtaposed with a potent symbol of life (i.e., Christmas); he is shown, symbolically, as a threat to it. Finally, Burton not only pays homage to *Frankenstein* (1818/1931), he reinforces the focus on death through the introduction of Jack's love interest, Sally (Catherine O'Hara, voice), a charming but unhallowed amalgam of body parts.[41]

Like *The Nightmare Before Christmas,* Burton's stop-motion feature *Corpse Bride* foregrounds death prominently, again personifying death in a main character. In this case, death takes residence in Emily (Helena Bonham Carter, voice), the "lovely" corpse bride. Whereas audiences are introduced immediately to Jack, they do not meet Emily at the onset of the film. Instead, they are first introduced to her eventual beloved, Victor Van Dort (Johnny Depp, voice), and his fiancée, Victoria Everglot (Emily Watson, voice). Emily is introduced only after Victor and Victoria's wedding plans go awry, after the awkward and unassuming Victor unknowingly weds the dead and conjures a tricky love triangle while practicing his vows in the forest. As in *The Nightmare Before Christmas,* Burton again elicits a powerful experience of the uncanny by foregrounding death to an unprecedented degree. Head over heels for her new husband, Emily whisks Victor, and the audience, away to the Land of the Dead, where corpses in varying degrees of decomposition abound. Wherever Victor turns his head, he finds heads and other body parts. Cadavers approach from all quarters, talking to him about life and death. A notable example, particularly if one is examining the parallel between Burton and classical examples of memento mori, is the skeleton Bonejangles (Danny Elfman, voice). Victor meets Bonejangles at the bar shortly after his arrival in the Land of the Dead. The lead singer in a classic line of dancing skeletons, Bonejangles sings a light-hearted tune with a sober message: "The Remains of the Day." Through its invocation of the uncanny with the classic Dance of Death, the chorus encourages Victor and the audience to move to a more congenial attitude toward mortality:

> Die, die, we all pass away
> but don't wear a frown 'cause it's really okay

you might try and hide
you might try and pray
but we all end up the remains of the day.

With the corpse bride, Emily, Burton fleshes out a full-figured cadaver who embodies love and death, a dead woman who, like Bonejangles, teaches Victor about life and death—in her case, by telling tales of love and loss. In the end, as a result of Emily's willingness to relinquish her accidental groom, Victor and Victoria are reunited and their love is cemented.

Dark Shadows differs from *The Nightmare Before Christmas* and *Corpse Bride* in that it is a live-action feature. Thus we cannot expect it to depict death in exactly the same form as in an animated film. In *Dark Shadows* death figures as yet another version of the walking dead: the vampire. As those acquainted with the film know, its vampire protagonist, Barnabas Collins (Johnny Depp), is not your typical bloodsucker. He's neither as terrifying nor as supernaturally bewitching as John Polidori's Ruthven or Bram Stoker's count; he isn't as sparkly as Stephenie Meyer's Edward, either; instead, he's a bumbling and uncanny personification of death in the form of the boy next door.[42] And death infiltrates all aspects of Barnabas's character. Death is not only what leads him to be a vampire; it is what he is. He is a dead man walking. And death is what he doles out, albeit apologetically.

At this juncture, it is useful to look at the way in which the foregoing works foreground death in such a way as to engender a productive experience of the uncanny, one that is more likely to prompt critical reflection and authentic reformation than heightened efforts at repression. As Heidegger notes, the uncanny is a powerful feeling that puts us in touch with being and thereby creates an epistemological and ontological opportunity. However, to the extent the experience of the uncanny is deeply unsettling, it can fuel escapism and denial as easily as invite us to authenticity. Burton's works elicit the uncanny but do so in a fashion that inspires delight. Though replete with material that might otherwise inspire horror, his corpus, particularly the aforementioned three films, remind viewers of the unpalatable truth of mortality in a manner that most can stomach, rather than one they will likely reject.

The first technique Burton uses to elicit an experience of the uncanny that calls us to greater acceptance of our mortality is his selection of medium and genre. Specifically, though Burton stamps every one of his works with his signature style, they are not pieces of pure innovation. Instead, and particularly in the case of the three films considered here, he utilizes traditional mediums and genres, most importantly ones with which audiences have positive associations, namely animation, comedy, and romance. For example, while *The Night Before Christmas* and *Corpse Bride* are packed with disarming reminders of death, the discomfort caused by these elements is mitigated by the fact that most adult viewers will not be inclined to fear animated characters, even if those characters are walking skeletons or corpses. As Burton is certainly aware, whereas viewers of works of the horror genre are primed for and anticipate the solicitation of that emotion, viewers of animation expect something entirely different, and this expectation predisposes them to react positively rather than negatively to characters, even characters who catalyze the uncanny because they are embodiments of death.

This positive reaction is furthered by the incorporation of comedic elements. As Redwine notes, classic works of memento mori frequently soften and diminish the disquietude and "unpleasantness" engendered by explicit symbols of death by incorporating "comic" elements.[43] This addition of comedic components tempers audience concern, reduces the likelihood of a defensive response, and allows these works to engender thoughts about death that are "difficult to forget" because they "slip into . . . consciousness like a whisper."[44] Though comedy is amply present in both *The Nightmare Before Christmas* and *Corpse Bride, Dark Shadows* employs it more obviously than they do. Perhaps because it lacks the insulating power of animation and introduces a greater volume of graphic violence, it relies more heavily on campy humor to counterbalance its blatant reminders of death and forceful solicitation of the uncanny. An example is Barnabas's fascination with his niece's lava lamp. Unaware of its true contents, Barnabas is driven by his vampiric instincts to drool over the blood-red liquid undulating lusciously inside the glass. Deftly counterbalancing the force of this comic moment, Burton maintains the uncanny by having Barnabas make reference to the symbolism of the lamp and to a traditional catalyst of the uncanny with which Barnabas is familiar—live burial—when he refers to the object as a "pulsating blood urn."

Just as he uses comedy, Burton also uses romantic interest to sweeten the uncanny and put death in a positive light. Specifically, he uses audience interest in romance to mitigate the disturbance engendered by characters who serve as reminders of death. In fact, in each of the films considered, Burton fosters a positive association with the uncanny, and with characters who embody death, by enmeshing them in a deeply romantic plot. Indeed, he galvanizes audience interest and virtually assures their sympathetic response to his catalysts of the uncanny by inverting the classical tradition of memento mori and turning characters who personify death into romantic protagonists rather than agents that threaten love's future.[45] This is nowhere more obvious than in *Dark Shadows,* which concludes with Barnabas and Victoria (Bella Heathcote), now both vampiric personifications of death, wrapped in an undying embrace.

Burton's use of the positive associations that audiences have with particular literary forms and characters to engender a productive reaction to a normally disarming subject can be explained more fully with reference to Greg Smith's "mood-cue approach" to aesthetic response.[46] In *Film Structure and the Emotion System,* Smith argues that films elicit affective and cognitive responses from audiences through the solicitation of emotion. Referencing Heidegger's account of moods, Smith notes that moods are cognitively relevant "preparatory states" that have an "orienting tendency," that is, they predispose individuals to feel and think in particular ways. According to Smith, films orient audiences primarily through "redundant emotive cues" that move them "toward an appropriate emotional orientation" as well as toward correct inferences regarding the moral status of particular characters and the message of the film as a whole. Smith notes that audience responsiveness to particular cues results primarily from the existence of genre "scripts" and audience members' cultural indoctrination to these largely durable structures. At the same time, Smith notes that innovative filmmakers can create a "complex emotional mix" and even elicit "nonprototypical emotions" by deviating from generic patterns and "liberally introducing [atypical] elements." He suggests that by "leav[ing] out cues we would normally anticipate or us[ing] emotion cues that are associated with other genres . . . filmmakers can play with the emotional possibilities" available and create works that are not only uncommon but also "densely informative."[47] In particular, Smith analyzes how *Ghostbusters* (1984) blends traditional horror cues with those of comedy to generate an atypical effect. Clearly, Burton employs a similarly innovative approach in *The Nightmare Before Christmas, Corpse Bride,* and *Dark Shadows.* These films mix horror, romance, and comedy to solicit an experience of the uncanny buoyed sufficiently through positive associations that viewers are inclined to allow the feeling of the uncanny to be sustained, and thereby to admit the thoughts of death that the uncanny engenders rather than try and suppress them. As advocates of TMT note, this is atypical of entertainment, which normally serves the "psychological function of bolstering an individual's . . . anxiety buffers"; that is, it tends to help us deny death rather than confront it.[48] Through his ingenious conditioning of audiences to new emotive cues (e.g., dead characters are made funny), Burton prompts them to experience an altogether uncommon response to uncanny catalysts of death-related thoughts. As advocates of TMT note, to the extent the uncanny arouses profound discomfort, individuals will normally try to "bypass the conscious experience of the emotion that reminders of mortality . . . create" by dissociating from it so "quickly . . . that the [formal] experience of anxiety is [effectively] circumvented" through either suppression or sublimation into another emotion.[49] By making his personifications of death pleasant, Burton forestalls this standard response. Audiences tend to flock to his works rather than flee them.

One of the reasons audiences might not resist Burton's work is that his repeated references to ghosts and places such as the Land of the Dead suggest the possibility of life after death. Clearly, not only *Dark Shadows* but also works such as *Frankenweenie* and *Beetlejuice* can be said to animate belief in this possibility. This potential seemingly confounds the claim that Burton's works promote authenticity. However, closer inspection reveals that Burton's animation of the dead does not necessarily engender belief in life after death. Instead, it can quite readily be interpreted as the vehicle he uses to allow death to speak directly to his audience and thereby call them to more open and productive engagement with their mortality. In addition, the way in which his works envision the possibility of life after death does not suggest Burton is trying to promote belief in this possibility.[50] His references to the possibility of life after death invite discussion of another way in which he manages death and the uncanny in such a way as to encourage positive audience response through a technique familiar to proponents of TMT: dual processing.[51]

As mentioned previously, advocates of TMT assert that virtually everyone is engaged in the denial of death at some level because unmitigated thoughts about death can engender paralyzing despair. They also assert that, depending on the individual's state of mortality salience—the degree to which thoughts about death occupy one's consciousness and subconsciousness—she or he will use primarily one of two types of defenses against an upsurge of death-related thoughts: proximal or distal. Distal responses actively deny death, whereas proximal responses merely defer attention from it. The most common form of distal defense is a death-denying ideology, such as a religion that endorses belief in life after death. Proximal defenses are used when distal ones are confounded, namely, when thoughts about death cannot be effectively suppressed. Distractions are common proximal defenses.

Obviously, works such as Burton's that foreground death hamstring viewers' distal defenses and prime them to utilize proximal ones instead. By animating the dead, Burton ingeniously gives audiences a little taste of a familiar distal defense, an anxiety buffer in the form of a death-denying ideology. This helps disable the spontaneous impulse to flee an explicit reminder of death. However, Burton then undercuts this distal defense and instead encourages a proximal means of distraction from death that is partial, not complete. Specifically, Burton's plots frequently allude to the possibility of life after death; however, they erode rather than embolden belief in this prospect due to their unmitigated emphasis on death. For example, consider Sally from *The Nightmare Before Christmas* and Emily from *Corpse Bride.* Rather than serve as beacons enlivening the hope that we can transcend death, they embody death and succumb to it. They are corpses who are literally falling apart. Sally lacks physiological integrity from the beginning insofar as she is composed of divergent parts and repeatedly falls apart at the seams. Worms erode Emily from the inside out and she "dies" at the end of the film when she dissolves into a thousand silver-blue butterflies. To be sure, Burton invokes a familiar anxiety buffer with stories that suggest the possibility of life after death, but he thins this buffer by saturating this other world and its representatives with death. Indeed, consistent with Smith's account, this sort of subversion catalyzes a powerful experience of the uncanny by virtue of the fact that it uses a vehicle of repression to prompt awareness of death.

Knowing individuals are reluctant to engage with death directly, Burton not only helps inhibit standard defenses and facilitates the encounter with mortality by incorporating psychologically satisfying references to life after death, he also embeds his reminders of death in otherwise familiar plots that redirect and largely command his viewers' occurrent attention but do not remove awareness of death altogether.[52] Like the skull on the banquet table in a classical work of memento mori, Burton's works put death on the table, indeed all over the table, but don't then talk about death itself very much. Instead, proverbially avoiding the elephant in the room, they serve up a story that refocuses the audience's attention and satisfies their predictable desire to put death out of immediate focus. This shift in attention alleviates the psychological stress associated with explicit thoughts about death but at the same time keeps death in sight, in the audience's peripheral vision.

Importantly, this is basically the way Heidegger describes how the authentic individual engages death. He makes it clear that authenticity does not require an unremitting focus on death. Instead, such brooding is indicative of a rare form of inauthenticity. Authentic being toward death requires one to keep one's finitude in mind but not in focus, so as to direct one's attention to life, heighten one's appreciation of time, and enhance one's sense of the fragility of being, the incommensurable opportunity of existence, and the ever-present necessity of care. Burton's works help audiences move toward this state. While he softens his presentation of death in various ways, Burton keeps the stakes high. In short, his works are so saturated with reminders of mortality that these reminders are virtually impossible to ignore. Indeed, he amplifies the uncanny by incorporating not only direct reminders of death but also multiple indirect catalysts of the uncanny (e.g., darkness, doubles, dismemberment). These reinforce disquietude through indirect allusion to death.[53] As we laugh at the comic antics of his characters and revel in the details of plot, Burton's examples of memento mori exercise our psyches and create an opportunity for us to exorcise some of the horror we harbor regarding mortality. Their uncanny presence initiates a "silent dialogue with death," concurrent with delight that helps open us to authenticity.[54]

"Disquieting Virtue": The Value of the Literary Uncanny

In *The Nightmare Before Christmas, Corpse Bride,* and *Dark Shadows,* Burton illustrates the power of the literary uncanny alluded to by figures such as Freud and Cixous. As Cixous notes, fiction has "a privileged relationship to the *Unheimliche*" because it "can multiply the uncanny effect" in such a way as to "leave the reader without any defense" against the transformation that the encounter with the uncanny can cause.[55] Indeed, one can argue that Burton is especially adept at conjuring what might be called the art uncanny, a term inspired by Noël Carroll's acclaimed work *The Philosophy of Horror* and its distinction between art horror and real horror.[56] Like art horror, literary experiences of the uncanny differ from their real counterparts in certain definitive ways. In particular, though the emotions we have in response to fiction are just as "genuine" as the ones we have in response to real events, they do not "move us to act" in the same way as those we have in response to real stimuli because we are aware that their catalysts are fictive.[57] Indeed, as Robert Solomon points out, precisely because they don't spontaneously motivate action, emotional responses to fiction "activat[e] our sensitivity" in a unique way; they "stimulat[e] and exercis[e] our sympathy without straining or exhausting [it]" and thereby help provide a "framework" for understanding.[58] In the case of the uncanny, the fact that audiences are not compelled to action by fictive catalysts of emotion is particularly relevant. As noted previously, the uncanny is a particularly volatile emotion. It can engender an epistemic advance on the part of the individual, but it often prompts precisely the opposite. Because the uncanny unsettles the individual, individuals frequently flee experiences of it as quickly as they come, and this precludes these experiences from operating in a revelatory capacity. However, when individuals experience the uncanny in response to fiction, they aren't as likely to try and escape the experience through prompt suppression or through the transference of attention into action or sublimated emotion (e.g., horror or fear).[59] Instead, they are likely to pause, in part because the experience brings with it other pleasures. This allows the uncanny to persist, and when the experience of the uncanny persists, its potential to influence understanding increases.

Of course, the main reason that encounters with fiction do not prompt action is because they tell their audiences stories that aren't real. As theorists of fiction such as Nussbaum indicate, literary works are also unique in their ability to foster understanding of challenging material because individuals are frequently more willing to grapple with disturbing subjects and uncomfortable emotions in conjunction with fiction as opposed to real life. As she argues in *Love's Knowledge,* our engagements with fiction can not only expand our opportunities for experience but also deepen them, because our defenses are not activated in response to fiction in the same way they are with events occurring in real life. Encounters with fiction are thus "free of certain sources of distortion that frequently impede our real-life deliberations."[60] This is particularly true of the uncanny. By virtue of the very real fear we have of dying, we regularly resist the uncanny and reminders of death in ordinary experience. Because such reminders are part of our real experience they strike too close to home, and all too often the experience of the uncanny that they elicit is quickly, and often unconsciously, deferred. However, while works of fiction elicit strong emotions and even encourage individuals to identify vicariously with their characters, they at the same time offer audiences an anxiety buffer by virtue of the fact that the stories they tell are "not ours."[61] In short, disturbing content presented in fiction does not prompt psychological resistance as quickly, or as forcefully, as would that same content encountered in real life. Here, of course, lies the magic of memento mori, Burton's examples in particular. His works serve to remind individuals of their mortality in a fashion that compels openness and acceptance rather than evasion and resistance. Indeed, by structuring symbols of death in such a way that we have as many positive associations with them as negative, his works serve to recondition audiences to better accept death as part of life and thus help them achieve equanimity, the affective indicator of authenticity, in the face of death. While one might interpret this as indifference, as Heidegger states, "indifference . . . is to be sharply distinguished from equanimity. This [latter] mood arises from . . . resoluteness . . . [and] has its view to the possible . . . [most notably] the anticipation of death."[62] Ultimately, indifference results from the repression of the uncanny. Ironically, it fails to eradicate the uncanny but succeeds in producing "numbness" toward life.[63] Equanimity produces exactly the opposite. It comes from accepting the uncanny.

The Nightmare Before Christmas, *Corpse Bride*, and *Dark Shadows* are examples of the literary uncanny and memento mori. As Royle notes, "There is something strangely singular, . . . valuable, and instructive about the uncanny." In his estimation, it possesses an "ineluctable significance."[64] Bowman agrees, asserting that the uncanny "can be revelatory in unexpected ways."[65] As this essay aims to show, the uncanny can be particularly instructive with respect to our mortality. The uncanny "is characterized by the return of the repressed," and the most powerful repressed truth that experiences of the uncanny unearth is that of our mortality.[66] Interestingly, when Burton offers the uncanny to his audiences, they tend to embrace rather than resist that return. Thus his films help his audiences reflect positively upon, and thereby make them more likely to accept, their mortality. As Bowman states, films that elicit the uncanny "act as aids to the understanding."[67] By acclimating audiences to symbols of death, Burton's works reveal a "secret once familiar but made alien [and sinister] by the process of forgetting."[68] Burton's morbid comedies build familiarity with, and thereby help dismiss, the sinister character of death. As Page notes, "Instead of hiding the subject of death . . . [Burton] brings it out in the open so as to dispel its taboo qualities." As such, his works show audiences that "the dead and death itself are not necessarily things to be feared."[69] One can also argue that Burton's uncanny works of memento mori are in some respects like the "experience machines" that the well-known philosopher Robert Nozick describes.[70] To be sure, Burton's films do not offer individuals a substitute for real experience in the way Nozick's experience machines do. Whereas Nozick's hypothetical experience machines are ones that would enable inauthenticity by affording individuals the opportunity to opt out of reality and enter virtual worlds crafted wholly according to their desires, Burton's films are instead ones that supplement our experience and may assist in the achievement of authenticity and efficacious functioning. For several hours at a time, Burton's films bring us into worlds that arouse the experience of the uncanny by surrounding us with the dead. These worlds initially upset our "ontological equilibrium," but eventually we become at home in them, and when they return us to our world we are "slightly changed" by virtue of our experience.[71] In the end, Burton's solicitation of the uncanny through symbols of death that delight may help audiences come to terms with their own end by acclimating them to death's unfettered expression in film.

Notes

I would like to express my thanks to Steve Csaki, Steve Benton, and Ken Hada for their insightful remarks and helpful suggestions on an earlier version of this essay. I also want to express my gratitude to East Central University, particularly the members of the administration and the Research Committee who approved my application for a research grant that helped facilitate the completion of this project. Finally, I would like to thank the staff of East Central University's Linscheid Library, as they were instrumental in locating many of the scholarly resources utilized in this work.

1. Sigmund Freud, *The Uncanny* (New York: Penguin Classics, 2003), 123.

2. Ibid., 123, 123, 123, 123, 123, 144, 123, 148, 147.

3. Surmounted beliefs refer to immature points of view that are eventually supplanted as an individual's (or culture's) understanding of the world matures.

4. Freud, *Uncanny,* 154, 154, 157, 157. See Lorne Dawson, "Otto and Freud on the Uncanny and Beyond," *Journal of the American Academy of Religion* 57, no. 2 (Summer 1989): 283–311, http://www.jstor.org/stable/1464384. Dawson indicates that due to the force of repression, "real experiences of the uncanny are . . . very rare, and experiences of the uncanny rooted in the reemergence of repressed complexes are even rarer" (296).

5. Freud, *Uncanny,* 157.

6. Ibid., 132, 139.

7. Hélène Cixous, "Fiction and Its Phantoms: A Reading of Freud's *Das Heimliche* (The 'Uncanny')," in "Thinking in the Arts, Sciences, and Literature," special issue, *New Literary History* 7, no. 3 (Spring 1976), 525–48, quote on 536, http://www.jstor.org/stable/468561, accessed March 13, 2012.

8. Nicholas Royle, *The Uncanny* (New York: Routledge, 2003), 22.

9. Diane Jonte-Pace, "At Home in the Uncanny: Freudian Representations of Death, Mothers, and the Afterlife," *Journal of the American Academy of Religion* 64, no. 1 (Spring 1996): 61–88, quote on 61, http://www.jstor.org/stable/1465246, accessed March 13, 2012.

10. Freud, *Uncanny,* 140, 148, 153, 149.

11. Various figures note Heidegger's contribution to the study of the uncanny. For example, though his article "The Return of Negation: The Doppelgänger in Freud's 'The "Uncanny"'" concentrates exclusively on Freud's account of the concept, in his notes to the essay Dimitris Vardoulakis states that "a more comprehensive study of the uncanny would have to account for Heidegger's use of the term" (115). Likewise, Nicholas Royle acknowledges, "it was Heidegger who, perhaps more than any other philosopher, was specifically concerned to explore the notion" (4). One of the few detailed examinations of Heidegger's account of the uncanny, and one to which this piece is indebted, is Curtis Bowman's "Heidegger, the Uncanny, and Jacques Tourneur's Horror Films." Here, while recognizing Freud's contribution, Bowman argues that Heidegger's account of the uncanny should also be given wider application. Asserting "Heidegger is to horror as Aristotle is to tragedy" (67), Bowman goes on to utilize Heidegger's theory of the uncanny to interpret Tourneur's horror films. For further consideration, Vardoulakis's essay can be found in *SubStance* 35, no. 2, issue 110 (2006): 100–116, http://www.jstor.org/stable/4152886. Royle's remarks can be found in his book *The Uncanny.* Finally, Bowman's article can be found in *Dark Thoughts: Philosophic Reflections on Cinematic Horror,* ed. Stephen Jay Schneider and Daniel Shaw (Lanham, MD: Scarecrow Press, 2003), 65–83.

12. Martin Heidegger, *Being and Time,* ed. Joan Stambaugh (Albany: State University of New York Press, 1996). Here Heidegger asserts that the being about which he is concerned "is always mine" (39).

13. Ibid., 49, 52, 37, 114, 114, 41.

14. Ibid., 213, 128, 127, 176, 128, 77. Heidegger argues that when we are productively engaged with the world things are "ready to hand" (ibid., 65) and our understanding is nonthematic. However, when presented with unfamiliar circumstances or problems, things lose their "handiness" (65) and anxiety erupts. Analogous to the way in which Jenefer Robinson discusses the startle response ("Startle," *Journal of Philosophy* 92, no. 2 [1995]: 53–75, http://www.jstor.org/stable/2940940), anxiety focuses attention and prompts reflection on the situation. This heightened attention motivates cognitive activity, most notably effort to understand the situation more fully so as to restore efficacious function. In short, cognitive activity is motivated by emotion and is, at least initially, pragmatic.

15. Heidegger, *Being and Time,* 127, 127.

16. Ibid., 216, 232, 215, 232, 228, 228.

17. Ibid., 253, 316, 263, 232, 235, 234.

18. Ibid., 18, 225, 157, 159, 161, 286, 357.

19. Prominent terror management theorists include Sheldon Solomon, Jeff Green-

berg, and Tom Pyszczynski. Sample articles that outline the theory include A. Rosenblatt, J. Greenberg, S. Solomon, T. Pyszczynski, and D. Lyon, "Evidence for Terror Management Theory I: The Effects of Mortality Salience on Reactions to Those Who Violate or Uphold Cultural Values," *Journal of Personality and Social Psychology* 57, no. 4 (1989): 681–90; J. Greenberg, T. Pyszczynski, S. Solomon, A. Rosenblatt, M. Veeder, S. Kirkland, and D. Lyon, "Evidence for Terror Management Theory II: The Effects of Mortality Salience on Reactions to Those Who Threaten or Bolster the Cultural Worldview," *Journal of Personality and Social Psychology* 58, no. 2 (1990): 308–18; and T. Pyszczynski, J. Greenberg, and S. Solomon, "Why Do We Need What We Need? A Terror Management Theory Perspective on the Roots of Human Social Motivation," *Psychological Inquiry* 8, no. 1 (1997): 1–20.

20. Ernest Becker, *The Denial of Death* (New York: Free Press, 1973), ix.

21. Heidegger, *Being and Time,* 15, 264, 235, 255, 389, 249.

22. Ibid., 259, 315, 316.

23. Susan Bernstein, "It Walks: The Ambulatory Uncanny," in "Comparative Literature," special issue, *MLN* 118, no. 5 (December 2003): 1111–39, quote on 1115, http://www.jstor.org/stable/3251857, accessed March 31, 2012.

24. Ibid., 1117.

25. Bowman, "Heidegger, the Uncanny, and Jacques Tourneur's Horror Films," 72.

26. Heidegger, *Being and Time,* 251.

27. Ibid., 241, 245, 316, 351, 351, 357, 352, 352, 285.

28. Harry Morris, "*Hamlet* as a *Memento Mori* Poem," *PMLA* 85, no. 5 (October 1970): 1035–40, quote on 1035, http://www.jstor.org/stable/1261544, accessed February 6, 2012.

29. Bruce Redwine, "The Uses of Memento Mori in *Vanity Fair,*" in "Nineteenth Century," special issue, *Studies in English Literature, 1500–1900* 17, no. 4 (Autumn 1977): 657–72, quote on 658, http://www.jstor.org/stable/450314, accessed February 6, 2012.

30. Ibid., 659.

31. Morris, "*Hamlet* as a *Memento Mori* Poem," 1035; Redwine, "Uses of Memento Mori in *Vanity Fair,*" 658.

32. Alison McMahan, *The Films of Tim Burton: Animating Live Action in Contemporary Hollywood* (New York: Continuum Press, 2005), 236; Edwin Page, *Gothic Fantasy: The Films of Tim Burton* (London: Marion Boyars Publishing, 2007), 7.

33. Tim Burton, *Burton on Burton,* ed. Mark Salisbury (London: Faber and Faber Limited, 2006), 124, 124, 124.

34. Page, *Gothic Fantasy,* 7.

35. Burton, *Burton on Burton,* 41, 253, 253.

36. Page, *Gothic Fantasy,* 120.

37. Ibid., 171. Arguably, some individuals may dislike Burton's work precisely because of its blatant preoccupation with death. As discussed, most individuals are engaged in the denial of death and resist formal consideration of their mortality. For this reason,

they may experience a predictable distaste for works that prompt either conscious or subconscious consideration of death, and Burton's work is an obvious example.

38. Redwine, "Uses of Memento Mori in *Vanity Fair*," 663; Horst Janson, "A 'Memento Mori' among Early Italian Prints," *Journal of the Warburg and Courtauld Institutes* 3, no. 3/4 (April–July 1940): 243–48, quotes on 243, 244, 246, http://www.jstor.org/stable/750277, accessed February 6, 2012.

39. Redwine, "Uses of Memento Mori in *Vanity Fair*," 657.

40. For examples of such classical works of art, see Hans Memling's *Triptych of Earthly Vanity and Divine Salvation* (1485) and Michael Wolgemut's *The Dance of Death* (1493). Other examples of memento mori include Hans Baldung Grien's *Death and the Maiden* (1517), Pieter Claesz's *Vanitas* (1625), and Frans Hals's *Youth with Skull* (ca. 1628).

41. Arguably, both Mary Shelley's text (1818) and James Whale's cinematic version (1931) of *Frankenstein* inspired and influenced Burton.

42. John Polidori, *The Vampyre* (London: Printed for Sherwood, Neely, and Jones, 1819), available at http://www.gutenberg.org/ebooks/6087; Bram Stoker, *Dracula* (New York: Barnes and Noble, 2003); Stephenie Meyer, *Twilight* (New York: Little, Brown, 2005).

43. Redwine, "Uses of Memento Mori in *Vanity Fair*," 664.

44. Ibid., 672, 672, 668.

45. While one can argue that Emily from *Corpse Bride* threatens Victor and Victoria's relationship, she does not do so intentionally, and in the end she acts in such a way as to further, rather than frustrate, their relationship.

46. Greg Smith, *Film Structure and the Emotion System* (Cambridge: Cambridge University Press, 2003), 13.

47. Ibid., 38, 39, 43, 43, 49, 51, 52, 51, 49, 52.

48. Sheldon Solomon, Jeff Greenberg, and Tom Pyszczynski, "A Terror Management Theory of Social Behavior: Functions of Self-Esteem and Cultural Worldviews," *Advances in Experimental Social Psychology* 24 (1991): 91–159, quote on 122.

49. Rosenblatt et al., "Evidence for Terror Management Theory I," 689.

50. He is not, however, explicitly denying the possibility of life after death either. Much like Heidegger, Burton seems to be emphasizing that the here and now needs to be our focal point and we need to deal with death because it affects our life.

51. For fuller examination of the concept of dual processing, as well as proximal and distal defenses, see T. Pyszczynski, J. Greenberg, and S. Solomon, "A Dual-Process Model of Defense against Conscious and Unconscious Death-Related Thoughts: An Extension of Terror Management Theory," *Psychological Review* 106, no. 4 (October 1999): 835–45.

52. Here I am referring to the distinction that David Novitz draws between occurrent and nonoccurrent awareness in *Knowledge, Fiction, and Imagination* (Philadelphia: Temple University Press, 1987). As he explains, objects that command our occurrent awareness are in our immediate focus whereas nonoccurrent content remains in consciousness but is not the focal point of conscious attention. Instead, nonoccurrent

content persists on the periphery of the individual's awareness. Novitz maintains that audiences are shaped by their encounter with literature as much by the way literature affects nonoccurrent awareness as occurrent awareness. Here the argument regarding the literary uncanny is the same. Insofar as Burton's works foreground death and elicit the uncanny they engender awareness of mortality. Audiences are more receptive than normal to this awareness, and it models authentic awareness of death by virtue of the fact that his works encourage explicit, but primarily nonoccurrent, awareness of death.

53. As Heidegger notes in *Being and Time,* things such as darkness can also solicit the uncanny by virtue of the fact that they refer to states that threaten the individual's being (177). Darkness elicits the uncanny because humans are more vulnerable to attack in the dark and it thereby heightens their mortality salience. Doubles offer a more conceptual threat to the self, namely, the threat embodied in a duplicate, an entity that removes one's ontological necessity. Dismemberment catalyzes the uncanny by referring to a state the individual would be unlikely to survive.

54. Cixous, "Fiction and Its Phantoms," 541.

55. Ibid., 546, 546, 547, 547. The phrase "disquieting virtue" is also Cixous's.

56. Noël Carroll, *The Philosophy of Horror* (New York: Routledge, 1990). Carroll distinguishes experiences of real horror from those we have in response to works of fiction. Attempting to resolve the paradox of horror, he argues that our interest in art horror is primarily cognitive. While our initial interest in literary examples of the uncanny might not be similarly epistemic (by virtue of our normal resistance to the truth the uncanny discloses), the literary uncanny's effect is cognitive to the extent it reveals information that was hitherto repressed. It should be noted that Cynthia Freeland, well-known critic of Carroll's stipulation that art horror involves monsters, nonetheless pays homage to Carroll by invoking a distinction between art dread and real dread similar to his distinction between art horror and real horror in her essay "Horror and Art-Dread." Though it is beyond the scope of this essay to examine the parallels in detail, there are interesting similarities between what Freeland describes as the "vague sense of impending doom" (189) characteristic of art dread and the feelings of anxious dislocation engendered by the art uncanny. As she states, though they resist them in real life, individuals enjoy experiences of art dread and could be argued to appreciate similar experiences of the art uncanny, because they "help us ponder and respond emotionally to natural and deep worries about the nature of the world" (192). Freeland's essay can be found in *The Horror Film,* ed. Stephen Prince (New Brunswick, N.J.: Rutgers University Press, 2004).

57. Robert Solomon, *In Defense of Sentimentality* (Oxford: Oxford University Press, 2004), 14, 59.

58. Ibid., 19, 19, 24.

59. As Bowman notes, the uncanny is a difficult emotion to elicit because it is subtle and "easily crowded out by [more] powerful emotions" ("Heidegger, the Uncanny, and Jacques Tourneur's Horror Films," 73). Indeed, as I have discussed, to the extent the feeling of the uncanny engenders a disarming degree of anxiety, individuals frequently

evade the feeling by shifting their attention away from their own internal vulnerability to external threats that they could conceivably escape. This shift engenders an emotional transition from the uncanny to horror or fear. The frequency of this sort of shift makes Burton's consistent solicitation of the uncanny that much more masterful to the extent it is actually one of the more challenging emotions to elicit and sustain.

60. Martha Nussbaum, *Love's Knowledge* (Oxford: Oxford University Press, 1990), 48.

61. Ibid.

62. Heidegger, *Being and Time,* 317.

63. Ibid., 316. Ernest Becker, in *The Denial of Death,* corroborates Heidegger's assessment, stating, "the ironic thing about the narrowing-down of neurosis is that the person seeks to avoid death, but he does it by killing off so much of himself and so large a spectrum of his action-world that he is actually isolating and diminishing himself and becomes as though dead" (181).

64. Royle, *Uncanny,* 23, 6.

65. Bowman, "Heidegger, the Uncanny, and Jacques Tourneur's Horror Films," 82.

66. Jonte-Pace, "At Home in the Uncanny," 78.

67. Bowman, "Heidegger, the Uncanny, and Jacques Tourneur's Horror Films," 81.

68. Maria Tatar, "The Houses of Fiction: Toward a Definition of the Uncanny," *Comparative Literature* 33, no. 2 (Spring 1981): 167–82, quotes on 176, 169, http://www.jstor.org/stable/1770438, accessed March 13, 2012.

69. Page, *Gothic Fantasy,* 231.

70. See Robert Nozick, "The Experience Machine," in *Introducing Philosophy through Film,* ed. Richard Fumerton and Diane Jeske (New York: Wiley-Blackwell, 2010), 122.

71. Bowman, "Heidegger, the Uncanny, and Jacques Tourneur's Horror Films," 73.

Affect without Illusion

The Films of Edward D. Wood Jr. after *Ed Wood*

David LaRocca

> A typical American film, naïve and silly, can—for all its silliness and even *by means of* it—be instructive. A fatuous, self-conscious English film can teach one nothing. I have often learnt a lesson from a silly American film.
>
> —Ludwig Wittgenstein

The director Edward D. Wood Jr. is derided for the films he made in the 1950s and otherwise notorious as the "worst director of all time"—a sort of patron saint of the B movie.[1] Part of the pleasure audiences derive from proclaiming Wood the worst practitioner of filmmaking seems linked with an expression of resentment: hidden in the criticism of his work lies a belief and expectation (perhaps unacknowledged or unarticulated) that filmmakers are supposed to show us our world by taking us out of it. To outer space if need be. Science fiction, for example, is a film genre in which the demands for simulated but necessarily convincing escape tend to be the highest. Partly the escape to another world serves the symbolic significance of plot and character: many science fiction films (including many disaster films) become ciphers for terrestrial problems such as marriage trouble, political upheaval, fraught race relations, and compromised environmental policy. These otherworldly film fictions seem more satisfying as allegories precisely because we are *sure* the film is about, well, some other world. Much the same could be said of horror films, where the division between worlds allows viewers to explore fears, desires, and curiosity into the unknown without a sense that they are present in those horrifying realms. With both science fiction and horror, we are then at peace to experience and judge our own allegorized problems at a safe distance. Yet Wood fails to satisfy audience expectations precisely because he fails to achieve this separation between worlds. He never really even gets off the ground. The viewer can see the wire holding the wobbling metallic disc meant to be a flying saucer ("Holy mackerel. . . . It's nothing from this world") as the disoriented airline pilot—whose acting is as wooden as the painted steering column he fumbles with—tries to avoid hitting it.[2] Wood's films are almost entirely without illusion, and so the audience remains in the world it sought to escape.

But this failure, one that was likely as evident to audiences in the 1950s as at present, masks Wood's success: creating a kind of documentary of creativity in the midst of constraint, and in that kind of realism showing—inadvertently—the emotional lives of his actors. His films excel not at moving us through illusion but rather through the awful reality of our encounter with the world we in fact inhabit. The science fiction world or the world of horror, it turns out, is our own strange world, a place where making films on one's own—with little money and few accomplices—is often disparaged and compromised. Wood's films reflect back to viewers the world they live in, and most viewers, it seems, ridicule him for it; those who are said to love his work may do so with the reassurance of knowing better work by other filmmakers. He was outspokenly committed to "realism" and continually attested to his audience that what they were about to see was "real," "true," and "based on fact." But he created a kind of realism that shows the strings, not the kind that hides them. As critic J. Hoberman has said, "The rich realism induced by Wood's failure to convince is of incomparably greater aesthetic interest than the seamless naturalism of conventional narrative film."[3] It seems an unpardonable offense to genre conventions and audience expectations to claim you have made a science fiction or horror film and instead to have shown what amounts to a documentary about the failure to do so. Wood's films are defiantly, though not intentionally, antispectacle.[4]

With *Ed Wood* (1994), however, Tim Burton reveals "the incomparably greater aesthetic interest" of Wood's films by creating a film with "the seamless naturalism of conventional narrative film."[5] By Hollywood means, Burton shows how and why we should be interested in Wood's work—above merely indulging in the pleasure of mocking it. Burton is a fan who clearly appreciates why it is fun to laugh at Wood's poorly made films, but he is also committed to exploring what Wood's films represent aside from their apparent failure to impress savvy audiences. Even midcentury filmgoers, despite differing expectations for what film could do, regarded his films as bad, poorly made, and worthy of ridicule. Burton's film makes clear and accentuates what is good and interesting about these "bad" films. Burton shows that the emotional core of Wood's films is discernible, evident, palpable even *without illusion,* without the viewer getting "lost" in the story. Burton's stylization heightens a viewer's sense of the documentary nature of Wood's work—that it is effectively the filming of the staging of people who *want* to make a movie, who want to convey emotion and ideas, but who do not achieve the degree of illusion that we expect of engrossing, accomplished films. *Ed Wood* is not a film that celebrates its eponymous hero (since celebration, in this case, is too often a form of condescension); rather, it is a work that seeks to understand the nature of his achievement.

Burton, already the renowned director of *Pee-wee's Big Adventure* (1984), *Beetlejuice* (1988), *Batman* (1989), *Edward Scissorhands* (1990), *Batman Returns* (1992), and *The Nightmare Before Christmas* (1993), creates in *Ed Wood* a film that succeeds in presenting the desired Hollywood illusion of division between worlds. The philosophical significance of this notion—and its effects—is partly elucidated in what follows by reference to work as ancient as Plato's *Republic* and as recent as Jean Baudrillard's *Simulacra and Simulation.* Aside from obvious culprits like proven directorial experience, higher production budgets, expert and inventive production crews, and a lot of very talented A-list actors, there are two attributes of Burton's film that aid the division of worlds and, more importantly for my purposes here, contribute to the way *Ed Wood* reveals what is compelling and philosophically interesting about a production by Edward D. Wood Jr. First, making a film about making a film puts the viewer into an intimate yet voyeuristic position—which is to say, at a distance from the subject of interest. Yet if Wood was so good at making science fiction and horror films that did not go much further than documenting his failures, why don't his films create this safe proximity? The answer comes in another attribute of Burton's film: a continual shift between genres that forces audiences to ask what *kind* of film they're watching. *Ed Wood* is part stylish period drama, part biopic, part genre parody, part pseudodocumentary, and part reenactment and creative integration of Wood's most notorious B movies. Having to determine the nature of the film we are watching intensifies an audience's commitment to the conditions of its creation. And yet a viewer may not even be *aware* that this need for definition and redefinition is what catalyzes the film's illusion—its capacity to draw a viewer into its world while keeping the viewer safely at home. These two metafilmic attributes underwrite the philosophical significance of Burton's film and help us revisit the nature—and postulate the success—of Ed Wood's own work.

A Disclaimer as Condition for Criticism

As if in exploring the philosophical significance of Burton's *Ed Wood* there arose a need to explain who it is I am referring to when I say "Ed Wood," I note here briefly, in good humor *and* seriousness, that the Ed Wood of my essay is a composite of fictions—drawn from the *Ed Wood* screenplay by Scott Alexander and Larry Karaszewski, Burton's *Ed Wood,* Wood's films, film criticism, documentary films, and oral histories taken from some of Wood's collaborators. (In their introduction to the screenplay, Alexander and Karaszewski emphasize that they "avoided the bane of the genre: the 'composite characters.'"[6] Yet, from where I stand, Ed Wood must be a composite: otherwise he would just be Ed Wood.) I inquire and posit inductively by reading texts to offer readings. I cannot say what Ed Wood said or meant, but only what I understand from what he has created and what others have created in thinking of him. I do not seek to convey authorial intention (for Wood or for Burton) but rather to draw my claims based on interpretations of texts. It may be useful, then, to think of the Ed Wood of Burton's film as a literary character: he is a fantasy of what Ed Wood might have been or what we should think him to be—since then the fantasy will reflect what we *need* him to be, thereby disclosing things about ourselves. But then, who Wood "really was" is neither that interesting nor that relevant for my purposes. Instead, the focus throughout my essay is on how Burton's fictitious film alters our understanding of the realities in Ed Wood's fiction films.

Furthermore, I should note (and emphasize) that Burton is the director—not the screenwriter—of *Ed Wood.* Consequently, when I speak of "Burton" I imagine the name to signify the director's approval and interest in the loving, sympathetic, philosophically informed portrait of Ed Wood that was written by Alexander and Karaszewski—whose work, in turn, was deeply influenced by Rudolph Grey's oral history *Nightmare of Ecstasy: The Life and Art of Edward D. Wood, Jr.*[7] Aside from the script, Burton likely had a tremendous influence on the tone and style of the film's visualization, but the degree to which that visualization is bound up with his endorsement of the screenplay should be kept in mind. Whether left unfilmed or left out in the editing process, significant portions of the screenplay did not end up in the finished film; the decisions about what constitutes the final work should be attributed, in part, to Burton's vision and understanding of Ed Wood.

Metaphysics and Metafilm

Tim Burton—by means of *Ed Wood*—transforms our relationship to Ed Wood's films. A long history of derision and condescension is suddenly put on hold to consider the accomplishments of Edward D. Wood Jr.'s films. What does Burton's film help us see? How does it illuminate what is filmically and philosophically pertinent in Wood's work? Because it is a metafilm, that is, a film about filmmaking, we seem to see *through* Burton's film to an interior Ed Wood film that never was. *Ed Wood* is a film that contains a revisualization of Ed Wood's films; it is Burton's attempt to create a simulacrum: a copy of something that does not have an original—a Wood film that is not derided for its kitsch but heralded as a work of high art. And as Hoberman claims, in *Ed Wood* "art is not reproduced as kitsch: living kitsch is reproduced as art."[8]

Yet Burton's film is not an instance of accomplished filmmaking—and a specimen of high art—simply because of its sumptuous production values and celebrated cast. Rather, it succeeds because Burton understands what is interesting about Wood's life: not the result of his efforts (his films) but, as it were, the nature of his efforts in making them. Burton is not the first to appreciate the entertainment—much less the philosophical—value of metafilm. In fact, there are enough films like *Ed Wood* that they amount to an important cycle. Among many metafilms, we could mention *8½* (Federico Fellini, 1963), *Day for Night* (Francois Truffaut, 1973), *The Player* (Robert Altman, 1992), *Lisbon Story* (Wim Wenders, 1994), *Living in Oblivion* (Tom DiCillo, 1995), *Boogie Nights* (P. T. Anderson, 1997), *State and Main* (David Mamet, 2000), *Timecode* (Mike Figgis, 2000), *Adaptation* (Spike Jonze, 2002), *Full Frontal* (Steven Soderbergh, 2002), *Incident at Loch Ness* (Zak Penn, 2004), and *Tristram Shandy: A Cock and Bull Story* (Michael Winterbottom, 2005). These are films that make themselves the condition for their own creation *and* criticism. *Ed Wood* is part of this cycle.

Burton, like all the directors noted above, creates a fictionalized encounter with the history or biography of a man. The metafilm, in this cycle, is always in significant measure a biographical film, or biopic. The films are also populated by fictional characters (sometimes alter egos, as in *8½*, or drawn from literature, as in *Tristram Shandy*). While the other films are about fictional directors (or others involved in film production), Burton's subject is about a real director, that is, a historically situated person. Early in *Ed Wood,* Wood (Johnny Depp) overhears secretaries discussing the "Christine Jorgenson story" and his interest is piqued when he learns that a producer is "trying to make a bio-pic" about "he/she/it."[9] This is another valence of metafilmmaking, a kind of Russian doll approach—Burton making a biopic about Ed Wood (the director) in which Ed Wood (the director-as-character) wants to make a biopic of Jorgensen by playing Jorgensen himself—and as a result transforms Wood's proposed biopic of Jorgensen into what should be called, more accurately, an *auto*biopic.

When the producer George Weiss (Mike Starr) learns that Christine Jorgenson has refused rights to the proposed film of her story, his solution is both necessary and elegant: "We'll fictionalize."[10] Wood, however, already sold himself as "more qualified to direct this than anyone else in town," based on the notion that his personal experience of transvestitism would, he presumes, give the film more credibility and more truth.[11] Wood does not want to fictionalize; he wants to *literalize,* so he casts himself in the lead role. The logic being that if Ed Wood *is* a transvestite then he will not really have to "play" at being a transvestite like an actor would. In fact, Wood would not act at all. He would just be himself. He tells the makeup man, "I don't want to look like a girl. I want to look like myself."[12] "Oh, just like the script!" is Dolores Fuller's exasperated declaration upon reading the screenplay, recognizing the isomorphism between Ed Wood (as Daniel Davis in *Glen or Glenda* [1953]) and Ed Wood (the director, her boyfriend).[13] Wood's forthright response is, "Exactly." For Wood the director, the equation is simple: film equals life. Wood does not see *Glen or Glenda* as representation but precisely as his story—as if it were a form of documentary footage of Wood in drag, which, in an important sense, it is.

Another kind of metafilm that should be mentioned, and that forms its own distinct cycle, includes documentaries such as *Burden of Dreams* (Les Blank, 1982), *Heart of Darkness: A Filmmaker's Apocalypse* (Fax Bahr, George Hickenlooper, Eleanor Coppola, 1991), *American Movie* (Chris Smith, 1999), *My Best Fiend* (Werner Herzog, 1999), and *Lost in La Mancha* (Terry Gilliam, 2002). These are not behind-the-scenes films but glimpses into the process of filmmaking. The films do not explain the films they are said to document. For example, *Burden of Dreams* does not tell us what *Fitzcarraldo* (Werner Herzog, 1981) means. Rather, these documentaries show; they are antididactic; they depict a process. There is no underlying thesis or theory that animates them or unlocks the mysteries of the film's subject. This cycle of documentaries is characterized by efforts to account for instances of and attempts at filmmaking—sometimes successes, but more often failures.

These two lists of metafilms—of feature fiction and documentary—represent films all dealing, in different ways, with the process of making films. With *Ed Wood,* Burton contributes something unique to the genre: taking the reimagining and stylization of Wood's biography as part of the process of remaking Wood's films. Burton does not make a film about Ed Wood so much as appropriate visual styles, plot treatments, acting mannerisms and pacing, qualities of the scores, and production attributes to make an ersatz Ed Wood film of his own. In this respect it is worthwhile to compare *Ed Wood* with *Boogie Nights,* where P. T. Anderson makes a film in which the genre of pornography film is depicted without making an outright porn film himself. Anderson creates a story for a film that is part of a genre defined (defiantly so) by antistory. *Boogie Nights* is a reply to the question, How do you make a film about pornography without a money shot, or rather, with more than a money shot? Just as a composer might write in the style of Bach, Chopin, or Dvořák, so Burton works to make a film in the style of Wood: not, of course, to imitate the poverty of those works, but the opposite—to illuminate what makes their existence pertinent to an understanding of filmmaking.

In Plato's *Republic,* Socrates's conversation with Glaucon in book 8 about the nature of reality yields consequential and unanticipated implications for the ontology of cinema. And, more particularly, the conversation sets up a distinction between visions of reality and truth that usefully distinguish Wood's view (in *Ed Wood*) from Burton's.

Socrates tells Glaucon that cave dwellers "would deem reality to be nothing else than the shadows of the artificial objects."[14] Wood is such a cave dweller. Imagine, then, Socrates's question to Glaucon as if Ed Wood were the subject: "What do you suppose would be his answer if someone told him that what he had seen was all a cheat and an illusion, but that now [viz., out of the cave, into the light of day], being nearer to reality and turned toward more real things, he saw more truly?"[15] Wood is, in fact, told this in the film, in effect, and is introduced to the world Burton inhabits. When Wood asks Criswell (Jeffrey Jones) "How'd you know we'd be living on Mars by 1970?" Criswell replies, "I made it up. . . . It's all about appearances."[16] Wood looks crestfallen—another person has told him that some work or idea is invented, when he thought it simply a fact to be revealed in due course. But then even

Wood, suspicious of the theory and not sure if it will work, puts it immediately to use. He too can make things up and present appearances. Wood holds a fund-raiser and just lies his way through it.

Wood insists that the filmed image is real, full of realism. That it is, as it were, coextensive with nonfilmed reality. Ed Wood, it seems, lives in one world (a world strictly of representation), whereas Burton is a dialectician (in Socrates's parlance), someone who posits two worlds (one represented, one real). And as artist, Burton sees his job as creating appearances that prompt us to fathom realities and truths; Wood, contrariwise, just thinks the appearances *are* realities and truths.

Wood's faith in the truth and reality of representation contributes to the didactic nature of his work. In fact, when Socrates defines a mistaken notion of education, it sounds like he is giving a pitch for a future Ed Wood film: "What [those with a flawed idea of education] aver is that they can put true knowledge into a soul that does not possess it, as if they were inserting vision into blind eyes."[17] The didacticism of Wood's work is, in this respect, underwritten by its diegesis. Wood often employs a narrator to explain the action: we hear, for example in *Plan 9 from Outer Space* (1959), the narrator say, "A woman startled by the sight in the sky telephones the police," as we see a woman startled by a sight in the sky telephoning the police. Sometimes characters narrate their own thoughts, as in *Glen or Glenda,* when a police inspector consults a psychiatrist: "I guess I've seen everything there is for a policemen to see. Yet I wonder if we ever stop learning, learning about which we see, trying to learn more about an ounce of prevention. I'm a man who thrives on learning. . . . Doctor, I'm hoping to learn something from you and with that knowledge maybe save some human from a fate which I just witnessed a few days ago."[18] Still another variation on Wood's didacticism is found when characters theorize about other characters in the film—"Then the way I get it, this Glen and the character he created, much as an author creates a character in a book, was invented as a love object to take the place of the love he never received in his early youth through lack of it from his parents."[19]

Bela Lugosi (played by Martin Landau in *Ed Wood*), the star of *Dracula* (Tod Browning, 1931), understands intuitively and experientially how "classic horror films" were much "spookier" than the then-current fascination with giant insects: "Who would believe such nonsense!"[20] As if he's telling Wood news, Lugosi explains: the classic horror films were "*mythic.* They had poetry to them."[21] We can read Lugosi's critique as befitting Wood's yet-to-be-made film since, as we will come to see in part through Burton's vision, Wood's films are not mythic or poetic or mythopoetic. Or rather, the degree to which they are mythic and possess poetry is a function of what a viewer, such as Burton, brings to them. Burton's film shows how Ed Wood's way of taking things straight and literal is, nevertheless, productive of thinking about mythic and poetic forms: identity, creativity, how one follows dreams and visions.

Compare Wood's literalist metaphysics of reality with Socrates's more literary, two-world, indirect, nondidactic, artistic view—one that exemplifies Burton's position and relationship with art and reality: "There must be an art, an art of the speediest and most effective shifting or conversion of the soul, not an art of producing vision in it, but on the assumption that it possesses vision but does not rightly direct it and does not look where it should, an art of bringing this about."[22] Wood believes in a naïve sense of "seeing is believing," where things on screen are self-same, as if there were no distortions (by anything from special effects to the imposition of literary narrative); whereas Burton, like Socrates, possesses a philosophical understanding of the relationship between art and reality: art is best understood as a provocation to thinking about the real and the true.[23] Art is not an end but a means to something else. When faced with an exceptional work of art, we find our attention is rightly directed and looks where it should. Not so much *at* the art as at what the art prompts us to consider.

Burton as a dialectician—as an artist who recognizes film's philosophical pertinence—employs film as a medium for provoking (or evoking) thought about both what is and is not screened. "The experiences that do not provoke thought," Socrates continues, "are those that do not at the same time issue in a contradictory perception. Those that do have that effect I set down as provocatives, when the perception no more manifests one thing than its contrary, alike whether its impact comes from nearby or afar."[24] The "contradictory perception" is precisely what a dialectical understanding of art provides: "some things are provocative of thought and some are not, defining as provocative things that impinge upon the senses together with their opposites, while those that do not I said do not tend to awaken reflection."[25] At this point we might seek an illustration: which understanding of film—Wood's or Burton's—seems to be more provocative for thought or awakens more reflection? Wood's didacticism does not invite reflection (though the nature of his didacticism does—that is one of the core interests of Burton's film), while Burton's provocative *Ed Wood,* full of "contradictory perceptions," continually represents dialectical investigation and invites it from viewers. Socrates notes one consequence for those, such as Wood, with a unified vision of reality and representation: "The clear waking vision of it is impossible for them as long as they leave the assumptions which they employ undisturbed and cannot give any account of them."[26] Burton, on the other hand, through an invigorating dialectic of metafilmmaking techniques, leaves few assumptions undisturbed.

We hear what might be called Socrates's disappointment in someone such as Ed Wood when he criticizes "the soul that hates the voluntary lie and is troubled by it in its own self and greatly angered by it in others, but cheerfully accepts the involuntary falsehood and is not distressed when convicted of lack of knowledge."[27] Socrates notes that "he who can view things in their connection is a dialectician; he who cannot, is not."[28] Burton's recognition of two types of metafilm, which I articulate below, confirms his status as a competent dialectician—that is, in a Platonic sense, someone capable of articulating a question, fathoming a reply to it, and recognizing precisely how two elements (such as content and form) are connected. Occasionally, and often quite effectively, we find Socrates's questions already latent with an answer—a feature usually understood as contributing to a form of irony (since Socrates's question anticipates his interlocutors' replies by providing an answer that, we presume, appears to be more clever than one they might have managed to generate on their own). The Socratic dialectician, then, is aware of his words—his text and context—in a metacritical fashion, much as we find in Burton's work, where he appears continually attuned to the layers or levels of reality he presents and represents. Burton's dialectical competency may be recognized as part of a postmodern attitude (and its forms of irony), but recourse to Plato suggests that one of Burton's philosophical preoccupations—principally his "view of things in their connection"—also engages the ancient practice of critical discourse known as dialectics.

Visual Duplicity and Cinematic Effect

Ed Wood is two kinds of metafilm interacting with one another—changing one another and together forming an impressive, coherent hybrid film. The first type I call biographical simulacra; the second type I refer to as mimetic reenactment.

Type 1. When Ed Wood appears as the biography of Ed Wood, the film is a simulacrum, not mimetic. Burton does not imitate a life but creates a new life with no original or referent. In other words, Burton's film is not historical but philosophical and literary. The biographical narrative is Burton's fantasy of Wood's life, and in important ways it becomes Burton's attempt to make his own Ed Wood–style film while importing his own, different sense of craft and humor.

Type 2. The portions of *Ed Wood* in which Burton re-creates or reenacts Ed Wood's films—*Glen or Glenda, Bride of the Atom / Bride of the Monster* (1955), *Plan 9 from Outer Space*—should be understood as remakes. Burton shows himself to be a careful and admiring student of Wood's films, and thus Burton's remakes are loyal to the original films—and as such are deeply mimetic. By "loyal," I mean imitative and referential: set design, casting, and other elements are meant to seem isomorphic—or as close to the original as possible.

These two kinds of film are important in their own right, since, for example, they show (regarding film type 1) Burton's biographical inventiveness both in terms of character and narrative and (regarding film type 2) Burton's skill at reconstituting and applying the filmmaking techniques of another director, in this case Wood.

Of Burton's two dozen or so feature films, including innovative, award-winning animated works, *Ed Wood* is by many accounts his most critically praised film. It is an easy move to note the irony that the subject of Burton's "best" film is the "worst" director of all of time. What is more interesting, and certainly more revealing about *Ed Wood*'s relation to Burton's other work, is Burton's parallel methodology or even care for what might be called the naïve arts. Burton's aesthetic—celebrated in a multimedia retrospective at the Museum of Modern Art (MoMA) in New York—bears strong ties to so-called outsider art. (If this is true, then the institutional celebration of his work at MoMA is a more satisfying irony to dwell on.) Burton's imagined worlds, and the manner in which he crafts them, suggest an artist who is deeply in tune with the handmade nature of art, and the proximity of the artist who creates it. Ed Wood worked as an outsider artist in Hollywood, a director at the margin or fringe of the mainstream. He made "realistic" films that engaged surreal problems and prospects—aliens who attack earth; the creation of atomic superhumans; very pointed social issues, such as the nature of human identity and its possible transformation (for example, in the mode of transvestitism). Burton clearly admires Wood's artistic process, and even the results! Yet, despite all of Burton's popularity and success in the mainstream as a weaver of tall tales and conjurer of alternate realities, his original works often have more cultural resonance than they do critical impact. *Ed Wood* seems to be the exception. Here Burton does not create an improbable fantasy world but stays very much on earth—with real people and their very real problems: something Wood, with his love of "realism," would have been flattered by. It would be a strange but very satisfying outcome if, for all of the colorful phantasmagoria of Tim Burton's other work, he were most admired for his black-and-white film about Ed Wood.

Part of that admiration, I suggest, derives from Burton's success in blending together type 1 and type 2 into a single, coherent film. The result of the combination is perhaps the primary reason why *Ed Wood* becomes a work of art: as a result of weaving the two types together, Burton makes the biographical story (type 1) seem more like one of Ed Wood's films and makes the "remakes" (type 2) seem more biographical. The finished film—*Ed Wood*—succeeds as a work of art because it both (a) transforms Wood's biography into a new kind of life (a simulacrum, a literary impression of a life) that is fascinating in its own right and revelatory of truths of human life and efforts at filmmaking (and importantly, that need not have any basis in facts or literal biographical details); and (b) puts Wood's otherwise dismissible, low-budget, poorly acted, awkwardly produced films into a context in which we can, as it were, enjoy them and see them anew. In fact, as my title suggests, Wood's original films are, I contend, more intriguing *after* watching Burton's film because Burton, in effect, has taught us (dialectically, not didactically) how to watch Wood's films and has shown us why we should appreciate them.

The Philosophical, not the Literal (Notes on Realism, Part I)

In the *Republic,* Plato creates an allegory that is meant to stand for the human condition: we are continually alternating between a world of projected representations and postulated realities. If only we were truly in the position of moviegoers and could step out of the theater. As it is, we never see the world directly but mediately and indirectly. All the world's a screen. And there is no way to look beyond the projection or peer behind the screen; we perceive only the surface of things. Later philosophers, such as Emerson and Nietzsche, would incorporate these kinds of tropes into their account of reality and representation.

With Plato, however, we find an early philosophical account of the ontology of representation; he is not as concerned with the aesthetics of representation (e.g., art's meaning, significance, or whether it is beautiful and well made) as with our understanding of the difference between seeing something and seeing something represented (or presented again). Plato, like Kant many centuries later, simply says that we never see anything presented but only ever see things represented. (Kant, in Platonic fashion, divides the world into noumena and phenomena—the former that which we never experience, the latter being all we ever experience.)

Ed Wood continually presents his films as showing the "real," as being "realistic." His promotion of this idea is linked with his underlying presumption that the more real something is the scarier (and more entertaining) it will be. He seeks to make films that will, in the language of Burton's Wood, "entertain, enlighten, and maybe even move people."[29] The problem, of course, is that realism has nothing to do with truth. Realism, in fact, undermines the drive to truth—either as the expression of ideas or as the hope for entertainment—by demanding a connection between realities. Wood seems to think that if the viewer believes the reality of what she sees on screen then she will be more frightened and more enlightened. Burton, on the other hand, thinks Wood's understanding is naïve and funny, but still interesting. Burton therefore adopts Wood's posture of realism in order to show us how it has nothing to do with the films he (that is, Burton) makes. But Burton does not stop there: by developing the type of film I call biographical simulacrum (type 1 above), Burton sidesteps the pursuit or claim of realism by simulating human experiences. While Wood seeks a literal isomorphism between realities, Burton aims to drive a wedge between them: to emphasize the degree to which what we see is a fabrication—a reality in its own right, not the reality we think we are being given, or even the reality we think we want. *Ed Wood,* then, is not a historical reenactment or a docudrama about Ed Wood but a simulation about a character named Ed Wood—a film that, of course, as noted, contains artful remakes and vignettes. The distance between the "real" Ed Wood and Burton's Ed Wood is irrelevant, part of the ongoing habit of viewers to desire an insight into art by way of a view of the artless (e.g., trivia and gossip). Wood celebrates the pursuit of realism (however misplaced, despite whatever poor results) with opening intertitles like the following from his first feature, *Glen or Glenda:*

> Many of the smaller parts are portrayed by persons who actually are, in real life, the character they portray on the screen. This is a picture

> of stark realism—taking no sides—but giving you the facts—All the facts—as they are today.
>
> You are society—Judge ye not.

Aside from the awkward grammar and earnest, chiding tone, Wood also demonstrates an evident lack of appreciation for the kind of realism one can achieve through simulation. In *Glen or Glenda* we don't seem to be watching a horror or science fiction film but something like an educational film, even an ethnological documentary. Over silent footage, accompanied only by doleful violin strings, the narrator comments on a man in drag, sustaining the effort to encourage the viewer to reserve judgment about what she sees:

> One might say "There but for the grace of God go I." . . . Nature makes mistakes; it's proven every day. This person is a transvestite: a man who is more comfortable wearing girl's clothes. The term "transvestite" is the name given by medical science to those persons who wear the clothing of the opposite sex. Many a transvestite actually wishes to *be* the opposite sex. The title of this can only be labeled "behind locked doors." Give this man satin undies, a dress, a sweater, and a skirt or even the lounging outfit he has on and he's the happiest individual in the world.[30]

It is a measure of the totemic significance of the white angora sweater featured in *Ed Wood* that it was displayed along with Batman's mask, Edward's scissorhands, and Betelgeuse's pinstripes in the Museum of Modern Art's retrospective of Tim Burton's body of work.[31] Burton appropriates Wood's opening proviso from *Glen or Glenda* about "real life," "stark realism," and "all the facts" but puts these notions to different use. At the outset of *Ed Wood,* Criswell the psychic bends up from an opening coffin to declare, "Greetings, my friend. You are interested in the unknown, the mysterious, the unexplainable . . . that is why you are here. So now, for the first time, we are bringing you the full story of what happened. . . . We are giving you all the evidence, based only on the secret testimony of the miserable souls who survived this terrifying ordeal. The incidents, the places, my friend, we cannot keep this a secret any longer. Can your hearts stand the shocking facts of the true story of Edward D. Wood, Jr.??"[32] While Wood wants to scare us with the reality of aliens resurrecting human corpses (*Plan 9 from Outer*

Space) or a mad scientist creating a race of atomic superhumans (*Bride of the Monster*), Burton wants to scare us with the realities of being a filmmaker.

> TOR: Dis is a nightmare.
> CRISWELL: It's showbiz.[33]

In Burton's vision the real problems, the real horror, are what takes place between takes: being unable to secure financing, contending with social stigma (for being a transvestite, or gay, or for wanting to get a sex change), being out of work (Bela Lugosi tells Wood, "In the afterlife, you don't need to look for work"), arguing with a lover about work, getting fired, losing one's unemployment benefits, losing one's lover, living without health insurance, being a drug addict (not always a horror in Hollywood, where bad news may be the condition for a comeback—in this case Bela makes front-page news as the first celebrity actor to check himself into rehab), and being in withdrawal from drugs (perhaps the most truly horrifying and emotionally difficult scene in *Ed Wood*).[34]

Because the typage in *Ed Wood* is so convincing, Burton's film seems to move beyond Wood's beloved and sought-after "realism" to achieve a work that has been praised as "impressively hyperreal."[35] Where Wood sought to show the "facts" of a "true story," he ended up showing us the "near-documentary atmosphere of genuine befuddlement" that plagues his productions.[36] Burton, on the other hand skips realism altogether and gives us instead a remarkable simulacrum of Wood's world and films. According to Jean Baudrillard in the essay "The Precession of Simulacra," the hyperreal is "a real without origin or reality."[37] In other words, simulacra suppress a connection to a referent and instead triumph as realities unto themselves. In Wood's films, the actors do not "become" characters; hence the documentary nature of his films. In *Ed Wood,* by contrast, the actors become more than the actors or characters they play: they inhabit a new hyperreality of their own. This phenomenon is what Baudrillard calls "the liquidation of all referentials."[38] Martin Landau does not, then, copy Bela Lugosi (and the characters he plays in Wood's films and non-Wood films such as *Dracula*) so much as become his own independent idea and instantiation of Lugosi. With simulation, Baudrillard notes, "it is no longer a question of imitation, nor duplication, nor even parody. It is a question of substituting the signs of the real for the real."[39] Baudrillard claims the evisceration of the real involves an "artificial resurrection," a notion that Wood likely would find compelling for its apparent connotations about the undead.[40] But it is an *artificial* resurrection, which is to say, a resurrection without a body. Meanwhile, Burton's regular preoccupation with adapting often well-known material (consider *Planet of the Apes* [2001], *Sweeney Todd* [2007], and *Dark Shadows* [2012], among other examples from the past decade or so) lends an additional valence to Baudrillard's notion of artificiality, since Burton's work involves remaking existing narratives in such a way that they become original—his own—by virtue of his signature styles and effects. In Burton's hands homage is incorporated so that the presence of the original is felt (palimpsestically) but not seen. The original film text is eclipsed by Burton's copy, which is very much its own independent, original creation: a thing in itself by means of artificial resurrection.

Baudrillard's distinction between the real and the hyperreal helps clarify the nature of what I refer to as biographical simulacra (type 1). There is a crucial difference between Wood's unintended documentary footage of actors (showing the realism of their experience making the film) and the hyperrealism of Burton's studied re-presentation of actors playing actors playing characters. Baudrillard's account of the difference between simulation and dissimulation adds to our understanding of these two kinds of realism: "To dissimulate is to pretend not to have what one has. To simulate is to feign to have what one doesn't have. One implies a presence, the other an absence. But it is more complicated than that because simulating is not pretending. . . . Therefore, pretending, or dissimulating, leaves the principle of reality intact: the difference is always clear, it is simply masked, whereas simulation threatens the difference between the 'true' and the 'false,' the 'real' and the 'imaginary.'"[41] Watching an Ed Wood film in the wake of *Ed Wood,* Baudrillard's distinction is abundantly and usefully evident. In Wood's work, the "difference" between actor and character, between film set and alternate world, is "always clear." Burton's film, contrariwise—largely in this case because he so masterfully interrelates film types 1 and 2—"threatens" our chances of discerning the difference. With Burton, the referent recedes into oblivion and *Ed Wood* becomes a new reality of its own. Art. Even high art.

Burton's combination of film types 1 and 2 creates at once a sense of familiarity (as if we are really watching Ed Wood's story and the making of Ed Wood's films) and a sense of alienation (because we are sure these artful impressions are decisively neither of Wood nor of his making). The alienation effect is related to what Hoberman calls the "deeply solipsistic" nature of *Ed Wood.*[42] We might gloss such a description by remembering that when

John Malkovich (the character) goes through the portal to his own body in *Being John Malkovich* (Spike Jonze, 1999), he only sees other Malkoviches speaking a language comprising only his name: "Malkovich, Malkovich, Malkovich." A similar lens is placed over Burton's camera so that anything it films in *Ed Wood* feels inspired by the life of Ed Wood or a transformative imitation of his films. Because "everything is stippled in noir lighting and awash in studio rain," Burton pushes the principle of reality into the hyperreal. We are put at a remove from the biography of Ed Wood and the making of his films: we enter into total simulation, where every scene is part of a noir/horror/sci-fi consciousness that passes for Wood's own. Burton has created a monster of his own by achieving the "artificial resurrection" of Ed Wood as simulacrum.

Nonacting versus Reenactment (Notes on Realism, Part II)

In trying to characterize the amateurism of many of Wood's actors, I might simply say it is a form of nonacting. At one point the character Ed Wood says, "I don't care if they're not actors. I want realism. I want this film to tell the truth."[43] Wood thinks that a real transvestite shows the truth better than an actor playing a transvestite; he could not have seen Johnny Depp as Bon Bon/Lieutenant Victor in *Before Night Falls* (Julian Schnabel, 2000) and realized his error. Yet Burton does that work for him, showing that actors ("the unreal," the simulacra, the imitative) show the truth through their *acting* performances.

There is a sense of nonacting in which we can, so to speak, see the actor him- or herself. For example, in the mimetic reenactment (type 2) scene in which Dolores Fuller plays the secretary, Margie, an *Ed Wood* viewer sees levels of imitation: Sarah Jessica Parker as Dolores Fuller as Margie.[44] We are, as it were, two removes from Parker as actor. But more interesting is the way Parker as Dolores performs the role of Dolores as Margie, thereby illuminating how Dolores is, well, not a very good actress (even as the performance intensifies our appreciation of the degree to which Parker is an exceptional actress). If you have never seen an Ed Wood film, then Burton's treatment here may seem like parody, as if he were satirizing the woodenness of Dolores's performance. Yet after watching the scene from Wood's *Bride of the Monster* that Burton has reenacted—which is, importantly, not to say re-acted—one realizes the skill and even the poignancy of the mimesis.[45] The extent to which Dolores Fuller (the actor) is not acting is easier to recognize in the wake of Burton's film, where Parker as Dolores as Margie acts Fuller's quality of nonacting. The reality of Fuller's nonacting is, then, better represented by the mimetic reenactment; with Parker as simulacrum we get a better glimpse of the truth of Fuller's performance in *Bride of the Monster.*

Seconds after Dolores finishes this scene in *Ed Wood,* Wood yells, "Cut. That was perfect." And Dolores responds with anger and irritation: "Of course it was." Her point being that Wood is satisfied with anything—usually the first thing—that gets shot. Always pressed for time and cash, always aware of the constraints that befall him as a moviemaker, Wood turns what for other directors would be compromise into a moment of achievement. "That was perfect" is almost a mantra in Burton's film, heard again and again.[46] (By contrast, one could never imagine canonical directors Robert Altman or Stanley Kubrick declaring, "That was perfect" after one take.) While it is clear that Wood's rush to move on is motivated in part by his awareness of limited resources, it is also indicative of his notion of realism in cinema. In an important sense, just saying the lines is enough, since he is not interested in acting so much as recitation—as if, again, "just saying" something makes it more real than if an actor transforms it through a sense of the character. In this way, Dolores Fuller's nonacted Margie might be considered more real for Wood than Parker's nuanced performance as Dolores as Margie.

The "just saying lines is enough" approach is related to the documentary nature of Wood's films: in documentary film, there is a presumption that scenes are not staged. (Of course, there are famous documentarians, such as Werner Herzog, who antagonize the established faith in fact as truth by doing multiple takes, giving actors lines, and adding other fabrications; Casey Affleck's documentary *I'm Still Here* (2010) offers another modification to the notion of "documentary" by creating a narrative feature film with actors playing themselves according to conventions of documentary film.) When asked by the crew if he wants to reshoot a scene because Tor Johnson as Lobo (George Steele) hit the door frame and moved the wall, Wood replies, "No, it's fine, it's real. You know in actuality Lobo would have to struggle with that problem every day."[47] A few minutes later, Wood says, "*The movie's getting made*—that's all that matters."[48]

After one of the instances in which Wood says, "That was perfect" about a substandard take, he is confronted by his financial backers: "Perfect? Mr. Wood do you know anything about the art of film production?"[49] To which Wood replies, "Well I like to think so." The backers, unconvinced, continue, "That cardboard headstone tipped over. This graveyard is obviously phony."

Wood tries to reassure them with insistence and a quick theory of his "art of film production": "Nobody will ever notice that. Filmmaking is not about the tiny details; it's about the big picture." When the backers remain skeptical, Wood lashes out: "What do you know? Haven't you ever heard of suspension of disbelief?" Wood's debate, as rendered here by the screenwriters, is a kind of miniaturized version of a conversation most viewers of Wood's films would like to have with him. The dialogue aptly contrasts two competing elements in film spectatorship: the tension between noticing something and suspending disbelief if the awareness compromises film reality. Plato has a version of this debate in *The Sophist* when he discusses the problem of the existence of things that are not real; the issue is also dramatized in *The Matrix* (Andy and Larry Wachowski, 1999) when Neo (Keanu Reeves) notices a black cat *again*. His experience of déjà vu is a clue that the signal of the matrix has been interrupted. Neo notices something, but it takes the others to interpret what it means. However, suspension of disbelief should not extend to ignoring the movement of door frames or falling headstones; they are, in fact, precisely what undermines the act of attention and involvement. When a viewer is riveted, caught up, then a lot of disbelief can be suspended, but when there is little to get lost in, even the slightest detail can distract and destroy the suspension of disbelief. And a disbelieving moviegoer, we might expect, will be in no mood to avoid noticing things that contribute to her disbelief.

All this is to make evident what should be clear from watching Burton's *Ed Wood*, namely, how it helps us see better the emotional reality of Ed Wood's films: not the emotional reality of the characters in Wood's films, we might say, but of the *actors* who portray them. When we are liberated from expecting a satisfying, immersive illusion, when we no longer force ourselves to suspend disbelief in the face of Wood's unconvincing production, we are then able to see what is powerful—even mythic and poetic—about Wood's work. Namely, it offers a glimpse into the realities of making films, the emotional qualities such work demands of its creators—actors, directors, screenwriters, producers, crew, friends, lovers, and the myriad tentative and transitional acquaintances who seem to make all the difference between being unemployed and alone and being at work, pursuing one's visions. Orson Welles (Vincent D'Onofrio) asks a disheartened Wood, "Why spend your life making someone else's dreams?"[50] One achievement of Burton's *Ed Wood* is the degree to which it puts Ed Wood's films in a new light. After watching *Ed Wood*, we watch the films of Ed Wood seeing all the strings and yet feeling the profound yearning that lies behind Wood's effort against great odds, in spite of constraints and criticism, to realize his dreams.

"He Tampered in God's Domain"

Early in *Ed Wood* we're given a clinic on how Wood makes a film from what the studios throw away. ("It's such a *waste.* If I had half a chance, I could make an entire movie out of this stock footage.")[51] Wood's imagination fuels a Victor Frankenstein–like capacity to make a vital whole from disparate parts; Wood can hue scattered and random elements to fit the line of a narrative. ("See, the story opens with these mysterious explosions. Nobody knows what's causing them, but it's upsetting all the buffalo. So the military is called in to solve the mystery." The technician notes, "Ya forgot the octopus," to which Wood replies, "No, I'm saving that for the big underwater climax!")[52] Of course, this much is true: Burton does use the octopus for the climax of *Ed Wood,* as Wood did in *Bride of the Monster.* But Wood's talent with found materials, like Dr. Frankenstein's, need not culminate in an elegant creation.

What is of more philosophical concern than the mere act of selection and assembly, then, is why Wood's stock-footage-laden film lacks the artistic impact of work by Woody Allen (such as *Zelig* [1983]) or Werner Herzog (such as *The Wild Blue Yonder* [2005]), which include large amounts of stock footage. The answer is not just technical (for example, a matter of editing) but theoretical: Wood has a different theory of truth than do Allen and Herzog. As we hear from Criswell at the beginning of *Night of the Ghouls* (1959), which serves as the model for the beginning of *Ed Wood:* "For many years I have told the almost unbelievable, related the unreal and showed it to be more than fact." In *Ed Wood,* Criswell begins by asking if the audience can "stand the shocking facts of the true story" it is about to witness and ends the film by noting how the story of Edward D. Wood Jr. is "stranger than fact."[53] Wood—both as an artist and as a character in *Ed Wood*—is not satisfied with the reality that film offers and so continually promises to go beyond it, to what is "more than" real, "stranger" than fact.

The film that *is* "stranger than fact" is none other than Tim Burton's *Ed Wood.* It is fiction "based upon" true stories. With Burton's realization of the story the viewer is, in effect, *dared to believe:* challenged to submit herself to the willing suspension of disbelief. As a conglomeration of fiction, dramatization, mimesis, diegesis, and metadiegesis, *Ed Wood* is stranger than fact. With *Ed Wood,* we have a formulation of Burton's theory of truth: that Wood's "real" life is not a correlate of Wood's life in *Ed Wood* but a point of inspiration. As fiction, *Ed Wood* is a philosophical and literary achievement because it transforms the viewer's relationship to facts: they are not things to overcome or outdo, but things to marvel at. Many critics have taken Ed Wood's apparently earnest and optimistic pursuit of realism as an invitation to mock him, to adduce his failures at achieving realism. Tim Burton, along with screenwriters Scott Alexander and Larry Karaszewski, shows us why Wood's vision does not deserve easy ridicule but is worthy of genuine inquiry. For after Plato, after Baudrillard, who does not wish to see things truly, to discern the difference between simulacra and things as they are? The insight of Wood's project is found not in the creation of filmic illusion but precisely in its absence—the space in which viewers get an unexpected glimpse of the real. Not the real Wood hoped to reveal, but its more modest counterpart: the real inherent in a convincing fake. Our satisfaction with movies full of fabricated illusion gives the lie to Wood's view: saying "it was so realistic" is a form of praise for exceptional deceit, for accomplished imitation.

The most useful, most literary (because self-referential) intertitle is the last one: Criswell "continued making highly inaccurate and bizarre predictions." For as we watch Criswell closing the casket he opened in the beginning of the film, the camera tracking back as it once tracked forward, we see that his prediction about *Ed Wood* might be understood this way: *Ed Wood* is not full of facts, realities, and realism (as the other intertitles encourage us to believe—trying to suppress the fact of the film as fiction and fabrication) but a dramatization that gives us a chance to see the truth of the realities in the fiction—the trials and tragedies of everyday life in filmmaking.

Notes

Epigraph: Ludwig Wittgenstein, *Culture and Value,* ed. G. H. von Wright, trans. Peter Winch (Chicago: University of Chicago Press, 1984), 57e. I sincerely thank Jennifer McMahon for offering helpful remarks and editorial input on an earlier version of this essay.

1. There are several documentaries about Ed Wood's life and work, including *Flying Saucers over Hollywood: The* Plan 9 *Companion,* directed by Mark Patrick Carducci (1993); *Ed Wood: Look Back in Angora,* directed by Ted Newsom (1994); and *The Haunted World of Edward D. Wood, Jr.,* directed by Brett Thompson (1995). See also Trent Harris's feature *Plan 10 from Outer Space* (1995) and Robert S. Birchard's

"Edward D. Wood, Jr.: Some Notes on a Subject for Further Research," *Film History* 7, no. 4 (Winter 1995): 450–55.

2. *Plan 9 from Outer Space,* directed by Ed Wood (1959), 00:05:05.

3. J. Hoberman, "Ed Wood . . . Not," *Sight and Sound,* no. 5 (May 1995): 11.

4. Of course, Ed Wood appears to have believed that his film effects were satisfying to viewers, and therefore he did not set out to create parody, camp, or documentary films. Even when critics and audiences contravened his judgment, Wood continued to make his signature low-budget productions—hence his defiance.

5. Hoberman, "Ed Wood . . . Not," 11.

6. Scott Alexander and Larry Karaszewski, *Ed Wood* (London: Faber and Faber, 1995), viii.

7. Rudolph Grey, *Nightmare of Ecstasy: The Life and Art of Edward D. Wood, Jr.* (Portland, OR: Feral House, 1994).

8. Hoberman, "Ed Wood . . . Not," 12.

9. Alexander and Karaszewski, *Ed Wood,* 9.

10. Ibid., 12.

11. Ibid., 10.

12. Ibid., 34.

13. Ibid., 31.

14. Plato, *The Collected Dialogues,* ed. Edith Hamilton and Huntington Cairns (Princeton: Princeton University Press, 1961), 515c.

15. Ibid., 515d.

16. Alexander and Karaszewski, *Ed Wood,* 65.

17. Plato, *Collected Dialogues,* 518b.

18. *Glen or Glenda,* directed by Ed Wood (1953), 00:07:39–00:08:24.

19. Ibid., 00:53:28–00:53:41.

20. Alexander and Karaszewski, *Ed Wood,* 17.

21. Ibid., 18.

22. Plato, *Collected Dialogues,* 518d.

23. The phrase "seeing is believing" also appears in Burton's *Sleepy Hollow* (1999), a repetition that suggests how Burton may have incorporated, consciously or not, an aspect of Wood's understanding of film reality.

24. Plato, *Collected Dialogues,* 523c.

25. Ibid., 524d.

26. Ibid., 533c.

27. Ibid., 535e.

28. Ibid., 537c.

29. *Ed Wood,* directed by Tim Burton (1994), 00:29:57.

30. Wood, dir., *Glen or Glenda,* 00:12:04–00:14:22.

31. For more on the MoMA retrospective and the work it contained, see the slim *Tim Burton,* with Ron Magliozzi and Jenny He (New York: Museum of Modern Art,

2009), and the massive *The Art of Tim Burton,* ed. Leah Gallo, Holly Kempf, and Derek Frey (Los Angeles: Steeles Publishing, 2009).

32. Alexander and Karaszewski, *Ed Wood,* 1.

33. Ibid., 136.

34. The Lugosi quote occurs in Burton, dir., *Ed Wood,* 01:21:00, and Lugosi makes front-page news at 01:24:00.

35. Hoberman, "Ed Wood . . . Not," 12.

36. Ibid., 10.

37. Jean Baudrillard, "The Precession of Simulacra," in *Simulacra and Simulation,* trans. Sheila Faria Glaser (Ann Arbor: University of Michigan Press), 1.

38. Ibid., 2.

39. Ibid.

40. Ibid.

41. Ibid., 3. For a related discussion of simulacra in light of Gilles Deleuze's remarks on the subject, see my "The False Pretender: Deleuze, Sherman, and the Status of Simulacra," *Journal of Aesthetics and Art Criticism* 69, no. 2 (Spring 2011).

42. Hoberman, "Ed Wood . . . Not," 12.

43. Burton, dir., *Ed Wood,* 00:24:26.

44. Ibid., 01:05:06.

45. *Bride of the Monster* (1955); the scene occurs between 00:19:49 and 00:20:12.

46. A few places where Wood says "That was perfect" include 01:05:10, 01:10:40, and 01:47:20.

47. Burton, dir., *Ed Wood,* 00:57:00.

48. Ibid., 01:03:48; italics from screenplay, Alexander and Karaszewski, *Ed Wood,* 91.

49. Burton, dir., *Ed Wood,* 01:47:24.

50. Ibid., 01:51:24.

51. Alexander and Karaszewski, *Ed Wood,* 8. Note that the header of this section is the last line of *Bride of the Monster.*

52. Ibid., 8–9.

53. Ibid., 1, 169.

Little Burton Blue

Tim Burton and the Product(ion) of Color in the Fairy-Tale Films *The Nightmare Before Christmas* and *Corpse Bride*

Debbie Olson

Color is the language of modern fairy tales. Color is also part of the language of consumer culture. Children's films, or films targeted toward children, particularly animated films, are constructed around and negotiated within capitalist consumer culture, intricately weaving commodities and consumption with fairy-tale lands and utopian spaces. Whenever an animated film hits the theaters it is "part of a package . . . that consists of various commodities attached to it: a program, an illustrated book, a doll, a poster," and many other products that seek to capitalize on children's desire to continue the experience of the film's fantasy world.[1] Product saturation resulting from feature films carries with it certain aesthetic properties—including color—that work to tie the fictional film space into the "real," lived material space of childhood. Film merchandising has been very successful for studios and directors. One of the earliest examples of media merchandising comes from the Disney corporation, which demonstrated the interconnectedness of color usage and product merchandising when it shifted its television series *Disneyland* (1954–1961) (which had been broadcast only in black and white) from ABC to NBC, renaming it *Walt Disney's the Wonderful World of Color* (1961–1990). At the time NBC was "heavily promoting" its color broadcasting because its parent company, RCA, was the largest maker of color televisions.[2] Marriages of manufacturers and filmmakers are today a regular occurrence (i.e., product placement). Such partnerships between filmmakers and merchandisers raise, for me, interesting questions about the aesthetics employed in films, commodity culture, and the connection to constructions of childhood.[3]

As a director, Tim Burton has created a specific color palette in many of his films. His first major hit, *Beetlejuice* (1988), introduced the viewer to deeply saturated colors that contrast markedly with monochrome images. The film is filled with deep lime greens, reds, purples, and midnight blues, a much different palette than that used in many other films geared toward children. Today, and in part due to the work of Burton, children's visual geography has transformed from pastel pinks, blues, and soft yellows and greens to the more urbanesque color schemes that signify a Burton film. Though broader cultural processes that developed in tandem help account for the palette shift—digital technologies, the rise of computer games, innovations in animation technology, and the rise in urban-themed popular culture—Burton's films mark the beginnings of the trend in children's films toward a more deeply saturated and adultified color palette. Are such changes in the color of childhood within visual media also reflected in the physical world that our children inhabit? How does the color of children's material space reflect their role within late capitalist consumer society? Do films influence a child viewer's future consumer choices? For example, do the pastel shades of the Disney palette or the deeply saturated colors of Burton's films help inform, construct, or motivate a child's future consumer tendencies? Though there are numerous studies that seek to gauge the effects of sex and violence on the child viewer, fewer studies have been done on how children negotiate, incorporate, or resist *color* associations that may precondition children as consumers. Are fairy-tale films, or films targeted at youngsters, propaedeutic in creating childhood preferences for certain palettes? And do those color preferences instill or inform broader ideological values that contribute to future product desire and loyalty? Few filmmakers rely on color as a signature of their oeuvre, but Burton is one of those rare filmmakers who has created to a certain extent an auteur signature based on a specific color palette pattern. Many of his films subvert what are considered "normal" color choices associated with children and childhood. Are such subtle but visually significant changes in the cinematic landscape of childhood then replicated in children's consumer culture? To answer some of these questions, I will examine the unique palette in Burton's films that I argue contribute to broader cultural processes that condition children to idealize and commodify their own childhood by creating product identification through color symbolism. I will look closely at how the unique palette in Burton's *The Nightmare Before Christmas* (1993) and *Corpse Bride* (2005) (both films targeted toward children) works to associate commodities with a belief in a childhood utopia visualized in the films.

Childhood as Commodity

Since World War II, film has visually reinforced the belief in childhood as a quasi-Victorian, untainted state of innocence and unknowingness. Portrayals of an idealized childhood speak seductively to adults, who often desire a nostalgic return to childhood as an imagined state of perfection. Until the nineteenth century, children were considered to be adults in miniature. Before then, childhood as a special time of life was not a part of the Western cultural landscape. But with the advent of the industrial era, accompanied by the rise of capitalism and the middle class, new notions of schooling and leisure time and widespread disapproval of child labor changed conceptions of childhood on a broad scale. Rather than a means of support, children in the nineteenth century became valued as emotionally important to the familial structure (a structure that itself became an American social ideal).[4] Daniel Thomas Cook argues that in the post-Depression era childhood became a "site for commercial activity" with the rise of industrialization and over time evolved in such a way that "a child's value was measured less and less in economic-monetary terms and became constituted increasingly in sentimental-emotional ones."[5] Notions of innocence and purity became cemented to this new state of childhood, which in turn created notions of a society-wide responsibility to protect childhood innocence from what was viewed as the corrupting influences of adult knowledge. For example, during the Depression Shirley Temple was the physical manifestation of the purity and spiritual innocence that childhood represented and that adults desired—Temple's identity and body, as a result, were commodified in both film and real life.

Victorian notions of perfect childhood are still in evidence today, represented by young, blonde and blue-eyed, cherub-faced girls and clean-cut, freckle-faced white boys and exhibited in a plethora of idealized, nostalgic images on postcards and in coloring books, picture books, commercials and other advertisements, television, and film. The result of this cultural saturation of images of perfect white childhood is a naturalized collective memory of childhood as a "time that refers back to a fantasy world where the painful realities and social constraints of adult culture no longer exist." This perfect Dick and Jane era is regularly presented to the consumer by products that are marketed with the promise to return adults to that whimsical, prelapsarian state.[6] Today, childhood as a site of consumerism has united with its long-standing romanticized emotional representation in products that are marketed effectively both to adults, for nostalgic reasons, and to children, who, by consuming products that represent cultural notions of an "ideal" childhood, become active participants in the creation of their own commodified mythology.

Throughout the postwar years the media industry increasingly shifted the notion of children as influencing agents who could persuade their parents to purchase goods and services, which were thus marketed to children, to children as "sovereign, playful, thinking consumers" who are now one of the fastest-growing market demographics, particularly in this age of niche markets and kids-only television networks like Nickelodeon, Nickelodeon's TV Land, The Cartoon Network, Noggin, Discovery Kids, and The Disney Channel.[7] The advent of children's cable networks afforded advertisers "a ripe environment through which to address children as consumers" in both programming and advertisements, as well as to construct those preferences through strategic product placement and association, among other things.[8] In early attempts in television and Hollywood films (mainly by Disney) to "mass market childhood . . . childhood got branded sweet and cuddly, cute and tiny" and took place in fantasy realms of pure Disney, pastel palettes that reinforced the whimsical notion of the perfect childhood, as well as notions of gender-specific colors, that is, pinks, reds, and violets for girls and blues, greens, and browns for boys.[9] As Ellen Seiter and Vicki Mayer argue, "Many aspects of children's toy and media worlds have remained unchanged since the 1950s" and are most visible in children's films.[10] The divinity and purity of a prelapsarian state is "at the heart of the bourgeois cult of the beautiful child" because "childhood itself" is one of the most successful products sold to American consumers.[11] It is my suggestion that the idealization of childhood *through color* in films like Burton's doubles as a marketing strategy that works to reinforce among children the desire for goods that allow them to revisit the utopia of the film world and to create among adults desire for products—packaged and advertised in the same color palette as the film—that promise a return to that idealized childhood.

In today's niche markets, advertisers mimic the visual colors present in popular films such as Burton's by creating ads that re-create the films' numerous contrasts of deep, saturated colors against drab monochromes, unconsciously "hailing" the child viewer, who then connects certain product coloring to the fantasy world portrayed within the films' mise-en-scène. John Fisk argues that "in responding to the call, in recognizing that it is *us* being spoken to, we implicitly accept the discourse's definition of 'us' . . . we adopt the subject position proposed for us by the discourse," a subject position that is immersed in and shaped by color.[12] Assuming the child viewer is placed in a particular subject position by a film's images and discourse presented through a particular palette, children may become preconditioned to favor certain product colors over others, colors associated with the desired fairy-tale utopia in children's film. As a marketing strategy, product advertisers work to "(re)define commodities as beneficial/functional for children. When goods become framed as 'useful' they become means to ends rather than intended for mere consumption."[13] As color is also one of the primary languages of advertising, Burton's distinctive palette in his fairy-tale films helps children learn to associate, identify, and desire products that are advertised and packaged using similar color palettes. Burton's unusual and highly stylized saturated palette, as a marketing strategy, increases the child viewer's idealization, mythification, and commodification of his or her own childhood.

The Color of Childhood

Childhood products (toys, games, clothing) come in a variety of colors, and the market has conditioned consumers to associate particular product palettes with childhood. Along with product logos and advertising jingles, "color is one of the many marketing tools that global managers use to create, maintain, and modify brand images in customers' minds. . . . [Companies] strategically use color to communicate desired images and reinforce them to consumers" in the hope of creating long-lasting brand or product loyalty, a marketing strategy that is also symbiotically connected to films' similar use of color palettes.[14]

The most dominant marketer of children's films and products is the Disney corporation. Disney's strategic marketing of products based on its films is one example of the use of the film palette as an advertising tool, guiding children toward products that are associated with the images they've seen in a particular Disney film. Media fantasy and fairy tales for children have been in the Disney company purview since its inception. Disneyland and Disneyworld are spatial re-creations of childhood, structured to reinforce the experience of Disney films' fantasy worlds within a cacophony of products. Disney is the symbol of childhood itself and markets a wide range of products to convince consumers they can recapture the essence of the idealized childhood. Disney animated films are a site of consumerism in that the films are the base from which products are then marketed that promise a chance to revisit the experience of the film. Jack David Zipes points out that "as commodity, the fairy-tale film sacrifices art to technical invention, innovation to tradition, [and] stimulation of the imagination to consumption for distraction."[15] As Henry Giroux argues, "Disney was one of the first companies to tie the selling of toys to the consuming of movies."[16] Many times, especially in recent years, Disney products associated with a film are released *before* the actual film itself, relying on film trailers and Internet promotions to communicate the desire for the fantasy world the film delivers. The heavy promotion of children's films are also heavy promotions for the specific palette within the film world.

The Disney film palette is rich with pastel pinks, blues, and light reds, greens, and yellows, all of the primary shades with just a few marginal colors on the side. Disney products replicate the film palette so as to reinforce product association and identification with the fantasy of the film. For Disney, "art . . . becomes a spectacle designed to create new markets, commodify children, and provide vehicles for merchandizing its commodities."[17] The strategic marketing of similar children's products by other companies who adopt the Disney color scheme counts on consumer association with the Disney palette to boost sales. "The meanings associated with different colors are important to marketers because the tools used to communicate brand image are mechanisms of meaning transfer," particularly meanings associated with nostalgia for utopian childhood.[18] Products that are marketed to children jump on the color coattails of the Disney palette in order to take advantage of the industry standardization of childhood, which is embodied in Disney colors. "As the fairy tale was 'standardized' so that it could transcend particular communities and interests, it structurally fit into the economic mode of production during the 1930s and 1940s known as Taylorism or Fordism. Films were [and are] intended to be mass-produced for profit as commodities," including all associated merchandise.[19] The palette used for children's products has reflected the Disney pastels for years. Even television cartoons and advertisements marketing children's products were mainly composed of pastels up through the late 1980s. With the advent of new computer technologies and graphics in the mid-1990s, however, new colors associated with childhood emerged.

Along with today's changing social conditions for children, the palette of childhood is also changing. The soft pastels of the 1940s and 1950s cult of Victorian childhood innocence are being replaced with bold, gritty, urbanesque, computer-enhanced, deeply saturated, dark, and often marginal, colors that reflect a change in the notion of childhood itself. Today's childhood is no longer viewed as a Victorian utopia; however, the nostalgic *desire* for the Victorian idealized childhood is still a viable marketing strategy. Today's children are growing up with a palette that represents a childhood mix of soft, comforting pastels framed or overrun by deeply saturated, dangerous marginal greens, reds, blues, and purples, and when they reach adulthood, that palette will be used to market *their* childhood utopias as a return to the fantasy worlds depicted in today's fairy-tale films. The advent of computer games and digital graphics has changed the color scheme associated with childhood—many toys, books, games, and especially clothing now reflect the color schemes of popular digitally generated worlds. Disney has been slow to adopt the deeply saturated, nonprimary colors and still produces almost all of its films and products in the same pastel primaries of the Victorian childhood ideal; however, in the 1990s a new crop of fairy-tale films emerged that I believe has been influential in changing the palette of American childhood. Burton is one of the top directors of this new style of fairy-tale film.

The Burton Hue

Part of Burton's success is his "ability to transform colour into a commodity . . . with high visibility in public space," a space that is beyond just the screening of his films.[20] Burton's highly stylized juxtaposition of deeply saturated, marginal colors against bland backgrounds of neutral peachy-beige or his trademark gray-blue work to create a new kind of fantasy realm full of contrasting colors that is then replicated and marketed to children in a variety of products (and not necessarily limited to products based on the film itself). Each new Burton film targeted toward children also brings with it a bevy of products based on the film, but the film's palette alone acts as an important tool to precondition its young audience to see the film's saturated colors, often marginal colors rather than primary, as desirable, thereby reinforcing their future adult tendencies to prefer colors that invoke nostalgia for the fantasy film world that "insinuates itself into [children's] lives as 'natural history.' It's as though the film has always been there."[21] The naturalization of the film's fantasy world, and its colors, is what later frames adults' product and color associations. According to Charlene Elliott, "Colour communication—and particularly its standardization—speaks to all . . . visions of communication. Colour itself circulates as a type of commodity and the 'information' contained within Starbucks green, for instance, is easily read by its target audience."[22] Color use in film is artistically strategic but also a tactic in the context of the consumer culture through which the film is received. Color communication in film, however, is a powerful, but often silent, aesthetic that functions at the liminal space of consciousness. Color is seen as an "unreality. . . . Its arbitrariness consists of a kind of unconnectedness . . . it is artificial," and though the human eye sees color, the mind negates it and experiences color as a violation of order or sense.[23] Burton uses color's unconscious discombobulation of the senses by juxtaposing its anarchic ambience with a dry, cold, concrete blandness that repels, even if that blandness characterizes the "socially correct" position, that is, the world of the living in *Corpse Bride* or the land of Halloween in *The Nightmare Before Christmas.*[24] In *Corpse Bride* the world of the living is a soft beige-white, a misty, milky, drab color that is visually unappealing. A similar coloration appears in Halloween Land in *Nightmare.* Halloween Town is soft oranges, beige, dirty white, and gray-blue, which is also visually unappealing. Burton juxtaposes both of these worlds with their exact opposite—vibrant color. For the *Corpse Bride* viewer, the Land of the Dead is more visually appealing (aurally also, as the songs the characters sing are upbeat and jazzy), as it is filled with vibrant color as well as vibrant characters. In *Nightmare,* Christmas Land resembles the idealization of all things Christmas—warm, brighter colors (reds, golds, greens) that sit on a bed of slightly bluish-white snow (which contrasts markedly with the grayish blue-white of Halloween Town).

Though Burton stops short of total free-range, abstract use of color, his vibrant objects and frenetic, colorful characters give the impression of wild chromatic flows (particularly in *Corpse Bride*). Color is "physiologically immersive" in Burton's films; in other words, color functions, according to Carolyn Kane (via Gilles Deleuze) at the precognitive level.[25] Burton's chromocentricity, then, titillates and teases the viewer, who oscillates between desire for difference and the unknown (color) and the safety, the knowingness, of cool, bland shades. Burton's color matrix is a complex web of desire, disgust, knowing, and negation. He challenges the viewer's color associations by applying unique color blends to situations and characters that would normally be portrayed in stereotypical ways (for instance, the "bad" character is always in dark, the "good" character is in lighter shades).

Though almost all of Burton's films utilize to varying degrees the contrast between deep, saturated colors and lackluster earth tones to emphasize his themes of dark versus light, I will look closely at the color usage in *The Nightmare Before Christmas* and *Corpse Bride* and suggest that Burton's color palette has manifested itself in the landscape of modern childhood through the panoply of products both connected and unconnected to the films.

The Color of Nightmares

In *The Nightmare Before Christmas,* color represents warmth, fulfillment, and happiness for Jack, which contrasts sharply with the stultifying, dull gray-blue of his Halloween world. Jack is unhappy with his life and just needs *something.* The film tells the viewer that the something Jack needs is *color,* and he finds it on the Christmas tree in the woods. The brightest, most vibrantly colored tree in the circle of holiday trees is the Christmas tree, and it is the deep, exuberant colors of that tree in contrast with the passive and lifeless gray-blue surroundings that bewitch Jack. Like the proverbial rabbit caught in a headlight of color, he is hypnotized by its beauty, its visual articulation of his very desire (color is his *objet a*), which draws him to it.[26] As Jack spirals down inside the tree, bright white snowflakes whiz past him until he lands in Christmas Town, where everything is warmly lit with deep, saturated, storybook shades. As Jack stands, the town is revealed to him and it is stunning. Yet as Jack begins to sing "What's This?," the splash of color hints a slightly discordant edge: red, blue, magenta, fuchsia, purple-violet, and green against the soft but deep bluish-violet-white of the snowy North Pole. Jack sings,

> What's this? What's this?
> There's color everywhere
> What's this?
> There's white things in the air
> What's this?
> I can't believe my eyes
> I must be dreaming
> Wake up, Jack, this isn't fair
> What's this? . . .
> The monsters are all missing
> And the nightmares can't be found
> And in their place there seems to be
> Good feeling all around . . .

The sights, the sounds
They're everywhere and all around
I've never felt so good before
This empty place inside of me is filling up
I simply cannot get enough

I want it, oh, I want it
Oh, I want it for my own

The song describes Jack's desire for the color that has unfolded in front of him, and rather than associate color with chaos or danger as is most often the case, color here functions as the Other for Jack. It becomes desirable, a difference he doesn't understand but wants to possess, a typically colonial attitude. For Jack, "appropriation of the Other assuages feelings of deprivation and lack."[27] This sense of lack fuels Jack's misguided attempt to permanently internalize those pleasure feelings by kidnapping that agent of Christmas color, Santa Claus.

In his animated films, Burton often incorporates a cinematographic strategy that was used in the early stages of color film technology (Technicolor) in *The Wizard of Oz* (1939), which "contrasted color and black and white—color Oz looked exotic; black and white Kansas looked ordinary. In the end, the fantasy land had more presence than the real land. . . . In these movies color gave the objects pictured a presence" that is just plain missing in the here and now, according to Burton's palette.[28] Burton's color strategy produces a proliferation of soft abstractions that are almost dreamlike in their contrast: deeply saturated colors of an idyllic place against the harsh, stale ennui of the blue-gray world. To Jack, the colorful world of Christmas Town is an exotic, exciting place, full of life and an aura of magic. Color here functions not as a discursive fracture but as an emergence of life, and for Jack it provides an aesthetic unity of spirit within the paradoxical chaos/control of the colors of Christmas Town. The color before him threatens to leap out of its defined space and engulf the surrounding world; the color is efficacious—at once terrifying and irresistible.

The palette in *Nightmare* contrasts the peachy-beige, blue-gray of Jack's Halloween world with the romantic and ethereal palette of Christmas Town. Christmas in today's postmodern age is more than anything else a holiday for and about commodities, and most are marketed specifically to recapture the fairy-tale, idealized warmth and happiness of a utopian, Dickensian notion of Christmas. Through color, *Nightmare* highlights the desirability and transformative quality of the Victorian-Dickensian vision of Christmas, but through the lens of a modern-day, technology-infused palette. Jack's discovery of the brilliant colors in Christmas Town works to demonstrate what David Goodwin calls the "motives of displacement," which creates an "invitation to consumers to identify themselves with a fantasy world."[29] Jack is attracted to the *color* of Christmas Town, though he has no understanding of the meaning of Christmas itself, a point that is significant by its glaring absence in the film. Indeed, Jack's attempt to "perform" Santa Claus produces very anti-Christmas results. This process of absence is an effect of what bell hooks describes as a "commodification of difference . . . [that] promotes paradigms of consumption wherein whatever difference the Other inhabits is eradicated, *via* exchange, by a consumer cannibalism that not only displaces the Other but denies the significance of that Other's history through a process of decontextualization."[30] This process works twofold within the film, as the Other (color, but not Christmas itself) becomes the commodified element. As Jack travels through Christmas Town he sings, "I want it, oh, I want it for my own!" The goal of the film is Jack's quest to capture (to *own*) the colors that give him such a feeling of warmth and fulfillment and not to understand the actual meaning of Christmas. This message "to own" functions almost like a commercial inside the film *for* the film's many spinoff products. Burton's palette, and Jack's dialogue, together offer to fill the consumer "lack" with similarly colored products that will replicate for the child consumer the happiness that such colored objects brought Jack in the film. Jack eventually, but briefly, goes on a mission to discover the meaning of the bright, happy colors. But Jack ultimately equates *ownership* of the brightly colored objects with capturing the essence of the feeling they invoke. To own color is the essence of happiness. Jack does not understand Christmas the concept, but when Jack puts on the red Santa suit he believes he then becomes Christmas. It is the *color* of the suit that, for Jack, makes the holiday and brings fulfillment, a message that implies satisfaction if consumers will only purchase products in similarly saturated colors.

The Palette of the Dead

Burton's common theme of light versus dark frequently manifests itself in the juxtaposition of the living versus the dead. The binary light/dark in *Nightmare* and *Corpse Bride* is also analogous to the juxtaposition of adulthood/

childhood. In *Corpse Bride* Burton pits the boring, strictly organized and controlled world of the living against the freedom and youthful vitality of the world of the dead. That contrast is reinforced through color. The color of the living (adult) world in *Corpse Bride* is rendered in Burton's trademark bland shades of gray-blue and peachy beige that, in contrast to the brilliant colors of the underworld, reflect the rigid, drab lifelessness of adulthood. In contrast, the vibrant colors of the underworld and the invigorating, jazzy liveliness of its inhabitants are punctuated by the deep, saturated palette of richly textured shades that weave together objects and (dead) people in a polychromatic, swirling dance of joie de vivre. The *Corpse Bride* palette draws the viewer into a world full of dissent and disruption (nothing in the underworld goes according to plan, in contrast to the almost neurotic scramble to stick to the plan in the world of the living) and makes that chaotic, lively underworld more desirable by its juxtaposition with the bland and painfully cold stiffness of the world above.

The protagonist in Burton films usually arrives at the color-filled world through some kind of transformation or journey (*James and the Giant Peach* [1996], *Beetlejuice, The Nightmare Before Christmas, Planet of the Apes* [2001], *Corpse Bride*) where "the descent into color often involves lateral as well as vertical displacement; it means being blown sideways at the same time as falling downward" in a swirl of color and exhilaration, where objects and creatures are discovered to be full of more life and character than those in the real world the protagonist left behind.[31] In *Corpse Bride* Victor is whisked away from the drab and stressful adult world and into the lush colors of the underworld through the kiss of his dead bride. Heather Neff argues that "children's filmmaking, which tends to encode its ideas in simplistic, emotionally charged images, provides a spectacular forum" for expressing the longing for an alternate world.[32] *Corpse Bride* uses "rich colors and textures, a panoply of visual messages [that] entice, exhort, and explain" the desirability of the alternate world of the dead using color contrast.[33]

Victor is as weak and neurotic as the adults who surround him in the living world, but through his time in the lively underworld he gains both confidence and strength, traits that the characters in the underworld possess in abundance. Socially, the message is a paradox in that death is made to seem preferable to life, that those who are living are actually very dead inside, and yet in the end, as Victor puts the cup of poison to his lips in order to be a part of the beautiful underworld forever, Emily stops him. She sacrifices her own happiness so that Victor can wed Victoria and live in the upper world. Yet the film has constructed an uncomfortable nostalgia for living in the land of the dead, paradoxically full of color and life, a much more desirable fate than to have to live in the sterile unpleasantness of the blue-gray world of the living.

Though *Corpse Bride* does not feature particular objects as the desired goal, the driving force of the film's plot is still economic. The film's conflict centers on two families vying for either wealth or status. Victoria's family is titled but has no money, whereas Victor's family is nouveau riche—no class but lots of cash. The humorous juxtaposition of Victor's middle-class family (they are brash, uncouth, and interestingly, the mother is overweight but not the father) and Victoria's literally stiff-upper-lipped, perpetually frowning, titled family (they are the reverse body types—the mother is thin and the father is overweight—body images that are subtle modern-day markers of class) personifies class distinctions that have a long history in Western culture.[34] Victoria's parents' cold and calculated desire "to commodify and appropriate any aspect of marginalized culture that might be 'useful'" for the salvation of the family fortunes is the sentiment that drives the frenetic race to marry Victoria to whoever can rescue the family from poverty.[35] In the adult world, Victoria and Victor do not choose their mates or their life path. They are bound by duty and responsibility and are not free in the living world. But Emily and the other characters in the underworld are free to choose their own path within their world. The film ends with Emily choosing to sacrifice her own happiness for Victor's and, as a result of her sacrifice, turning into a flock of butterflies (pale, gray-blue) that soar up in the sky, disappearing into the insipid gray-white moonlight. Burton "make[s] extensive use of the interplay of neutral (black and white) and weighted [color] domains," and buttresses the color symbolism with the upbeat jazzy songs that the dead characters sing, reinforcing audience longing for the more colorful underworld in *Corpse Bride*.[36] Despite the macabre overtones of the underworld, the film leaves the viewer saddened at the thought of Victor and Victoria living a long, drab, colorless life in the above world. The vibrant, fun, *alive* world of color that exists just below the drab surface of the living (dead) world remains ever present, just out of reach, yet comforting and desirable. One can imagine that the memory of the dynamic underworld will haunt Victor's life aboveground, much as it will stay with young viewers when the film is over.

The message of *Corpse Bride,* however, is problematic for a child audience in that the film creates a disturbing desire to return to the land of the dead rather than stay with the living. The film sets up a "displacement, then, [which] 'neutralizes' a real hierarchy and substitutes, instead, an inverted, imaginary one" that privileges death over life.[37] That privileging is largely the result of the use of deeply saturated colors that draw the viewer to identify "real" life with color, the opposite of traditional notions of color, which as "always meant the less-than-true and the not-quite-real."[38] Burton's films are part of a technology-infused chromatic aesthetic that has created a new dimension of the idealized visual memory of childhood by "directing the meaning of the visual, anchoring hue to a particular idea, theme, or message." In Burton's films, color becomes much more than just a cinematographic style—it "becomes obviously commodified, packaged and sold as a vehicle for increased sales, while verbally rooted in a particular time."[39] Burton's frequent juxtaposition of death and life (as in his 1988 film *Beetlejuice,* where the underworld is an infectiously fun place compared to the crazy mean-spiritedness of the living world) functions to subvert the Victorian idealized childhood into a strange reversal of innocence—Burton presents a childhood utopia that is dark, necromantic, gritty, and *knowing.* Burton's protagonists tend to gain knowledge or insight that separates them from the self-absorbed adults and the adult world's superficiality. Gaining special knowledge in Burton films comes not from *believing* in magic but from *experiencing* the magical through color in a way that can, ultimately, be more easily associated with products that reflect the film's dark, saturated, urbanesque, and slightly ominous color palette.

Toy Store(y)

Though the Victorian ideal of childhood is still very much marketed, the reality of childhood today is much further away from the time of utopian innocence it was perceived to be in the 1950s through the 1970s. Today childhood is filled with technology that in some instances replaces socialization and discovery of the world with an internal isolation that relies on stimuli from sources other than human to achieve a sense of adventure, belonging, camaraderie, and culture (i.e., social networking or online role-playing games such as World of Warcraft). Computer games, iPods, iPads, television, and film all provide quasi-social connections for the modern child, which has resulted in the adultification and, almost by default, the urbanization of today's childhood. The vision of children innocently dancing through green fields of brightly colored flowers wearing pastel colors and white

Keds, catching butterflies or playing in the sand, has evolved into images of children dancing to rap and hip-hop heard through their iPod earphones, crowded together in front of a TV playing video games, negotiating around traffic and through malls, or being bullied by cyber-gangs, all while wearing dark street colors and adorned with a variety of flashy bling. Changes in the social, political, and economic experience of childhood within the disappearing middle class are visually expressed by the changing color aesthetic in children's films or films targeted toward children. Childhood the concept, though always a space where adult desires intersect with adult fantasy, has experienced a transformation that places children in the interstice between attitudes old and new. Preindustrial era conceptions of the child as mini-adult (revisited within contexts of criminal justice and the law, where children as young as eight are convicted as adults) dance with post-Fordist attitudes about the helpless, unknowing child whose innocence must be protected at all costs (which has resulted in the suppression of such natural child behaviors as hugging or roughhousing in the public school system). These seemingly disparate attitudes about the childhood experience, however, merge in Burton's films, where the childlike character occupies the liminal spaces of both adulthood and childhood. That liminal space is then replicated in products bearing the distinct palette of the film adventure.

The film's distinct palette appears replicated on store shelves as marketers "anticipate a viewer who knows certain pictorial conventions and who shares visual experiences" in a community of color associations.[40] The deeply saturated and marginal colors of music videos, TV shows, and films also mimic the dark reality of drugs, crime, sex, school shootings, isolation, bullying, and technology that inhabit today's childhood. As Elliott argues, "Between sixty-two and ninety percent of a person's first impression of an item comes solely from its colour."[41] Children learn color preferences through a complex process of association over time. As babies, the toys, bedding, clothing, stuffed animals, and other items that adults surround their child with also help that child learn to associate comfort, fulfillment, and happiness with the color of the objects surrounding them. As the child grows and is exposed to visual media of various types, the color associations are expanded, as are the child's experiences while viewing. Depending on the visual media, color association involves a "simple motion of relaxation-tension-release [that] is created by moving from and to points of dynamic symmetry, from one point of visual [color] balance in spatial composition to another."[42] And though "reactions to color are considered highly individualized," there is evidence of some level of universal color associations, as works by Thomas Madden, Kelly Hewett, and Martin Roth and by Patti Bellantoni suggest.[43] Bellantoni concludes that "color influences our choices, our opinions, and our emotional state. Our feelings of euphoria or rage, calm or agitation can be intensified or subdued by the colors in our environment. This is powerful information in the hands of a filmmaker."[44] A child's experience within the cacophony of media color functions in part to establish his or her palette preferences later in life. Films play a significant role in establishing those color preferences, particularly in today's visual culture and especially the highly saturated and stylized color palettes that occupy Burton's films.

In capitalism's quest for constant consumers, marketers rely on consumers' "learned vocabulary of pictorial symbols and . . . complex cognitive skills. . . . Thus, advertising images can be understood as a discursive form, like writing, capable of subtle nuances in communications or, like numbers, capable of facilitation of abstraction and analysis."[45] As Elliott argues, use of color by either a filmmaker or product manufacturer is a systematic process of developing color associations between a product and a desired fantasy through certain stages of color association. Color analysts have theorized three types of color consumers: Color Forwards—"the twenty percent of the population who are generally younger, attuned to new colour trends and willing to embrace them; Color Prudents wait for a color to gain acceptance before adopting it" and make up a little over half the population. Color Prudents "depend on the 'information' conveyed by degrees of display or by high visibility, which might come from a combination of media/marketing use (in retail or the like) . . . As such, the information flow in question is not verbal . . . but purely visual; and Color Loyalists, who comprise twenty-five percent of the population and are profiled as middle-aged with busy lifestyles who have no interest in fashionable colour culture."[46] Product manufacturers produce products in the palette of popular children's films to take advantage of children as Color Forwards, who are color malleable—their loyalty to specific colors has not yet been established. Child viewers are often presented with the color schemes of imagined utopian worlds within fantasy films, such as Burton's. Though the filmic world itself may not actually *be* utopian, the color scheme may suggest such perfection, hence creating a desire, like Jack's, to experience and belong to such a world. To further this desire, products are then created and marketed in those palettes that may create color loyalty in young viewers that will last through the other two stages of color consumption.

And it can only help if the film's characters and plot reinforce the desire to belong to such colorful worlds and to "own" things.

Films are important devices in the cultural production of color association. Visual media function as a vehicle for the cultural production of color and for color associations, which have the potential to influence consumers worldwide. Burton's films are far-reaching and one can assume the color palette of his films has lasting associations among a great majority of his young viewers. The cultural production of color association is only "one mechanism for creating [brand] logos that are recognizable and evoke positive brand and/or corporate images" in relation to products that promise to deliver a return to the childhood adventure on the big screen.[47] In a consumer culture, that production of color becomes persuasively entwined with the ideologically coded desire for eternal youth. That strategy depends on the idealization of childhood, no matter how it changes, which then becomes an "*artefact* of colour . . . a social phenomenon, a vivid expression of place and space" that, in Burton's films, becomes the chromocentric vision of childhood that young viewers today will desire to return to (through consumption) as they grow into the unfortunate and unmagical condition of adulthood.[48]

Notes

This essay previously appeared in slightly different form in *MP: A Feminist Journal Online* (June 2007) and is reprinted here by permission.

1. Jack David Zipes, "Towards a Theory of the Fairy-Tale Film: The Case of Pinocchio," *Lion and the Unicorn* 20, no. 1 (1996): 8.

2. J. P. Tellotte, "Minor Hazards: Disney and the Color Adventure," in *Color: The Film Reader,* ed. Angela Dalle Vacche and Brian Price (New York: Routledge, 2006), 37.

3. See the Walling chapter in this volume for further discussion of Burton's representation of childhood.

4. Karen Sánchez-Eppler, *Dependent States: The Child's Part in Nineteenth-Century American Culture* (Chicago: University of Chicago Press, 2005), xviii–xxii.

5. Daniel Thomas Cook, "The Rise of 'The Toddler' as Subject and as Merchandising Category in the 1930s," in *New Forms of Consumption: Consumers, Culture, and Commodification,* ed. Mark Gottdiener (Lanham, MD: Rowman and Littlefield, 2000), 112, 113.

6. Lyn Spigel, *Make Room for TV: Television and the Family Ideal in Postwar America* (Chicago: University of Chicago Press, 1992), 185.

7. Jyotsna Kapur, "Out of Control: Television and the Transformation of Childhood in Late Capitalism," in *Kid's Media Culture,* ed. Marsha Kinder (Durham, NC: Duke University Press, 1999), 125.

8. Spigel, *Make Room for TV,* 204.

9. Jyotsna Kapur, *Coining for Capital: Movies, Marketing, and the Transformation of Childhood* (New Brunswick, NJ: Rutgers University Press, 2005), 57.

10. Ellen Seiter and Vicki Mayer, "Diversifying Representation in Children's TV: Nickelodeon's Model," in *Nickelodeon Nation,* ed. Heather Hendershot (New York: New York University Press, 2004), 120.

11. Kapur, 49.

12. John Fiske, *Television Culture: Popular Pleasures and Politics* (New York: Routledge, 1987), 52.

13. Cook, "Rise of 'The Toddler,'" 115.

14. Thomas J. Madden, Kelly Hewett, and Martin S. Roth, "Managing Images in Different Cultures: A Cross-National Study of Color Meanings and Preferences," *Journal of International Marketing* 8, no. 4 (2000): 90–107, quote on 90.

15. Zipes, "Towards a Theory of the Fairy-Tale Film," 8.

16. Henry A. Giroux, *The Mouse That Roared* (Lanham, MD: Rowman and Littlefield, 1999), 118 n20.

17. Ibid., 158.

18. Madden, Hewett, and Roth, "Managing Images in Different Cultures," 91.

19. Zipes, "Towards a Theory of the Fairy-Tale Film," 6.

20. Charlene Elliott, "Crayoned Culture: The 'Colour Elite' and the Commercial Nature of Colour Standardization," *Canadian Review of American Studies* 33, no. 1 (2003): 37–61, quote on 47.

21. Zipes, "Towards a Theory of the Fairy-Tale Film," 8.

22. Elliott, "Crayoned Culture," 38.

23. David Batchelor, *Chromophobia* (London: Reaktion Books, 2000), 15.

24. See the Jenkins chapter in this volume for further discussion of how Burton uses techniques that disorient to engender a unique aesthetic effect.

25. Carolyn L. Kane, "The Synthetic Color Sense of Pipilotti Rist; or, Deleuzian Color Theory for Electronic Media Art," *Visual Communication* 10, no. 4 (2011): 475–97, quote on 481.

26. In Lacanian theory, the *objet petite a,* the object cause of desire, is the unattainable object that fuels desire. Jacques Lacan introduced this theory in his 1957 lecture "Les formations de l'inconscient."

27. bell hooks, *Black Looks* (New York: Routledge, 1992), 26.

28. Flo Leibowitz, "Movie Colorization and the Expression of Mood," *Journal of Aesthetics and Art Criticism* 49, no. 4 (1991): 364.

29. David Goodwin, "Toward a Grammar and Rhetoric of Visual Opposition," *Rhetoric Review* 18, no. 1 (1999): 93.

30. hooks, *Black Looks,* 31.

31. Batchelor, *Chromophobia,* 41.

32. Heather Neff, "Strange Faces in the Mirror: The Ethics of Diversity in Children's Films," *Lion and the Unicorn* 20, no. 1 (1996): 56.

33. Linda M. Scott, "Images in Advertising: The Need for a Theory of Visual Rhetoric," *Journal of Consumer Research* 21, no. 2 (1994): 252.

34. For more on the correlation of obesity and class, see David Freedman et al., "Trends and Correlates of Class 3 Obesity in the United States from 1990 through 2000," *JAMA: The Journal of the American Medical Association* 288, no. 14 (2002):1758–61; J. Sobal and A. J. Stunkard, "Socioeconomic Status and Obesity: A Review of the Literature," *Psychological Bulletin* 105, no. 2 (1989): 260–75; D. J. Hruschka, "Do Economic Constraints on Food Choice Make People Fat? A Critical Review of Two Hypothesis for the Poverty-Obesity Paradox," *American Journal of Human Biology* 24, no. 3 (2012): 277–85.

35. Neff, "Strange Faces in the Mirror," 54.

36. Brian Evans, "Temporal Coherence with Digital Color," in "Digital Cinema," supplemental issue, *Leonardo* 3 (1990): 46.

37. Goodwin, "Toward a Grammar and Rhetoric of Visual Opposition," 96.

38. Batchelor, *Chromophobia,* 52.

39. Elliott, "Crayoned Culture," 57.

40. Scott, "Images in Advertising," 256.

41. Elliott, "Crayoned Culture," 39.

42. Evans, "Temporal Coherence with Digital Color," 46.

43. Madden, Hewett, and Roth, "Managing Images in Different Cultures," 93.

44. Patti Bellantoni, *If It's Purple, Someone's Gonna Die: The Power of Color in Visual Storytelling for Film* (Burlington, MA: Focal Press, 2005), 24.

45. Scott, "Images in Advertising," 254.

46. Elliott, "Crayoned Culture," 39.

47. Madden, Hewett, and Roth, "Managing Images in Different Cultures," 103.

48. Elliott, "Crayoned Culture," 53.

Contributors

KIMBERLEY BALTZER-JARAY is an instructor at the University of Guelph and King's University College (Western University) whose area of expertise is early phenomenology and existentialism but who has interests in just about every area of philosophy. She even likes Kant, and she often admits that fact out loud, in public. She is president of the North American Society for Early Phenomenology, a writer for *Things & Ink Magazine*, and author of the blog *A Tattooed Philosopher's Blog: Discussion of the Type I Ink, Therefore I Am.* The first philosophical tattoo she got was of Jack Skellington. She explains its significance by saying that she has an affinity with Jack—she is always asking metaphysical questions and she, too, doesn't understand Christmas.

STEVE BENTON is assistant professor of English and the director of the University Honors Program at East Central University in Ada, Oklahoma. He received his B.A. from Texas Christian University, his M.A. from the University of Chicago, and his Ph.D. from the University of Illinois at Chicago. His most recent publications have appeared in the *Atlantic* (online) and the *Journal of Popular Film and Television.*

PAUL A. CANTOR is the Clifton Waller Barrett Professor of English and Comparative Literature at the University of Virginia. He received his B.A. and Ph.D. in English from Harvard University, where he taught as an assistant professor of English from 1971 to 1977 and as a visiting professor of government in 2007 and 2012. He served on the National Council on the Humanities from 1992 to 1999. He is the author of *Shakespeare's Rome: Republic and Empire* (Cornell University Press, 1976), *Creature and Creator: Myth-Making and English Romanticism* (Cambridge University Press, 1984), the *Hamlet* volume in the Cambridge Landmarks of World Literature series (1989; 2004), and *Gilligan Unbound: Pop Culture in the Age of Globalization* (Rowman and Littlefield, 2001), which was named by the *Los Angeles Times* one of the best nonfiction books of the year. He is the coeditor along with Stephen Cox of *Literature and the Economics of Liberty: Spontaneous Order in Culture* (Ludwig von Mises Institute, 2009). His most recent book, *The*

Invisible Hand in Popular Culture: Liberty vs. Authority in American Film and TV (University Press of Kentucky, 2012), contains a fuller version of his essay on *Mars Attacks!*.

KEVIN S. DECKER is associate professor of philosophy and associate dean of the College of Arts and Letters at Eastern Washington University. His teaching and research interests include American pragmatism, applied and normative ethics, philosophy of social science, and philosophy and popular culture. He is the coeditor of Star Wars *and Philosophy* and Star Trek *and Philosophy* (Open Court), Terminator *and Philosophy*, and *The Ultimate* South Park *and Philosophy* (Wiley-Blackwell) and the editor of the upcoming Ender's Game *and Philosophy* (Blackwell). He has published chapters in similar books on tattoos, James Bond, Transformers, *The Daily Show, Doctor Who*, the films of Stanley Kubrick, and *30 Rock*. His book *Who Is Who? The Philosophy of* Doctor Who (I. B. Tauris) was published in late 2013.

KEN HADA is professor at East Central University in Ada, Oklahoma, where he teaches American literatures and various courses in humanities and directs the annual Scissortail Creative Writing Festival. His latest poetry collection is *Margaritas and Redfish* (Lamar University Press, 2013). He is a contributor to *The Philosophy of the Western* (University Press of Kentucky, 2010), and some of his additional critical essays may be found in *College Literature, Southwestern American Literature, Ethnic Studies Review, Journal of the West*, and *American Indian Culture and Research Journal* (http://kenhada.org).

JENNIFER L. JENKINS is associate professor and faculty fellow at the University of Arizona, where she teaches American literatures and film. In addition to pursuing a long-standing interest in gothic domesticity on page and screen, she works on regional archival film in the southwestern United States and northern Mexico. Her current project is *Celluloid Pueblo: Western Ways Film Service and the Invention of the Postwar Southwest*. In 2011 she became curator of the American Indian Film Gallery. Recent publications examine domesticity and divorce in *Invasion of the Body Snatchers* and the first sound films shot in Arizona.

DEBORAH KNIGHT is associate professor of philosophy at Queen's University, Kingston, Canada. She has published on topics including philosophy and literature; philosophy and cultural studies; *The Matrix; The Simpsons;* the horror film; Hitchcock; *Blade Runner* and *Dark City;* Scorsese's *The Age of Innocence;* the Western, with a focus on Robert Altman's *McCabe and Mrs. Miller;* and *The Third Man.* Other recent publications focus on sentimentality, the genres of tragedy and comedy, and personal identity in relation to the philosophy of film.

DAVID LaROCCA is writer-in-residence at the New York Public Library and fellow at the Moving Picture Institute in New York. He is the author of *On Emerson* (Wadsworth, 2003) and *Emerson's English Traits and the Natural History of Metaphor* (Bloomsbury, 2013) and the editor of Stanley Cavell's *Emerson's Transcendental Etudes* (Stanford University Press, 2003) and *Estimating Emerson: An Anthology of Criticism from Carlyle to Cavell* (Bloomsbury, 2013). LaRocca is the editor of *The Philosophy of Charlie Kaufman* (University Press of Kentucky, 2011) and the forthcoming *The Philosophy of War Films*—also for the Philosophy of Popular Culture series. Additionally, he has contributed essays to *The Philosophy of Spike Lee* (2011), *The Philosophy of the Coen Brothers* (updated edition, 2012), and *The Philosophy of Michael Mann* (2014). His articles on aesthetic theory, American philosophy, autobiography, and film have appeared in *Epoché, Afterimage, Transactions, Liminalities: A Journal of Performance Studies, Film and Philosophy, Midwest Quarterly, Journal of Aesthetics and Art Criticism,* and *Journal of Aesthetic Education.* And he is the director of the documentary *Brunello Cucinelli: A New Philosophy of Clothes* (A Fine Print Film Production, 2013). More details at www.davidlarocca.org.

GEORGE McKNIGHT is emeritus professor of film studies in the School for Studies in Art and Culture at Carleton University, Ottawa, Canada. He is the editor of *Agent of Challenge and Defiance: Films of Ken Loach* (Praeger, 1997). Besides his research interests in British cinema and the film industry, he has published on Hitchcock, suspense, *CSI,* the philosophy of horror, the Western, and *Memento.*

JENNIFER L. McMAHON is professor of philosophy, English, and humanities at East Central University in Ada, Oklahoma. McMahon has expertise in existentialism, aesthetics, and comparative philosophy. She has published articles in journals including *Asian Philosophy* and the *Journal of the Association for Interdisciplinary Study of the Arts,* as well as numerous essays on philosophy and popular culture in volumes including *Seinfeld and Philosophy* (Open Court, 2000), The Matrix *and Philosophy* (Open Court, 2002), The Lord of the Rings *and Philosophy* (Open Court, 2003), *The Philosophy of Martin Scorsese* (University Press of Kentucky, 2007), *The Philosophy of Science Fiction Film* (University Press of Kentucky, 2007), House M.D. *and Philosophy* (Blackwell, 2008), and *Death in Classic and Contemporary Film* (Palgrave, 2013). She coedited *The Philosophy of the Western* (University Press of Kentucky, 2010) with Dr. B. Steve Csaki.

DEBBIE OLSON is lecturer of English at the University of Texas at Arlington. Her research interests include West African film, images of African and African American children in film and popular media, transnationalism, and New Hollywood Cinema. She is the coeditor of *Lost and Othered Children in Contemporary Cinema* (Lexington, 2012) and *Portrayals of Children in Popular Culture: Fleeting Images* (Lexington, 2012). She is the editor of the forthcoming volume *Hitchcock's Children: The Child in the Films of Alfred Hitchcock.* Her articles appear in *The Tube Has Spoken: Reality TV as Film and History* (University Press of Kentucky, 2009) and *Facts, Fiction, and African Creative Imaginations* (Routledge, 2009). She is the editor in chief of *Red Feather Journal,* an international journal of children's visual culture. She is currently completing her dissertation on the transnational circulation of the black child image.

DANIEL SULLIVAN is assistant professor of psychology at the University of Arizona. His empirical research interests include the motivations and consequences of death denial and enemyship, as well as the cultural conditioning of experiences of existential threat. His psychological analyses of film and literature have appeared in the *Journal of Popular Film and Television, Literature Interpretation Theory,* and the *Journal of Humanistic Psychology.* With Jeff Greenberg, he is the editor of an anthology entitled *Death in Classic and Contemporary Film: Fade to Black* (Palgrave, 2013).

MARK WALLING is professor of English at East Central University in Ada, Oklahoma. His area of expertise is creative writing. Walling has a wide variety of publications, including numerous pieces of short fiction and an award-winning screenplay. He also specializes in film studies and recently published a critical article titled "All Roads Lead to the Self: Zen Buddhism and David Lynch's *Lost Highway*" in *The Philosophy of David Lynch* (University Press of Kentucky, 2011).

RYAN WELDON received his M.A. in rhetoric and technical communication, B.A. in philosophy, and B.A. in English literature from Eastern Washington University, where he is currently a career advisor for the College of Arts, Letters, and Education. His usual academic obsession revolves around exploring feminist and queer descriptions of identity in popular culture, entertainment media, and advertising.

INDEX

The Philosophy of Popular Culture

The books published in the Philosophy of Popular Culture series will illuminate and explore philosophical themes and ideas that occur in popular culture. The goal of this series is to demonstrate how philosophical inquiry has been reinvigorated by increased scholarly interest in the intersection of popular culture and philosophy, as well as to explore through philosophical analysis beloved modes of entertainment, such as movies, TV shows, and music. Philosophical concepts will be made accessible to the general reader through examples in popular culture. This series seeks to publish both established and emerging scholars who will engage a major area of popular culture for philosophical interpretation and examine the philosophical underpinnings of its themes. Eschewing ephemeral trends of philosophical and cultural theory, authors will establish and elaborate on connections between traditional philosophical ideas from important thinkers and the ever-expanding world of popular culture.

Series Editor

Mark T. Conard, Marymount Manhattan College, NY

Books in the Series

The Philosophy of Stanley Kubrick, edited by Jerold J. Abrams
The Philosophy of Ang Lee, edited by Robert Arp, Adam Barkman, and James McRae
Football and Philosophy, edited by Michael W. Austin
Tennis and Philosophy, edited by David Baggett
The Philosophy of J. J. Abrams, edited by Patricia Brace and Robert Arp
The Philosophy of Film Noir, edited by Mark T. Conard
The Philosophy of Martin Scorsese, edited by Mark T. Conard
The Philosophy of Neo-Noir, edited by Mark T. Conard
The Philosophy of Spike Lee, edited by Mark T. Conard
The Philosophy of the Coen Brothers, edited by Mark T. Conard
The Philosophy of David Lynch, edited by William J. Devlin and Shai Biderman
The Philosophy of the Beats, edited by Sharin N. Elkholy
The Philosophy of Horror, edited by Thomas Fahy
The Philosophy of The X-Files, edited by Dean A. Kowalski
Steven Spielberg and Philosophy, edited by Dean A. Kowalski
The Philosophy of Joss Whedon, edited by Dean A. Kowalski and S. Evan Kreider

The Philosophy of Charlie Kaufman, edited by David LaRocca
The Philosophy of Clint Eastwood, edited by Richard T. McClelland and Brian B. Clayton
The Philosophy of Tim Burton, edited by Jennifer L. McMahon
The Philosophy of the Western, edited by Jennifer L. McMahon and B. Steve Csaki
The Philosophy of Steven Soderbergh, edited by R. Barton Palmer and Steven Sanders
The Olympics and Philosophy, edited by Heather L. Reid and Michael W. Austin
The Philosophy of David Cronenberg, edited by Simon Riches
The Philosophy of Science Fiction Film, edited by Steven Sanders
The Philosophy of TV Noir, edited by Steven Sanders and Aeon J. Skoble
The Philosophy of Michael Mann, edited by Steven Sanders, Aeon J. Skoble, and R. Barton Palmer
The Philosophy of Sherlock Holmes, edited by Philip Tallon and David Baggett
Basketball and Philosophy, edited by Jerry L. Walls and Gregory Bassham
Golf and Philosophy, edited by Andy Wible